Auditor's Guide to IT Auditing

Founded in 1807, John Wiley & Sons is the oldest independent publishing company in the United States. With offices in North America, Europe, Asia, and Australia, Wiley is globally committed to developing and marketing print and electronic products and services for our customers' professional and personal knowledge and understanding.

The Wiley Corporate F&A series provides information, tools, and insights to corporate professionals responsible for issues affecting the profitability of their company, from accounting and finance to internal controls and performance management.

Auditor's Guide to IT Auditing

Second Edition

RICHARD E. CASCARINO

WILEY

John Wiley & Sons, Inc.

For general information on our other products and services or for technical support, please contact our Customer Care Department within the United States at (800) 762-2974, outside the United States at (317) 572-3993, or fax (317) 572-4002.

Wiley also publishes its books in a variety of electronic formats. Some content that appears in print may not be available in electronic books. For more information about Wiley products, visit our web site at www.wiley.com.

Library of Congress Cataloging-in-Publication Data:

Cascarino, Richard.
    Auditor's guide to IT auditing / Richard E. Cascarino. — 2nd ed.
        p. cm. — (Wiley corporate F&A series)
    Rev. ed. of: Auditor's guide to information systems auditing.
    Includes index.
    ISBN 978-1-118-14761-0 (hardback); ISBN 978-1-118-22584-4 (ebk);
    ISBN 978-1-118-23907-0 (ebk); ISBN 978-1-118-24425-8 (ebk)
    1. Electronic data processing—Auditing.   I. Cascarino, Richard. Auditor's guide to
        information systems auditing.   II. Title.
    QA76.9.A93C37 2012
    658′.0558—dc23   2011042683

ISBN 978-1118-14761-0

Printed in the United States of America

10 9 8 7 6 5 4 3 2 1

I wish to take this opportunity to dedicate this book to my wife, Max, who has, over the last 33 years, put up with my bad temper when the computer would not do what I programmed it to do, my ego when it did eventually work, my despair when the system crashed again and again, and my complacency when the problems were solved.

I would also like to thank those who molded my career over the years, particularly Jim Leary for showing me what an IS manager could be and Scotch Duncan Anderson for showing me what an internal auditor should be.

And in grateful thanks to my friend, the late Gene Schultz, who died before being able to review the second edition of this book having given such a sterling review to the first edition. He was an inspiration and will be sadly missed.

Contents

Chapter 3: IT Risk and Fundamental Auditing Concepts   33

Chapter 4: Standards and Guidelines for IT Auditing   47

Chapter 5: Internal Controls Concepts Knowledge   57

Preface

I N TODAY'S BUSINESS ENVIRONMENT, computers are continuing the revolution started in the 1950s. Size and capacity of the equipment grows on an exponential curve, with the reduction in cost and size ensuring that organizations take advantage of this to develop more effective and responsive systems, which allow them to seek to gain competitive advantage by interfacing more closely with their customers. This second edition has been brought up to date with the latest in information technology (IT) approaches such as cloud computing as well as the latest in standards and regulations. The section on risk management has been expanded to include varying risk-analysis techniques available to the IT auditor.

Net technologies such as cloud computing, electronic data interchange (EDI), electronic funds transfers (EFTs), and e-commerce have fundamentally changed the nature of business itself and, as a result, organizations have become more computer dependent. The radical changes to business are matched only by their impact on society.

It has become impossible for today's enterprises of any size and in any market sector to exist without computers to assist with their fundamental business operations. Even the old adage that "we can always go back to manual operations" is today a fallacy. The nature of today's business environment obviates that option. Even the smallest businesses have found that the advent of personal computers (PCs) with increased capabilities and processing speed, while at the same time reduced pricing and sophisticated PC software, has revolutionized the concept of what a small business is.

In order for organizations to take full advantage of the new facilities that computers can offer, it is important that their systems can be controlled and are dependable. They require that their auditors confirm that this is the case. The modern auditor therefore requires significantly more knowledge of computers and computer auditing than did auditors of earlier years.

CONTROLS IN MODERN COMPUTER SYSTEMS

The introduction of the computer has brought fundamental changes to the ways organizations process data. Computer systems:

- Are frequently much more complex than manual systems, the larger systems at least requiring a number of highly skilled computer technicians to develop and maintain them.
- Process large volumes of data at high speed, and can transmit data effectively and instantaneously over extreme distances, commonly between continents.
- Hold data in electronic form, which, without the appropriate tools and techniques, is often more complex for the auditor to access than paper records. In addition, modern systems have reduced the volumes of printed outputs by the incorporation of online access and online inquiry facilities. Indeed, many modern EDI-type systems have no paper audit trail whatsoever.
- Process data with much less manual intervention than manual systems. In fact large parts of sophisticated systems now process data with no manual intervention at all. In the past, the main justification for computerization was frequently to reduce the number of staff required to operate the business. With modern decision support and integrated systems, this is becoming a reality not at the clerical level, but at the decision-making and control level. This can have the effect that the fundamental business controls previously relied upon by the auditor, such as segregation of duties or management authorization, may no longer be carried out as previously and must be audited in a different manner. In computer systems, the user profile of the member of staff as defined within the system's access rights will generally control the division of duties while managerial authorities are, in many cases, built into systems themselves.
- Process consistently in accordance with their programs providing the computer has been programmed correctly and change control is effective.
- In large minicomputer and mainframe systems, there is a significant concentration of risk in locating the organization's information resources in one format, although not necessarily in one place. Organizations then become totally reliant on their computer system and must be able to recover from failure or the destruction of their computer system swiftly and with minimal business disruption.
- Are often subject to different legal constraints and burdens of proof than manual systems.
- May operate within a cloud environment within which control over the availability, security, and confidentiality of systems and data may be handed over to a third party and may be subject to laws of a differing country.

These changes brought about by computerization can greatly increase the opportunity for auditors to deliver a quality service by concentrating the risk and allowing the auditors to correspondingly concentrate their efforts. For example, harnessing the power of the computer to analyze large volumes of data in the way the auditor requires is commonly now the only practical way of analyzing corporate data, and this was not only impractical but also impossible while data was spread around the organization in a myriad of forms.

In addition, the use of computer systems with built-in programmed procedures permit the auditor to adopt a systems approach to auditing in that the controls within the computer system process in a more consistent manner than a manual system. In manual systems the quality of the control procedure can change on a day-by-day basis, depending on the quality of the staff and their consistency of working. This can result in the auditor having to undertake a substantial amount of checking of transactions, to confirm transactions have processed correctly.

Controls within computer systems are commonly classified in two main subdivisions:

1. **General controls.** The controls governing the environment in which the computer system is developed, maintained, and operated, and within which the application controls operate. These controls include the systems-development standards operated by the organization, the controls that apply to the operation of the computer installation, and those governing the functioning of systems software. They have a pervasive effect on all application systems.
2. **Application controls.** The controls, both manual and computerized, within the business application to ensure that data is processed completely, accurately, and in a timely manner. Application controls are typically specific to the business application and include:
   ▪ Input controls such as data validation and batching
   ▪ Run-to-run controls to check file totals at key stages in processing, and controls over output

Ultimately, the auditor's job is to determine if the application systems function as intended, the integrity, accuracy, and completeness of the data is well controlled, and report any significant discrepancies. The integrity of the data relies on the adequacy of the application controls. However, application controls are totally dependent on the integrity of the general controls over the environment within which the application is developed and run.

In the past, the auditor has often assumed a considerable degree of reliance on controls around the computer, that is, in the application controls. This is sometimes referred to as auditing "around" the computer because the auditor concentrates on the input and output from the computer, rather than what happens in the computer.

This has never been truly justified but has become, over recent years, a lethal assumption.

With the spread of online and real-time working, and of the increasing capacity of fixed disks, all of the organization's data is commonly permanently loaded on the computer system and accessible from a variety of places, with only systems software controls preventing access to the data. This system is increasing in technical complexity, and the ability to utilize any implemented weaknesses is also growing.

It is critical that the auditor is assured of the integrity of the computer operational environment within which the applications systems function. This means that the auditor must become knowledgeable of the facilities provided in key systems software in the organization being audited.

This book is designed for those who need to gain a practical working knowledge of the risks and control opportunities within an IT environment, and the auditing of that environment. Readers who will find the text particularly useful include professionals and students within the fields of:

- IT security
- IT audit
- Internal audit
- External audit
- Management information systems
- General business management

Overall, this book contains the information required by anyone who is, or expects to be, accountable to management for the successful implementation and control of information systems.

It is intended that the text within this book forms the foundation for learning experience, as well as being your reference manual and student text. The emphasis is therefore on both the principles and techniques as well as the practical implementation through the use of realistic case studies.

 ## OVERALL FRAMEWORK

Within the book the terms Information Technology (IT) and Information Systems (IS) are both used because both are in common use to mean virtually identical functions. The book is split into eight parts, namely:

Part I: IT Audit Process

This part covers the introduction to the technology and auditing involved with the modern computer systems. It seeks to establish common frames of reference for all IT students by establishing a baseline of technological understanding as well as an understanding of risks, control objectives, and standards, all concepts essential to the audit function. Internal control concepts and the planning and management of the audit process in order to obtain the appropriate evidence of the achievement of the control objectives is explained as is the audit reporting process.

Chapter 1 covers the basics of technology and audit. The chapter is intended to give readers an understanding of the technology in use in business as well as knowledge of the jargon and its meaning. It covers the components of control within an IT environment and explains who the main players are and what their role is within this environment.

Chapter 2 looks at the laws and regulations governing IT audit and the nature and role of the audit charter. It reviews the varying nature of audit and the demand for audits as well as the need for control and audit of computer-based IS. The types of audit and auditor and range of services to be provided are reviewed together with the standards and codes of ethics of both the Institute of Internal Auditors (IIA) and the standards specified by the Information Systems Audit and Control Association (ISACA).

Chapter 3 explores the concepts of materiality and risk within the IT audit function and contrasts materiality as it is commonly applied to financial statement audit such as those performed by independent external auditors. In this context, the quality and types of evidence required to meet the definitions of sufficiency, reliability, and relevancy are examined. The risks involved in examining evidence to arrive at an audit conclusion are reviewed as are the need to maintain the independence and objectivity of the auditor and the auditor's responsibility for fraud detection in both an IT and non-IT setting. A variety of differing risk assessment methods is examined.

Chapter 4 explores in detail the ISACA Code of Professional Ethics and the current ISACA IS Auditing Standards and Guidelines Standards and discusses the IIA Code of Ethics, Standards for the Professional Practice of Internal Auditing, and Practice Advisories. In addition, standards and guidelines other than the ISACA and IIA models are explored.

Chapter 5 introduces the concepts of corporate governance with particular attention to the implications within an IT environment and the impact on IS auditors. Criteria of Control (COCO), Committee of Sponsoring Organizations of the Treadway Commission (COSO), King, Sarbanes-Oxley Act of 2002, and other recent legislative impacts are examined together with the structuring of controls to achieve conformity to these structures. Control classifications are examined in detail together with both general and application controls. Particular attention is paid to COBIT (Control Objectives for Information and Related Technology) from both a structural and relevance perspective.

Chapter 6 introduces the concept of computer risks and exposures and includes the development of an understanding of the major types of risks faced by the IT function including the sources of such risk as well as the causes. It also emphasizes management's role in adopting a risk position, which itself necessitates a knowledge of the acceptable management responses to computer risks. One of the most fundamental influencing factors in IT auditing is the issue of corporate risk. This chapter examines risk and its nature within the corporate environment and looks at the internal audit need for the appropriate risk analysis to enable risk-based auditing as an integrated approach. This includes the effect of computer risks, the common risk factors, and the elements required to complete a computer risk analysis

Chapter 7 examines the audit planning process at both a strategic and tactical level. The use of risk-based auditing and risk-assessment methods and standards are covered. The preliminary evaluation of internal controls via the appropriate information-gathering and control-evaluation techniques as a fundamental component of the audit plan and the design of the audit plan to achieve a variety of audit scopes is detailed.

Chapter 8 looks at audit management and its resource allocation and prioritization in the planning and execution of assignments. The management of IS Audit quality through techniques such as peer reviews and best-practice identification is explored. The human aspects of management in the forms of career development and career path planning, performance assessment, counseling, and feedback as well as professional development through certifications, professional involvement, and training (both internal and external) are reviewed.

Chapter 9 exposes the fundamental audit evidence process and the gathering of evidence that may be deemed sufficient, reliable, relevant, and useful. Evidence-gathering techniques such as observation, inquiry, interviewing, and testing are examined and the techniques of compliance versus substantive testing are contrasted. The complex area of statistical and non-statistical sampling techniques and the design and selection of samples and evaluation of sample results is examined. The essential techniques of computer assisted audit techniques (CAATs) are covered and a case study using the software provided is detailed.

Chapter 10 covers audit reporting and follow-up. The form and content of an audit report are detailed and its purpose, structure, content, and style as dictated by the desired effect on its intended recipient for a variety of types of opinion are considered as well as the follow-up to determine management's actions to implement recommendations.

Part II: Information Technology Governance

This part details the processes involved in planning and managing the IT function and the management issues faced in a modern IT department. The techniques used by management and the support tools and frameworks are examined with respect to the need for control within the processes.

Chapter 11 covers IT project-management, risk management including economic, social, cultural, and technology risk management as well as software quality-control management, the management of IT infrastructure, alternative IT architectures and configuration, and the management of IT delivery (operations) and support (maintenance). Performance measurement and reporting and the IT balanced scorecard are also covered as are the use of outsourcing, the implementation of IT quality assurance, and the socio-technical and cultural approach to management.

Chapter 12 examines IT strategic planning and looks at competitive strategies and business intelligence and their link to corporate strategy. These, in turn, influence the development of strategic information systems frameworks and applications. Strategic planning also includes the management of IT human resources, employee policies, agreements, contracts, segregation of duties within IT, and the implementation of effective IT training and education.

Chapter 13 looks at the broader IS/IT management issues including the legal issues relating to the introduction of IT to the enterprise; intellectual property issues in cyberspace: trademarks, copyrights, patents as well as ethical issues; rights to privacy; and the implementation of effective IT governance.

Chapter 14 introduces the need for support tools and frameworks such as COBIT: Management Guidelines, a framework for IT/IS managers and COBIT: Audit's Use in Support of the Business Support Cycle. International standards and good practices such as ISOI7799, IT Infrastructure Library®(ITIL®), privacy standards, COSO, COCO, Cadbury, King, and Sarbanes-Oxley also play a vital role in ensuring the appropriate governance.

Chapter 15 covers the need for, and use of, techniques such as change control reviews, operational reviews, and ISO 9000 reviews.

Part III: Systems and Infrastructure Lifecycle Management

IT is essential to an organization only in so far as it can effectively assist in the achievement of the business objectives. This means that the business-application systems need to be appropriate to the business needs and meet the objectives of the users in an effective and efficient manner. Part III explores the manner in which application systems are planned, acquired externally, or developed internally and ultimately implemented and maintained. In all cases such systems have an objective of being auditable in addition to the other unique business objectives. This part also examines the variety of roles that the auditor could be called on to undertake and the circumstances and controls appropriate to each.

Chapter 16 covers the IT planning and managing components and includes developing an understanding of stakeholders and their requirements together with IT stay planning methods such as system investigation, process integration/reengineering opportunities, risk evaluation, cost-benefit analysis, risk assessment, object-oriented systems analysis, and design. Enterprise Resource Planning (ERP) software to facilitate enterprise applications integration is reviewed.

Chapter 17 covers the areas of information management and usage monitoring. Measurement criteria such as evaluating service level performance against service-level agreements, quality of service, availability, response time, security and controls, processing integrity, and privacy are examined. The analysis, evaluation, and design information together with data and application architecture are evaluated as tools for the auditor.

Chapter 18 investigates the development, acquisition, and maintenance of information systems through Information Systems' project management involving the planning, organization, human resource deployment, project control, monitoring, and execution of the project plan. The traditional methods for the system development life cycle (SDLC) (analysis, evaluation, and design of an entity's SDLC phases and tasks) are examined, as are alternative approaches for system development such as the use of software packages, prototyping, business process reengineering, or computer-aided software engineering (CASE). In addition system maintenance and change-control procedures for system changes together with tools to assess risk and control issues and to aid the analysis and evaluation of project characteristics and risks are discussed.

Chapter 19 examines the impact of IT on the business processes and solutions, business process outsourcing (BPO), and applications of e-business issues and trends.

Chapter 20 looks at the software-development-design process itself and covers the separation of specification and implementation in programming, requirements specification methodologies, and technical process design. In addition database creation and manipulation, principles of good screen and report design, and program language alignment are covered.

Chapter 21 looks at the audit and control of purchased packages to introduce readers to those elements critical to the decision taken to make or buy software. This includes a knowledge of the systems-development process and an understanding of the user's role in training required so that the outsource decision on the factors surrounding it may be made to best effect.

Chapter 22 looks at the auditor's role in feasibility studies and conversions. These are perhaps the most critical areas of systems implementation, and audit involvement should be compulsory.

Chapter 23 looks at the audit and development of application-level controls including input/origination controls, processing control procedures, output controls, application system documentation, and the appropriate use of audit trails.

Part IV: Information Technology Service Delivery and Support

This part examines the technical infrastructure in a variety of environments and the influence the infrastructure has on the management and control procedures required to attain the business objectives. The nature and methodologies of service center management are exposed for discussion.

Chapter 24 examines the complex area of the IS/IT technical infrastructure (planning, implementation, and operational practices). IT architecture/standards over hardware including mainframe, minicomputers, client-servers, routers, switches, communications, and PCs as well as software including operating systems, utility software, and database systems are revealed. Network components including communications equipment and services rendered to provide networks, network-related hardware, network-related software, and the use of service providers are covered as are security/testing and validation, performance monitoring, and evaluation tools and IT control monitoring and evaluation tools, such as access control systems monitoring and intrusion-detection-systems monitoring tools. In addition, the role of managing information resources and information infrastructure through enterprise management software and the implementation of service center management and operations standards/guidelines within COBIT, ITIL, and ISO 17799 together with the issues and considerations of service center versus proprietary technical infrastructures are explored.

Chapter 25 introduces the areas of service center management and the maintenance of Information Systems and technical infrastructures. These involve the use of appropriate tools designed to control the introduction of new and changed products into the service center environment and include such aspects as security management, resource/configuration management, and problem and incident management. In addition, the administration of release and versions of automated systems as well as the achievement of service-level management through capacity planning and management of the distribution of automated systems and contingency/backup and recovery management are examined.

The key management principles involved in management of operations of the infrastructure (central and distributed), network management, and risk management are outlined as are both the need for customer liaison as well as the management of suppliers.

Part V: Protection of Information Assets

This part examines the essential area of IT security in all of its manifestations. The administration of security focusing on information as an asset is commonly problematic and may frequently be observed as a patchwork of physical and logical security techniques with little thought to the application and implementation of an integrated approach designed to lead to the achievement of specific control objectives.

Chapter 26 looks at the area of information assets security management. This covers information technology and security basics and the fundamental concepts of IT security. The need for securing IT resources and maintaining an adequate policy framework on IT asset security, the management of IT security, and security training standards are examined as are the major compliance and assurance issues in IT security.

Chapter 27 covers the critical area of the components of logical IT security. Logical access control issues and exposures are explored together with access-control software. The auditing of logical access to ensure the adequate control of logical security risks using the appropriate logical security features, tools, and procedures is detailed.

Chapter 28 looks at the application of IT security including communications and network security. The principles of network security, client-server, Internet and web-based services, and firewall security systems are all detailed together with connectivity protection resources such as cryptography, digital signatures, digital certificates, and key management policies. IT security also encompasses the use of intrusion-detection systems and the proper implementation of mainframe security facilities. Security is also a critical element in the development of application systems and involves both the systems development and maintenance processes and database design.

Chapter 29 examines the concepts of physical IT security including physical access exposures and controls.

Part VI: Business Continuity and Disaster Recovery

In many organizations, the ongoing continuity and availability of an information-processing capability is critical to the corporate survival of the entity. This part explores the need for and techniques utilized in the protection of the information technology architecture and assets through both disaster recovery planning and the transfer of risk by utilizing the appropriate insurance profile. The auditor's role in examining corporate continuity plans is examined in detail.

Chapter 30 introduces the activities required to ensure the protection of the IT architecture and assets. These include backup provisions involving business-impact analysis and business-continuity planning leading to IT disaster recovery planning, obtaining management support and commitment to the process, plan preparation and documentation, obtaining management approval, and distribution of the plan. In addition, the testing, maintenance, and revision of the plan together with audit's role in all of these activities are investigated.

Chapter 31 looks at insurance and the variety of insurance coverage that can be obtained. Issues such as the valuation of assets, including equipment, people, information processes, and technology, are examined.

Part VII: Advanced IT Auditing

The final part explores the technical auditor's function and role in auditing specialized areas such as the audit and control of e-commerce systems, auditing operating systems at both micro and mainframe levels, securing systems against outside penetration, and investigating security breaches.

Chapter 32 examines the tasks required to establish and optimize the IT audit functions including defining the scope of IP auditing, setting the objectives, staffing, and training. Measuring the effectiveness of the IT audit and the role of the specialist are critical in producing an effective IT audit function. It also introduces readers to the concepts of the paperless society inherent in e-commerce, business-2-business (B2B), business-2-consumer (B2C), and electronic data interchange (EDI) in general. These concepts change the internal control structure required in such an environment as well as changing the sources of what audit and legal evidence is available. The auditor will be required to implement the correct program to bring the contoured auction in line with this changing business environment.

Chapter 33 takes the reader through the advanced concepts of auditing within a UNIX / Linux environment including the major threat categories and control opportunities as well as the use of the appropriate audit tools.

Chapter 34 covers in detail the theory and practice of auditing within a Windows Vista or Windows 7 environment. This again includes the major control opportunities, controls to be sought, and audit tools to be used.

Chapter 35 addresses the major risk of computer hackers including definitions of how hackers gain entrance and the design of the appropriate security hierarchy in order to effectively manage this critical risk.

Chapter 36 examines the problem of computer fraud and countermeasures to prevent, detect, and alleviate the problems. This includes the effect of the risk of fraud on the business control objectives, the techniques applicable for determining higher risk, as well as the impact of computer fraud on an organization. The ability to distinguish between types of computer fraud, and the nature and effect as well as identification of likely fraud indicators enables the structuring of an appropriate antifraud security environment. The auditor must be capable of distinguishing between fraud and forensic auditing and applying the appropriate techniques. This involves an understanding of the rules that influence the acceptability of computer evidence as legally acceptable and binding evidence.

Appendices

Five appendices will be found at the back of the book including the appropriate ethics and standards for the IT auditor as well as sample audit programs for:

- Application Systems Auditing
- Logical access control
- UNIX / Linux environments
- Windows Vista and Version 7

Auditor's Guide to IT Auditing

PART ONE

IT Audit Process

CHAPTER ONE

Technology and Audit

THIS CHAPTER COVERS the basics of technology and audit. The chapter is intended to provide an understanding of the technology currently in use in business as well as knowledge of the jargon and its meaning. It also covers the components of control within an information technology (IT) environment and explains who the main players are and what their roles are within this environment.

After reading this chapter you should be able to:

- Understand the technology currently in use in business
- Understand the jargon and its meaning
- Define the components of control in an IT environment
- Briefly explain who the players are and what their roles are
- Define the fundamental differences between batch and online systems
- Explain the principal business risks within each processing type
- Describe the components that make up the online system and the effect these have on control objectives
- Explain the controls within each type of computer system
- Contrast the basics of batch and online security
- Demonstrate an ability to:
  - Identify the differing types of database structures
  - Identify the principal components of each type of Database Management System (DBMS)
  - Identify the primary threats to each of these components

- Relate DBMS components to the operating system environment in which they operate
- Identify potential control opportunities and select among control alternatives
- Identify the principal DBMS products in the market
- Recognize vulnerabilities in multiple DBMS environments and make appropriate recommendations

 ## TECHNOLOGY AND AUDIT

Before the auditor can make an effective start in auditing the technology, it is critical that both Audit and IT speak a common language and that the auditor understands the technical jargon with which they will be confronted.

Some Computing Jargon

Before we can start to discuss the audit and control of computer systems, we must have a common understanding of the jargon used.

Hardware

Hardware consists of those components that can physically be touched and manipulated. Principles among those components are:

- **CPU.** The Central Processing Unit is the heart of the computer. This is the logic unit that handles the arithmetic processing of all calculations.
- **Peripherals.** Peripheral devices are those devices that attach to the CPU to handle—typically—inputs and outputs. These include:
  - Terminals
  - Printers
  - Disk and tape devices
- **Memory.** Memory takes the form in modern computers of silicon chips capable of storing information. In commercial computers, this information takes the form of 1 and 0 in the notation known as *binary.* Memory comes in various forms including:
  - **RAM.** Random Access Memory whose contents can be changed but which is vulnerable to loss of power where the contents of memory may also be lost. This type of memory is also known as *dynamic* or *volatile* memory.
  - **ROM.** Read-Only Memory is a form of memory whereby instructions are "burned-in" and not lost in the event of a power loss. These programs cannot be changed. This is also known as non-volatile memory.
  - **PROM.** Programmable Read-Only Memory is similar to ROM but can have the contents changed.
  - **EPROM.** Erasable Programmable Read-Only Memory is similar to PROM but the instructions can be erased by ultra-violet light. There is another version of

memory known as ***nonvolatile RAM.*** This is memory that has been attached to a battery so that, in the event of a power loss, the contents will not be lost.

▪ **Mainframe.** Mainframe computers are the large (physically as well as in power) computers used by companies to carry out large-volume processing and concentrated computing.

▪ **Mini.** Minicomputers are physically smaller than mainframes, although the power of many minicomputers exceeds that of recent mainframes.

▪ **Micro.** Microcomputers are physically small computers with limited processing power and storage. Having said that, the power and capacity of today's micro is equivalent to that of a mainframe only five years ago.

▪ **LANs.** Local Areas Networks are collections of computers linked together within a comparatively small area.

▪ **WANs.** Wide Area Networks are collections of computers spread over a large geographic area.

Storage

Data is stored in a variety of forms for both permanent and temporary retention:

▪ **Bits.** Binary Digits, individual ones and zeros
▪ **Bytes.** Collections of Bits making up individual characters
▪ **Disks.** Large-capacity storage devices containing anything from 10 Mb to 150 Gb of data
▪ **Diskettes.** Small-capacity removable disks containing from 360 k to 100 Mb of data
▪ **Optical Disks.** Laser-encoded disks containing between 650 Mb and 9 GB of data
▪ **Tapes.** Reel-to-Reel or cassettes that store data
▪ **Memory.** See Memory under the Hardware section

Communications

In order to maximize the potential of the effective use of the information on computers it is essential that isolated computers be able to communicate and share data, programs, and hardware devices.

▪ **Terminals.** Remote devices allowing the input and output to and from the computer of data and programs.

▪ **Modem.** MOdulator/DEModulator, which translates digital computer signals into analog signals for telephone wires and retranslates them at the other end.

▪ **Multiplexer.** Combining signals from a variety of devices to maximize utilization of expensive communication lines.

▪ **Cable.** Metallic cable, usually copper, which can carry the signal between computers. These may come in the form of "twisted pair," where two or more cables are strung together within a plastic sleeve, or in the form of coaxial, where a cable runs within a metallic braiding in the same manner as a television aerial cable.

- **Fiber Optics.** These consist of fine strands of fiberglass or plastic filaments that carry light signals without the need for electrical insulation. They have extremely high capacity and transfer rates but are expensive.
- **Microwave.** This form of communication involves sending high-power signals from a transmitter to a receiver. They work on a direct line-of-sight basis but require no cables.

Input

Inputs to computer systems have developed rapidly over the years. The IT Auditor will still occasionally encounter some of the earlier types:

- **Cards.** Rarely seen nowadays, punch cards were among the first input and output media and consisted of cardboard sheets, some 8 inches by 4 inches with 80 columns, where rectangular holes could be punched in combinations to represent numeric, alphabetic, and special characters.
- **Paper Tape.** Another early input/output medium, paper tape was a low-cost alternative to punch cards and consisted of a one-inch wide paper tape with circular holes punched in it to form the same range of characters.
- **Keyboards.** The most common input device today (although that is changing). Most keyboards are still based on the original typist's QWERTY keyboard design.
- **Mouse.** An electromechanical pointing device used for inputting instructions in real time.
- **Scanners.** Optical devices that can scan pictures into a digitized computer-readable form. These devices may be used in combination with OCR (Optical Character Recognition) software to allow the computer to interpret the pictures of data into actual characters.
- **Bar Codes.** Optically recognizable printing that can be interpreted by low-cost scanners. Common in retail operations.
- **Voice.** Perhaps the future of computer input whereby the computer user, programmer, or auditor simply dictates into a microphone and the computer responds appropriately.

Output

As with inputs, outputs are changing rapidly. In the earliest of computing times, output came in three basic forms. The most common of these was paper, however, quantities of cards and paper tape were output for subsequent reprocessing. Nowadays most outputs are via screens or directly onto magnetic media.

- **Paper.** Still a popular output medium, paper may be in continuous stationery form, cut sheet form, or preprinted business stock such as invoices or negotiable instruments such as checks.
- **Computer.** Output directly to another computer is a growing trend with the coming of age of electronic data interchange (EDI).

- **Screen.** Output to screen is the current norm for the majority of outputs with graphics, tables, charts, and three-dimensional forms possible.
- **Microfilm/fiche.** For permanent, readable recording of outputs with a small storage space required, microfilm is a popular output medium. Each frame contains one page of printed output. An alternative is the creation of microfiche, measuring approximately 6 inches by 4 inches and containing some 200 pages of printout.
- **Magnetic Media.** Output to disks, diskettes, and tapes is commonly used to store large volumes of information.
- **Voice.** Another new output medium is voice, where a permanent record is not required.

Control

Within the computer systems, control is exercised at a variety of points within the overall architecture. At each stage, opportunities exist to vary the manner in which the computer systems perform to meet the needs of the users.

- **Operating System.** The Operating System is the set of programs that control the basic operations of the computer. All other software runs under the direction of the Operating System and rely on its services for all of the work they undertake.
- **Applications.** These systems perform the business functions required of the computer. They run under the direct control of the Operating System but may contain many powerful control elements themselves.
- **Parameters.** These are user-defined variations adjusting the manner in which programs normally operate.
- **Run Instructions.** These are instructions to operators of computers instructing them on the jobs to be run and responses to machine questions to be entered.
- **JCL.** Job Control Language is a means of automating the job-running process by giving the computer the instructions in the form of batch programming language.
- **Human Element.** Ultimate control is exercised by the people who use, operate, program, and manage computers.

People

As pointed out in the Criteria of Control (CoCo) report referenced in Chapter 15, control is exercised by people and, as such, the auditor must understand the roles and responsibilities of the individuals involved in the development and processing of computer systems.

- **Operators.** Use the computers on a day-to-day basis.
- **Programmers.** Write the application programs that run on the computer.
- **Systems Designers.** Design the overall structure of the application systems and specify the programs required.
- **Systems Analysts.** Analyze the business structures, applications, and procedures to determine what, if any, contribution IT can make. They also design the outline of business specifications of new systems.

- **Systems Programmers.** Are responsible for the well-being of the Operating Systems and programs, the related systems software components.
- **Database Analysts.** Are responsible for maintaining the DBMS, which is the systems software that controls access to and format of the data.
- **Network Analysts.** Are responsible for ensuring availability, performance standards, and security are achieved on networks.
- **Management.** Plan, organize, and direct to ensure corporate objectives are achieved.

Data

Data consists of:

- Fields held in
  - Records held in
    - Files held on
      - Disks

 ## BATCH AND ONLINE SYSTEMS

Batch versus Online

In the early days of commercial computing, and up to the late 1960s, most processing took place on a batch basis only. This meant that all inputs were collected centrally and input together in "batches" of documents. This would typically take place using a centralized data preparation function to convert the data from written form into holes punched into either cards or continuous paper tape. The process was highly error prone and the input medium was fragile. In later batch systems the data was entered via a terminal onto a file, which would later be processed in batch mode. In this type of system, the primary control objectives were the *accuracy* and *completeness* of capture.

Many highly effective controls were designed and implemented to ensure completeness of data capture of batches of data, complete capture of all batches, and accurate capturing of batches of input data. These controls included the manual preparation of batch header documents for later comparison to computer-generated information, and double keystroke verification, whereby an operator entered the data into a batch of cards or directly onto a file containing a batch of input transactions. This data was then re-inputted by an independent data capture clerk and compared by the system to ensure accuracy and completeness.

With the advent of online systems, such controls fell away because they were deemed to be no longer appropriate. In many cases within an online environment very few alternative controls were implemented and frequently the auditor would find that large assumptions were made as to the adequacy of the controls surrounding the accuracy and completeness of data input.

In today's systems, capture and processing will normally take place using online, real-time data capture with a small batch component. Input is typically via a terminal with instantaneous updates. Overnight report production in batch mode is common. The terminals may be local or remote and the remote terminals may be either dial-up or dedicated. The terminals themselves may be of differing types, but the principal control objectives remain:

- Availability
- Security
- Confidentiality
- Accuracy

In online systems there is an additional component to the system that comes complete with its own concerns, and that is the communications component. This may take the forms of microwave links, satellite hookups, or the more basic cables, which themselves may be either dedicated or dial-up.

Computers communicate in a digital form where a signal is either on or off, whereas normal telephone cables operate in an analog mode where the signal is moderated either by changing the height of the curve (amplitude modulation or AM) or by changing the frequency of the signal (frequency modulation or FM). Communications may operate in a *Simplex* mode where traffic is one way only. This means effectively that a circuit must make a complete circle to get there and get a reply back. This form of circuit is inexpensive but vulnerable. *Half-duplex* communication allows two-way traffic, but only one way at a time. This is the type of signal used in citizens' band (CB) radio. *Duplex* communications involves simultaneous two-way communication. Computer systems typically use half-duplex communication.

Other communication concepts that will be of interest to the auditor are:

- *Synchronous communications.* High-speed transmission and reception of long groups of characters
- *Asynchronous communications.* Slow, irregular transmissions, one character at a time with start and stop bits
- *Encryption.* Scrambling of data into unreadable forms such that it can be unscrambled
- *Protocol.* A set of rules for message transmission in the network

Networks themselves may be of varying types including Private Networks; Public Switched Networks (PSNs), such as the telephone systems; Value Added Networks (VANs), such as Beltel, where the service provider adds on additional services instead of simply providing point-to-point connection; and Local Area Networks (LANs), where the connections are both private and nearby. Where there is a significant physical distance involved the network may be referred to as a Wide Area Network (WAN). In recent years, the Internet has become of increasing concern as well as use to the Internal Auditor. The Internet is a collection of computers worldwide connected together loosely and provides both a source of information as well as a source of external risk.

Networks may be configured as point to-point with separate direct links. An alternative configuration could be a multi-drop configuration with multiple terminals sharing a single line. Ring Networks have no central computer; each machine is classed as a "node" on the network, and Star Networks have a single, central computer coordinating all communications.

Where an online system exists, there may be capabilities for:

- **Online inquiry,** which allows a remote user to retrieve data directly. In this case the primary concern should be **Confidentiality** of information.
- **Online data entry** permits remote entry of data and allows concurrent processing of data. In this case the primary concerns would be **Transaction Authenticity** as well as **Accuracy** and **Completeness.**
- **Online update** is similar to online data entry but with immediate effect of transactions. The primary concerns here would be **Concurrency Control** (prevention of two users updating the same record at the same time) and **Availability.**

The basic online concerns are:

- Availability
- Security
- Unauthorized access
- Accidental or intentional changes

Security-threatened areas would include the operating system and particularly its management features, intercomputer communication including dial-up access and gateways, as well as poor network performance.

In any networked operation, availability is a major concern. This includes availability of the hardware components, the software, the data, the networking capability, and the human resources.

Typical controls in this area to protect against unavailability are the ensuring of:

- An adequate physical environment
- Adequate backups
- Multiple redundancies in equipment to ensure no reliance on a single piece
- Peer-to-peer networking to permit mutual backup
- Adequate disaster-recovery planning
- Appropriate training

Security itself is a factor of the hardware, the software, and the human element. **Hardware** is liable to theft, sabotage, and penetration. On the **software** side, the operating system software may itself be stolen, corrupted, or bypassed, while applications software may suffer a similar fate and may additionally be replaced by an alternative application.

Data is one of the organization's most valuable assets and may be liable to theft, corruption, substitution, or manipulation.

Such security threats may come from normal users of the systems (deliberately or accidentally), specialist insiders such as the IT staff, legitimate outsiders such as computer engineers, customers and suppliers who have been granted access to the site, or outside hackers who attempt to penetrate the organization's security for fun or profit.

Database Management Systems

A DBMS is a software or hardware structure controlling the nature of, and access to, the information required by a user application system. Given the manner in which the systems developed over the years, it helps to have a clear understanding of what each component is.

Definition of Terms

Access Methods: Software logic procedures used to retrieve, insert, modify, and delete data on a storage device.

Data Dictionary/Data Directory Systems (DD/DS): Software that manages a repository of information about data and the database environment.

Data Independence and Data Sharing: A technique allowing diverse users with different logical views to access the same data in different ways. This is achieved by divorcing the definition of the nature and location of the data from the programs using it. The definitions, views, access rules, locations, logical views, and other information describing the actual data are located in one file of ***Metadata***, or data about the data. This enables new users with new logical views to be accommodated as well as changing logical views and changing physical representation.

Data Structure: The interrelationships of data.

Database: A collection of data logically organized to meet the information requirements of a universe of users.

Database Administration: A human function involved in the coordination and control of data-related activities.

Database Management System (DBMS): A hardware/software system that manages data by providing organization, access, and control functions.

Storage Structures: Methods and techniques used to physically represent data structures on storage devices.

User System Interfaces: Components of the database environment that request, manipulate, and transform data into information for an end user.

Conceptual Level of Database Design

Individual Database Management Systems vary widely in data structuring capabilities. Selection among these will depend on both the ***Entry Access Methods*** (Randomizing, Indexing) and the ***Navigational Access Methods*** (Read the First, Read the Next, Embedded Links, Inverted Index).

Principals of Data Structures

Data Structures are used to model a business (function) in terms of information and follow the general business structure, namely:

- Sequential
- Hierarchical
- Network
- Relational Model

Data Structures then become the basis for Database Type selection:

- Sequential
- Hierarchical
- Network
- Relational Model

All of these database types have generic components, although each component is different for each branded product:

- Data Definition Language (DDL)
- Storage Structure Definition Language (SSDL)
- Data Manipulation Language (DML)
- DBMS Nucleus and Utilities

Database Structuring Approaches

Over the years the form in which we have looked at data has evolved from the original ***sequential approach*** to today's ***relational approach.*** The auditor may still find examples of all such database approaches in the course of auditing.

Sequential Approach

- Fundamental Assumption
  There is a Direct Relationship between data:

Hierarchical Approach

■ Fundamental Assumption

There is some Hierarchical Relationship between data:

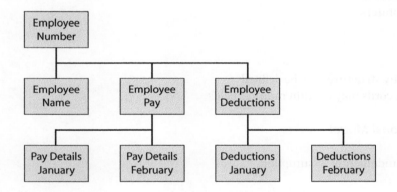

Terminology

■ Root Segment
■ Parent Segment
■ Child Segment
■ Twins

Network Approach

■ Fundamental Assumption

There is some General Relationship between data:

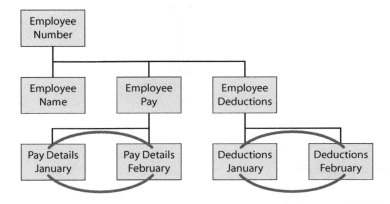

Terminology

- Records
- Pointers

Note

- Any structure may be defined
- Records may contain multiple fields

Relational Model

- Fundamental Assumption

There is some Mathematical Relationship between data:
Data is held in Tables with each individual line being a Table Entry or Tuple

Emp. No.	Dept. No.	Name
12	15	F Bloggs
25	43	J Smith

Employee Table	
Dept. No.	**Dept. Name**
43	Internal Audit
47	IT

Department Table

Data Manipulation	
SELECT	— All Retrieval
UPDATE	— Change
INSERT	— Create new Tuple
DELETE	— Delete Tuple
FROM	— Specifies Table
WHERE	— Conditions
AND	— Conjunction of Conditions
OR	— Disjunction of Conditions

Example

SELECT — EMPLOYEE = NAME FROM EMPLOYEE-DB WHERE
—DEPT = "B03" AND POSITION = "MANAGER"

The result is always a table:

Packages and Vendors

DB2	—IBM
DATACOM	—ADR

INVERTED LIST

Record	Make	Color	Model
1	BMW	Red	528I
2	Ford	Blue	Laser
3	Ford	Red	Laser
4	BMW	Blue	328i

Can be indexed by Make, Color, Model

Make	Records
BMW	1,4
Ford	2,3

Color	Records
Red	1,3
Blue	2,4

Model	Records
328I	4
528I	1
Laser	2,3

Terminology

■ Indexes and Pointers

Data Dictionary/Directory Systems

The ***Data Dictionary*** (DD) tells what is in a database/file. It deals with the description of the logical view (i.e., the partial view of the data that a user has and includes such items as the data Name, Description, Synonym, etc.).

The ***Data Directory*** tells where and how to access data. It deals with the description of the physical aspects of data such as Location, Address, and Physical Representation.

Entities of the DD/Directory Systems (DS) are defined by ***Attributes***, which describe data's:

■ Identification
■ Source
■ Classification
■ Usage
■ Qualification
■ Relationship

A DD/DS can be a useful tool independent of the need for a DBMS in the areas of documentation support, coordination of shared data usage, and control over modification of programs and files. The DD/DS has become popular with the advent of DBMS packages with the greater recognition of opportunities to share data, leading to a greater need to control data usage, the future introduction of computer privacy legislation, as well as the complexity of relationships involved.

Who Looks After the Database System?

Database Administrator

Functions of the database administrator (DBA) include coordinating the information content of the database. This does not mean that the actual data itself is the DBA's concern, but rather that the DBA is responsible for deciding the storage structure and access strategy. The DBA will liaise with computer users and, following their business requirements, will define authorization checks and validation procedures as well as a strategy for backup and recovery. The DBA is also responsible for monitoring performance and responding to changes in requirements.

In order to achieve all these objectives, DBAs have at their disposal tools specifically designed to facilitate these tasks. These tools include *utility programs* to permit the loading of raw data onto the database, *reorganization routines* to keep the database access efficient as well as effective, and *statistical analysis* to determine when maintenance is required. In addition, *journaling* (e.g., logs) can keep records of who did what and when on the database. Although these logs are optional, they can be of major assistance to the DBA in database recovery in the event of problems. The *Data Dictionary* itself, in addition to *database analyzers*, will also assist in recovery.

Database Recovery

The objective of database recovery is to reinstate databases to a known state while minimizing lost work. This means that it must permit recovery on a transaction basis and provide fast recovery in order to minimize manual work while ensuring the safety of recovery data. At the same time, it is inevitable in such a process that some data will eventually go missing and recovery must provide a mechanism to inform users of "lost" transactions. Recovery must cater for various types of failures including hardware as well as software disasters.

Recovery procedures come in various forms to cater to the various forms of failure and include:

- **Checkpoints.** The DBMS will either determine or force a point in time where all transactions have been affected, committed to disk, and all memory buffers have been flushed. At this point a record is made that the database is "quiet" or has been "quiessed" and that any recovery only needs to go back this far. It is used to define a "stable" state of the database for recovery.
- **Roll Back.** The log is processed backward and completed transactions are rolled out to the last checkpoint.
- **Roll Forward.** Log is processed forward to reinstate the system.
- **Update Backup copy.** (e.g., Media Failure)
- **Compensating Transactions.** (e.g., Journal Entries)
- **Salvation Routine**

For effective log recovery, before the database is updated a log of the *before* image is made to enable undoing the change if necessary (e.g., failure before update). After the database is updated a log of the *after* image is made to redo change if necessary (e.g., media failure). These logs contain audit trail information for manual followup (e.g., Program Id, Transaction Id).

Auditing Databases

With the advent of DBMSs, these have been a migration of controls from individual application to the general database environment. This migration of controls improves control opportunities overall and permits the centralized administration of the control environment.

In order to review relevant database designs, the auditor would:

- List all the record types
- Read and analyze their descriptions and names
- Identify the key of each record and verify requirement for uniqueness
- Study the relationships (and sets)
- Identify all the relationships, which are:
  - One:Many
  - Many:Many
- Evaluate the strength of each relationship
- Verify consistency of the design with business information needs

Documentation of the Database Environment

The Data Dictionary/Directory System can be used to accept, record, and generate a variety of documentation, including:

- Requirements and specifications
- Data documentation
- Metadata generation

It can automate the documentation process and enable cross-referencing of programs to individual data elements as well as report generation. It can also assist in enforcing **change control.**

The Data Dictionary can be effective in **active** or **passive** mode. In active mode, all database access must be made via the DD/DS. In passive mode the DD/DS is there as a record, but has very little effective control. The obvious advantages of an Active DD/DS include improved accuracy, timeliness, completeness, and control over updates.

Administration and Coordination Functions

The auditor would also review the Administration and Coordination Functions by examining the review and monitoring activities of the DBA, which would include reviews of database designs, reviews of system design, reviews of program design and coding, monitoring the general quality of data, and monitoring overall database performance.

Organizational issues such as the roles that require segregation would also be examined. These would typically include:

- Database Administration
- Systems Development
- Programming
- Operations
- End Users
- Internal Audit

This can only be effectively done by assigning responsibility for data ownership. This can mitigate the control concern of uncoordinated sharing of data-update responsibility by assigning responsibility for data definition. Such coordinating of shared usage ensures the uniform application of the appropriate level of controls.

Operational Controls for the Database Environment

In the operation of a database-structured business system, the auditor must ensure the existence and effectiveness of controls for ensuring against unauthorized access, controls over ensuring accuracy and completeness, Recovery and Restart tools and techniques, and controls over access to data.

The impact of a database environment on privacy and security is complicated by the need to assess requirements among multiple users. Sharing of data may cause control concerns; however, it is possible to describe security specifications using the Declarative Data Definition Language (DDL), thus centrally ensuring clearer specifications and making the environment easier to audit. This is brought about by the migration of the implementation of controls from the application to the environment.

Impact of Database on Completeness and Accuracy Issues

Database technology can have a marked effect on the quality of information provided. This is a concentration of risk due to sharing of data and an increased cost of error correction due to the system's complexity. In addition, there can be a deteriorating effect on user reliance and confidence due to database erosion and cascading errors.

Mitigating the concerns involving completeness and accuracy means that not only the risks but also the controls must migrate. These may be generalized in the environment and implemented in the DBMS, DD/DS, and so on.

The benefits from the auditor's viewpoint include the potential for:

- Consistency of data
- Enhanced quality of audit by increased accessibility
- More accurate systems-development process
- Data resource management will accrue benefits through formalized discipline
- Migration of controls

Disadvantages from the auditor's viewpoint include:

- New Technology/Pioneer syndrome (technology lust)
- Implementation cost control
- Access to DBMS managed data
- Data integrity tradeoffs
- Change in scope/timing of audit

The role of the auditor in such a changed environment is to consult with the database user on requirements, check the edit and validation rules, determine whether there is partial acceptance or rejection on error, determine who has the responsibility for correctness and consult with DBA on the implementation plan.

Qualities that assist the auditor in these tasks include the capability for edit and validation element by element, the error response, the procedures for edit and validation maintenance, and the procedures for adding new data elements.

Common DBMS edit and validation controls include:

- Uniqueness checking for Key and Nonkey
- Structural/Relational checking
- Picture string and simple format checking
- Edit and validation performed according to declaratively specified criteria

Metadata generation can provide the desired control environment.

Controlling Initial Database Content

Usually the user is responsible for providing initial database content and should spot-check the loaded database for correctness. The auditor will determine whether there have been sufficient checks by using statistical methods when appropriate.

 ## ELECTRONIC DATA INTERCHANGE

Electronic data interchange (EDI) can be formally defined as the transfer of structured data, by agreed message standards, from one computer system to another without human intervention. It is used to replace conventional business documents with the transfer of electronic documents or business data from one computer system to another computer system (i.e., from one trading partner to another trading partner without the need to re-capture transactions or, indeed, without human intervention). To utilize this technology successfully, agreed standards were required between trading partners to ensure accuracy, completeness, and nonrepudiation of transactions. Under normal circumstances, human intervention is required only in the handling of error conditions within application systems, as would be the case regardless of the method of input.

In order to facilitate the transmission of information between disparate hardware and software architectures, EDI standards were designed to operate independently of communication and software technologies.

There are four major sets of **EDI standards:**

1. The UN recommended ***UN/EDIFACT*** is the main international standard and is predominant outside North America.
2. In North America, the predominant. standard is ***ANSI ASC X12 (X12).***
3. Within the European automotive industry, the ***ODETTE*** standard is common.

4. In the retail industry, the **EANCOM** standard, based on EDIFACT, is the generally accepted standard and has superseded the earlier **TRADACOMS** standard, although this is still used extensively in the United Kingdom.

From both a business control and auditing perspective, the existing business processes designed to handle paper transactions may not be appropriate for EDI and typically require changes to accommodate electronic processing of business documents. Audit trails, where they exist, will be electronic and will require the use of the appropriate interrogation software rather than manual scrutiny of paper documents. In many cases, these audit trails may exist for a very short period of time unless a control system has been designed to accommodate electronic recordkeeping.

 ## ELECTRONIC BUSINESS

Electronic business, often referred to as "**eBusiness,**" "**e-business,**" or "**internet business,**" is generally defined as the application of information and communication technologies (ICT) in support of all the activities of business in order to enable businesses to better satisfy the needs and expectations of their customers by linking their internal and external data processing systems more efficiently. E-business may involve a variety of business processes that could include the entire value chain from electronic purchasing and supply chain management through processing orders electronically to handling customer service.

E-business generally takes one of three forms:

1. **Electronic Commerce** in the form of either business-to-business interactivity (B2B) or business-to-consumer (B2C) interactivity. Internet shopping, online marketing, and supply chain management would all be seen as forms of Electronic Commerce.
2. **Internal Business Systems** ranging from human resource management through financial systems could all be handled as e-business depending on the nature of the organization.
3. **Enterprise-wide Communications** ranging from email to web conferencing and Voice over Internet Protocol (VoIP) may also be classified as forms of e-business.

In all of these cases, the risk profile of e-business differs from conventional business risks due to the nature of the systems. Access is typically granted to greater numbers and a wider variety of individuals over whom direct control may not be exercised. At the same time, the wider exposure of systems and information increases the risk exposure in a variety of areas. These would typically include:

▪ **Systems Availability** becomes critical since the expectation is that all system functionality will be available to all users at the time of their choosing and service disruptions can have a severe impact on the business.

- ***Access Control*** to specific functionality may require restrictions that in many organizations have not traditionally been implemented on the basis that "we trust our staff." When this is combined with changes to privacy legislation and the potential access of an unknown population, control in this area becomes of paramount importance.
- ***Privacy and Confidentiality*** become a complicated exercise with businesses potentially giving other businesses and individuals direct access to information that would normally be seen as company confidential or individually private.
- ***Data Integrity*** becomes more difficult to maintain and to ensure that data, either in transit or at the organization's system, cannot be compromised or corrupted accidentally or deliberately.
- ***Authenticity of Transactions*** becomes critical because of the potential alteration, duplication, or deletion of transactions. It is essential that both parties in a transaction can have confidence that the other party is who they claim to be. Traditional authentication techniques such as password protection, digital signatures, or other biometric authentication mechanisms may require use in multiple layers in order to ensure appropriate authentication.
- ***Nonrepudiation*** is a general requirement for business transactions ensuring that neither party can deny participating in the transaction or argue that the transaction does not reflect what was agreed to. This typically involves advanced authentication techniques such as the use of digital signatures.

 ## CLOUD COMPUTING

Cloud Computing originally evolved as an extension of the traditional ***Client-Server*** approach to computing in which a network-friendly client version of a particular application system was lodged on client computers. These utilized the client system's memory and CPU for processing while the resultant data files were stored centrally on the corporate data servers. This meant that multiple user licenses of an application had to be purchased for use by many users on a network.

The concept of Cloud Computing differs from this model in that the application systems are provided from the server and executed and managed by the clients' web browsers with no need for an installed client version of the application system. This form of application centralization gives the cloud service providers absolute control over the versions of an application system provided to clients, thus removing the need for license agreements on an individual client basis as well as easing software version control. This form of Cloud Computing is commonly known as ***Software as a Service (SaaS)***. As a result of this, both the hardware and software requirements on the user's side decrease, with the cloud's network taking the bulk of the load.

In terms of risk, client computing once again exacerbates the risks of information security and privacy since the data as well as the applications are maintained within the cloud itself. This can expose both the user of the system as well as the service provider to potentially serious risks of data loss as well as cyber espionage. In addition, where the data resides in a country other than that of the cloud user, the user may be exposed to legal issues regarding future access to his or her own data as well as ownership of the intangible property under the terms of another country's legislation. A further complication arises should access to the clouded services be, for any reason, unavailable. Potentially this could leave the user of the service in an untenable position where his or her ability to do business may be severely restricted. Should a client decide to migrate the data to another cloud provider, further complications may ensue due to the lack of porting standards.

Further details of cloud computing will be covered in Part III.

CHAPTER TWO

IT Audit Function Knowledge

T HIS CHAPTER LOOKS at the laws and regulations governing information technology (IT) audits and the nature and role of the audit charter. It reviews the varying nature of audits and the demand for audits as well as the need for control and audit of computer-based IT. The types of audit and auditor and range of services to be provided are reviewed together with the standards and codes of ethics of both the Institute of Internal Auditors (IIA) and the standards specified by the Information Systems Audit and Control Association (ISACA).

 INFORMATION TECHNOLOGY AUDITING

Effective management of information and related IT has become of critical importance to the survival and long-term success of any organization. This has arisen because of the increasing dependence on information and the associated systems that deliver this information, together with the costs and size of future use of IT. As a result, management has a heightened expectation of delivery from IT functions and demands improved quality with a decreased delivery time and improved service levels at reduced costs. In addition, the increasing potential from threats such as information warfare or cyber terrorism has added a new awareness. At the same time, the potential for technology to revolutionize organizations and their business practices creates new business opportunities and offers the chance to massively reduce costs.

IT Audit has traditionally been based upon the paradigms that control equals **management** control, that management control starts with governance, that top management can control everything, and that control is imposed.

Today's business environment suggests that a more appropriate re-engineered paradigm might be that continuous improvement focuses control with owners of the process.

The role of IT Audit must change to reflect this new reality. That IT Audit is ultimately responsible to the organization will not change; however, the owners of the process are becoming the custodians of internal control and not necessarily traditional management structures.

IT Auditors frequently become experts at describing the best design and implementation of all types of controls. IT Auditors are not, however, expected to equal—let alone exceed—the technical and operational expertise pertaining to the various activities of the organization. Nevertheless, they may help the responsible individuals achieve more effective results by appraising the existing controls and providing a basis for helping to improve those controls.

WHAT IS MANAGEMENT?

Management has been described as optimizing the utilization of corporate resources through the planning, organizing, leading, and controlling of the members of any organization. It is a process of continuous improvement whereby the business itself is constantly adapting to its environment and management must change in a similar order.

MANAGEMENT PROCESS

The management process begins with an *understanding of the organization's business.* Until this is achieved, any attempt to determine organizational needs will be at best misleading and at worst disastrous. Once the overall objectives and environment of the business have been established, *establishing the needs* becomes a comparatively easy task. The organization's needs may be determined by identifying and examining the *key activities* whose effective performance can make or break the organization. These key activities must themselves be monitored and therefore ambitious *performance objectives* must be established early in the planning process. For every performance objective there will be a range of threats which, if fulfilled, will either reduce the effectiveness or totally negate the objective. These must be assessed in a formal *risk assessment* to determine the appropriate corporate coping strategy. The coping or *control strategies* must be determined by management and the appropriate controls themselves selected. The actual controls must be *implemented and monitored* and there should exist controls to ensure this happens. Controls, once implemented, must be effective in performance and periodically management must *evaluate and review performance* with this in mind.

UNDERSTANDING THE ORGANIZATION'S BUSINESS

This is a combination of a theoretical approach utilizing literature searches on the organization and its functions on the business press, if possible, combined with a reading of annual reports in order to obtain the whole picture.

This theory will be combined with a more practical approach involving interviewing staff in order to both evaluate their understanding of the business as well as to confirm the auditor's understanding. Site visits to observe the operation of specific business functions will also assist in this endeavor. Further information and confirmation may be derived by comparing the current understandings to those in effect during previous reviews.

 ## ESTABLISHING THE NEEDS

Once the overall objectives and environment of the business have been established, the overall needs must be determined. A study of the organizational mission statement permits the general performance objectives to be derived. Management should have established strategic plans and objectives in order to ensure these are achieved. By interviewing executive management, employees, and perhaps even customers and suppliers, the business needs for the successful accomplishment of the objectives may be determined.

 ## IDENTIFYING KEY ACTIVITIES

The major products and services provided to meet the business objectives need to be identified. Once again this will involve determining the level of management's understanding of customer needs and sizes, the competition and their probable response patterns, as well as their understanding of which are their own key performance areas (KPAs). The KPAs are those activities that will make or break those activities.

 ## ESTABLISH PERFORMANCE OBJECTIVES

For each KPA, Performance Objectives must be established. This involves seeking core activity targets that are both achievable and stretching. Key Performance Indicators (KPIs) will be required to measure performance appropriately. The risks and threats that could lead to non/under-achievement must be assessed including both external and internal threats.

 ## DECIDE THE CONTROL STRATEGIES

Once the full risk analysis is complete, management is in a position to decide what activities must be ensured, which risks must be managed, and which transferred. This, in turn, will dictate which risks can be cost-effectively prevented, which must be detected, and how a materialized risk can be corrected.

Business risks must be prioritized and tradeoffs will be required because control measures are commonly contradictory, so that efficiency may trade off against effectiveness.

IMPLEMENT AND MONITOR THE CONTROLS

For controls to be effective, they must be monitored and wishing them into existence will not accomplish the fact. Controls result from the planned and thoughtful intervention of management to achieve a specific end.

Monitoring may take several forms including self-assessment, the use of regular audits, and the introduction of continuous improvement programs. Controls must be frequently reviewed for ongoing relevance as well as for their effectiveness and must be modified and adapted where required.

EXECUTIVE MANAGEMENT'S RESPONSIBILITY AND CORPORATE GOVERNANCE

Corporate Governance may be defined as the relationship among various participants in determining the direction and performance of companies and includes:

- Shareholders
- Management
- Board of Directors
- Employees

Under this definition, the objectives of a corporation may be further defined as including the attainment of human satisfaction in a social structure. Efficiency and effectiveness, flexibility, and continuity then form a significant part of fulfilling a corporation's objectives.

Management then becomes the link between the providers of capital (owners and shareholders) and users of capital (operational or functional management). The review and approval of financial and operating objectives are normally carried out by executive management. They will also offer advice to general management, recommend board candidates, and review the adequacy of internal controls.

AUDIT ROLE

Auditing may take the form of IT, internal, external, and public sector auditing. Internal auditing examines the adequacy and effectiveness of the management system of internal control. The role of the external auditor is primarily one of ensuring the fairness of representation of the financial accounts of the entity audited. Within the public sector, much auditing is aimed at ensuring the effectiveness and efficiency of management processes in order to ensure service delivery. IT Auditing may be used in any of the other areas.

The auditing process is also designed to determine where to audit as well as what to audit, and may use any and all of:

- Control Strategy Assessment
- Control Adequacy and Effectiveness
- Performance Quality Assessment
- Unit Performance Reporting
- Following Up

Overall the standards of audit performance must be up to a professional level. For IT Audit, this typically means to a level laid down in the ISACA standards.

CONCEPTUAL FOUNDATION

The Conceptual Foundation is provided by implementing a structured Risk Analysis. This involves the assessment of the risk of expressing an incorrect audit opinion that comprises both the risk of audit misstatement as well as the risk of failure to discover. In addition, this includes the evaluation of business risk that comprises risks to both the auditee as well as to third parties.

PROFESSIONALISM WITHIN THE IT AUDITING FUNCTION

IT Auditing responsibilities include the development and implementation of a risk-based IT Audit strategy and objectives in compliance with generally accepted audit standards (GAAS) in order to provide a statement of assurance that the organization's information technology and business processes are controlled, monitored, and assessed adequately, and are aligned with the organization's business objectives. This would also facilitate the monitoring of the implementation of risk management and control practices within the organization.

In addition, IT Auditing involves the planning of specific audits to ensure that the IT Audit strategy and objectives are achieved and that information is obtained that is sufficient, reliable, relevant, and useful in order to achieve the audit objectives. This will typically involve the analysis of information gathered in order to identify reportable conditions and reach appropriate conclusions. IT management will be required to review the work performed in order to provide a reasonable assurance that objectives have been achieved. A critical function within IT Auditing is the communication of audit results to key managers and stakeholders.

The professionalism of IT Auditing is demonstrated by adherence to both the ISACA *Code of Professional Ethics* and the ISACA IT *Auditing Standards* (see Chapter 4).

RELATIONSHIP OF INTERNAL IT AUDIT TO THE EXTERNAL AUDITOR

The external auditor is primarily responsible to the organization and all of its stakeholders. While the external auditor has a statutory responsibility to report on financial matters, IT Auditing forms a key role in achieving that statutory responsibility. As such, while IT Auditing is an integral part of an internal audit function, it must also be seen as an integrated function within the execution of the work of the independent external auditor.

RELATIONSHIP OF IT AUDIT TO OTHER COMPANY AUDIT ACTIVITIES

An understanding of the relationship between IT Auditing and other company audit activities is required in order to fully understand the nature of IT Auditing. The IT Auditor may be seen as an integral part of the IT Audit function, playing an external consultant's role or playing an internal role but independent of the IT Audit function.

Overall, the roles and responsibilities of the audit function typically are found within the *audit charter*.

AUDIT CHARTER

Charters tend to be common in approach, although individual charters are tailored to meet the unique needs of the organization for which they are designed. Because of its role—to define the relationship and responsibilities that should exist among the Chief Executive, the head of IT Audit, and the line managers—it is normally seen to be highly desirable that the Chief Executive takes a close interest in the drafting of the charter. In practice, many audit functions draw up their own charter and seek ratification from the Chief Executive and audit committee. In most organizations, it is commonly perceived to be the defining terms of reference for the head of the audit function and provides top management with a measurement of the level of assurance regarding the reliability and quality of internal control within the organization. It also acts as a point of reference when the audit function's structure, plans, or reports are being reviewed.

To the operational managers of an organization, the charter indicates the level of authority to act delegated to the audit function in reviewing each of their systems of internal control over the computer and manual systems. They may expect to see constraints within the body of the document, which preserves their own rights as decision makers.

CHARTER CONTENT

The form, content, and wording of the charter will normally be selected by the audit function itself. These will typically be influenced by IT Audit standards and should encourage best professional practice as defined by the appropriate professional bodies. The IT Audit charter may be an independent publication or, in the case of a formally constituted Internal Audit function, be part of the Internal Audit charter. The document is normally signed off by both the Chief Executive and the Chairman of the Audit Committee. The document itself would typically consist of:

- A formal definition of IT Audit within the organization and its key objectives.
- The authority under which the head of IT Audit acts, including the line of reporting as well as rights of access to people, properties, assets, and records.
- Terms of reference describing, at a detailed level, the role and working objectives of the head of IT Audit.

 ## OUTSOURCING THE IT AUDIT ACTIVITY

Many organizations have decided to outsource the IT Audit function. In some cases, this decision has been made because of a lack of expertise within the internal audit function. In other cases it is not cost effective for the organization to maintain internally the skills and disciplines required to keep the IT Audit function up to date and effective. In all cases where the function has been outsourced, management requires assurance that the control of the function is being maintained at a professional level. The method of achieving this is the same as if the function were internal, in compliance with international accepted standards for professional practice. Ensuring compliance with such standards is part of the role of the audit committee and is normally achieved by commissioning of a quality assurance review to be carried out on the IT Audit function.

 ## REGULATION, CONTROL, AND STANDARDS

Increasingly, accreditation and audit of IT services must be provided by internal or third parties to ensure that adequate security and control exists. Several evaluation methods exist that can be used to determine adequacy including ITSEC, TCSEC, and ISO 9000 evaluations using standards such as COBIT (*Control Objectives for Information and Related Technology*), ISO 17799, ITIL (IT Infrastructure Library), COSO *Internal Control—Integrated Framework* and COSO *Enterprise Risk Management—Integrated Framework*, and so forth.

CHAPTER THREE

IT Risk and Fundamental Auditing Concepts

THIS CHAPTER EXPLORES the concepts of materiality within the IT audit function and contrasts materiality as it is commonly applied to financial statement audits such as those performed by independent external auditors. In this context, the quality and types of evidence required to meet the definitions of sufficiency, reliability, and relevancy are examined. The risks involved in examining evidence to arrive at an audit conclusion are reviewed as are the need to maintain the independence and objectivity of the auditor and the auditor's responsibility for fraud detection in both an Information Technology (IT) and non-IT setting.

 COMPUTER RISKS AND EXPOSURES

"Control" comprises all the elements of an organization (including its resources, systems, processes, culture, structure, and tasks) that, taken together, support people in the achievement of the organization's objectives. Control is "effective" to the extent that it provides reasonable assurance that the organization will achieve its objectives reliably. Leadership involves making choices in the face of uncertainty. "Risk" is the possibility that one or more individuals or organizations will experience adverse consequences from those choices. Risk is the mirror image of opportunity.[1]

All entities encounter risk regardless of their size, structure, nature, or industry. In common with this, all business decisions involve elements of risk including such elements as financing, product lines or sources, and methods of supply.

All businesses, products, and processes involve some degree of risk. Risk management involves assessing a product, process, or business by:

- Identifying processes
- Identifying the types of risks associated with each process
- Identifying the controls associated with each process
- Evaluating the adequacy of the system of control in mitigating risk
- Determining the key controls associated with each process
- Determining the effectiveness of the key controls

Three types of risk are normally considered when using a risk-based audit approach. They are *inherent risk, control risk,* and *audit risk.*

Inherent Risk

Inherent risk is the likelihood of a significant loss occurring before taking into account any risk-reducing factors. In evaluating inherent risk, the auditor must consider what are the types of and nature of risks as well as what factors indicate a risk exists. To achieve this the auditor must be familiar with the environment in which the entity operates.

Control Risk

Control risk measures the likelihood that the control processes established to limit or manage inherent risk are ineffective. In order to ensure that internal audit evaluates the controls properly, the auditor must understand how to measure which controls are effective. This will involve identifying those controls that provide the greatest degree of assurance to minimize risks within the business. Control effectiveness is strongly impacted by the quality of work and control supervision.

Controls in business operations provide the major line of defense against inherent risk. In general, the auditor may assume that stronger controls reduce the amount of risk; however, at some point the cost of control may become prohibitive (in terms of both monetary and staff resources as well as customer satisfaction).

Audit Risk

Audit risk is the risk that audit coverage will not address significant business exposures. Pro-forma audit programs may be developed in order to reduce audit risk. These provide guidance as to which key controls should exist to address the risk, and the recommended compliance and/or substantive test steps to be performed. These programs should be used with care and modified to reflect the current business risk profile.

EFFECT OF RISK

In general, business risks may affect a company's ability to successfully compete, to maintain financial strength and a positive public image, and ultimately, its ability to survive. Risks will impact the overall quality of an organization's products, people, or services. Risks cannot be eliminated—only managed.

Auditors have traditionally been tasked with gaining and confirming an understanding of the system of internal control as fundamental to evaluating the adequacy and effectiveness of management's internal controls. Internal control has been presumed to be a response to business risk. In order to evaluate the effectiveness of risk-control measures, the auditor must have a comprehensive understanding of the underlying business risks.

Within a heavily computerized organization, such an understanding requires, initially, a thorough understanding of the business process in order to identify critical processes where less-than-optimum performance could have severe consequences. In addition, an understanding of the risks inherent within a computerized environment is essential in order to assess the appropriateness and mitigating effects of the control environment.

Such understandings of both the business process and the IT environment imply a collaborative approach because the internal auditor is rarely as knowledgeable about the process as the manager who routinely controls it or the IT staff implementing the IT control environment. By the same token, the management and IT teams who are involved in a business or IT process on a day-to-day basis will normally lack the independent perspective an internal auditor can bring to risk evaluation.

One of the major cornerstones of IT governance is the management of risks. This is increasingly being seen as a strategic issue to be addressed at board level in order to ensure the ongoing viability of the organization because failure within IT can have a catastrophic effect on the organization.

For many business executives, understanding the risks relating to the use of IS remains a challenge. In some cases, this results from a basic lack of understanding of the uses and potential abuses of such information systems. Many executives derive their understanding of IT risk from the popular media, who tend to focus on risk areas of high visibility and human interest and neglect the underlying flaws in control strategies that allowed those risks to materialize.

Elimination of risk is neither possible nor desirable because it is by careful management of risks that organizations achieve their objectives. The risk of not using IT in an appropriate way is as great or possibly greater than the risk of the existing technology failing or being penetrated.

Because of the increasingly complex business environment coupled with growth in the use of advanced technological solutions, the management of information risks has become one of the most challenging areas within which management must operate. Conducting business, particularly at an international level, requires the demonstration of high levels of good governance. As a result of this requirement for good governance, organizations place a growing emphasis on *enterprise risk management* (ERM).

Enterprise risks come in a variety of forms including operational, financial, and systemic risk. Within these, technology risk and the risk of failures within information security are critical.

COSO has defined the *ERM Framework* as encompassing:

- *"Strategic.* High level goals, aligned with and supporting its mission
- *Operations.* Effective and efficient use of its resources
- *Reporting.* Reliability of reporting
- *Compliance.* Compliance with applicable laws and regulations"[2]

As can be seen, IT plays an important role in all of these areas. As such, IT risks could be defined as:

- **Strategic.** The risk that IT either developed in-house or purchased is not aligned with the organization's goals and does not support the achievement of its mission.
- **Operations.** The risk that the information systems in use by the organization impose unacceptable overheads on the organization or result in sub-optimal service levels. At the same time, the dependency of organizations on the information systems means that unavailability of those systems within appropriate timescales can also prove a major operational risk.
- **Reporting.** The risk that IT cannot be relied on to produce information in an accurate, complete, and timely manner.
- **Compliance.** The risk that IT, in itself, leads to breaches of laws and regulations with a result of losses to the organization, either financial or in reputation.

 ## AUDIT AND RISK

The Institute of Internal Auditors (IIA) Practice Advisory 2100-6: Control and Audit Implications of E-commerce Activities highlights the challenges facing internal auditors in organizations that increasingly use IT in business operations and provides guidance as to the role and responsibilities of internal audits.

> Continuous changes in technology offer the internal auditing profession both great opportunity and risk. Before attempting to provide assurance on the systems and processes, an internal auditor should understand the changes in business and information systems, the related risks, and the alignment of strategies with the enterprise's design and market requirements. The internal auditor should review management's strategic planning and risk-assessment processes and its decisions.[3]

It is the responsibility of operational management to identify, assess, and manage risk. It is IT audit's responsibility to assist management in this process by facilitating the identification and assessment of risk and by assisting management to monitor how well risks are actually being managed by the business.

Many organizations do not have the resources available to identify, analyze, and control all business risks from an IT perspective. Implementing a formal risk-assessment process assists by providing a consistent method for selecting high-impact risks on which to focus audit resources.

During the risk assessment, IT auditors develop an understanding of the operation's business in order to facilitate the identification and assessment of significant risks to and from the information systems. This assessment is then used to allocate audit resources to areas within the organization that provide executive management and the Audit Committee with the most efficient and effective level of audit coverage.

Auditors must always keep in mind that individual managers have differing attitudes toward risk. Some managers or even organizations see the acceptance of risk as fundamental to the making of profits, whereas others are highly risk-averse and consider reducing risk a fundamental component of the business. This is referred to as *risk tolerance.* Unless the auditor understands this concept, it is likely that management and auditors will talk at cross purposes on risk and that audit recommendations may be deemed impractical or unacceptable.

Based upon the individual risk positions adopted, companies will have many different risk-mitigation interventions, such as insurance coverage, financial instruments, compliance, and internal audit functions. Management must understand that internal audit does not replace management's responsibility to control its own risk to acceptable levels.

Risks themselves are commonly categorized based on the organization's response, thus:

- **Controllable risks.** Risks that exist within the processes of an organization and that are wholly in the hands of the organization to mitigate.
- **Uncontrollable risks.** Risks that can arise externally to the organization and that cannot be directly controlled or influenced but that nevertheless call for a risk position to be taken by the organization.
- **Influenceable risks.** Risks that arise externally to the organization but that can be influenced by the organization.

 ## AUDIT EVIDENCE

IT auditors are frequently expected to express an opinion on the adequacy and effectiveness of internal controls in mitigating risk. For this the auditor must gather audit evidence. Evidence may be defined as *information intended to prove or support a belief.* Individually, items of evidence may be flawed by a personal bias or by a potential error of measurement and each piece may be less competent than desirable so the auditor will look in total at the "body of evidence," which should provide a factual basis for audit opinions.

CONDUCTING AN IT RISK-ASSESSMENT PROCESS

Multiple methodologies exist for the execution of an IT risk assessment. We will examine several of these, together with the author's own methodology, which has proved effective in both risk evaluations and control-management design.

NIST SP 800 30 FRAMEWORK

Under the SP 800 30 framework of the National Institute of Standards and Technology (NIST), risk assessment, involves the determination of the likelihood of a future adverse event. *Threats* to an IT system must be evaluated in conjunction with the potential *vulnerabilities* and the *controls* in place for the IT system.

Impact refers to the magnitude of harm that could be caused by a threat's exercise of vulnerability. The level of impact is governed by the potential mission impacts and produces a relative value for the IT assets and resources affected (e.g., the criticality sensitivity of the IT system components and data). The *risk-assessment* methodology encompasses nine primary steps:[4]

Step 1. System Characterization
Step 2. Threat Identification
Step 3. Vulnerability Identification
Step 4. Control Analysis
Step 5. Likelihood Determination
Step 6. Impact Analysis
Step 7. Risk Determination
Step 8. Control Recommendations
Step 9. Results Documentation

Once risk has been quantified, risk mitigation is seen to be a systematic methodology used by senior management to reduce mission risk that can be achieved through any of the following risk-mitigation options:

- **Risk Assumption**. To accept the potential risk and continue operating the IT system or to implement controls to lower the risk to an acceptable level.
- **Risk Avoidance**. To avoid the risk by eliminating the risk cause and/or consequence (e.g., forgo certain functions of the system or shut down the system when risks are identified).
- **Risk Limitation**. To limit the risk by implementing controls that minimize the adverse impact of a threat exercising a vulnerability (e.g., use of supporting, preventive, detective controls).
- **Risk Planning**. To manage risk by developing a risk-mitigation plan that prioritizes, implements, and maintains controls.

- **Research and Acknowledgment**. To lower the risk of loss by acknowledging the vulnerability or flaw and researching controls to correct the vulnerability.
- **Risk Transference**. To transfer the risk by using other options to compensate for the loss, such as purchasing insurance.

The object is to address the greatest risks and strive for sufficient risk mitigation at the lowest cost, with minimal impact on other mission capabilities.

 ## ISO 27005

ISO 27005 is the name of the standard covering information security risk management drafted and published by the International Organization for Standardization (ISO) and the International Electrotechnical Commission (IEC).

The standard provides guidelines for information security risk management (ISRM) in an organization, specifically supporting the requirements of an information security management system as defined by ISO 27001. It defines risk as "a combination of the consequences that would follow from the occurrence of an unwanted event and the likelihood of the occurrence of the event." The risk analysis process outlined in the standard indicates the need to identify information assets at risk, the potential threats or threat sources, the potential vulnerabilities, and the potential consequences (impacts) if risks materialize.

Overall, it defines *information security risk assessment* as being a combination of risk analysis and risk evaluation.

Risk analysis is, itself, defined as combining risk identification and risk estimation where risk identification involves risk characterized in terms of organizational conditions. This would typically involve the identification of assets: Assets within the defined scope as well as the identification of threats based on incident reviewing, asset owners, asset users, external threats, and so on. In addition, ISO 27005 requires the identification of existing controls and testing that the controls are working correctly.

Identification of Vulnerabilities involves the short-listing of the vulnerabilities within organizational processes, IT, personnel, and so forth, as well as the identification of consequences of risks.

Risk Estimation specifies the measure of risk in terms of both qualitative and quantitative estimations, while *Risk Evaluation* involves the comparing and prioritization of *Risk Level* based on *Risk-Evaluation Criteria* and *Risk-Acceptance Criteria.*

The standard does not specify, recommend, or even name any specific methodology, although it does specify that a structured, systematic, and rigorous method of analyzing risks must exist and must include creating the risk treatment plan.

 ## THE "CASCARINO CUBE"

The following discussion is a generic approach to risk identification and prioritization. Its use needs to be tailored to the requirements of an individual organization. It is referred to here as a "cube" although it is, in actuality, a cuboid with the numbers of layers dependent on the individual architecture, components, and risks that the organization is exposed to.

In general, information processing uses an architecture which is shown in Exhibit 3.1.

▪ The core is the *organization's data,* which is the major asset to be protected.
▪ This exists within, and under the control of, the *mainframe* computer itself.
▪ In order to gain access to the Mainframe, *mainframe communications* channels are used.
▪ This communication is typically conducted from *servers* or intermediate processors.
▪ These in turn, communicate via routers and cabling through *wide area networks*

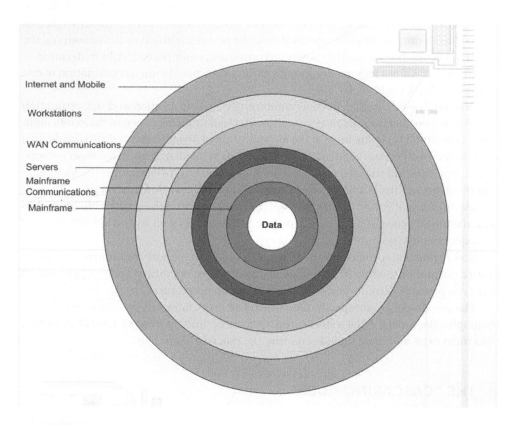

Internet and Mobile
Workstations
WAN Communications
Servers
Mainframe
Communications
Mainframe
Data

EXHIBIT 3.1   Typical IT Infrastructure

Networking Communications

Workstations are the point from where users can enter the system. In addition there are frequently users who will access the data via the Internet and mobile computing. These rings, then, make up the first layer of the cube (see Exhibit 3.1).

The architecture itself will consist of a number of components including among others, typically:

▪ Data
▪ Software
▪ People
▪ Hardware

Each of these architect layers and components will be exposed to risks in a variety of forms. Commonly the risks may include:

▪ System non-availability
▪ Loss of confidentiality
▪ Loss of integrity
▪ Inaccuracy and incompleteness
▪ Lack of monitoring
▪ Lack of compliance
▪ Under-performance

These are shown three dimensionally in Exhibit 3.2. Based on the discussions with operational and technical staff at the organization, a cube of risks, systems components, and architectural components can be identified and risk-ranked. Higher ranked risks to more critical components form the upper left-hand corner of each architectural slice.

This will typically result in a cuboid such as that shown in Exhibit 3.3.

When prioritized and structured, the organization's risk profile may be represented by higher-ranked risks to more critical components that form the upper left-hand corner of each architectural slice.

Each architectural slice may then be evaluated separately and the operational, security, and technical controls identified and allocated to the specific cell representing a risk (such as unavailability) to a system component (such as data). At this stage, no attempt is made to determine whether the controls that are believed to exist actually do exist and function as intended.

Examples of the cells indicating specific controls are shown in Exhibit 3.4.

The objective of the exercise is to determine whether the accumulation of controls *intended* to mitigate a particular risk to a particular component, would be adequate to reduce the risk to acceptable levels *if they function as intended.* Inadequacy of controls indicate a level of risk too high even if all of the controls work as intended, and such a vulnerability must then be addressed.

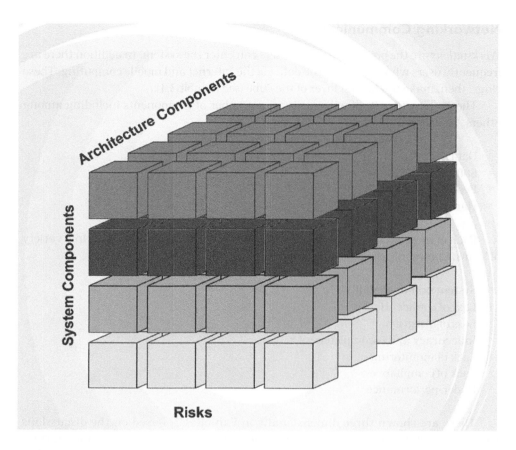

EXHIBIT 3.2 Cascarino's Cube

Once all mitigating controls have been identified, they can be evaluated in order to determine which controls can give management the *most* assurance (whether it be from a preventative, detective, or corrective perspective). These are designated the *key controls* and form management's most critical defenses against those specific risks. From management's perspective, these controls would be subject to the most stringent monitoring in normal operations. From an audit perspective, these would typically be the controls selected to be tested for *effectiveness.*

If these controls function as intended, management may gain the assurance that risk is being controlled to the desired level in an *adequate* and *effective* manner.

Where such testing of controls determines that the key controls are *not* functioning as intended, the cause of failure must be determined and rectified. In the meantime the other controls in that particular cell can be evaluated to determine whether they have

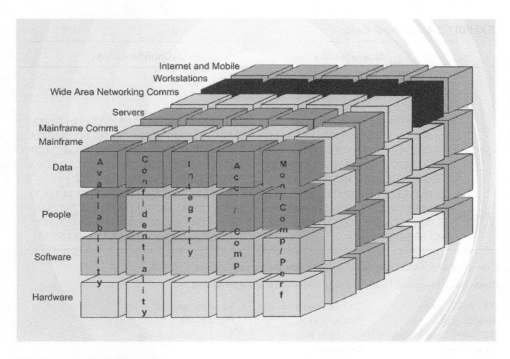

EXHIBIT 3.3   IT Security

sufficient cumulative impact to maintain the overall control at the desired level. If so, then the effectiveness of these controls must also be tested.

Once key controls have been identified within each of the individual cells, they may be traced three dimensionally into other cells within other system components and architectural components. This then permits a three-dimensional map of the impact that the failure of the key control could have across all system components and architectural components facing a variety of risks.

Additionally, the three-dimensional nature of the cuboid enables the auditor to examine control adequacy and effectiveness in vertical slices of system components indicating all risks and architectural components affected, horizontal slices of risks to all components indicating the system and architectural components affected or sliced by architectural components showing all risks and system components affected.

By maintaining the Cube and associated controls as risk levels change with the business, and by keeping the control list current and tested, the overall risk and control architecture can be monitored in order to ensure that the overall residual risk to the organization is maintained at acceptable levels.

EXHIBIT 3.4 Control Cells

	Unavailability	Confidentiality
Data	T1,T2,T3,T4,T5,T6,T7,T8,T9,T10,T11,T12,T13,T14,T15,T16,T17,T18,T21,T22,T23,T26,T27,T28,T29,T30,T33,T34,T35,T36,T37,T39,T40,T41,T42,T43,TK45,TK46,T4K9,TK56,T57,T58,T60 - O1,O2,O3,O4,O5,O8,O9,O11,O12,O14,O16,19,O23,OK25,O26,O27,O28,O29,OK30,O31, - S3,S4,S5,S6,S11,SK12	T11,T12,T16,T17,T18,T22,T23,T24,T25,T27,T28,T26,T31,T32,T33,T34,T35,T40,T41,T44,T47,T58,T60 - O1,O2,O3,O4,O5,O6,O7,O8,O9,O10,O11,O12,O13,O14,O15,O16,O21,O22,O33 - S1,S2,S3,S4,S5,S6,S7,S8,S9,S10,S11
People	T16,T17,T22,T21,T28,T30,T31,T32,T34,T35,T36,T41,T43,T47,T49,T57,T62 - O1,O5,O8,O11,O25,O27,O28,O30, - S1,S3,S11,S12,	T11,T12,T22,T23,T24,T31,T32,T33,T34,T28,T35,T36,T39,T41,T42,T43,T47,T51,T58,T60 - O1,O2,O3,O4,O5,O7,O8,O10,O11,O14,O15,O21,O22,O26,O32, - S1,S3,S4,S5,S6,S7,S8,S9,

Examples of controls identified may include terms such as: the

Controls List (legend T=technology, S=security, O=operations)

T1 - APC Power Monitoring

T2 - APC Cold Water Monitoring

T3 - APC Temperature Monitoring

T4 - APC UPS

T5 - Generator - Natural Gas Powered

T6 - APC UPS Generator Monitor

T7 - Multiple Power Paths (N+1 config)

T8 - Air Conditioning (N+1 config)

O1 - Policies and Procedures

O2 - User Access Approval

O3 - Key Fob Access

O4 - Security Cameras in Retail Areas

O5 - Human Resources Policies

O6 - Location Security Officer Checklist

O7 - Confidential Shredding

O8 - Training

S1 - Policies and Procedures

S2 - Log Monitoring

S3 - User Access Approval Review

S4 - Reoccurring User Access Review

S5- Security Camera Monitoring

S6 - Key Fob Access Review

S7 - Shred Bin Monitoring

S8 - User Awareness Training

RELIABILITY OF AUDIT EVIDENCE

Audit evidence may be classified as:

▪ **Sufficient.** Factual, adequate, and convincing such that a prudent person would reach the same conclusions as the auditor.

▪ **Competent.** Reliable and the best attainable through the use of appropriate audit techniques.

- **Relevant.** Supports audit findings and recommendations and is consistent with the objectives for the audit.
- **Useful.** Helps the organization meet its goals.

Evidence, for the IT auditor, is frequently thought of as being obtained by direct interrogation of computer data files. Although this is a common technique, evidence may also be obtained by observing conditions, interviewing people, and examining records. Such evidence is typically classified as:

- **Physical evidence.** Generally obtained by observation of people, property, or events, and may be in the form of photographs, maps, and so on. Where the evidence is from observation, it should be supported by documented examples or, if not possible, by corroborating observation.
- **Testimonial evidence.** May take the form of letters, statements in response to inquiries, or interviews, and are not conclusive in themselves because they are only another person's opinion. They should be supported by documentation where possible.
- **Documentary evidence.** The most common form of audit evidence and includes letters, agreements, contracts, directives, memoranda, and other business documents. Such documented evidence may also be derived from computerized records using the appropriate audit tools and techniques. The source of the document will affect its reliability and the trust we place in it. The quality of internal control procedures will also be taken into account.
- **Analytical evidence.** Commonly derived from computations, comparisons to standards, past operations, and similar operations. Once again, in this area, computerized tools will normally prove a highly effective aid to the auditor. Regulations and common reasoning will also produce such evidence.

It is worth noting that a common concept within the gathering of evidence, namely *materiality*, may differ among the varying types of audit. For financial auditing, materiality is generally taken to be a sum of money and is used to determine levels of significance in assessing audit evidence. From an internal audit perspective, materiality relates rather to weaknesses or failures within the internal control structures of the organization. Any evidence, however small, indicating a failure within a major control relied upon by management would be deemed significant evidence.

 ## AUDIT EVIDENCE PROCEDURES

The auditor relies heavily on gathering evidence. This is done in a variety of ways and follows the *audit program*. The audit program is a set of detailed steps that the auditor will follow in order to gain the appropriate evidence and, for the IT auditor, may well include the use of computerized techniques, although this is not always the case.

The actual program used will vary from audit to audit depending on what the auditor wishes to find out and must always include a degree of flexibility to allow for changes based on the evidence already acquired. For example, the auditor may wish to examine data files in order to determine that the printouts relied upon by management match the live data files. In such a case, the use of computer-assisted tools and techniques would be appropriate. In a different scenario, an auditor wishing to examine the authorization of transactions may use such tools to do extractions of records in order to do a follow-up on the documentary evidence of original documents seeking authorization signatures.

In gathering evidence, auditors must ensure that they maintain an independent and objective attitude both in fact and in appearance. Such independence is normally taken to be in jeopardy when an auditor is charged with auditing an area where there has been line responsibility within the previous year. Many auditors interpret this as indicating that they cannot be too detailed in making recommendations because this would preclude their conducting subsequent audits due to a perceived lack of independence and objectivity. This may indeed be the case, and both management and auditors must understand that, where detailed assistance is given in designing audit implementing control structures, the auditor is functioning primarily as an internal control consultant. Subsequent auditing of these structures should be done independently of the consultant.

 ## RESPONSIBILITIES FOR FRAUD DETECTION AND PREVENTION

It must be clearly understood that the primary responsibility for the prevention and detection of all frauds, including IT frauds, is the responsibility of operational management. Nevertheless, the auditor has a role to play in assisting management in establishing a control environment in which fraud is unlikely to occur, but where it does occur, it will be quickly detected.

This contrasts to the approach of the forensic auditor whose primary obligation is the resolution of fraud with sufficient proof to prove or disprove allegations of fraud. Forensic auditors must presume that all cases eventually will end up in litigation and the quality of evidence gathered must take this into account. Forensic IT Auditing is covered in more detail in Chapter 36.

 ## NOTES

1 W. Bradshaw and A. Willis. *Learning about Risk: Choices, Connections and Competencies.* Toronto: Canadian Institute for Chartered Accountants, 1998.
2 Committee of Sponsoring Organizations, Enterprise Risk Management, September, 2004, executive summary.
3 Institute of Internal Auditors: Advisory 2100-6: Control and Audit Implications of E-commerce Activities: Altamonte Springs, FL 2001.
4 NIST SP 800-30 Risk Management Guide for Information Technology Systems - http://csrc.nist.gov/publications/nistpubs/800-30/sp800-30.pdf.

CHAPTER FOUR

Standards and Guidelines for IT Auditing

T HIS CHAPTER EXPLORES in detail the Information Systems Audit and Control Association (ISACA) *Code of Professional Ethics* and the current ISACA Information Technology (IT) *Auditing Standards and Guidelines Standards* as well as the Institute of Internal Auditors (IIA) *Code of Ethics, Standards for the Professional Practice of Internal Auditing* and *Practice Advisories.* In addition, standards and guidelines other than the ISACA and IIA models are explored.

IIA STANDARDS

In 1978 the IIA introduced *the Standards for the Professional Practice of Internal Auditing* to be used around the world in order to provide international consistency and as a measurement tool for audit quality assurance. These consisted of five general and 25 specific standards together with numerous *Statements on Auditing Standards.* Standards were considered mandatory while non-mandatory *Guidelines* were also included.

The IIA standards were intended to establish a yardstick for consistent measurement of internal auditing operations. This allowed the unification of internal auditing worldwide by improving internal audit practice, proclaiming the role, scope, performance, and objectives of internal auditing, promoting the recognition of internal auditing as a profession, and promoting responsibility within the internal auditing profession.

As part of its ongoing research into the evolving role of internal auditing, an extensive research project known as the *Competency Framework for Internal Auditing (CFIA)* was undertaken by the IIA. It was intended to update the *Common Body of Knowledge (CBOK)* expected from a professional internal auditor.

The CFIA included not only the competencies needed by auditors, but also how these competencies would be assessed. Based upon this research, the IIA brought together an international group of audit professionals, the *Guidance Task Force (GTF)*, to formulate a guidance framework for the future.

This resulted in the *Professional Practices Framework*, which comprises mandatory, advisory, and practical guidance in the forms of the *Standards, Practice Advisories*, and *Development and Practice Aids*, respectively.

 ## CODE OF ETHICS

Compliance with both the *Code of Ethics* and the *Standards* are mandatory. All mandatory statements are first promulgated for discussion by the entire profession through the issuance of exposure drafts. Compliance with these statements is considered essential to the delivery of professional services by both the individual auditor and the internal audit function.

 ## ADVISORY

The *Guidelines* were replaced with *Practice Advisories* representing the best approaches to implementation of the *Standards*. Essentially, the *Practice Advisories* are designed to assist the auditor by interpreting the *Standards* in a variety of internal auditing environments. *Practice Advisories* will continue to be issued from time to time, both as general aids as well as to meet specialized needs within a given industry, geographic location, or audit specialty.

 ## AIDS

The IIA has also developed or endorsed *Development and Practice Aids*. These include educational products, research studies, seminars, conferences, and other aids related to the professional practice of internal auditing. These are not intended to be either compulsory as are the *Standards*, nor advisory as are the *Practice Advisories*. They are intended solely to assist in the development of internal audit staff by introducing them to techniques and processes developed by a variety of experts in their fields.

 ## STANDARDS FOR THE PROFESSIONAL PERFORMANCE OF INTERNAL AUDITING

The *Standards* themselves have been regrouped and redefined into:

- **Attribute Standards.** These address the attributes of organizations and individuals performing internal audit services and apply to all internal audit services.

- **Performance Standards.** These describe the nature of internal audit services provided and provide quality criteria against which the performance of these services can be measured.
- **Implementation Standards.** These prescribe *Standards* applicable to specific types of engagements in a variety of industries as well as specialist areas of service delivery.

Full details of the *Standards for the Professional Practice of Internal Auditing* can be found at www.theiia.org.

ISACA STANDARDS

The framework for the IT auditing standards provides multiple levels of guidance:

- *Standards* define mandatory requirements for IT auditing and reporting. They inform:
  - IS auditors of the minimum level of acceptable performance required to meet the professional responsibilities set out in the ISACA Code of Professional Ethics for IT auditors
  - Management and other interested parties of the profession's expectations concerning the work of practitioners
  - Holders of the Certified Information Systems Auditor™ (CISA®) designation of requirements. Failure to comply with these standards may result in an investigation into the CISA holder's conduct by the ISACA Board of Directors or appropriate ISACA committee and, ultimately, in disciplinary action.
- *Guidelines* provide guidance in applying IT auditing standards. The IT auditor should consider them in determining how to achieve implementation of the standards, use professional judgment in their application, and be prepared to justify any departure. The objective of the IT auditing guidelines is to provide further information on how to comply with the IT auditing standards.
- *Procedures* provide examples of procedures an IT auditor might follow in an audit engagement. The procedure documents provide information on how to meet the standards when performing IT auditing work, but do not set requirements. The objective of the IT auditing procedures is to provide further information on how to comply with the IT auditing standards.

Control Objectives for Information and related Technology (COBIT®) resources should be used as a source of best practice guidance. Each of the following is organized by IT management process, as defined in the COBIT *Framework*. COBIT is intended for use by business and IT management as well as IT auditors; therefore its usage enables the understanding of business objectives and communication of best practices and recommendations, to be made around a commonly understood and well-respected standard reference. COBIT includes:

- **Control objectives.** High-level and detailed generic statements of minimum good control
- **Control practices.** Practical rationales and how-to-implement guidance for the control objectives
- **Audit guidelines.** Guidance for each control area on how to obtain an understanding, evaluate each control, assess compliance, and substantiate the risk of controls not being met
- **Management guidelines.** Guidance on how to assess and improve IT process performance, using maturity models, metrics, and critical success factors

Full details of the *IS Standards, Guidelines and Procedures for Auditing and Control Professionals* can be found at www.isaca.org.

 ## ISACA CODE OF ETHICS

ISACA also has its own code of ethics, which requires that members, Certified Information Security Managers (CISMs), and CISAs shall:

- Support the implementation of, and encourage compliance with, appropriate standards, procedures, and controls for information systems.
- Perform their duties with due diligence and professional care, in accordance with professional standards and best practices.
- Serve in the interest of stakeholders in a lawful and honest manner, while maintaining high standards of conduct and character, and not engage in acts discreditable to the profession.
- Maintain the privacy and confidentiality of information obtained in the course of their duties unless disclosure is required by legal authority. Such information shall not be used for personal benefit or released to inappropriate parties.
- Maintain competency in their respective fields and agree to undertake only those activities that they can reasonably expect to complete with professional competence.
- Inform appropriate parties of the results of work performed, revealing all significant facts known to them.
- Support the professional education of stakeholders in enhancing their understanding of information systems' security and control.

Failure to comply with this *Code of Professional Ethics* can result in an investigation into a member's or certification holder's conduct and, ultimately, in disciplinary measures. Full details of the *Code of Professional Ethics* can be found at www.isaca.org.

 ## COSO: INTERNAL CONTROL STANDARDS

In 1992, the American Institute of Certified Public Accountants, the Institute of Internal Auditors, the American Accounting Association, the Institute of

Management Accountants, and the Financial Executives Institute issued a jointly prepared study entitled *Internal Control—An Integrated Framework.* This document identifies the fundamental objectives of any business or government entity. These include economy and efficiency of operations, safeguarding of assets, achievement of desired outcomes, reliability of financial and management reports, and compliance with laws and regulations.

Internal control was defined by the Committee of Sponsoring Organizations (COSO) as a broadly defined process, effected by people, designed to provide reasonable assurance regarding the achievement of the three objectives that all businesses strive for, namely:

1. Economy and efficiency of operations, including achievement of performance goals and safeguarding of assets against loss;
2. Reliable financial and operational data and reports; and
3. Compliance with laws and regulations.

In order to achieve these objectives, COSO defined five components that would assist management in achieving these objectives. These consisted of:

▪ **Sound Control Environment.** A sound control requires the correct level of attention and direction from senior management. The control environment is implemented by employing managers and employees who possess integrity, ethical values, and competence. It is a function of management's philosophy and operating style. For this to be effective, proper assignment of authority and responsibility coupled with the proper organization of available resources is required. The training and development of people to the required standard is essential in ensuring the competence of people in exercising control.

▪ **Sound Risk Assessment Process.** A sound risk-assessment process requires the implementation of an awareness of the risks and obstacles to successful achievement of business objectives and the development of an ability to deal with them. As such management must establish a set of objectives that integrates all of the organization's resources so that the organization operates in unison. The risk assessment itself involves the identification, analysis, and management of the risks and obstacles to successful achievement of the three primary business objectives.

▪ **Sound Operational Control Activities.** Sound operational-control activities involve the establishment and execution of sound policies and procedures. These help ensure effective implementation of actions identified by management as being required to address risks and obstacles to achievement of business objectives. These include such concepts as authorization, reviews of operating performance, security of assets, and segregation of duties.

▪ **Sound Information and Communications Systems.** Information systems facilitate the running and control of a business by producing reports containing financial-, operational-, and compliance-related information. They deal with both internally generated data as well as with the external activities, conditions, and events necessary to make informed business decision making and external reporting. For this to happen, appropriate information must be identified, captured, and communicated in a manner and time frame that enables people to carry out their responsibilities

Effective communication must flow down, up, and across the organization. (This includes a clear message from top management to all personnel that control responsibilities must be taken seriously.) This means that all personnel must understand their own role in the internal control system, as well as how their individual activities relate to the work of others. Personnel also require a means of communicating significant information upward as well as with external parties.

■ **Effective Monitoring.** To ensure the efficacy of the control process, the entire control system must be monitored to assess the quality of the system's performance over time. Deficiencies must be reported, with serious matters reported directly to top management.

In addition, there should be separate, independent evaluations of the internal control system. The scope and frequency of these independent evaluations depend primarily on the assessment of risks and obstacles, and the effectiveness of ongoing monitoring procedures.

BS 7799 AND ISO 17799: IT SECURITY

Both British Standard (BS) 7799 and International Standards Organization (ISO) 17799 were developed to assist companies by ensuring that, when electronic commerce is entered into, some degree of assurance regarding the security and control is implemented at either end within the trading partners' own systems.

The standards break down IT security into 10 main areas, namely:

1. Security Policy
2. Security Organization
3. Asset Classification and Control
4. Personnel Security
5. Physical and Environmental Security
6. Computer and Network Management
7. Systems Access Control
8. System Development and Maintenance
9. Business Continuity Planning
10. Compliance

Within each of these areas, key controls are identified to be considered mandatory and additional controls considered optional dependent on the level of risk sustainable by the organization. The detailed standard explains what is required to provide a secure organization but at minimum, the standards require the existence of:

- Written information-system security policy
- Allocation of responsibility for information security
- Users trained appropriately on information-security risks and controls
- A feedback mechanism for the reporting of security-related issues
- Fully tested and effective business-continuity plans
- Controls to ensure compliance with the appropriate data-protection legislation
- Controls to ensure safeguarding of records in line with corporate statutory requirements
- Controls to prevent and detect malicious software such as viruses and spyware
- Review procedures

 NIST

With the passage of the Federal Information Security Management Act (FISMA) of 2002,[1] there is a statutory provision to ensure that agencies comply with mandatory Federal Information Processing Standards (FIPS). The National Institute of Standards and Technology (NIST) is the federal technology agency that works with technology measurements and standards. The Computer Security Resource Centre (CSRC), a division of the NIST, has assisted by producing both a handbook on IT security as well as multiple security standards.

The NIST Handbook covers very similar ground to BS 7799 and ISO 17799, but goes into considerably more detail on subjects such as:

- Elements of computer security
- Roles and responsibilities
- Common threats

Management Controls

- Computer security policy
- Computer security program management
- Computer security risk management
- Security and planning in the computer-system life cycle
- Assurance

Operational Controls

- Personnel/user issues
- Preparing for contingencies and disasters
- Computer security incident handling

- Awareness, training, and education
- Security considerations in computer support and operations
- Physical and environmental security

Technical Controls

- Identification and authentication
- Logical access control
- Audit trails
- Cryptography

The NIST Handbook also includes sections on the practical implementation of assessing and mitigating risks within the computer system.

Another recent standard, *Minimum Security Requirements for Federal Information and Information Systems,* specifies minimum security requirements for federal information and information systems in 17 security-related areas. Federal agencies are required to meet the minimum security requirements as defined therein. All such standards are available from NIST at www.csrc.nist.gov.

 BSI BASELINES

The British Standards Institution (BSI) Baseline Controls for Information Security can be obtained from www.bsi.bund.de. They describe a minimum set of controls to provide medium-level protection for information systems and cover:

IT Security Management

- IT security process
- Responsibilities and authorization in the IT security process

IT Baseline Protection for Generic Components

- Organization
  - Personnel
  - Contingency Planning
  - Data Protection
- Infrastructure
  - Buildings
  - Cabling
  - Rooms
- Office
  - Server room
  - Storage media archives

- ▪ Technical infrastructure room
- ▪ Protective cabinets
- ■ Home working place
  - ▪ Non-networked systems
  - ▪ DOS PC (single user)
  - ▪ UNIX system
  - ▪ Laptop
  - ▪ DOS PC (multiuser)
  - ▪ Non-networked Windows NT computer
  - ▪ PC with Windows 95
  - ▪ Local Area Networks (LANs)
- ■ Server-Based Network
  - ▪ Networked UNIX systems
  - ▪ Peer-to-peer network
  - ▪ Windows networks
  - ▪ Novell Netware
  - ▪ Heterogeneous networks
- ■ Data Transfer Systems
  - ▪ Data carrier exchange
  - ▪ Modem
  - ▪ Firewall
  - ▪ E-mail
- ■ Telecommunications
  - ▪ Telecommunication systems
  - ▪ Fax machine
  - ▪ Telephone answering machine
  - ▪ LAN integration of an IT system
- ■ Other IT Components
  - ▪ Standard software
  - ▪ Databases
  - ▪ Telecommuting

It should not be thought that the standards are definitive. From time to time new standards are created and old ones updated and it is part of the job requirement of the IT auditor to keep abreast of the latest developments in internationally recognized standards.

 NOTE

1 Federal Information Security Management Act (FISMA): www.csrc.nist.gov/policies/ FISMS-final.pdf: 2002.

5

Internal Controls Concepts Knowledge

T HIS CHAPTER INTRODUCES the concepts of Corporate Governance with particular attention to the implications within an Information Technology (IT) environment and the impact on IT auditors. Criteria of Control (COCO), Committee of Sponsoring Organizations (COSO), King, Sarbanes-Oxley Act of 2002, and other recent legislative impacts are examined together with the structuring of controls to achieve conformity to these structures. Control classifications are examined in detail together with both general and application controls. Particular attention is paid to Control Objectives for Information and Related Technology (COBIT) from both a structural and relevance perspective.

 INTERNAL CONTROLS

Confusion commonly arises as to what exactly a control is. A control may be defined as *any action taken by management to enhance the likelihood that established objectives and goals will be achieved.* It results from management's planning, organizing, and directing, and the many variants (e.g., management control, internal control, etc.) can be incorporated within the generic term.

Management controls are intended to ensure that an organization is working toward its stated objectives:

- Corporate objectives and goals are the statement of corporate intent (market penetration will increase by 10 percent in the coming year).
- Management objectives define how the corporate objectives will be met (market penetration will be increased leveraging the information within the data warehouse in order to determine customers' current and future wants and needs).
- Internal control ensures that programs to ensure management objectives are properly planned and executed (periodic checks will be made of the integrity of the data contained within the data warehouse and marketing will be trained in full use of data-mining tools in order to satisfy their information needs).

Control responsibility is clearly management's job and encompasses planning, organizing, and directing.

Planning in this case is taken to mean the establishing of objectives and goals as well as choosing the preferred methods of utilizing resources.

Organizing involves the gathering of the required resources and arranging them in such a way that the objectives may be attained.

The *directing* process of management includes authorizing, instructing, and monitoring performance as well as periodically comparing actual to planned performance.

Within the IT environment, this involves ensuring that systems function as intended, data integrity is maintained, confidentiality is maintained, systems are available as and when required, data accuracy and completeness are maintained, and access is granted only on an authorized basis.

Management decisions may be classified as *strategic, tactical,* or *operational* and all decisions at any level are impacted by the IT designed to provide the basis upon which the decisions are made.

IT audit must then ensure that the system of internal control will be effective and function as intended.

The level of control needed will be affected by overall objectives.

Corporate objectives and goals are the statement of corporate intent and are generally very broad, while *management objectives* define how the corporate objectives will be met and are normally much more detailed. Internal control is designed to ensure that programs to ensure management objectives are properly planned and executed.

Again, at an even more detailed level, **operating objectives** are the drivers dictating the normal day-to-day activities and may, in themselves, conflict so that we find a conflict between, for example, the need for confidentiality and the need for data availability; similarly there are conflicts between efficiency of data processing versus effectiveness. The prioritization of operating objectives directs the development of controls and will affect the final, overall system of controls.

Assume the organization operates in a high-security environment. Control objectives may be such that the permanent loss of information would be preferable to leakage of information. In a lower-security environment, availability may be the key concern and loss of confidentiality may be a comparatively minor matter. It is the evaluation of this risk profile that dictates the nature and direction of the internal control structures and therefore the IT audit work.

COST/BENEFIT CONSIDERATIONS

Objectives must take into consideration the cost of attempting to achieve them. *As quickly as possible* implies zero controls other than for speed while *No errors* implies strong internal controls covering all aspects of quality. Controls must therefore be practical, useful, achievable, and compatible with both operating and control goals and there is always a trade-off between cost and benefit. Because all controls cost resources in terms of money, personnel, computing power, and time, controls always imply a trade-off between cost and benefit. (Is it worth spending $200 to prevent a possible loss of $100?)

 ## INTERNAL CONTROL OBJECTIVES

Overall, internal control objectives, at a detailed level, can be seen to encompass:

- **Reliability and Integrity of Information.** If management cannot trust the reliability and integrity of the information held and processed within the IT, then all information must be deemed suspect and, in some cases, this may be more detrimental to the organization than a loss of information systems.
- **Compliance with Policies, Plans, Procedures, Laws, and Regulations.** Laws and regulations are imposed externally and must be complied with. Inadequate information systems may lead to the organization inadvertently breaching the laws of the country with result of losses in terms of fines, penalties, and possibly imprisonment for corporate officers.

    The organization's internal policies, plans, and procedures are designed to ensure planned, systematic, and orderly operation. From time to time the manager may be required to evaluate the adequacy of such policies, plans, and procedures since the nature of the business may have changed, risks may have to be reassessed and control objectives re-prioritized.
- **Safeguarding of Assets.** Loss of assets is typically one of the most visible risks an organization can face and typically these lead to the implementation of the most visible controls, such as locks on doors, safes, security guards, and so forth. In an IT-dependent organization, asset controls may also include non-tangibles such as dual custody, segregation of duties, and computer authentication techniques. Few organizations would be in a position to declare the information held as a corporate asset on the balance sheet. Nevertheless, the corporate information warehouse may be the largest asset the organization can claim if leveraged appropriately. In addition, for many organizations the financial records held within the computer systems are indeed actual assets in that, for example, the total value of inventory is commonly taken to be whatever the computer system says the inventory value is. Similarly, debtor and creditor valuations are largely based upon the information contained within the appropriate computer systems.

■ **Effectiveness and Efficiency of Operations.** *Effectiveness* involves the achievement of established objectives and should be the ultimate focus of all operations and controls. Many information systems, at the time of the original design, were focused upon achieving the corporate objectives. Over time these objectives may have changed and the information systems may become counterproductive to achieving those objectives. Computer systems therefore required constant monitoring as to their alignment with corporate strategic directions and intent.

Efficiency is classed as a measurement of the optimization of utilization of "scarce resources" and includes reduction of waste as well as the reduction of underutilization of resources. In many organizations information systems have become the proverbial "sledgehammer to crack a nut" and, taking only the case of office automation, have served to reduce efficiencies instead of improving them.

With those control objectives in mind, management can structure the system of internal controls to improve the probability of achieving all of those objectives.

TYPES OF INTERNAL CONTROLS

Internal controls can be classified into various types and it is the combination of these controls that go to make up the overall system of internal controls designed to achieve the general control objectives. Such controls can be classified into:

■ *Preventative controls*, which occur before the fact but can never be 100 percent effective and therefore cannot be wholly relied upon. These could include controls such as restrictions on users, requirements for passwords, and separate authorization of transactions.
■ *Detective controls*, which detect irregularities after occurrence and may be cheaper than checking every transaction with a preventative control. Such controls could include effective use of audit trails and the use of exception reports.
■ *Corrective controls* ensure the correction of problems identified by detective controls and normally require human intervention within the IT. Controls in this area may include such processes as Disaster Recovery Plans and transaction-reversal capabilities. Corrective controls are themselves highly error-prone because they occur in unusual circumstances and typically require a human decision to be made, and an action decided upon and implemented. At each stage in the process a subsequent error will have a multiplier effect and may compound the original mistake.
■ *Directive controls* are designed to produce positive results and encourage acceptable behavior. They do not themselves prevent undesirable behavior and are normally used where there is human discretion in a situation. Thus, informing all users of personal computers that it is their responsibility to ensure adequate backups are taken and stored appropriately does not, of itself, enforce compliance. Nevertheless, such a directive control can be monitored and action taken where the control is breached.

▪ *Compensating controls* can be seen to exist where a weakness in one control may be compensated by a control elsewhere. They are used to limit risk exposure and may trap the unwary evaluator. This is particularly true where the auditors are faced with complex integrated systems and the control structures involve a mixture of system-driven and human controls scattered over a variety of operational areas.

In general, then, management and the auditor must always bear in mind that under-control is cheap to implement but may cost you the organization, while over-control is expensive and ultimately paralyzing.

SYSTEMS OF INTERNAL CONTROL

It is the overall combination of the individual elements of control that go to make up the *Systems of Internal Control*. These are, in turn, influenced by the *Control Environment*. This may be defined as the overall infrastructure within which the other control elements will function and establishes the conditions under which the rest of the internal controls will operate. Primary elements within this include the *Organizational Structure*. This defines individual managers' responsibilities, sets limits of authority, and allows the ensuring of appropriate segregation of duties. If the organizational structure is inappropriate, with excess powers granted to individuals or if poor segregation of duties exists, the effectiveness of the individual controls may be weakened irreparably. It is impossible to enforce, for example, division of duties within the computer system by using detailed access rights if one individual has been granted access rights across incompatible duties as part of the normal operating procedures. The *Control Framework* includes the policies and procedures that describe the scope of a function, its activities, interrelationships with other departments, as well as the external influences of laws and regulations, customs, union agreements, and its competitive environment. The structures enforcing controls may be complex or simple. Large organizations tend to have highly structured control frameworks, while smaller organizations frequently use personal contact between employees.

ELEMENTS OF INTERNAL CONTROL

Given the overall control objectives noted in the preceding section, control structures must be designed in order to ensure:

▪ **Segregation of duties.** Controls to ensure that those who physically handle assets are not those who record asset movements. Nor are they the same people who reconcile those records nor even those who authorize such transactions. Within a modern computer system this is normally achieved by a combination of user identification, user authentication, and user authorization.

- **Competence and integrity of people.** Underpinning the control system are the people who enforce it. In order for controls to be effective, those who exercise control must be capable of doing so and honest enough to consistently do so. This means that simply having users follow procedures is inadequate in a modern information systems environment, and a high degree of risk and control awareness is required in order to ensure that the controls function as intended.
- **Appropriate levels of authority.** A common mistake in control structures is the granting of too much authority within control boundaries. Authorities should only be granted on a need-to-have basis. If there is no need for a particular individual to have specific authorities, they should not be granted. Obviously this requires effort on the part of those individuals who assign authorities in identifying which levels of authority are in fact needed and which are simply desired. It is, unfortunately, still true in many sites that access control is limited to user authentication and subsequent to such authentication the user will then have unrestricted access into all functional areas within IT.
- **Accountability.** For all decisions, transactions, and actions taken, there must be controls that will allow the determination of who did what with an acceptable degree of confidence. This normally involves the use of control logs and audit trails. Simply maintaining such logs and records can be counterproductive because they can lull the organization into a false sense of security. For such records to be an effective control they must be scrutinized regularly and appropriate action taken to remedy any discrepancies noted.
- **Adequate resources.** Controls that are attempted with inadequate resources will typically fail whenever they come under stress. Adequate resources include manpower, finance, equipment, materials, and methodologies. Management frequently underestimates cost of resources to implement controls, and IT auditors commonly recommend controls giving no thought to the cost of such control and management's lack of resources to implement.
- **Supervision and review.** Adequate supervision of the appropriate type is fundamental to the implementation of sound internal control. It is unfortunately still true that in many cases people do not do what is *expected*, but only what is *inspected*.

 ## MANUAL AND AUTOMATED SYSTEMS

Within our information systems there are two primary software components that add to or subtract from control. These components are:

- **Systems Software.** Systems software includes computer programs and routines controlling computer hardware, processing, and non-user functions. This category includes the operating systems, telecommunications software, and data-management software.
- **Applications Software.** Applications software includes computer programs written to support business functions such as the general ledger, payroll, stock systems, order processing, and other such line-of-business functions.

In addition, many organizations are becoming more and more dependent upon application systems created within the user's own environment.

▪ **End-User Systems.** End-user systems are special types of application systems that are generated outside the IT organization to meet specific user needs. These include micro-based packages as well as user-developed systems. In many cases these systems were designed to achieve specific operational goals and may or may not have been designed with appropriate controls implemented.

 ## CONTROL PROCEDURES

In order to ensure that control over the corporate computer investment is adequate, a range of controls is required, including:

▪ **General IT Controls.** Covering the environment within which the computer systems are utilized
▪ **Computer Operations.** Covering the day-to-day operations of the machine
▪ **Physical Security.** Covering the security of the physical hardware, software, buildings, and staff
▪ **Logical Security.** Covering the manner in which data and software are protected from access via the systems themselves
▪ **Program change control.** To ensure that systems that are correct and functional continue to be so
▪ **Systems development.** To ensure that the systems in use by the organization are effective, efficient, and economical

 ## APPLICATION CONTROLS

Application systems have their own sets of built-in controls that are primarily business-systems oriented. Generally they include such control objectives as accuracy, completeness, and authorization. In addition, the auditor may find compensating controls, where weak controls in one area may be compensated for by other controls.

As previously stated, controls are usually classified into the general categories of *preventative, detective,* and *corrective.* It can be useful to the auditor in determining the degree of reliance to be placed on control structures to categorize controls in other ways. Controls may be classified as *discretionary* or *non-discretionary,* where discretionary controls are those that are subject to human discretion. These would include such controls as supervisory review of signatures. Non-discretionary controls are provided by the system and cannot be overridden. They include controls such as the use of personal identity numbers (PIN) numbers.

Other classification types could be *voluntary* or *mandated.* Voluntary controls are chosen by the organization to support its business, while mandatory controls are those that are required by laws and regulations.

Controls may be *manual* or *automated*, where manual controls are implemented by manual intervention and automated controls are implemented by the computer system itself.

Controls may be *application* or *general* IT, with application controls having to do with the business function and general IT controls being about the running of the IT function.

A control may be a preventative, discretionary, voluntary, manual, general control if it:

- Prevents errors
- Could be changed or omitted
- Is not required by law
- Is performed by a human
- Addresses the environment in which other controls operate

 ## CONTROL OBJECTIVES AND RISKS

All computer environments face a variety of risks, which include such dangers as:

- Fraud
- Business interruption
- Errors
- Customer dissatisfaction
- Poor public image
- Ineffective and inefficient use of resources

These are controlled via a variety of control objectives that address specific threat areas.

 ## GENERAL CONTROL OBJECTIVES

These objectives, general in nature, cover the overall aspects of the integrity of information, computer security, and compliance with policies, plans, rules, laws, and regulations.

 ## DATA AND TRANSACTIONS OBJECTIVES

The processing of transactions and the handling of data are also subject to control procedures at each stage of processing.

At the *input* stage typical examples of control objectives might be that:

- All transactions are initially and completely recorded
- All transactions are completely and accurately entered into the system
- All transactions are entered only once

Input methods could include a mixture of on-line input, batch input, input from interfacing systems, and electronic data interchange. Controls at this stage would typically include:

- Use of pre-numbered documents
- Reconciliation of control totals
- Data validation in all its forms
- Activity logging
- Document scanning
- Access authorization
- Document cancellation

At the *processing* stage typical examples of control objectives might be that:

- Approved transactions are accepted by the system and processed
- All rejected transactions are reported, corrected, and re-input
- All accepted transactions are processed only once
- All transactions are accurately processed
- All transactions are completely processed

Processing types may include batch processing, interactive update (real time), as well as on-line batch processing where the data is captured on-line but the processing takes place in a batch environment.

Controls at this stage would typically include:

- Control totals
- Programmed balancing
- Segregation of duties
- Restricted access
- File labels
- Exception reports
- Error logs
- Reasonableness tests
- Concurrent update control

At the *output* stage typical examples of control objectives might be that:

- Assurance that the results of input and processing are output
- Output is available only to authorized personnel

Outputs could include hard-copy printouts, file output for onward processing, or on-line inquiry replies.

Controls at this stage would typically include:

- Complete audit trail
- Output distribution logs

PROGRAM CONTROL OBJECTIVES

The development and running of computer programs are subject to their own control objectives and procedures. Control objectives would include ensuring:

- Integrity of programs and processing
- Prevention of unwanted changes
- Ensuring adequate design and development control
- Ensuring adequate testing
- Controlled program transfer
- Ongoing maintainability of systems

    Typical controls around the development of programs would include:

- Use of a formal Systems Development Life Cycle (SDLC)
- User involvement
- Adequate documentation
- Formalized testing plan
- Planned conversion
- Use of post-implementation reviews
- Establishment of a quality assurance (QA) function
- Involvement of internal auditors

    If these control objectives are adequately addressed and the appropriate controls are affected, then the risks within the computer systems should be effectively minimized.

CORPORATE IT GOVERNANCE

The importance of good governance has become a watchword internationally and has been driven by the requirements of the global economy for transparency and account-ability in organizational stewardship.

    Corporate governance involves the mechanisms by which a business enterprise is directed and controlled. It concerns the mechanisms through which corporate man-agement is held accountable for corporate conduct and performance and provides the framework within which the objectives of the company are set, and the means of attain-ing those objectives and monitoring performance are determined.

    Good corporate governance ensures that the board and management pursue objec-tives that are in the best interests of the organization and its stakeholders and facilitates effective monitoring.

The corporate governance framework rests on the legal, regulatory, and institutional environment and includes factors such as business ethics and corporate awareness of the environmental and societal interests of the communities within which the organization operates because these can also have an impact on the reputation and the long-term sustainability of an organization.

Following the lead taken by the Treadway Commission's 1987 report into Fraudulent Financial Reporting in the United States, a number of commissions were established in various countries to investigate corporate governance practices and make recommendations inter alia regarding: changes to legislation; recommending corporate codes of "ethical" conduct; and criteria for evaluating and reporting on corporate governance practices worldwide.

These include the Cadbury Report on Corporate Governance (United Kingdom, 1992), the Hampel Report (United Kingdom, 1998), the King Report (South Africa, 1994), the Blue Ribbon Report (United States, 1998), the King II Report (South Africa, 2002), and the recent Smith Report (United Kingdom, 2003)[1] *Audit Committees Combined Code Guidance* dealing with the role and responsibilities of "effective" Audit Committees, and the Higgs Report (2003)[2] providing a *review of the role and effectiveness of non-executive directors.* In Europe there has similarly been much activity to strengthen corporate governance and company law standards. These include the Cromme Code in Germany and the Bouton Report "[P]romoting better corporate governance in listed companies" in France in September 2002.

The Cadbury Committee was commissioned to report specifically on the financial aspects of corporate governance in response to some spectacular company collapses in the United Kingdom such as BCCI Plc, Polypeck Plc, and Barings Bank.

In many cases these reports called for a strengthening of the board's conformance and compliance role. The reports advocated the strengthening of the role of independent non-executive directors, the creation of compliance committees using these non-executive, independent directors in audit committees, remuneration committees to oversee directors' remuneration, and nomination committees concerned with the nomination of new directors to the board. In addition they called for greater transparency of board matters and the separation of the roles of the chairman of the board from the chief executive officer of the business.

The various reports all contain recommendations for enhancing corporate governance practices, some of which have subsequently been incorporated into changes in corporate legislation and the listing requirements of stock exchanges.

The far-reaching Sarbanes-Oxley Act[3] in the United States provides stringent legal requirements to enforce sound corporate governance requirements on all U.S. Securities and Exchange Commission (SEC) registrants as well as their subsidiaries and associated entities, wherever established and operating in the world.

Sarbanes-Oxley provides for new corporate governance rules, regulations, and standards for specified public companies including the SEC registrants. The SEC has made the use of a recognized internal control framework mandatory and, in its final rules regarding the Sarbanes-Oxley Act, made specific reference to the recommendations of COSO.

COSO AND INFORMATION TECHNOLOGY

COSO specifically addresses IT control requirements in certain components of the COSO framework (e.g., control activities).

While there are many sections within the Sarbanes-Oxley Act, sections 302 and 404 probably have the most impact on information systems.

Section 302:

> ... Requires a company's management, with the participation of the principal executive and financial officers (the certifying officers), to make the following quarterly and annual certifications with respect to the company's internal control over financial reporting:
>
> ■ A statement that the certifying officers are responsible for establishing and maintaining internal control over financial reporting
> ■ A statement that the certifying officers have designed such internal control over financial reporting, or caused such internal control over financial reporting to be designed under their supervision, to provide reasonable assurance regarding the reliability of financial reporting and the preparation of financial statements for external purposes in accordance with generally accepted accounting principles
> ■ A statement that the report discloses any changes in the company's internal control over financial reporting that occurred during the most recent fiscal quarter (the company's fourth fiscal quarter in the case of an annual report) that have materially affected, or are reasonably likely to materially affect, the company's internal control over financial reporting

Section 404 goes on to state that:

Management's report on internal control over financial reporting is required to include the following:

■ A statement of management's responsibility for establishing and maintaining adequate internal control over financial reporting for the company
■ A statement identifying the framework used by management to conduct the required assessment of the effectiveness of the company's internal control over financial reporting
■ An assessment of the effectiveness of the company's internal control over financial reporting as of the end of the company's most recent fiscal year, including an explicit statement as to whether that internal control over financial reporting is effective
■ A statement that the registered public accounting firm that audited the financial statements included in the annual report has issued an attestation report on management's assessment of the company's internal control over financial reporting

Management should provide, both in its report on internal control over financial reporting and in its representation letter to the auditor, a written conclusion about the effectiveness of the company's internal control over financial reporting. The conclusion about the effectiveness of a company's internal control over financial reporting can take many forms; however, management is required to state a direct conclusion about whether the company's internal control over financial reporting is effective.

Management is precluded from concluding that the company's internal control over financial reporting is effective if there are one or more material weaknesses. In addition, management is required to disclose all material weaknesses that exist as of the end of the most recent fiscal year.[4]

As can be seen, these sections that address internal control over financial reporting require the management of public companies specified by the act to assess the effectiveness of the organization's internal control over financial reporting and annually report the result of that assessment. For listed companies, this means assessing the effectiveness of the organization's internal controls over their information systems because these form the base source for the financial information contained within the financial reports.

While Sarbanes-Oxley requires management to state that it has implemented a control framework that is compatible with COSO, there is no guidance on what framework it should use. The IT Governance Institute (ITGI) addressed in *IT Control Objectives for Sarbanes-Oxley: The Importance of IT in the Design, Implementation and Sustainability of Internal Control for Financial Reporting and Disclosure.*[5]

Within this document, ITGI points out that:

Organizations need representation from IT on their Sarbanes-Oxley teams to ensure that IT general controls and application controls exist and support the objectives of the compliance effort. Some of the key areas of responsibility for IT include:

- Understanding the organization's internal control program and its financial reporting process
- Mapping the IT systems that support internal control and the financial reporting process to the financial statements
- Identifying risks related to these IT systems
- Designing and implementing controls designed to mitigate the identified risks and monitoring them for continued effectiveness
- Documenting and testing IT controls
- Ensuring that IT controls are updated and changed, as necessary, to correspond with changes in internal control or financial reporting processes
- Monitoring IT controls for effective operation over time
- Participation by IT in the Sarbanes-Oxley project management office

It then becomes critical to demonstrate how the IT controls implemented support the COSO framework. An organization should have IT control competency in all COSO components. As noted in Chapter 4, COSO identifies five essential components of effective internal control being:

1. Control environment
2. Risk assessment
3. Control activities
4. Information and communication
5. Monitoring

COSO itself does not give sufficient detail for implementation of an appropriate control framework within IT. As such, IT management will be required to implement a more detailed control framework as defined within Chapter 4 such as COBIT, which aligns with the intentions of the Sarbanes-Oxley Act and facilitates the designed control structure in compliance with section 404. Always bear in mind that COBIT was designed to provide control over operational and compliance objectives. Financial reporting is only one of those objectives.

 ## GOVERNANCE FRAMEWORKS

Three frameworks have become widely recognized as "IT governance frameworks." While each has significant IT governance strengths, none may be looked on as a complete IT governance solution.

ITIL

IT Infrastructure Library® (ITIL®) was developed by the United Kingdom's Office of Government Commerce to be a library of best practice processes aimed at IT service management. ITIL is one of the worldwide de facto standards for service management and includes broad and publicly available professional documentation on how to plan, deliver, and support IT service features.

CobiT

Control Objectives for Information and related Technology® (CobiT®) is an IT governance framework and supporting toolset designed to enable managers to bridge the gaps between control requirements, technical issues, and business risks. It emphasizes regulatory compliance, facilitates organizations increasing the value attained from IT, enables alignment, and simplifies implementation of the CobiT framework.

ISO/IEC 38508

ISO/IEC 38508 was developed by the joint technical committee ISO/IEC JTC1, information technology, subcommittee SC 7, software and systems engineering. Designed as a worldwide formal international IT Governance Standard, ISO/IEC 38500 was published in June 2008 and sets out a clear framework for the Board's governance of Information and Communications.

These frameworks are covered more fully in Chapter 14.

 NOTES

1 Audit Committee's Combined Code Guidance, a report and proposed guidance by a Financial Reporting Council appointed group chaired by Sir Robert Smith, London, January 2003.
2 Review of the Role and Effectiveness of Non-executive Directors, report and recommendations to the Secretary of State for Trade and Industry, Derek Higgs, London, January 2003.
3 The Sarbanes-Oxley Act (2002), 107th Congress of the United States, Washington, January 2002.
4 Ibid.
5 IT Governance Institute, IT Control Objectives for Sarbanes-Oxley: The Importance of IT in the Design, Implementation and Sustainability of Internal Control for Financial Reporting and Disclosure, www.itgi.org, 2004.

CHAPTER SIX

Risk Management of the IT Function

T HIS CHAPTER INTRODUCES the concept of computer risks and exposures and includes the development of an understanding of the major types of risks faced by the Information Technology (IT) function, including the sources of such risk as well as the causes. It also emphasizes management's role in adopting a risk position, which itself necessitates a knowledge of the acceptable management responses to computer risks. One of the most fundamental influencing factors in IT auditing is the issue of corporate risk. This chapter examines risk and its nature and the corporate environment and looks at the internal audit need for the appropriate risk analysis to enable risk-based auditing as an integrated approach. This structured approach includes the effect of computer risks, the common risk factors, and the elements required to complete a computer risk analysis.

> Leadership involves making choices in the face of uncertainty. "Risk" is the possibility that one or more individuals or organizations will experience adverse consequences from those choices. Risk is the mirror image of opportunity.[1]

 NATURE OF RISK

Ultimately, all entities encounter risk regardless of their size, corporate structure, nature of business, or type of industry. All business decisions involve elements of risk whether it is a decision regarding the financing of the business, addition or deletion of product lines, or the sources and methods of supply to the organization. All these must be assessed at an entity level by the executive management of an organization and related to the business activity desired.

These risks can affect the ability to successfully compete, the ability to maintain financial strength and the corporation's positive public image, and ultimately the organization's ability to survive. The overall quality of products, services, and people will all be affected. Risks cannot be eliminated, only managed, but this requires an entity-wide *risk identification.* The overall risk will largely depend on entity objectives, and the identification must be seen as an iterative process carried out on an ongoing basis.

Risk identification may be done as part of the planning process either on a "zero base" or as incremental to the last review. Risks may arise from internal or external factors and the factors themselves may be interrelated.

The Institute of Risk Management (United Kingdom) recommends in its risk management standard the following responsibilities for boards:

> The Board has responsibility for determining the strategic direction of the organization and for creating the environment and the structures for risk management to operate effectively. This may be through an executive group, a non-executive committee, an audit committee, or such other function that suits the organization's way of operating and is capable of acting as a "sponsor" for risk management. The Board should, as a minimum, consider, in evaluating its system of internal control:

> - The nature and extent of downside risks acceptable for the company to bear within its particular business
> - The likelihood of such risks becoming a reality
> - How unacceptable risks should be managed
> - The company's ability to minimize the probability and impact on the business
> - The costs and benefits of the risk and control activity undertaken
> - The effectiveness of the risk management process
> - The risk implications of board decisions[2]

RISK-ANALYSIS SOFTWARE

There are multiple types of risk-analysis software available in the current market. We will look at two versions for comparison purposes (Cost of Risk Analysis [CORA] and World Modeler). I was biased in my selection. Both software companies are based in Denver, Colorado, as am I and I am therefore most familiar with these products. Other popular products include Primavera™ from Oracle, @RISK™ from Palisade, as well as many ERM risk-modeling software tools.

Cost of Risk Analysis (CORA)

CORA™ software, originally developed by International Security Technology Inc. (IST), is now distributed by All Hazards Management, a specialist list company based in Colorado. CORA helps risk managers perform sophisticated analyses of risks in order to optimize operational risk-management strategies. It utilizes a combination of "expert rules files" generated by risk experts in a given field and "data files" provided by field personnel to estimate the cost of risk, permitting the optimization of the selection of businesses resumption plans, IT system backup modes, insurance coverage, and other mitigation measures.

It consolidates its cost-of-risk estimates for individual facilities on projected income statements to show the overall impact of risk in a realistic context. Its normal use is to maximize the quality and minimize the cost of full-scale quantitative risk-analysis projects by constructing a dynamic risk model of the organization and then facilitating the development of the required information to make informed decisions.

World Modeler

World Modeler™, distributed by Quantellia, integrates enterprise data with expert knowledge in a desktop environment in order to build three-dimensional interactive simulations to assist decision makers to understand the future impact of their choices as they play out over time within a complex organization. World Modeler is designed to assist decision makers acquire an intuitive understanding of the system under consideration, and provides both individuals as well as decision-making teams with a much clearer picture of where the uncertainties in decision outcomes lie, thus facilitating risk modeling in a graphical manner.

Using an interactive, exploratory environment, it integrates with both transactional and analytical data sources in order to combine quantitative data with human judgment.

It is designed to permit managers to make risk decisions in the face of missing information as well as uncertain information and its multi-scenario planning facilitates the location of the decision's sensitivity points to build a risk mitigation strategy.

 AUDITING IN GENERAL

Auditing in general involves an annual risk assessment and planning exercise to determine the overall audit coverage required. This is followed by individual audit planning. The preliminary review is used to obtain and record an understanding so that an audit area may be broadly evaluated. From this evaluation, the extent of compliance testing or substantive testing required may be determined. After the testing is completed and the results evaluated, audit reporting must take place. This is typically addressed to the first level of management able and empowered to take effective action. After the report is agreed and issued, a follow-up is required to ensure any agreed action has taken place.

The auditor needs to identify the appropriate control objectives, then to identify what is needed to accomplish control; to identify where responsibility lies; and whether a management, system, or physical control is appropriate.

Identifying control objectives is done via the risk profile. The control objectives will have unique weightings for your site, although the fundamental objectives of availability, completeness, accuracy, confidentiality, and integrity will not change. All controls implemented will involve cost/benefit trade-offs.

Problems that will commonly be encountered as a result of computer risks include:

- Erroneous record keeping
- Unacceptable accounting
- Business interruption
- Erroneous management decisions
- Fraud and embezzlement
- Loss or destruction of assets
- Competitive disadvantage
- Excessive costs
- Paralysis of the business

Typical causes of computer risks in companies include no risk evaluation having been done. This commonly results in an incorrect view of computer controls. No allocation of responsibilities and a lack of management involvement lead to inadequate segregation of duties. Poor supervision and poor personnel procedures can lead to problems with inadequate access control. Open systems and a lack of user awareness coupled with the common problem of human errors combine to leave an unacceptable risk position.

Auditors normally consider three types of risks when utilizing the risk-based audit approach. *Inherent risk* is *the likelihood of a significant loss occurring before taking into account your risk-reducing factors.* In order to evaluate inherent risk the auditor must be familiar with the environment within which the risk could occur in order that the nature of risk, indicators suggesting the likelihood of such a risk, and the severity of such an implied risk may be assessed. *Control risk* measures *the likelihood that the control processes established to manage inherent risk are proved to be ineffective.* In order to evaluate whether the controls designed and implemented by management have adequately reduced the inherent risk to within tolerance levels, the auditor must identify those controls relied upon by management to reduce the likelihood or impact of the risk. Once these controls have been identified, an audit program to test the known effectiveness of these controls may be designed and implemented. The auditor must always bear in mind the cost of controls in reducing risks and that, at some point, a management decision may be taken to implement no further controls and accept the *residual risk. Audit risk* is *the risk that significant business exposures have not been adequately addressed by the audit process.* While the IT auditor will take all steps to ensure that audit risk has been minimized, it can never be guaranteed.

ELEMENTS OF RISK ANALYSIS

Risk analysis involves the estimating of the significance of a given risk and assessing the likelihood or frequency of the risk occurring. Risk analysis in an organization involves process analysis, which requires the identification of key dependencies and control nodes. It looks at the processes within a business entity and identifies cross-organizational dependencies. It looks at where data originates, where it is stored, how it is converted to useful information, and who uses the information. These processes can be positively affected by quality control programs. At this stage, risks are normally evaluated before the mitigating effects of controls are considered in order to establish the inherent risk.

Management and auditors must then consider how the risk should be managed, what actions need to be taken, and what controls need to be implemented. Should they be preventative procedures to reduce the significance or likelihood of the risk occurring, or displacement procedures to offset the effect if it does occur? Mitigation of risk by internal control involves decisions regarding costs and benefits. Of these, cost is normally easier to quantify and theoretically costs should be incurred until they exceed benefits.

In practice this is a management decision where cost-benefit analysis usually results in some portion of the risk being managed and some portion remaining. Management should review the residual risk on an ongoing basis and from an exposure standpoint. Risk analysis is not a universal panacea. No matter how good the analysis, poor judgment in decision making may still occur after the risks are known. The analysis itself may have been made in the light of data that was incomplete, inaccurate, or untimely. People tire and make mistakes. Most risk analysis ignores collusion (two or more people acting collectively) or management override of the system of internal control.

Nevertheless, meaningful risk analysis substantially increases the probability of achieving objectives. It alerts management to changes needed to control procedures and links activity objectives to action. It focuses effort on control procedures and should become second nature. The analysis itself may be formal or informal; it is the results, not the degree of formality, that matter.

DEFINING THE AUDIT UNIVERSE

In order to commence the risk-analysis process, an "inventory" must be taken of all auditable units. This may be by cost center, business function, subsidiary, or cost center within subsidiary. How the audit universe is regarded depends on several organizational factors such as the nature of the industry, the degree of pre-defined structure within the entity, the degree of autonomy granted to business units, the types of management processes and organizational relationships, as well as the information systems usage. At a more detailed level, computers of all kinds within an organization are constantly faced with a variety of risks and exposures. It is helpful if we first define these terms:

- **Computer risk.** Probability that an undesirable event could turn into a loss.
- **Computer exposure.** Results from a threat from an undesirable event that has the potential to become a risk.
- **Vulnerability.** A flaw or weakness in the system that can turn into a threat or a risk.

The total impact of computer risks range from minor to devastating and could affect the organization's ability to successfully compete, maintain its financial strength, maintain a positive public image, and, ultimately, to survive. Such risks could include any or all of:

- Loss of sales or revenues
- Failure to meet government requirements or laws
- Loss of profits
- Loss of personnel
- Inability to serve customers
- Inability to sustain growth
- Inability to operate effectively and efficiently
- Inability to compete successfully for new customers
- Inability to stay ahead of the competition
- Inability to stay independent without being acquired or merged
- Inability to maintain present customer/client base
- Inability to control costs
- Inability to cope with advancements in technology
- Inability to control employees involved in illegal activities
- Damage to business reputation
- Complete business failure

Computer risks, exposures, and losses may be characterized as intentional or unintentional and may involve actual damage, alteration of data or programs, as well as unauthorized dissemination of information. Objects that can be affected include physical items such as the hardware or hard-copy outputs, which are both vulnerable to risks such as theft or loss; the telecommunications system, which can cause major corporate grief if unavailable for any reason as well as being vulnerable to internal or external penetration; the applications software, which is vulnerable to sabotage; systems software such as the operating system itself, which can also be amended or circumvented; computer operations, where control procedures may be amended or bypassed; and the data itself, where virtually anything could happen.

The risks in IT are the opposite of the control objectives and may be expressed as either. For example, a risk may be expressed as "loss of confidentiality" or the control objectives as "maintaining confidentiality." Either way these must be treated as risks to the business. As such they are the responsibility of executive management with enforcement occurring at an operational or technical level. Obviously, the relative importance of risks will vary and the control techniques will differ from industry to industry and from company to company. The risks may be minimized but they can never be totally eliminated and indeed it is normally not cost effective to attempt to eliminate risks and in some cases not even desirable.

COMPUTER SYSTEM THREATS

Threats may come from either external or internal sources and may be intentional or unintentional as well as malicious or non-malicious.

Internal threats may come from users, management, IT staff, IT auditors, and others, either acting alone or in collusion.

Users

Threats from this source are the most commonly occurring and include errors, fraud, breach of confidentiality (commonly accidentally), or malicious damage.

The most common causes of these threats are poor supervisory control combined with poor personnel procedures. In many cases far too much power has been granted to users who already have access to the assets. In many cases the users have an in-depth knowledge of the system's control weaknesses and are in a position to exploit them.

Management

Threats here again include error and fraud but may also include systems manipulation for "corporate" reasons such as profit smoothing or advance booking of sales or delayed recording of costs. Again breach of confidentiality is a hazard together with malicious damage.

Common causes here are likely to involve inadequate segregation of duties with management, in many cases unquestioned regarding decisions they make and transactions they authorize. This, combined with poor personnel procedures and too much power granted, can lead to major problems, particularly when combined with management's access to assets and its authority to override conventional control levels.

IT Staff

Threats here include the normal problems of error, fraud, and breach of confidentiality as well as malicious damage. In this case, however, the impact of errors and so forth tends to be further reaching because they may affect not only a single transaction, but every transaction passing through a system. Once again the most common problem is accidental destruction rather than deliberate sabotage. Common causes are typically too much power granted, for example, granting of access to live data, poor change control, and ineffective division of duties. In many cases computer staff have control because they have the power associated with knowledge of the system.

IT Auditors

A commonly ignored threat, IT auditors again are in a position to commit errors or fraud, to breach confidentiality, or cause malicious damage. In many cases there is little or no supervisory control exercised and far too much power granted. The auditors have access to the assets and a detailed knowledge of system weaknesses. In addition, they have the right to attempt to break the system, although it is not supposed to be for their gain.

Others

Other people also have access to computer systems, including engineers, salespersons, and so forth. Threats here include again errors, fraud, and loss of confidentiality, as well as malicious damage and accidental destruction. Common causes in these cases include poor disposal of outputs, careless talk, inadequate access control both physical and logical, publicity, and the advent and promotion of open systems.

External Threats

Threats may come from legitimate external users as well as inter-computer links such as the Internet, electronic data interchange systems, system hackers, and viral attacks as well as from natural causes. Such threats are commonly caused by inadequate logical access control resulting in high-value systems being unguarded. A poor security attitude within staff coupled with an incorrect concept of computer security and an incorrect risk evaluation can also open up such exposures.

 ## RISK MANAGEMENT

With such a plethora of risk exposures, management must adopt a position on risk. It may involve any or all of *accepting the risk, reducing the risk* (normally by increased internal control), or *transferring the risk*. The option that is NOT acceptable is simply *ignoring the risk*. In order to adopt an appropriate position, management must *know and understand the risk*.

Risk-Based Audit Approach

Risk assessment must be carried out in order to permit the efficient allocation of limited IT audit resources and to ensure that all levels of management have been checked and that the audit effort is focused on areas of highest business impact. Risk assessment is then the basis for audit department management because it summarizes the impact of the selected subject on the overall business.

The initial audit activity gathers or updates information about the organization in order to determine the audit strategy. This determination includes forming audit judgments regarding the organization and assessing the inherent and control risks in order to determine the appropriate audit-testing plan. Inherent risk may be seen as the risks the organization faces without the mitigating impact of internal controls. Control risks involve those elements of inherent risk not successfully mitigated by the internal control structures.

The initial information required would include knowledge of the organization's business and place within its industry, as well as a knowledge of the applicable accounting, auditing, and regulatory standards within the industry. These allow the determination of the overall business objectives of the organization or departmental function. Once the business objectives have been determined, the auditor may proceed to identify and isolate the individual detailed control objectives. For example, the overall objective of the purchasing function is to buy items for the organization. The control objectives for this function would include ensuring that only the right items are purchased, at the right price, in the right quantity, of the right quality, in an authorized manner, for delivery to the right place at the right time.

The risks then become those factors that can prevent fully or partially the achievement of the control objectives. The auditor must then determine which controls will mitigate those risks and what source of evidence exists as to the adequacy and effectiveness of that mitigation.

Risk Factors to Consider

Among the risk factors normally considered are the:

- Date and results of last audit
- Financial exposure and potential loss and risk
- Requests by management
- Major changes in operations, programs, systems, and controls
- Opportunities to achieve operating benefits
- Quality of the internal control framework
- Competence of management
- Complexity of transactions
- Liquidity of assets
- Ethical climate and employee morale

There are two possible assessment methods for the auditor to choose from. *Objective assessment* utilizes only quantitative attributes of auditable units such as the value of throughputs, the value of assets under control, the number of personnel, or the volume of transactions. In this methodology, there is no weighting of risk factors undertaken. The alternative assessment method uses *subjective assessment*, whereby each risk factor may be weighted on a scale representing degrees of concern, thus allowing the auditor to express his or her (or management's) feelings regarding risk materiality.

Risk-Based Auditing

Risk-based auditing involves integrating the concepts of high-level risk analysis into the development of the overall audit plan. The audit plan itself may be differentiated between *mandatory audit activities* and *discretionary audit activities.* Mandatory audit activities are those activities that must be carried out within the time span of the audit plan and include legal or regulatory requirements, senior management requirements, and external auditor liaison requirements. These may be assigned the greatest risk value to ensure automatic selection but the auditor must be careful to ensure that senior management requirements are in fact requirements and not just nice to have.

Discretionary audit activities should be decided upon using risk factors that should be limited to the most important 10 or fewer to keep the process manageable. Risk factors must apply to a variety of products and services across the company.

One common risk factor within information systems includes the *monetary values* handled within individual applications. This is an easily quantified criterion for evaluation and, as such, is one of the more frequently used risk factors. *Disclosure of information* to a third party could seriously impact the organization and could, in some cases, jeopardize the future viability of the organization. *Loss of information* could, under some circumstances, also threaten the existence of the business. *Failure to comply with legal statutes* or regulations will normally result in some form of sanction, frequently monetary. The *technical complexity of systems* is very much a judgment call for a system classed as extremely complex by one organization but may be seen to be the norm at another. Nevertheless, such complexity can add greatly to the risk of failure of parts or all of the information-processing structures. System stability is commonly overlooked as a risk factor because rarely does it threaten the survival of the organization. Despite this, the costs involved in constant maintenance and adjusting of unstable systems, hardware, software, or a combination of both, can make this a significant threat. For many modern organizations, *unavailability of systems* has become a major threat and for many businesses an extended period of unavailability could result in their rapid closure of the business. In addition, there are always risk factors unique to a given organization and these must also be taken into consideration.

These risks result from a variety of sources and causal factors and initial risk analysis is intended to measure inherent risk, that is, risk without taking into consideration the effects of internal control processes. Sources of threats also include fire, flood, sabotage, natural disaster, and the biggest threat of all—human error.

Logical threats such as user abuse, time bombs, data peeking, Trojan horses, salami techniques, and data diddling must also be considered, as must the mitigating effect of such control elements as change control.

The high-level risk analysis should therefore be seen as a broad-brush approach designed to arrive at an approximate risk evaluation of a business entity. This determines the frequency of audit but not necessarily depth or focus areas.

The detailed risk analysis identifies the control processes designed to mitigate risk and involves the design of the audit steps to test such control processes. Basic controls within computer systems include edit checks on inputs, reconciliations on outputs, backup, and recovery controls to ensure ongoing continuity. Disciplinary controls such as segregation of duties, physical and logical access restrictions, and authorization are essential to ensure adequacy of risk control.

Establishing a detailed risk profile involves assessment of a range of security-threatened areas including:

- Physical security
- Personnel security
- Data security
- Applications software security
- Systems software security
- Telecommunications security
- Operations security

In order to mitigate risk in these areas, control procedures may be classified under the headings of general organization-control procedures, access controls to data and programs, use of the appropriate systems-development methodologies, data-processing operations controls, systems-programming and technical-support functions, as well as data-processing quality assurance procedures.

In assessing the quality of internal controls, the nature and quality must be examined including whether the controls are manual or automated. Weak or unknown internal controls indicate a higher risk. The audit experience of this business area as well as the time since the last audit and the significance of findings at that time may have a major impact on the evaluation of risk. Visibility and scope may be measured by the volume of transactions, the size of master files, the types of input, and processing. Visibility may be assessed by considering the number of users of services, systems interfacing with other audit units, and any major changes since last audit. The effect on accounting data may be shown by the booking duration of accounting entries, the degree of automation in processing, and the condition of suspense accounts in terms of both size and movements.

Assessing the risk could involve measuring and evaluating the number of users on the system, the security awareness of those users, the value of assets under the direct control of the systems, the degree of user sophistication, and outsider access. In addition, the effectiveness of password management and change control must be considered as well as the access rights of both operations and development staff. Controls such as the scrutiny of logs may also be seen to reduce risk.

 NOTES

1   W. Bradshaw and A. Willis. *Learning about Risk Choices, Connections, and Competencies.* Toronto: Canadian Institute for Chartered Accountants, 1998.
2   The Institute of Risk Management (IRM), The Association of Insurance and Risk Managers (AIRMIC), and ALARM. The National Forum for Risk Management in the Public Sector, Risk Management Standard, London, 2002.

CHAPTER SEVEN

Audit Planning Process

THIS CHAPTER EXAMINES the audit-planning process at both a strategic and tactical level. The use of risk-based auditing and risk-assessment methods and standards are covered. The preliminary evaluation of internal controls via the appropriate information gathering and control evaluation techniques as a fundamental component of the audit plan and the design of the audit plan to achieve a variety of audit scopes is detailed.

BENEFITS OF AN AUDIT PLAN

Planning is fundamental to successful auditing. Bad planning typically results in a failure to achieve the audit objectives as well as the conducting of audits being either insufficient in scope with unidentified risks resulting in incomplete audits, or alternatively over-auditing and making inefficient use of resources.

One of the more common mistakes made by Information Technology (IT) auditors is proceeding to implementation of the audit without having a clearly thought-out plan.

Planning is one of the most fundamental management techniques and yet one of the most badly executed techniques. In order for an audit to be effective it must, by definition, achieve its objectives. It is critical that the auditor fully understand these objectives before the audit commences. A structured, well-documented audit plan identifies and establishes the criteria against which a successful audit will be measured. The planning process involves:

- Identifying the tasks to be performed in the course of an audit
- Allocation of those tasks to specific auditors
- Deciding when a task should commence
- Quantification of the duration of each individual task based on the auditor allocated

The primary stage of planning any audit, computer or non-computer, is obtaining a clear understanding of the business objectives of the area under review. For example, the overall business objective of a procurement function may be seen as buying things. This, in turn, leads to the definition of the control objectives of the business area, for example, ensuring that goods are procured at the right price, at the right time, in the right quantity, in the right quality, for delivery to the right place.

Once the control objectives of the area under review are clearly and fully understood, the auditor may then proceed to identify those controls relied upon by the user to ensure that the control objectives are achieved. Many of these controls will be preventative and will not themselves leave a clear audit trail of the control efficiency and effectiveness. As a result, the auditor may have to look elsewhere for evidence that the controls are achieving that which was intended, and that the control objectives in fact are being achieved.

Once the auditor has identified the source of evidence as to the achievement of the control objectives, the appropriate audit technique and audit tools may be selected.

If these steps are omitted and the auditor proceeds directly to the interrogation of computer systems and the running of Computer Assisted Audit Techniques (CAATs), an audit will result that cannot be seen to be achieving its goals and objectives because the goals and objectives were unknown when the audit took place.

Only with careful consideration and planning can a successful audit occur.

The Elements

An audit plan should include:

- Tentative determination of the objectives and scope of the audit. This includes determining the objectives of the audit in consultation with the auditees as well as what is to be included within the scope of the audit and what will not be included. Once the objectives and scope have been finalized and agreed to, an *engagement letter* clarifying the agreed scope and objectives should be sent to the client so that, at a later stage, no misunderstanding will arise as to what had been agreed would and would not be audited.
- At this stage, the auditor will seek to determine the overall business objectives of the area to be reviewed as well as the control objectives. The background information regarding the area to be audited must be gathered. This involves a reading of operating procedure manuals and discussions with operating management in order to obtain the whole picture. This theory will be combined with a more practical approach involving interviewing user staff in order to both evaluate their understanding of the business and to confirm the auditor's understanding. Site visits to

observe the operation of specific business functions will also help. Further information and confirmation may be derived by comparing the current understanding of the controls to those identified and in operation during previous reviews.

The major products and services that are the key activities involved in meeting the business objectives must be identified. Once again, this will involve determining the level of management's understanding of their own *key performance areas* (*KPAs*).

■ For each KPA, performance objectives must be established. This involves seeking core activity targets that are both achievable and, at the same time, stretching. *Key performance indicators* (*KPIs*) must be identified that will enable the performance to be measured appropriately. The risks and threats that could lead to non-achievement, underachievement, or even failure must then be assessed. Both external and internal threats must be considered.

> *Internal threats* are those over which management has complete control, such as choice of vendor.
> *External threats are* those that management cannot directly control, but for which they must nevertheless develop a coping strategy, such as interest rate fluctuations or actions by competitors.

■ The overall intention of a specific audit may be classified as reviewing the design of the internal control system for adequacy, tests of compliance with the designed control system, and evaluation of the effectiveness of the implementation of the control system.

■ The selection of the audit team. In many cases the audit will be conducted by a team of auditors that will include a mixture of disciplines. Each team has typically several functions to perform, usually by different members of the team. These will include determining of objectives and scope, coordinating the work including assigning team members, coordinating the project with other work going on in the department at the same time, and reviewing all documentation for the audit process. In addition to these administrative functions, the conducting of the extended audit tests will be carried out by individual team members. In many smaller audits, or in departments where IT auditors are few, these functions are typically combined so that a single auditor will carry out all those functions. It is only once the team has been selected that the full time extent of the audit can be determined because that time taken will be dependent upon the skills and experience of the individual team members.

■ Initial communication with the auditees and others involved in the audit. Courtesy, as well as good business practice, indicate that the auditor should notify the auditee and selected others prior to the commencement of the audit. This permits the auditees to make necessary preparation and arrange access to records, employees, and facilities. At this point it is appropriate for the audit team leader to draft an engagement letter outlining the information pertaining to the forthcoming audit. This letter confirms discussions with the auditees and agreements reached on scope and objectives.

Obviously there are times—for example, fraud audits—where such preliminary communication would not be carried out in the same manner if, indeed, at all.

- Preparation of the preliminary audit program. One of the most critical areas in the planning process is establishing the audit program. This program is a detailed list of analytical steps to be carried out during the course of the audit. Preparation of this program enables the assignment of individual auditors to individual tasks within the overall audit. This is essential in time management because individual auditors do not work at the same rates. Auditor productivity will be heavily dependent on the individual auditor's experience and knowledge of the areas under review.

  It should be stressed that this audit program is purely preliminary and will be modified during the course of subsequent audit operations as new information comes to light. As such, time estimates at this stage are precisely that, estimates.

  One of the most common mistakes in preparing the preliminary audit program is to simply list the questions to be asked. While this is part of an audit program, the critical element is the determination of which evidence will be examined, and how, in order to answer those questions. An example of a bad audit program would include a step to "determine if all purchase orders are appropriately signed." A better step would be "take a statistically significant sample of purchase orders and compare the signatures to the authorized signatures list in order to determine whether all purchase orders are appropriately signed."

- The planning of the audit report. The best audit in the world is a waste of time and money if necessary improvements do not take place. In order for management to be convinced that changes to control procedures are necessary, the auditor must produce a report that is objective but persuasive, clear, concise, constructive, and timely. The audit report communicates the result of the audit to the auditees and others in the organization. The planning for the audit report begins at the preparation stage of the audit process. Ultimately, all audit work is carried out in anticipation of the final audit report. Many auditors see the audit report as largely non-productive work and a task to be rushed and disposed of as soon as possible at the end of the audit. Nothing could be further from the truth. If this stage is rushed, a poor-quality report will result. In many cases it will lie unread on a manager's desk and will have very little impact on the organization as a whole. A well-written audit report will typically result in a rapid response from the appropriate management levels to resolve the issues included therein. The contents of the final report are obviously unknown at the planning stage. However, because most audit departments use standardized report layout, it should be possible for the auditor to envisage the structure and appearance of the final report even if the actual contents are unknown.

- Approval for the audit approach. It is the responsibility of the in-charge auditor to review and approve the audit program prior to the commencement of actual work by the audit team. This review includes determining that the audit objectives and scope are as required and that the specific audit procedures included in the audit program will lead to those audit objectives being accomplished.

STRUCTURE OF THE PLAN

The structure of the planning will, in general, follow the structure of the audit process. It will therefore include the preliminary survey of operations, the internal control description and analysis, the expanded tests control systems, the development of findings and recommendations, the report production, following up, and audit evaluation.

Preliminary Survey

The objectives of the preliminary survey are to gain an initial understanding of the auditee's operations and to gather preliminary evidence for further audit planning. Where the area has been audited in the past, the preliminary survey may take the form of confirmation of the auditor's understanding. The survey itself will typically include an opening conference between members of the audit team and auditee management to outline the audit assignment with management and coordinate audit activities with auditee operations. An on-site tour of the premises is normal to familiarize the auditor with the nature of the operations and personnel involved. This tour permits the auditor an initial assessment of the overall standard of internal control. Care must be taken at this stage not to start the audit process prematurely. Further studies of selected documents will provide a basis for written descriptions of the auditee's operations. Documents such as job descriptions, organization charts, policy manuals, and critical operating documents would be examined at this stage in order to determine if they exist, how well they are maintained, if they are appropriately secured, and if they are ever used. Written descriptions of the auditee's operations prepared by the auditor can clarify the auditor's understanding and confirmation can be sought directly from auditee management.

Internal Control Description and Analysis

From the preliminary survey the auditor should have a good understanding of the business and control objectives of the area under review. This stage allows the preparation of detailed descriptions of the auditee's internal controls related to the areas under review. Limited testing of such controls may take place at this stage in order to determine the size of subsequent testing required. Based on this information the auditor would evaluate the system of internal controls in order to determine whether the control structures in place, if effective, would lead to the desired level of control. At this point a risk reassessment can be carried out in order to determine the need for any changes in the objectives and school of the audit and how much, if any, expanded audit tests are required before conclusions can be drawn.

Expanded Tests

In order to determine whether the internal control structure is effective, a certain amount of expanded audit testing will be required. These are the tests that would be included in the final audit program as an addition to the preliminary audit program. Such testing would include the examination of records and documents, interviews with auditee management and other personnel, observation of operations, examination of assets, interrogation of computer files, comparisons of audit results to auditee's reports, and other procedures designed to test the effectiveness of the system of internal control. The auditor would make use of all the previously discussed tools and techniques at their disposal.

Findings and Recommendations

Based on the work carried out, the auditors will develop the findings and determine what changes, if any, are necessary to improve internal controls. A finding consists of four distinct parts. *Criteria* are those standards against which observed conditions will be measured. *Conditions* refer to what was actually observed during the course of audit testing. The *effect* refers to the impact on the business associated with any observed problems. The *cause* of the problem addresses failures of internal control or weaknesses within the internal control structures.

Based on these findings the auditor may choose to make recommendations. These typically take four forms:

1. *Make no changes in the control system* where controls are deemed to be both adequate for a given level of a risk and effective in controlling that risk and the current control system is seen to be cost effective.
2. *Improve control* and reduce risk either by modifying current controls or by adding new ones.
3. For those areas where risk is not at acceptable levels, but control is impractical or not cost-effective to implement, the auditor may recommend the *transfer of risk* either by insurance or outsourcing.
4. Should there remain an element of risk uncovered by the system of internal control but nevertheless at an unacceptable level, the auditor may be able to recommend changes that would improve the rate of return for accepting that level of risk.

Report Production

The reporting phase of the audit includes documenting and communicating the final results. This is not, as is often believed, the "final product." The overall objective of the audit was to assist management to improve control within the organization. As such, communication via the audit report is a critical element. It is the audit report that will persuade management to take effective action or conversely fail to persuade management. The reputation of the audit function is largely based on the audit report because this represents a formal presentation of the auditor's professional competence. In most audit reports it is found beneficial to include the comments of the auditee to any recommendations raised. This ensures the objectivity of the final report by permitting the auditee to disagree formally with the auditor's observations. Failure to include auditee comments may result in the auditee finding other ways of expressing their disagreement with the audit report, the audit process, and the auditors themselves. The audit report itself must be produced in a timely manner and no unwarranted delays should be permitted to occur within the process. A 24- to 48-hour production schedule should be aimed for.

Following Up

It is critical that any recommendations made within the audit report be followed up in order to determine whether management has accepted the risk of taking no further action, taken the appropriate remedial steps to resolve any control weakness, or taken no action and left the weakness as an unacceptable risk. This follow-up will itself result in the production of a report, albeit a short one, which will hopefully state that all outstanding issues have now been resolved.

Audit Evaluation

The final stage of the audit relates to the evaluation made by the auditors of themselves. No audit is complete until the full audit process has been executed. It is an essential control within the audit function itself that self-assessment be carried out at the end of each audit project. Coming as it does at the end of the process, the step is often omitted to the detriment of future audit performance.

 TYPES OF AUDIT

Again, to a large extent the development of the audit plan will depend upon the nature of the audit being conducted. *Financial audits* tend to involve the verification of figures produced by the computer systems. This will commonly involve the auditor using CAATs to extract information directly from data files for comparisons to reported figures. *Operational audits* focus on the effectiveness and efficiency of business operations and could include IT in itself as a business function. These audits will normally involve identifying performance evaluation criteria and KPAs and matching the performance achieved against that intended. *General control audits* focus on the management controls around the information processing function and facility and may be either operational or compliance based. *Application audits* can take the form of reviews of live application systems within the user arena, audits of application systems under development, or audits of the applications systems development process itself. *Audits involving operating systems* are less concerned with audits of the operating system itself but rather the way in which the installation has chosen to implement operating system options. This typically involves examining the parameters selected and the selection process for appropriateness. *Physical access audits* are performed in the same manner as physical access audits to any corporate asset for the primary objective and safeguarding of the corporate asset. *Logical* access audits, however, will typically involve interrogation of computer systems control files in order to match access rights granted against job requirements.

CHAPTER EIGHT

Audit Management

THIS CHAPTER LOOKS at audit management and its resource allocation and prioritization in the planning and execution of assignments. The management of Information Technology (IT) audit quality through techniques such as peer reviews and best practice identification is explored. The human aspects of management in the forms of career development and career-path planning, performance assessment, counseling and feedback, as well as professional development through certifications, professional involvement, and training (both internal and external) are reviewed.

PLANNING

It is important to emphasize that computer auditing is only one part of the total internal or external audit function. The IT audit group's responsibility is to provide support to the general audit side on computer-related aspects of their work, by providing adequate audit coverage of the organization's information systems. Audit management must ensure that general and computer audit work complement each other, dovetailing together to provide adequate audit coverage for the enterprise.

Planning the IT audit function involves defining the areas of audit involvement. These could be the review of:

- Business systems
- Systems under development
- IT facilities management
- Security and recovery controls
- Efficiency and effectiveness of IT

 ## AUDIT MISSION

To review, appraise, and report on:

- Soundness, adequacy, and application of controls
- Compliance with established policies, plans, and procedures
- Accounting for and safeguarding corporate assets
- Application of proper authority levels
- Reliability of accounting and other data
- Quality of performance of assigned duties
- Extent of coordinated effort between departments
- Safeguarding of corporate interests in general

 ## IT AUDIT MISSION

To review, appraise, and report on:

- Soundness, adequacy, and application of IT operational standards
- Soundness, adequacy, and application of systems-development standards
- The extent of compliance with corporate standards
- Security of the corporate IT investment
- Adequacy of contingency arrangements
- Completeness and accuracy of computer-processed information
- Whether optimum use is being made of all computing resources
- Soundness of application systems developed

The scope of work undertaken includes installation reviews, systems reviews, audits of systems under development, as well as audits of the development process. Auditing of the contingency planning arrangements, provision of in-department expertise, and training of non-IT auditors may also be IT audit responsibilities. The specialist may be required to assist in computerizing the internal audit function, to review logical security, and to liaise with external IT audit functions.

Specialist tasks would include reviews of logical security, IT strategic planning, efficiency/effectiveness, communications systems security, and IT technical support functions.

ORGANIZATION OF THE FUNCTION

The dividing line between what is a computer audit function and what is a general audit function can vary significantly between audit groups. Some groups include what in other audit departments would be a computer audit function in the general audit responsibilities. There are three different views on computer audit as a discrete discipline.

The first view, and one often held by computer auditors themselves, is that any review of computer controls should be carried out by a specialist computer auditor. Therefore, as computer systems are continuing to spread and increase in complexity, the number of staff working as professional, full-time computer auditors must increase correspondingly.

The contrary view is that computer auditors and general auditors must integrate fully. Because most business systems are computer based, all auditors must be computer auditors. Extreme proponents of this view see no future for separate computer audit specialists, even for the most technical work.

Between these views is a third view, which has much to commend it. There is some benefit in some areas of audit work involving the review of computer systems being carried out by computer-literate general auditors. This includes the review of personal computer (PC) systems, which tend to be highly integrated into the workings of user departments, and many aspects of the review of both developing and live systems, which again benefit from a detailed knowledge of the business environment. Some straightforward file interrogations can now easily be carried out by general auditors. However, there is still a continuing and major role for specialist computer audit staff, particularly in the more technical areas of developing or live application reviews, and for mainframe computer installation and systems software reviews.

Such an organization will typically report independently to a level sufficiently high to ensure adequate authority for access. Normally it is seen as a part of internal audit and reports within that structure. The structure of IT audit itself is a factor of size, which will determine the need for specialists as opposed to generalists, the complexity of systems and the uniqueness of systems, and the extent of use of packaged systems.

 ## STAFFING

Depending on the size and complexity, staffing could consist of a mix of:

- Computer audit manager
- Application auditors
- Trainee auditors
- Audit application development staff
- Technical support

Skill levels required of the manager of such a department would include specialized skills in both conventional and computer auditing as well as the managerial skills appropriate to handle a mix of technical specialists. Knowledge of the corporation would be absolutely essential to ensure adequacy of risk coverage.

Tasks of the IT manager include the planning of the strategic direction of the section, which must take into account corporate priority setting as well as the liaison internally and externally to ensure effective IT coverage in an efficient manner. As with any line manager, the review and approval of all IT audit work and the controlling and monitoring of the workflow are part of the normal managerial function. The staffing of the department, defining of roles, sourcing of staff and training, motivating, and career planning for acquired staff are part of the normal managerial process.

Once the audit universe has been defined, it will be possible to work out the types of skill required to review the audit areas that have been identified.

Assuming typical IT audit coverage in a large organization, the following skills or knowledge may be required in an IT audit department:

- **IT security and control principles.**
- **Audit principles.** Auditors need to understand how to plan and undertake audits, and how to document their work.
- **Good interpersonal and communications skills**, both oral and written, because very complex technical information often has to be communicated in a jargon-free way.
- **Good sense of judgment** because they need to analyze complex technical and business issues, and to conclude on the security and control implications.
- **Business-specific skills,** for example, a bank will benefit in application reviews if some staff have banking training.
- **Systems-analysis skills** to assist in understanding computer systems and reviewing the development process.
- **Data-analysis skills** to assist the auditor in understanding the design and development process, as data-analysis techniques are in widespread use.
- **Some programming skill** to assist in preparing computer-assisted audit techniques (CAATs) and reviewing systems under development.
- **Computer operations experience** to help the auditor to review computer installations.
- **Networks** for the review of data communications.
- **Systems software** to assist in the review of the systems software infrastructure of the organization.
- **PCs and minicomputers.** This has now become a very significant area in many organizations.
- **Interfacing with the Internet.** The extension of the Internet into all aspects of business computing requires a knowledge of both the technology and the risks faced.
- **Cloud computing.** The variations within cloud computing are rapidly becoming the technology of choice for many organizations. Knowledge of the expanding risk that comes with such technology is of paramount importance to the modern IT auditor.

In-depth and varied skills are therefore required and are rarely found in one individual. Many computer audit departments are thus staffed by auditors from a variety of different computing and audit backgrounds. It is management's job to develop missing skills in the group, and bring the group together as a team. Ongoing training is essential to keep skills current in an ever-changing data processing environment.

In order to discharge their responsibility of identifying and analyzing risk in computer systems, the computer auditor must, as is the case with all auditors, be able to write reports in simple, jargon-free language. The auditor must be able to report on risk in terms that management can understand; insofar as is possible, the effect of the risk must be described in business terms for business management. While the final report of findings to management, both orally and in writing, may take only a small percentage of audit time, if it is not done professionally, much of the potential benefit of the audit will be lost. Good written and oral communications skills are therefore essential.

 ## IT AUDIT AS A SUPPORT FUNCTION

IT audit may also be viewed as support function to the rest of the internal audit function and may be involved in the development of CAATs, the provision of assistance to non-IT auditors, and even the internal training of non-IT auditors. They may also assist in the development of control procedures for internal computer usage while ensuring the appropriate research in advanced IT and IT audit techniques is conducted.

Organizational structures may be centralized or decentralized. Centralized has the advantages of independence from local management and the maintenance of close ties with corporate management. Availability is flexible but the centralized auditor may be seen as an outsider by local management and this could offset all the aforementioned advantages.

Decentralized IT audit with each division with its own IT auditors permits close ties at the local level with an enhanced perception of benefits. The auditors may have a better understanding of the local business functions but there is a possible loss of objectivity and standard audit approach. It is also a costly approach.

The hybrid approach uses generalist groups in the field with technical support at the head office. Rotation of staff through the specialist section may give the best of both worlds, but it may fragment audit efforts and result in a loss of cohesion.

 ## PLANNING

Planning the computer audit function involves defining the areas of audit involvement. These could be the review of:

- Business systems
- Systems under development
- IT facilities management

- Security and recovery controls
- Efficiency and effectiveness of IT

Of these we will focus primarily on the review of business information systems.

BUSINESS INFORMATION SYSTEMS

Reviews of business systems include audits of application systems, fraud audits, compliance audits, financial audits, operational audits, recovery audits, and systems-development audits.

Auditing computer systems of any kind is a systematic process commenced by obtaining a *business understanding* of the system under review. From this understanding, the auditor can define the business objectives of the system and verify them with user management. The next stage would be the definition of the specific *control objectives* and from there the auditor may proceed to identify and evaluate critical *controls/processes/ apparent exposures* and design the audit procedures to test the critical facets. Evaluation of the results, reporting, and follow-up complete the process.

In designing the audit procedures, the auditor is testing to obtain evidence. This means that the auditor must know what he or she is looking for. It must always be understood that not all controls need to be tested and that, to provide cost-effective auditing, the auditor should look for common controls, that is, controls that address a variety of control objectives. As individual controls are identified, the auditor should try to identify control structures or combinations of controls that serve to mitigate risk areas and should establish the degrees of control effectiveness.

INTEGRATED IT AUDITOR VERSUS INTEGRATED IT AUDIT

For many years confusion has arisen as to the difference between integrated audit and the integrated auditor. Contrary to what some believe, there are some simple and realistic answers to this question.

There are two readily identifiable approaches to integrated audit that have been tried with varying degrees of success: integrated auditor and integrated audit.

Integrated Auditor

The basic concept is to develop an expanded auditor skill set, basically to train financial/ operational auditors to be "partial" IT auditors. Armed with a basic understanding of computers—and general and application controls—all auditors would be able to include IT control considerations in each and every audit, as well as use basic CAATs (without being totally dependent on the IT audit staff). Basic training on information technology and IT audit remains the first step in developing IT auditors (including integrated auditors) at all skill levels.

Audit programs may then be modified to include IT control considerations, as well as to identify opportunities for CAATs.

If extensive IT audit education is provided for the integrated auditor, standard "off the shelf" IT audit programs might be used without modification. If the education provided is less extensive, audit programs may require significant modification to ensure the auditor fully understands both the question and possible answers, and knows what to do next based on the answer given.

The complete integrated auditor fully understands and will use CAATs in all audits. Undertrained integrated auditors rely on others to do CAATs for them.

In today's world, all auditors must have some level of IT expertise. All organizations base audit staffing and training requirements on the audit mission and audit requirements, and are becoming increasingly sophisticated in accomplishing that process. Thus, in reality, all auditors have become integrated IT auditors—some just have greater knowledge and skills than others. Effective integration is therefore dependent on:

- Expanding the IT knowledge base of each and every auditor
- Realistic audit assignments based on knowledge and skill level
- Extensive IT audit tools and support
- Effective technical supervision

Integrated Audit

The alternate solution chosen by some organizations is to focus their resources more directly by providing an integrated audit *product* rather than developing an integrated *auditor*. Rather than attempt to expand the knowledge base of an individual, they seek to apply the knowledge base that currently exists within their organization by assembling an audit team including IT audit-trained as well as financial/operationally trained auditors working together. This approach is obviously preferred by those organizations that already use cross-functional teams extensively. Though it is not always a viable alternative for smaller audit staffs, including a technical expert in an audit can have major internal assurance and risk management advantages.

The key to successful team auditing is the building of team participation skills to assure functional groups. Not all auditors are used to working as members of cohesive groups, and some have had no training or experience whatsoever of working in a group setting. This means that effective team building will involve expanding the group process knowledge base of both staff and management. Realistic audit team assignments based on knowledge and skill level are a prerequisite as IT audit management involvement and participation.

The biggest barriers to achieving effective auditing in an IT environment include the assumption that IT Audit is a separate and unique and special audit discipline, while the fundamental internal auditor skill set is accounting and general business oriented, with limited IT knowledge required.

Many organizations are redefining internal audit as the business processes are re-engineered throughout the rest of the organization. The internal audit discipline is also undergoing a massive re-engineering and reorganization as new philosophies, methodologies, and techniques such as control self-assessment are tested and implemented. What better time to restructure based on an IT philosophy?

IT is pervasive within the organization. Structures that seek to make IT distinct and special are obsolete and counterproductive. As auditors we have created the artificial functional designations of financial audit, operational audit, and IT audit because that suited our purposes at the time. In today's business environment we must use functional specialization to our advantage, not be ruled by it. We must eliminate over-specialization and correctly reclassify IT as a pervasive and critical organization resource rather than a special organization function that can only be audited by function specialists.

 ## AUDITEES AS PART OF THE AUDIT TEAM

Effective internal control can only be achieved when everyone wants to have effective internal control and work together to achieve that goal. Team-based auditing has long been a preferred integrated audit approach. As in any team effort, success is dependent on shared objectives and full participation. In today's world, however, the team audit approach needs to be taken to the next level, including management and staff of the area undergoing evaluation.

True team audits can provide team access to the broader specialized knowledge content of its individual members, and also identify those areas where critical specialized knowledge is absent.

 ## APPLICATION AUDIT TOOLS

The tools available for computer auditors include not only CAATs but also the standard tools such as interviews, system questionnaires, control questionnaires, and documentation. Control evaluation tools such as CAATs, test data generators, and flowcharting packages may be combined with specialized audit software, generalized audit software, utility programs, and non-audit-specific software such as reporting programs and general query languages.

Risk analyzers, audit planning software, and automated working papers may also prove useful tools in this environment.

 ## ADVANCED SYSTEMS

The audit of advanced systems such as paperless systems (e.g., electronic data interchange [EDI]) or decision support systems (e.g., Executive Information Systems) involves a risk-multiplier factor. The risk is limited only by the corporate dependency on the system. This is normally unevaluated and normally understated because risks in these areas could threaten the ongoing existence of the organization. The use of cloud computing and enterprise resource management (ERM) systems to drive the fundamental business of the organization means the risks within these areas must be clearly understood by the IT auditor and that the IT audit program must be tailored to meet these advanced risks.

Advanced systems are an enormous corporate investment designed to maintain the corporate competitive edge. In some cases they may lead to a complete re-engineering of the organization with major impacts on efficacy, efficiency, and economy.

 ## SPECIALIST AUDITOR

Many organizations make use of specialists within their IT audit function to carry out tasks classed as being beyond the scope of the conventional IT auditor. These include such audit areas as performance auditing of computerized systems, auditing logical computer security, auditing telecommunications, auditing that technical specialist's area, and auditing IT strategic planning. In all of these areas a higher level of technical competence is normally required and for many organizations it is neither cost effective nor desirable to retain such skill levels in-house. In these circumstances, the organization would rather outsource to a technical specialist or use consultancy skills as required. Where the specialist IT audit capability is in-sourced, career progression can be a problem because such high levels of technical skills are normally only required within IT audit, IT security, or IT itself.

 ## IT AUDIT QUALITY ASSURANCE

As with any other audit area, quality assurance remains the responsibility of the audit manager. In practice, this will normally involve review of audit work by other IT auditors as well as audit management. It is critical, to maintain the confidence of the auditee and the IT department in the IT audit function, that IT audit work be seen to be technically competent in all of the areas addressed. Once more, where such assurance cannot be given in-house, outside sources may be used as external quality assurance (QA) reviewers. Such external resources can come from a variety of sources including specialist consultancy firms and independent external auditors.

9

Audit Evidence Process

THIS CHAPTER EXPLORES the fundamental audit evidence process and the gathering of evidence that may be deemed sufficient, reliable, relevant, and useful. Evidence-gathering techniques such as observation, inquiry, interviewing, and testing are examined and the techniques of compliance versus substantive testing are contrasted. The complex area of statistical and non-statistical sampling techniques and the design and selection of samples and evaluation of sample results is examined. The essential techniques of computer-assisted audit techniques (CAATs) are covered and a case study using the IDEA© software downloadable with the book is included on the download.

 ## AUDIT EVIDENCE

As noted in Chapter 3, IT auditors must gather audit evidence in order to express opinions. Audit evidence itself may be classified as *sufficient*, *competent*, *relevant*, or *useful* and evidence is typically classified as *physical*, *testimonial*, *documentary*, or *analytical*.

 ## AUDIT EVIDENCE PROCEDURES

As has been stated, the auditor gathers evidence by following the audit program, which is a set of detailed steps that the auditor will follow in order to gain the appropriate evidence and, for an IT auditor, may well include the use of computerized techniques, although this is not always the case.

The evidence gathered permits the expression of an opinion on the efficiency, economy, and effectiveness of the activities. It lists directions for the examination and evaluation of information and provides the primary link between the audit fieldwork and the audit report.

Steps in formulating the audit program involve determining the results from the preliminary survey, determining what, if any, risk is indicated; determining what types of controls best manage the risks; determining what, if any, additional evidence the auditor would like; and selecting the audit tests.

Like a route map, the audit program must fit the need of the traveler. It states what is to be done, when it is to be done, how it is to be done, who will do it, and how long it will take. The audit program helps the auditor stay on schedule/budget. It may be pro-forma or specifically tailored, but in either case it provides the following benefits:

- It is a systematic plan for each phase of audit work providing a basis for assigning work to the team members.
- It is a means of controlling and evaluating progress and assisting in training inexperienced staff members.
- It provides a summary record of work done.
- It reduces the direct supervision requirement by providing a clear path for subordinates and provides internal audit quality assurance information.

The final audit program should be prepared immediately after the preliminary survey, although even then the program may be modified during the audit. Where new pro-forma audit programs are to be introduced, they should be prepared well in advance and field tested. Programs that are prepared too late will be rushed and have steps missing.

Preparation of the audit program should focus on what is hazardous to the corporation. The program should be thoughtful, relevant, effective, and economic, remembering again that not every item need be checked and that reasonableness and relevance should be maintained.

 ## CRITERIA FOR SUCCESS

In order for the audit program to be successful, the objectives of the operation should be stated and agreed to by the auditee up front. The programs should be tailor-made where possible and the reasoning behind each work step should be shown. A common failing of audit programs is the creation of a list of questions to be answered. The audit program is a series of detailed instructions to be followed in the obtaining of audit evidence. These work steps should be prioritized to seek evidence of the most important control objectives first. All audit programs should be flexible because circumstances may change based on evidence uncovered. Supervisory approval must be shown for all audit scheduling and staffing, and the audit constraints must be agreed to by all parties.

Audit supervision will typically utilize standard project management techniques in order to match resources to requirements. This will include the defining, organizing, and monitoring of tasks and training staff as well as approval of the audit program.

The audit supervisor must be satisfied with the:

- Audit subject
- Audit objective
- Audit scope
- Pre-audit planning
- Selection of audit procedures
- Procedures for evaluation or testing
- Procedures for communication
- Report preparation
- Follow-up review

The audit program provides for the collection of audit evidence of:

- Structures
- Documentation standards
- Systems documentation

This may involve interviewing personnel, observing performance, or statistical sampling.

The overall audit approach must be:

- Simple
- Practical
- Quick
- Commonsense
- Business oriented
- Technically competent

 STATISTICAL SAMPLING

In many cases the auditor can gain adequate assurance regarding the mitigation of risk without having to examine every single record or transaction. Under such circumstances, the auditor may choose to use a variety of sampling techniques in order to obtain evidence that is satisfactory and competent. The auditor may choose to use either non-statistical or statistical sampling techniques.

Non-statistical sampling involves the auditor making a judgment call as to the number of items to be selected and which items. The sampling technique is valid where the auditor wishes to examine a few examples without necessarily drawing conclusions about the whole population.

Statistical sampling itself is the process of testing a portion of a group of items to evaluate and draw conclusions about the population as a whole.

Statistical sampling may be defined as follows:

> The auditor is performing either a compliance test or a substantive test of either documented internal accounting controls or accounting source records by applying procedures to less than 100 percent of the items in the class of transactions or account balance for the purpose of forming a conclusion about some characteristic of the class or balance.

 ## WHY SAMPLE?

The underlying assumption of sampling is that the results of a sample yield accurate information about the population from which the sample was taken. Sampling, therefore, can be viewed as an effective method of gathering audit evidence.

If auditors did not use sampling, every item comprising an account balance or every transaction occurring within a class of transaction would need to be reviewed. The cost of such an examination would (a) be prohibitive due to the amount of time required to perform such an examination and (b) far outweigh the benefit obtained. Sampling provides the auditor with a means of obtaining almost identical information, but at a much lower cost. Thus, sampling is also an efficient method of gathering information.

There are two basic sampling approaches:

1. Judgmental/nonmathematical
2. Statistical

Each approach represents a different way of handling audit risk. Therefore, each may be appropriate for some populations but not for others. Choosing the appropriate approach involves answering some critical questions about risk, population characteristics, and the objectives of our testing. The answers lead us to the best approach and the most efficient audit plan.

 ## JUDGMENTAL (OR NON-STATISTICAL) SAMPLING

In judgmental sampling, the auditor relies solely on his or her professional judgment to assess the risk of sampling error and evaluate the population. Because the sample is not intended to be representative of the whole population, sample results cannot be extrapolated to the whole population. This approach is normally used where the auditor intends to use the sample for limited purposes.

Where the auditor is aware that a section of the population is higher risk, the auditor may choose to direct the sample to that particular area. Once again, the auditor has exercised professional judgment in selecting the population to be reviewed and conclusions drawn must be carefully judged to ensure their validity.

Judgmental sampling should not be used as a primary audit procedure if the auditors have no special knowledge about which items in the population are more likely to contain misstatements.

Again, judgmental sampling may be used for limited purposes (i.e., when sampling is not the primary audit procedure) such as corroboration of the outcome of other analyses by examining a few detailed transactions to check the validity of forecasts.

 ## STATISTICAL APPROACH

In statistical sampling, the sample is selected in such a way that it can be expected to be representative of the population. By doing so, the auditor intends that the relevant characteristics of the sample, such as the sizes or rates or errors, should be mathematically proportional to those of the population. For this to be valid an appropriate sample-selection technique, such as random selection, and an adequate sample size must be chosen. The sample results may then be used to project to the population (extrapolate) in order to estimate a specific value for the population. The more representative the sample is, the more accurate the extrapolation. This effectively means the larger the sample size, the more accurate the extrapolation.

Obviously statistical sampling is less than 100 percent assured and the auditor must take into consideration the effect of sampling risk.

 ## SAMPLING RISK

All auditing involves a certain amount of risk or uncertainties. The risk that material irregularities or errors will not be detected either by internal control or by the use of the appropriate auditing procedures is always present. The uncertainty that exists in applying the audit procedures is commonly referred to as audit risk. When auditors choose to use statistical sampling, they face the possibility that, due to the fact that there is less than 100 percent certainty, the conclusions drawn about the population may contain some material error. This audit risk comprises two specific subsets. Sampling risk is the risk that the sample chosen does not appropriately reflect the population as a whole, while non-sampling risk is the risk that, having obtained a representative sample, the auditor still misses a significant error.

In the case of statistical sampling as opposed to judgmental sampling, an attempt is made to control the risk of sampling error. Because the auditor has accepted that 100 percent certainty is either not desirable or not possible, an auditor working at a 95 percent certainty level has accepted a 5 percent chance that the sample drawn does not accurately or completely reflect the population. This risk exists because of the nature of sampling certainty.

In a normal distribution, a 95 percent certainty indicates that, should the auditor draw a sample of twenty 100 times, 95 of those times the full sample would be drawn from a representative part of the population. Five of those times the sample would include one or more items that are not representative of the population.

On the occasions when this happens, caused by the random chance in the selection of the sample, it is classed as the risk of sampling error. This risk always exists regardless of how the sample is selected. The auditor's justification for accepting this risk involves a judgment call regarding the level of assurance that in the chosen combination of substantive testing and reliance and internal control there is a reasonable probability of detection. By choosing the appropriate sampling technique and by applying their professional judgment after consultation with auditee management, the auditor attempts to minimize the risk of sampling error. In addition, by choosing an appropriate statistical model and by following the correct sampling selection methodology, the auditor can quantify the likelihood of sampling error in order to determine that it is within acceptable limits.

In the case of judgmental sampling, the risk of sampling error still exists but, because the auditor did not explicitly state the confidence level, the risk is not quantifiable. This means that, in this case, the risk of sampling error is dependent on the experience, skill, and judgment of the individual auditor but that the auditor's evaluation cannot be independently and quantifiably substantiated.

Whether the sample chosen is based upon statistical methods or the auditor's judgment, every use of sampling is also subject to the risk of non-sampling error. This type of error is a result of other uncertainties that are not caused by the sampling process. Causes of this type of error could include:

- Mistakes in selecting the sample
- Use of incorrect audit procedures for a given objective
- Failure to recognize misstatements or irregularities included in the sample items
- Improper definition of the population

Non-sampling error therefore includes any misjudgments or mistakes on the part of the auditor that may lead them to an incorrect conclusion based upon the tests carried out on the sample. These errors would have occurred even if sampling had not been chosen as the technique and the full population examined. By careful planning and use of the appropriate audit techniques, this risk can be minimized, although not eliminated.

ASSESSING SAMPLING RISK

Institute of Internal Auditors (IIA) Standards state that auditors should use their professional judgment in assessing sampling risk. The two main aspects of sampling risk in compliance tests of internal controls are:

1. The risk of over-reliance on controls (beta risk), which is the risk that the sample leads the auditor to place reliance on the control when it is not justified.

2. The risk of under-reliance on controls (alpha risk) is the risk that the sample leads the auditor to evaluate the population as beyond tolerance levels erroneously.

The auditor should also be concerned with sampling risk when performing substantive tests. The risks are classified as:

- The risk of incorrect acceptance (beta risk) is the risk that the sample supports the auditor's conclusion that the amount or quantity is not materially misstated when in fact it is.
- The risk of incorrect rejection (alpha risk) is the risk that the sample leads the auditor to believe that the amount or quantity is materially misstated when in fact it is not.

Alpha characteristics of the population relate to the efficiency of the audit, while beta risks relate to the effectiveness of the audit in the detection of material errors.

 ## PLANNING A SAMPLING APPLICATION

Once an auditor has made the decision to use sampling, consideration must be given to both the audit objectives and the characteristics of the population.

Audit Objectives

As with any audit, the auditor starts off by considering the control objectives of the area under review. From this can be derived the source of audit evidence and the nature of the audit testing required to evaluate that evidence. Where the audit testing needs to use sampling techniques, the auditor may focus on the specific objectives to be achieved by the tests to be carried out on the sample selected.

The sampling technique chosen will be dependent on the nature of the opinion the auditor wishes to express. An opinion on error rates within our population would normally dictate the use of attribute-sampling techniques, while expressing an opinion on the probable values of our population may call for the use of monetary unit sampling or variable sampling.

Population Characteristics

The second stage of planning is to define the population about which an opinion will be expressed in terms of the population's characteristics. For example, the auditor may choose to express an opinion about high-value items, low-value items, or all items. Any opinions expressed based on a sample can only be in terms of the population that was sampled in the first place. Should the auditor sample invoices within the previous six months, any opinion expressed can only be valid in terms of the previous six months' invoices. Any conclusions drawn about invoices beyond this period would be invalid.

Again, if the auditor wishes to express an opinion regarding customers exceeding their credit limit, the appropriate population to examine would be the creditors' records and not the invoices.

In testing to ensure that all orders have been invoiced, the sample would be drawn from the orders and checked forward against the invoices. If the auditor wishes to express an opinion regarding the authorization of payments, the sample must be drawn from payments and checked backward against the authorized input documents.

In any population, a common evaluation technique is to determine the average value of the population. Three averages are possible: the *mean*, the *median*, and the *mode*. In statistical sampling, the most commonly used average is the mean.

The mean or arithmetic average value of a data set may be calculated as the sum of all values, divided by the number of data points. For example, if three selections are made by the auditor of invoices with values of R 100, R 140, and R 180, then the average value would be (100 + 140 + 180)/3, or R 140.

The median represents the middle value in a population range. The mode represents the most frequently occurring value in a population.

In a census of a population, for example, there may be individuals with ages ranging from 10 to 80 with a predominantly young population and an arithmetic average age of 35. In such a population, the median may be found to be 45, the mean is 35, and the mode may be as low as 20 because of the population being skewed toward younger people.

Deviations from the Mean

The *amount of variability* in the population defines the spread of values. One method of determining the variability of a population is to examine its variability from the mean. *Standard deviations* measure dispersion around the mean. The standard deviation can be calculated as the square root of the average of squared deviations of each member of the population from the mean. In the case of our invoices, this would involve:

$$100 - 140 = (40)^2 = 1600$$
$$140 - 140 = (0)^2 = 0$$
$$180 - 140 = (40)^2 = 1600$$
$$3200 / 3 = 1066.67$$
$$\sqrt{1066.67} = 32.66$$

The main use from an audit perspective is the statistical fact that in a normal (unskewed) population, 68 percent of the population will lie within 1 standard deviation from the mean, and 95 percent of a population will lie within 1.96 standard deviations from the mean. In other words, when an auditor samples such a population, there is a 95 percent probability that all items selected will be drawn from within ± 1.96 standard deviations from the mean.

The skewness of a distribution refers to its lack of symmetry. A perfectly symmetrical distribution will result in a normal bell curve with a skewness of zero. Most distributions have some degree of skew. A distribution with the majority of the population distributed to the right of the mean is said to be negatively skewed, and a distribution with the majority of the population distributed to the left of the mean is said to be positively skewed.

The computation of skewness involves taking the deviations from the mean, dividing them by the standard deviation, and raising them to the third power; these figures are then added together and divided by the number of data points.

 ## CALCULATING SAMPLE SIZE

For any sample design, deciding on the appropriate sample size will depend on certain key factors that must be considered together in order to ensure that the sample objectives are met. As previously stated, the amount of variability in the population defines the spread of values. This will also affect accuracy and consequently the size of the sample required when estimating a value. The greater the variability, the larger the sample size required.

The *confidence level* represents the likelihood that the results obtained from the sample lie within the associated precision. The higher the confidence level desired, the larger the sample size required. Auditors normally operate at a 95 percent confidence level but where a situation is evaluated as low risk, a lower level such as 90 percent is acceptable. Conversely, in a higher risk situation, the auditor may operate at a 99 percent confidence level.

Contrary to popular belief, the *population* size does not normally affect sample size. Statistically, the larger the population size, the greater is the likelihood that the sample will be representative. Where the population to be sampled is less than 5,000, the population size begins to have an impact on the sample size. The effect is to slightly increase the required sample size. Where population size is very low, standard sampling techniques may be invalid and non-parametric sampling techniques may be required. Some audit software does not take this into consideration in calculating sample size, and the auditor must be aware that such sampling will only be appropriate in larger populations.

Differing methods of sampling are appropriate in different circumstances and the auditor must be aware of the advantages and disadvantages of each so that the appropriate sampling method can be selected, as can be seen in Exhibit 9.1.

 ## QUANTITATIVE METHODS

In addition to statistical analysis, a variety of quantitative methods are also available to be selected by the internal auditor. These mathematical tools are commonly used to obtain an understanding of operations and permit the drawing of conclusions in a variety of circumstances through analyzing the complexities of situations. Of the many quantitative methods available to the auditor, the most common are examined in the following sections.

EXHIBIT 9.1 Table of Sampling Methods

Method	Definition	Advantages	Disadvantages
Judgmental sampling	Based on deliberate choice of the auditor	• Normal application is for small samples from a population that is well understood and there is a clear method for picking the sample • Is used to provide illustrative examples or to check forecasts	• Sample is typically small and can be misleading • Prone to bias • Sample results cannot be extrapolated to give population results
Attribute sampling	Used to determine error rates in the population	• Results in the minimum sample size needed to express an opinion of a given confidence level	• Only valid for populations > 5,000 • May result in a larger sample size than judgmental sampling • Requires random selection to remain valid
Variable sampling	Used to estimate values of a population	• Results in the minimum sample size needed to express an opinion of a given confidence level	• Only valid for populations > 5,000 • May result in a larger sample size than judgmental sampling • Requires random selection to remain valid
Cluster sampling	Units in the population can often be found in geographical groups or clusters (e.g., schools, households, etc.). A random sample of clusters is taken, then all units within those clusters are examined	• Quicker, easier, and cheaper than other forms of random sampling • Does not require complete population information • Useful for face-to-face interviews	• Works best when each cluster can be regarded as a microcosm of the population • Larger sampling error than other forms of random sampling • If clusters are not small, it can become expensive • A larger sample size may be needed to compensate for greater sampling error

Method	Description	Advantages	Disadvantages
Probability proportional to size (PPS) or monetary unit sampling (MUS)	Samples are drawn in proportion to their size giving a higher chance of selection to the larger items (i.e., the chance of being selected is proportional to the individual item's size)	• Unit to be selected is a single monetary unit (e.g., dollar) • Where you want each element to have equal chance of selection rather than each sampling unit • Powerful to identify over-exaggeration	• Can be expensive to get the information to draw the sample • Only appropriate if you are interested in the elements • Not appropriate if elements are underexaggerated
Stratified sampling	The population is subdivided into mutually exclusive layers. The strata can have equal sizes or you may wish a higher proportion in certain strata	• Ensures units from each main group are included and may therefore be more reliably representative • Should reduce the error due to sampling • Typically results in lower sample sizes	• Selecting the sample is more complex and requires good population • Estimates involve complex calculations
Simple random selection	Ensures each member of the population has an equal chance of selection	• Produces defensible estimates of the population and sampling error • Simple sample design and interpretation	• Need complete and accurate population listing • May not be possible in an unnumbered population • May not be practical if remote items selected for something
Systematic selection	After randomly selecting a starting point in the population between 1 and n, every nth unit is selected, where n equals the population size divided by the sample size	• Easier to extract the sample than simple random selection • Ensures cases are spread across the population	• Can be costly and time-consuming if the sample is not conveniently located • Cannot be used where there is a pattern to the population distribution

Trend Analysis

Trend analysis is used to evaluate the behavior of a variable such as turnover of a period of time. Such analyses can serve as evaluation criteria to determine the reasonableness of fluctuations of an extended period. Comparisons of this year's turnover to last year's turnover or, alternatively, this month's turnover to the same month last year are popular.

Chi-Square Tests

Chi-square analyses are *non-parametric tests* capable of analyzing relationships between qualitative data. For example, do operating units in the South have particular patterns of operation different from those in the North?

Chi-square tests can check for the independence of normal classifications and ordinal data, and require no particular distributional pattern for the data.

Correlation Analysis

The measurement of the extent of association of one variable with another is known as correlation analysis. Two variables are said to be correlated when they move together in a detectable pattern. A direct correlation is said to exist when both variables increase or decrease at the same time, although not necessarily by the same amount or, indeed, in the same direction. For example, one would expect inventory to decrease as sales increased or for sales of soft drinks to increase as temperatures rise.

Correlation analysis is used by internal auditors to identify those factors that appeared to be related. An operational auditor, for example, may use correlation analysis to determine whether corporate performance is in line with industry standards by comparing the correlation of company costs of imported parts with the exchange rate fluctuations. Problems with how these statistics are computed, shortcomings in the internal auditor's understanding of auditees' operations, or real inefficiencies or misstatements can be pinpointed through correlation analysis.

Graphical Analysis

Graphical analysis can be useful to the internal auditor in identifying interrelationships in data, anomalies, and simple data errors.

A common form of graphical representation used by the auditor is a *scatter diagram*, which refers to any graph of data points. The more discernible a pattern appears in the graph, the more likely one variable is related to another and therefore can be used to predict the other's value. Where no pattern can be noted, there would appear to be little, if any, correlation between the two variables.

Where a strong correlation exists, either positive or negative, the correlation value will approach 1. Where little correlation exists the correlation value will approach 0. Unfortunately, correlation values only measure linear patterns. Where there is a nonlinear relationship, correlation statistics will not disclose this. Occasionally the correlation value can be distorted by a single data point not conforming to the general pattern.

While this can be readily seen on the graph, it may be less obvious in examining the correlation value.

Learning Curves

In conducting operational audits of performance levels of the implementation of new procedures for the quality of training of new staff, a learning curve would normally be expected to be observed. As employees gain experience with the new procedures or as the new employee becomes more experienced, the length of time taken to complete a task should decrease.

Learning curves are evaluated by computing the time required per unit of production each time that the cumulative output is doubled. A decrease in production time per unit of 25 percent would result in a 75 percent curve. A 60 percent curve would result if the production time was reduced by 40 percent.

By measuring this curve the auditor can determine how quickly a new procedure or employee becomes productive. When a new procedure is recommended, calculating the initial time per unit under the old system and comparing it to a series of observations over time using the new procedures can objectively determine the impact of the revision to the procedures.

Ratio and Regression Analysis

Ratio analysis assumes a given proportional relationship between two numbers and is normally used for comparisons over time. A more advanced form of ratio analysis attempts to quantify the interrelationship in order to facilitate predictions in a *regression analysis*. Regression analysis is used to estimate the effect that a movement in one variable (the independent variable) causes a movement in the other variable (dependent variable); for example, if the sun shines, more cool drinks will be sold: but how many more? By performing the regression analysis, the relationship, if any, can be identified and quantified and sales levels predicted.

Regression analysis can thus assist the auditor in understanding and quantifying data interrelationships. Unusual variations between expectations and recorded values may be noted for further investigation.

Using software, the auditor can additionally conduct a multiple discriminant regression analysis relating the independent variable to a number of dependent variables simultaneously. By determining the comparative strength of the relationships, the auditor can choose the focus area to achieve greatest impact in performance improvement. Such analysis has also been used to attempt to predict bankruptcy.

As with most statistical tools, regression analysis is based on a set of underlying assumptions that must be met for its use and interpretations to be valid.

Linear Programming

Linear programming is an operations research tool used for the allocation of scarce resources or to determine optimal blends of raw materials. The constraints applicable are reduced to algebraic formulae, which are then solved by simultaneous equations. For example, in a production environment, machining may be capable of processing 100 units per machine, while finishing can handle 35 units per machine. The question of how many of each machine should be used for optimum production can be solved using linear programming.

 ## PROJECT-SCHEDULING TECHNIQUES

Accurate project-scheduling techniques have long been a goal in project management. Internal auditing frequently works in project teams that often suffer from the same poor project scheduling.

Program Evaluation Review Techniques

The program evaluation review technique (PERT) is used to diagrammatically identify dependent and independent activities. By showing graphically which activities cannot be started until the previous activities have been completed and, at the same time, which activities can proceed simultaneously, the planner can allocate resources to those tasks having the most impact on the final completion deadline. This technique also takes into consideration operational constraints placed on the resources needed to carry out the tasks.

In Exhibit 9.2, the shortest time to get from A to E while completing all tasks is calculated by calculating the longest path, in this case A-H-I-E (9 days). Other times and paths include A-B-C-D-E (8 days) and A-F-G-D-E (5 days).

This means that the bottom path would be the most critical. The reason for this is that any delay in this path will postpone the final completion date. Any delay in the middle path that does not exceed four days will have no effect on the final completion date. Should the top path experience a delay in any of the processes of, for example, three days, then the top path will now take 11 days to complete and will become the critical

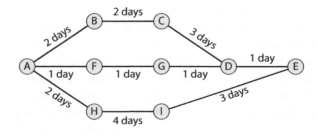

- Path A-B-C-D-E takes 8 days
- Path A-F-G-D-E takes 5 days
- Path A-H-I-E takes 9 days

EXHIBIT 9.2 PERT Chart

path. If, by the same token, the time taken for the critical path can be reduced, then the final completion date can be brought forward.

Critical Path Method

The critical path method (CPM) is a scheduling tool that was developed independently of PERT but uses a similar diagram. CPM, however, uses two time estimates: one for normal effort and one for *crash* effort. Crash time is the time required for completion if all available resources were committed to that task.

GANTT or Bar Charts

One of the simplest planning tools requiring no mathematical calculations is the Gantt chart. It is commonly used in organizing work and monitoring progress through the various stages of a simple project and involves the production of bar charts showing the start and completion times of individual project activities. The major drawback to these charts is the poorer representation of interdependencies.

 SIMULATIONS

Monte Carlo Simulations

Computers can be used to accelerate timescales by repeatedly carrying out activities very rapidly. By combining this with the probability of events occurring, a sophisticated model can be built.

One such approach is referred to as the Monte Carlo Method. It uses the computer to simulate uncertainty via random behavior based on the probabilities entered and then estimates specified models several times to determine average performance.

Game Theory

The term *game theory* refers to mathematical models of optimal strategies under various incentive schemes. This is used in competitive environments to explore "what if" solutions.

A non-zero-sum game is said to exist when a profit is generated in which it is possible for both participants to share. A zero-sum game denotes a situation where a profit simply transfers from a loser to a winner. Game theory is used to assist the internal auditor in understanding the reasons that particular strategies are pursued in negotiation sessions or competitive price setting.

Queuing Theory

Businesses often have queues at service points. Elimination of these queues by increasing the number of service points would result in service points frequently being unused and costs increasing. Management frequently must decide how many service points should be provided.

Queuing theory facilitates the use of mathematical models to minimize the *total cost* for a given rate of arrivals; the minimized cost includes both *service costs* (facility and operating costs) and *waiting costs* (the idle resources waiting in line or having service points idle).

COMPUTER-ASSISTED AUDIT SOLUTIONS

In today's environment, a review of business systems will almost inevitably involve the use of appropriate information retrieval and analysis programs and procedures. The auditor will use test transaction techniques to review system-level activity. In advanced auditing, the use of knowledge-based systems will permit the distribution of advanced audit techniques to less skilled staff. Confusingly, these are commonly referred to as Computer-Assisted Audit Tools (CAATs), Computer-Assisted Audit Techniques (CAATs), or more correctly Computer-Assisted Audit Tools and Techniques (CAATTs)

Computer-Assisted Audit Tools and Techniques (CAATTs) are needed because of the large volumes of data in multiple locations involved in the managing of a complex business environment.

The use of computer-assisted audit solutions involves the merging of software into an audit program. In order for this to prove effective, key control questions must be pre-defined in order to facilitate the use of the technology to analyze the data and provide the answers.

Advantages from the auditor's perspective include increased auditor productivity, creativity, and the application of a consistent methodology.

Information retrieval and analysis programs and procedures include programs that organize, combine, extract, and analyze information. This includes generalized audit software as well as application and industry-related software. Customized audit software and information retrieval software as well as standard utilities and on-line inquiry may also be utilized for information retrieval and analysis. Where the auditor has computer skills in programming, conventional programming languages may provide a viable alternative, but a lack of such skills does not preclude auditors from utilizing such techniques. The ready availability of microcomputer-based software, which provides computing power without the requirement of technical expertise, puts direct data analysis within the toolkit of any auditor. The primary requirement is an understanding of the business application and how data relates.

GENERALIZED AUDIT SOFTWARE

Generalized audit software (GAS) is software designed specifically for auditors in order to provide a user-friendly audit tool to carry out a variety of standard tasks required by the auditor such as examining records, testing calculations, and making computations.

A common audit technique is to take a copy of a file of standard data for later comparison to a changed version of the same data. GAS can conduct the comparison and analysis.

Selecting, analyzing, and printing audit samples are techniques that can significantly improve the quality of an audit by allowing the quantification of audit and sampling risk. In a high-volume system, these techniques may be the only method the auditor can employ to achieve audit satisfaction. In such systems the use of computerized sampling simplifies both the usage and interpretation of results. Most GAS comes complete with sampling and analysis functions to handle the complexities for the auditor.

The auditor will commonly have to handle data that is not in a suitable format for analysis. Summarizing and re-sequencing data are required to put the information into a more usable format. Once reformatted, the software can also perform the appropriate analyses.

GAS cannot resolve all of the auditors' problems, but it can assist considerably in many of the common problem areas. It is specifically designed for the handling of volumes of data. The output can be used for further computer processing allowing audits to be linked together. The time to audit can be reduced and the auditor freed to spend time interpreting results. Because there are limited programming skills required, the audit reliance on IT staff is reduced.

There are, however, limitations. Hardware and software environments may be restrictive if an inappropriate package is selected. The number of files that can be handled may be restrictive and the types of record structures may not be comprehensive. The numbers of computations may be limited and the number of reports per "pass" may be restrictive. This makes the selection of software a critical element in the effective use.

CAATs Case Study

Supplied with this book is access to a demonstration version of IDEA via website download (see About the Website). IDEA is one of the world's most popular and powerful GAS packages. This is included so that the IT auditor maintains hands-on experience in order to become familiar with such tools. The software and educational case study is supplied with the kind permission of CaseWare IDEA Inc.

 ## APPLICATION AND INDUSTRY-RELATED AUDIT SOFTWARE

In addition to GAS, audit procedures are commonly available for standard business applications such as accounts receivable and payable, payrolls, general ledgers, and inventory management. Such software is available stand alone or as add-ons to standard GAS packages.

Specific industry-related audit software is available for industries such as insurance, health care, and financial services. Most such packages require conversion of input to standard package layouts and selection of appropriate parameters. This means that a degree of IT skill is required for conversion. The software itself is normally both cost effective and efficient. Other non-audit-related software such as SPSS Clementine, a Data Mining toolkit, MS Access, and MS Project Manager may also be readily adapted for audit purposes.

 ## CUSTOMIZED AUDIT SOFTWARE

Customized audit software is software designed to run in unique circumstances and to perform unique audit tests. Where output is required in unique formats, customized audit software may be required. Such software may be expensive to develop and normally requires a high level of IT skills. It must be handled with care because running it may not tell you what you think it does; however, it may be the only viable solution in a unique processing situation.

 ## INFORMATION-RETRIEVAL SOFTWARE

Standard information-retrieval software such as report writers and query languages, while not specifically written for auditors, can perform many common audit routines. This category of software includes report writers, program generators, and fourth-generation languages.

 ## UTILITIES

Utilities are programs written to perform common tasks such as copy, sort, print, merge, select, or edit. These programs are normally parameter driven and may be used in combination with other software. They are extremely powerful and the right to use them should be restricted. From an audit perspective, they see data as it exists, which adds to the degree of reliance that auditors can place on their results.

 ## ON-LINE INQUIRY

Interactive interrogation can provide comparison data for audit reports, can provide confirmation of corrective action taken, and can be an additional source of audit information. Effective use requires few IT skills but an understanding of the information is essential. Armed with the appropriate access authority auditors can obtain adequate audit evidence to meet their requirements. Auditors, however, need to be sure what they are looking at because there is ample opportunity for drawing erroneous conclusions.

 ## CONVENTIONAL PROGRAMMING LANGUAGES

Standard languages such as COBOL, BASIC, RPG, PASCAL, C, and so on, can prove effective audit tools but require a degree of programming experience. Such programs are normally slow to develop and expensive and may not be reliable because the auditor is not a professional programmer. They can, however, perform any audit test the auditor can envisage and may be used in conjunction with any other type of audit software.

MICROCOMPUTER-BASED SOFTWARE

Microcomputer-based software can prove a flexible and powerful tool for the auditor and may include GAS, Computer-Aided Software Engineering (CASE), spreadsheet packages (analysis, manipulation, recalculation, etc.), specialized packages (NCSS, etc.), and specialized software for auditing micros (CSAN, etc.).

They have the advantages of being able to use input from multiple hardware/software platforms, are comparatively inexpensive, and result in one set of portable software to learn. Disadvantages include the fact that the auditor is not looking at the live data and that the software may not handle all data formats from mainframes.

TEST TRANSACTION TECHNIQUES

Test transaction techniques may be used to confirm processing controls functioning and include the evaluation of edit and validation controls, the testing of exception reports, and evaluation of data integrity controls. Total and calculation verification may be performed.

The transaction test techniques could include:

- **Test data.** This technique involves the utilization of a copy of the live computer system through which a series of transactions is passed in order to produce predetermined results. This technique, while effective in searching for defects, is limited by the volume of data that can be handled. In addition, the results may be biased by the results the auditor expects.
- **Integrated Test Facility (ITF).** This technique, while similar in nature to test data, is effected by creation within the live system of a dummy entity (department, warehouse, etc.), and the processing of test data against the dummy entity *together with the live data*. This technique has the advantages of testing the system as it normally operates and testing both the computer and manual systems. It has distinct disadvantages as well. All test transactions must be removed from the live system before they affect live totals, postings, or the production of negotiable documents such as checks. In addition, there may be a very real danger of destroying the live system. ITFs must be used with great care.
- **Source-code review.** This computer audit technique involves the review of the source code originally written by the programmer. In the past this has meant browsing through piles of printout. In today's environment, sophisticated searches can be implemented using generalized audit software to establish weaknesses in the source code.

- **Embedded audit modules (SCARFs [System Collection Audit Review Files]).** In systems where audit trails may only exist as computer records and then only for a short time or discontinuously, it may be necessary for the auditor to have built in a facility to collect and retain selected information to serve as an audit trail for subsequent examination. This obviously makes the collected data a target for destruction or manipulation and it must be treated as such.
- **Parallel simulation.** Parallel simulation is a technique involving the creation of software to simulate some functional capability of the live system such as a calculation. The live data is processed through the simulating program in parallel with the live system and the outputs are compared.

Review of system-level activity involves the examination of control areas with a pervasive influence such as telecoms, the operating environment itself, the systems-development function, and change control. End-user computing, although not in the same category of general control, can be treated in the same manner as a general threat.

CHAPTER TEN

Audit Reporting Follow-up

T HIS CHAPTER COVERS AUDIT REPORTING and follow-up. The form and
content of an audit report are detailed and its purpose, structure, content, and
style as dictated by the desired effect on its intended recipient for a variety of types
of opinion are considered, as well as the follow-up to determine management's actions
to implement recommendations.

 AUDIT REPORTING

Ultimately, the value of an audit lies in the improvements to the business situation
brought about as a result of the audit. Where no such improvements take place the
audit may well have been a waste of time, resources, and money. Improvements will only
take place where the individuals authorized and empowered to take effective action have
been convinced that some form of action is appropriate to improve the control situations.

A variety of individuals will use audit reports for a variety of purposes. Executive
management will typically use an audit report to gain an insight into the overall status
of internal controls within a given business area and for the organization as a whole.
Operational management uses audit reports to determine the adequacy and effectiveness of specific controls in achieving specific performance and control objectives. Other
agencies may use audit reports to gain insight into the inner workings of specific operations and the degree of reliance that can be placed on the outputs of those business areas.

In general, auditors communicate the overall findings together with recommendations for actions to be taken using the audit report. These reports are sent to those individuals who are in a position to take effective action or ensure that corrective actions are taken. Senior executives within the organization may also receive either copies of the report or summaries of the reports. Results of the audit are usually reported orally in the form of interim reports and closing conferences as well as in writing.

 ## INTERIM REPORTING

Interim reports are those reports prepared and issued while the audit is in progress. They are typically used to either report progress on an extended audit or to notify the auditee of a finding that warrants immediate attention. They may be either written or verbal, although a written memo-form report can be a useful proof of delivery of a finding. The main advantages of interim reports are the provision of timely feedback to the auditee coupled with a higher probability of immediate action. This can, in turn, result in a more favorable final report if appropriate action is taken. Interim reports effectively provide a follow-up opportunity during the audit itself.

 ## CLOSING CONFERENCES

Before the final audit report is issued, a closing conference is common. This permits an overall review of the audit objectives and findings and is the final opportunity to clear up any misunderstandings or omissions prior to report issuance. It ensures a fair and balanced presentation and allows auditees to express their opinion. It also gives the auditor feedback on the way the audit was handled from a client's perspective.

 ## WRITTEN REPORTS

Written reports at a minimum should be produced at the end of an audit. Reports generally should be:

- Accurate
- Objective
- Clear
- Concise
- Complete
- Constructive
- Timely

Written reports should include the audit purpose, scope, results, auditor's opinion, recommendations for potential improvements, acknowledgment of satisfactory performance, and the auditee's reply to the auditor's opinions and recommendations. Because the issued audit report is a reflection of the competence and professional image of the whole Information Technology (IT) audit function, it should be reviewed and approved by the in-charge auditor prior to issue.

For many managers the audit report is the only demonstration they will see that IT audit has fully discharged its responsibilities. This impression will be based not only on the technical competence of the report, but also the clarity of writing and the tone and style of the report. The report must communicate the auditor's message in a clear and unambiguous way without leaving any questions unanswered in the reader's mind.

CLEAR WRITING TECHNIQUES

Given that the objectives of audit communications are to inform, persuade, and influence, the writer of a report must utilize clear writing techniques to get the message across as effectively as possible. Our normal, human method of communication uses a conversational style that tends to be more retainable than other, formal methods of communication. Unfortunately, human nature being what it is, everyday conversation takes the form of statements, questions, and answers. In a written communication the auditor is not available to answer questions that the written statements raise in the mind of the reader. As such, written communications must anticipate questions raised and answer them within the report.

In order to be persuasive the auditor must, while ensuring that the point is gotten across, avoid antagonizing the recipient of the audit report. Improvements come about as a result of implemented recommendations, and recommendations will not willingly be implemented if the person responsible reacts negatively to the audit report. Where control deficiencies are reported, care should be taken to avoid personal references and the audit report should criticize poor practices rather than individuals.

There is a rough rule of thumb that says that the more words there are, the less persuasive the report will be. The auditor's aim is to ensure that appropriate action is taken, which requires first that the report be read. When a manager is faced with a plethora of thick reports with very little content the most likely scenario is that these reports will be consigned to the wastepaper basket. Writing a short, high-impact report is much more difficult than writing a long, meandering essay. In order to achieve the desired results the audit report must be written with impact in mind.

Sentences should be kept short, averaging 15 to 20 words, with one basic idea per sentence. Long sentences tend to be foggy, dull, and boring. When the reader gets bored he or she will start to skip through the report seeking any keywords of interest. This does not mean that the auditor should count every word in a sentence and artificially cut long sentences in two. Most auditors know the size of their writing and can see at a glance if the sentence is too long. Here is a general rule of thumb: If the sentence were read aloud and the reader ran out of breath before the end of the sentence, it is too long.

Generally, active voice verbs assist in making sentences more readable because they are normally shorter, livelier, and more conversational. Instead of writing

"...were asked for by the manager," which uses a passive form of verb, try *"the manager asked for...."* Passive voice verbs tend to be dull, unclear, and less emphatic. They also tend to be extremely formal in writing style. Some audit reports are deliberately written to be extremely formal and structured in order to emphasize the impartial and impersonal nature of the report, and under such circumstances passive voice verbs would be highly appropriate. An example of this is fraud audit reports where a deliberate effort is required to show that the opinion expressed is a professional judgment based upon the evidence gathered and not a personal opinion.

A common fault with audit reports is the use of impressive words, which the reader may not understand or may misinterpret. *"Unless the paradigm is changed the situation may be exacerbated"* actually says *"unless we change the way we do things, things could get worse."* The writer should use clear, familiar words in order to get across the intended message. While we have already noted that fewer words can have more impact, the auditor should never sacrifice clarity for brevity. If that requires 10 words to be specific rather than five words to be vague, then take the 10 words. Some audit reports become so cryptic that the reader has to guess the auditor's meaning. IT auditing in particular will involve report recipients who come from a variety of backgrounds and who may or may not understand computing jargon. Wherever possible jargon should be avoided and, where it is unavoidable, it should be explained for the non-technical. The writer must always bear in mind that the onus of communication is on the auditor, not the reader.

Long, monotonous sections of report can cause the reader to skip and browse rather than read and digest. Use of white space and headings can break up the monotony of long sections and facilitates the location of specific information. *Scanning* the report, speed-reading looking for keywords of interest may not, in fact, be a problem. Where the reader does not need to read the full report but only certain sections, it is useful if the auditor can draw the attention directly to those sections. This can substantially speed up the reading process and may result in parts of a report being read that would otherwise be ignored. Some auditors feel that, having written the report, all readers must read the full thing. The alternative may be that the report is not read at all.

In the same way as keeping sentences short, keeping paragraphs short can make the report more reader-friendly. Other techniques to assist in ensuring the readability of reports include the use of bullets, emphasis, white space, graphics, and color. At the same time these techniques should not be used simply to pad the report or make it appear overly fancy. The objective of the report is to communicate and persuade, not to impress with the auditor's ability to create a piece of artwork.

 ## PREPARING TO WRITE

From the start of the audit the auditor will already have a mental picture of the report in mind. At the time that the scope and objectives are approved the anticipated audience is known and subsequently all audit work should be carried out with the audit report in mind. The subject matter is known and the scope and objectives are known and, although the actual results of the audit are unknown at this stage, the probable areas to be included in the report should be clear by the end of the preliminary survey.

Writing the audit report comes at the end of the audit after the close of field work when time is running out, and this frequently results in audit reports that are rushed and of poor quality. Adequate time must be budgeted from the start to allow the production of a high-quality, communicative audit report. Most auditors agree that the hardest part about writing an audit report is actually starting. Some auditors find an exercise known as free writing assists in loosening up the mental muscles. This technique involves writing some piece of unrelated text such as a letter prior to starting on the actual report. The theory is that this ensures that the brain is working in logical communication mode prior to the report writing being commenced and that idea flow is eased.

 BASIC AUDIT REPORT

The contents of most audit reports follow a similar pattern and include:

- Background, scope, and objectives
- Summary of major findings
- Audit opinion
- Detailed findings and recommendations
- Acknowledgments of satisfactory performance
- Detailed technical appendices

A cover is almost always desirable because it sets a professional tone from the start. It should include the report title, name and location of auditee, and the date of audit coverage.

A formalities section normally constitutes an introduction and is typically one to three pages in length. It includes the date of the report; the addressee (get it right); and the background, scope, and objectives of the audit. A brief audit opinion and the general nature of the findings together with the reply expectations and a signature are required. The names of participating auditors, distribution list, and contents of the body of the report are also a normal part of the formalities section.

 EXECUTIVE SUMMARY

Most audit reports include an executive summary covering the most important issues and findings from an overall business point of view. The executive summary provides a preliminary perspective to the whole report and focuses on risks to the organization and the specific effect of control weaknesses. It may be all that is read and, in many cases where such summaries go to senior executives, it is all that should be read.

Two approaches are possible in the executive summary, depending on the nature of the executive audience. With a knowledgeable executive, a *condense and eliminate* approach may be used. This involves an abbreviated explanation of major audit findings, in order of importance to the executive and cross-referenced to the body of the report. A *briefings* approach that informs, advises, and interprets may be more appropriate in a specialized audit where the executives may not be fully conversant with the implications of findings.

 ## DETAILED FINDINGS

Detailed findings usually constitute the body of the report. Strange as it sounds, a finding is not something that was found. An audit finding is comprised of four distinct parts:

1. **Condition.** Records what was found by the auditor (i.e., what the evidence showed)
2. **Criteria.** Indicates what should have happened in terms of control considerations
3. **Cause.** Indicates whether the condition was caused by the absence of an internal control or the failure of one and, if so, which
4. **Effect.** Indicates the impact on the business of the cause of the condition

Many auditors struggle to decide how much detail should be included in the body of the report. The detailed findings should include sufficient information for the reader to understand the nature of the finding, the relative importance of the finding, and what needs to be done about the finding. There can be no clear-cut rule on this because it depends on the knowledge level and experience of the audience being communicated with. During the course of the audit, the auditor should assess how much detail will be required in the final report. In order to ensure the final report is readable, exhibits and attachments are usually placed in an appendix if placing the information in the body of the report would make it overly lengthy or unreadable. All graphics, charts, photographs, and financial tabulations should be clearly labeled within the report in case they are referenced in two or three places. Where appendices are used they should be cross-referenced to the report.

One of management's common requirements is the expression of an audit opinion. This normally takes the form of an opinion on the adequacy and effectiveness of the internal control structures. The auditor must bear in mind that an opinion on adequacy is an indication that the control structures do or do not achieve *management's* desired level of control. Many auditors express an opinion on whether the control structures meet their own definition of adequacy. The audit opinion provides an overall perspective to the rest of the report and forces auditors to commit themselves, but can cause a management overreaction resulting in important parts of the report being ignored because, by their nature, audit results are normally mixed.

Auditee responses to findings and recommendations are normally included in the final report. This assists provision of a balanced report and can lend credibility to the report. Where such comments are included, they must be reviewed with and agreed to by the auditee. This does not mean, however, that the auditee must agree with all of the auditor's findings and recommendations. In some cases the two parties must agree to disagree with both opinions expressed within the report so that the managerial decision can be made. If the manager decides to accept the risk expressed within the report and take no action, and if such a decision is within their area of authority, the auditor has done his or her work in drawing the risk to management's attention and no further audit effort is required in this area.

 ## POLISHING THE REPORT

Because the audit report is a reflection on the professionalism and competence of the whole IT Audit function, the report must appear as professional as possible. Polishing the report involves a rigorous review prior to issue. This can be done by using a checklist to ensure the readability and understandability of the report or by using a peer group, which normally involves one auditor with no knowledge of the specific audit area so that assumptions may be challenged. Ultimately the report will be signed off by the in-charge auditor or a designated deputy. One of the major auditee complaints is that reports containing critical issues are issued late and that they are expected then to implement the recommendations with immediate effect. It is therefore critical that the auditor does not build in delays to report issuance.

Commonly the audit report will involve the coordination of several writers' efforts. In such cases is may be wise to read the report aloud and recognize the differences where individual contributors change.

 ## DISTRIBUTING THE REPORT

Audit reports are normally distributed to a variety of managerial levels. The report should be directed at the first authority level able to take appropriate action. The full distribution list is normally known early in the audit process; however, auditee chains of command can cause internal political ramifications. Many IT audit reports are sent to the recipients by e-mail. In general, the delivery method should take into account both the confidentiality of the reported information as well as the remoteness of the recipient. Couriering or hand-delivery may be preferred but impractical. If e-mail is used, adequate encryption techniques should be implemented to ensure the confidentiality and integrity of the message delivered.

If the audit report contents are highly confidential, detective controls can be implemented to trace individual copies should a leak occur. The most obvious of these techniques is copy numbering, but intentional misspellings or rewording of critical areas may also be used.

 ## FOLLOW-UP REPORTING

It is, unfortunately, a truism that people do not do what is expected; they do what is inspected. The IT audit executive should establish a follow-up process to monitor progress and ensure that management actions have been effectively implemented or that senior management has accepted the risk of not taking action. These two alternatives lead to different follow-up activities. Where management chooses to *take appropriate action on the audit findings,* auditors must find out what action was taken and determine if it was appropriate. They would typically issue follow-up reports normally directed to the recipients of the original report and the key focus must be on the attainment of the control objectives, not necessarily on the implementation of audit recommendations. Where management *accepted the risk of not taking action*, no follow-up report may be required. Given the mixed nature of audit findings, it is to be expected that management will implement some recommendations and accept some risks. This should be noted in the follow-up report.

Follow-up reports are normally directed to the recipients of the original report and the key focus is on resolution of the audit findings, not necessarily on the implementation of specific audit recommendations. It may well be that, subsequent to the audit report being issued, management circumstances may have changed in terms of risk prioritization or resource availability and an alternative course of action has been implemented leading to achievement of the same control objectives.

Where the auditor feels that the alternative course of action has not adequately addressed the control objective, the auditor will need guidelines for rejecting the auditee's corrective measures. Under the circumstances care should be taken not to attempt to force audit preferences on management. The audit focus should be on control objectives and principles; management should focus on the controls themselves. To do otherwise is to risk becoming the approver. Management must decide, not the auditor. Where a management action is rejected, the auditor must take care never to attack the individuals concerned. The auditor must avoid becoming emotionally involved in disagreements. State specifically in rejections why the rejection has occurred and which control objectives are still threatened.

TYPES OF FOLLOW-UP ACTION

The auditor will commonly review auditee responses and corrective actions, evaluate the adequacy of those responses and corrective actions, and report follow-up findings. Follow-up actions will vary significantly for differing audits in terms of the breadth, degree of focus, depth, and extent of follow-up examination. Practical considerations such as time available must be taken into consideration. Auditors tend to be optimists as far as time is concerned and follow-ups are often used to take shortcuts. In many cases follow-ups are completely omitted. In order to reduce the time required for follow-ups, the auditor should attempt to:

- Follow up as many as possible during the audit itself
- Review written responses prior to the review
- Review only the documentation of corrective action for less critical findings
- Avoid performing audit work at all on minor items
- Limit follow-up tests to only the problems noted

It is not necessary that the follow-up be done by the original auditor or audit team. In some lower-risk cases all that may be required is confirmation from management that the agreed action has been taken. In other cases the audit committee itself may seek reassurance from management that agreed actions have been implemented.

PART TWO

Information Technology Governance

CHAPTER ELEVEN

Management

T HIS CHAPTER COVERS Information Technology (IT); project management; risk management including economic, social, cultural, and technology risk management; software quality-control management; the management of the IT infrastructure; alternative IT architectures; and configuration and the management of IT delivery (operations) and support (maintenance). Performance measurement and reporting and the IT balanced scorecard are also covered, as are the use of outsourcing, the implementation of IT quality assurance, and the socio-technical and cultural approach to management.

IT INFRASTRUCTURES

Control Objectives for Information and Related Technology (COBIT®) defines control over the IT process as involving the need to "determine the technology direction to support the business. This requires the creation of a technological infrastructure plan and an architecture board that sets and manages clear and realistic expectations of what technology can offer in terms of products, services and delivery mechanisms."

IT staff require specialist expertise and skills in order to develop a technology infrastructure plan. The impact of emerging technologies must be taken into account and validated in order to identify anticipated deviations from the plan. The development and maintenance of a technology infrastructure plan is not to be taken lightly. The infrastructure must be responsive to change and human resources strategy must also be aligned with the technology direction so that technology changes can be properly managed. This includes the use of outsourcing and partnering in order to access missing expertise and skills.

The architecture itself will constantly change in order to ensure the best approach is taken to satisfy user requirements as they change with increasing rapidity. A continuous improvement program will probably be required in order to ensure the rapidly changing technology is utilized in order to keep pace with a similar speed of change in user requirements. Under these circumstances, flexibility and the ability to adapt are of paramount importance.

Changes to infrastructures obviously incur significant costs and cannot be achieved piecemeal. Management support at the highest level is essential in order to make the resources available to minimize resistance to cross organizational boundaries.

The use of differing technology platforms within one organization can make integration a major problem, which can be most easily resolved by utilizing a common business strategy with related architectures.

As such, policies are required to ensure that appropriate choices are made among internal development, use of external infrastructures, and outsourcing. This includes the identification of dependencies on key system components, hardware, software, or personnel, which are available only from a limited number of sources. Ideally, the architecture will make extensive use of interchangeable and reusable components.

As with all IT, the sole constant is change and, accordingly, the management of change becomes a key control opportunity. Adequate control over the selection, acquisition, testing, installation, and ultimately disposal of individual parts of the overall architecture is now critical. Even a simple expansion of capacity to meet growing volume or performance requirements requires careful planning.

Within any given architecture, IT can be split broadly into three infrastructure areas: project-based functions, operations and production, and technical services.

 ## PROJECT-BASED FUNCTIONS

Confucius is quoted as stating: "In all things, success depends upon previous preparation—and without such preparation there is sure to be failure." This is the basis for all project planning.

A *project* may be defined as a temporary endeavor undertaken to accomplish a unique purpose, involving several people performing interrelated activities. In IT terms this would normally involve bringing together a variety of user and IT skills to work together in order to develop new or improved information systems. IT projects cover the specification, supply, and installation of "off-the-shelf" systems and the development of bespoke software (i.e., software uniquely developed for a specific purpose). As with any other project-based development process, the primary focus is the development of a quality system, as specified by the user, on time and within budget.

Each individual project will be unique inasmuch as the system being developed will be unique and the individual combination of resources put together to achieve it will be unique. The project may be seen as a *finite*, *pre-defined* set of *activities* to lead to a *specific outcome*. It is finite in that it has a fixed beginning and a fixed end. It is pre-defined in that each individual facet of the project can be planned in advance and allowances made for changes during the development process. It is a set of individual activities that can be individually controlled but which must be coordinated in order to ensure that all areas fit together appropriately so that the project may achieve its specific outcomes.

Computer projects, either involving the development or acquisition of new systems or the maintenance of existing systems, consume resources in terms of money, manpower, materials, machines, and methods. Many of these resources will be drawn from cross-departmental boundaries and will involve a mixture of skills and disciplines.

Although project control is designed to minimize the risk of non-achievement of the project objectives, there is always a degree of uncertainty throughout the project. At the commencement of the project, this uncertainty will be high because the final outcome may be seen only in outline. As the project progresses, the degree of uncertainty reduces overall and specifically for the next phase of the project. In order to ensure that delivery risk is minimized, a project sponsor is required to handle the primary role of direction setting with a project manager handling task scheduling and performance monitoring. These form the fundamentals of project management. Aligned to these are the processes and practices. "Soft" issues, such as teamwork and leadership tend to be emphasized less partly due to the small size of many IT projects. Typically these processes and practices are formalized in a specific methodology. Originally these methodologies were predominantly focused on technical issues, while nowadays they focus more on the organizational benefits and management activities.

Managing people, information, and resources as they proceed through the project development cycle involves tasks such as:

- Aligning the development of the project strategy with the sponsor's (and other stakeholders') business strategy
- Defining the requirements (in a testable manner)—these lead to specifications and solutions being designed and developed
- Defining and managing the project scope, schedule, resource requirements, and budget (ensuring this represents optimal financing)
- Installing and progressing project control systems
- Procuring/inducting resources into the project
- Building effective project teams
- Exercising leadership
- Ensuring effective decisions and efficient communications

In any project management activity the most critical component is an effective project manager who works with the project sponsor and others in determining and delivering the scope and objectives of the project. In determining the scope and objectives, the project sponsor largely dictates services and performance required. These will serve as measurement criteria to determine the effectiveness of the development process. All projects consume resources, and the quantity of resources in terms of manpower, skill levels, costs, and timescales may place limiters on the degrees of effectiveness achieved. In other words, the requirement for efficiency will have a mitigating effect on the degrees of effectiveness of the project as a whole. It is the balancing of the need for efficiency while maintaining an effective development process that is the project manager's most difficult task because it is in this area that trade-offs must be negotiated between the project sponsor and the suppliers of resources. Because projects develop over time as business requirements change and skill levels improve, resource budgeting is an iterative process whereby nearby expenditures should be predictable in detail but long-term expenditures of resources can be led by as much as 100 percent.

In essence, project management is "the application of knowledge, skills, tools and techniques to project activities in order to meet or exceed stakeholder's needs and expectations from a project."[1]

IT projects normally follow a common development cycle. Partly because of the special challenges posed by the intangible nature of software, and the importance of getting user involvement in a structured manner, this process tends to be both consistent and dominant. There are various versions of this: the spiral, the waterfall, and the vee.

In his definitive work in 1976, Archibald[2] defined the project life cycle as having identifiable start and end points and passing through six distinct phases, namely:

1. Concept
2. Definition
3. Design
4. Development
5. Application
6. Post-completion

This led to the development of the *waterfall* cycle in Exhibit 11.1 where it can be seen that each activity "cascades" from the previous activity to lead ultimately to fully deployed information systems. In this model the difference is that the major activities overlap significantly. The major difficulty with this model is software development's need to progress iteratively is not catered for because each project remains with the identifiable start and end points.

In 1988 Boehm proposed an iterative spiral model for the development and enhancement of computer software.[3] Boehm's spiral involved four major functions, namely: next stage planning; determining objectives, alternatives and constraints/evaluation of alternatives; identifying and resolving risk issues; developing and verifying the next level product. These functions started with the development of a baseline product and then moved through several iterations until the final product was implemented.

An alternative development based upon the waterfall cycle was suggested by Fish[4] and is known as the vee cycle, and it follows a sequence such as that shown in Exhibit 11.2. Business strategy dictates the formulation of business requirements, which will usually incorporate explicit user requirements. These then lead to the definition of systems requirements and specifications. These allow the formation of the architectural design of the software and coding then creates the individual components of the sys-

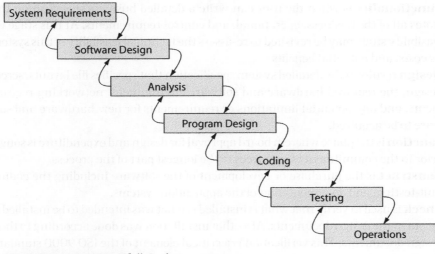

EXHIBIT 11.1 Waterfall Cycle

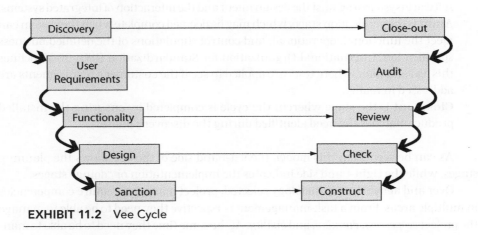

EXHIBIT 11.2 Vee Cycle

tem, which is then tested "up" the waterfall against the different levels of specification. From a control and audit perspective this form of systems development is considered the easier to audit because at each level there are standards to match against and there is a separate audit stage.

Within an IT environment, this approach would typically involve:

- **Discovery** is the point in the process when the IT or user area finds there is a market for a specific system. This phase is brief; there are few decisions to be made.
- **Requirement** is when the user can write an outline system specification that states: "We need a system capable of the following functionality A, B, C " At this stage a feasibility study may include an assessment of the technical feasibility of this system, its costs, and potential benefits.

- **Functionality** is when the user can write a detailed business specification that states all of the business, operational, and control requirements. At this stage the feasibility study may be revisited to re-assess the technical feasibility of this system, its costs, and potential benefits.
- **Design** results in the detailed system specification that specifies file layouts, screen design, the required hardware and software environment, networking requirements, and any potential limitations or requirements for new hardware and software to be acquired.
- **Sanction** is the phase wherein board approval for design and expenditure is sought prior to the commitment of resources to the longest part of the process.
- **Construct** is the purchase or development of the software including the coding, unit-testing, and documentation of the application systems.
- **Check** is used to verify that what is installed is what was intended to be installed as set out in the design documents. Also, that installation was done according to those design documents. This verification is a critical element of the ISO 9000 standard.
- **Review** involves testing sub-systems, usually with a test material to ensure that the intention of the system has been met. This phase tests collections of hardware and software (systems) against the design intent and the interaction of integrated systems.
- **Audit** is the verification stage, which may be deemed complete when the system can meet the functional, operational, and control stipulations of the detailed business specification. International Organization for Standardization (ISO) 9000 defines this as validation, where tests are applied to see if the customer's requirements are addressed in reality.
- **Close-out** is the stage wherein the cycle is completed by ensuring the installed product matches the need identified during the discovery phase.

As can be seen from this model, the left-hand side of the vee shows the planning stages, while the right-hand side indicates the implementation or "doing" stages.

Over and above the methodology selected, project managers require competencies in multiple areas. From a task-management perspective they need to be able to manage the project *scope*, *cost*, *duration*, and *quality*. At the same time they need to be able to manage their human resources with good communication while simultaneously ensuring risk is controlled and that the whole project is adequately integrated.

Many of the quantitative tools discussed in Chapter 9 such as Gantt charts, PERT charts, and critical path analysis are used by management to control time and budgets. Overall the management areas of planning, leading, and controlling remain fundamental to the development process.

 ## QUALITY CONTROL

One of the most difficult areas within project-based functions is the achievement of appropriate levels of quality. One reason for this is the wide variety of interpretations of the meaning of the word. The International Organization of Standardization (ISO)

defines quality as "the totality of characteristics of a product or service that bear on its ability to satisfy stated or implied needs."[5] Quality involves ensuring that the customer's agreed requirements and expectations are achieved. This may sound simple but involves two main performance areas, namely: *process quality* and *product quality*. Process quality involves the effectiveness and efficiency of the process that creates the end product. Product quality is a measurement of the degree to which customer needs and expectations are satisfied. It is possible to produce a quality product even with a flawed process but such achievements are rare. Under normal circumstances comprehensive standards such as COBIT™ must be combined with a thorough understanding of the business and functional requirements of the new system.

Issues of systems development are more fully covered in Part Three of this book.

 ## OPERATIONS AND PRODUCTION

Operations and production include the day-to-day running of the information processing facility (IPF), data communications, input and output controls, output distribution, and backup and recovery including the disaster recovery plan. At its most fundamental, computer alterations could include:

- Mounting and dismounting data files
- Loading paper into printers
- Aligning special forms
- Scheduling runs
- Loading programs
- Balancing run priorities
- Responding to operating system prompts
- Responding to application system prompts
- Maintaining incident logs
- Performing routine housekeeping tasks
- Responding to equipment failures
- Production of backup copies as defined
- Restoration from backup when authorized
- Handling "unpredictable" conditions

They are also responsible for handling remote site libraries containing backups of data files, program source code, and object code. The sites may have automated library functions or may rely on manual records. In all cases, because operations are handling live data files, segregation of duties must be maintained. One critical area for operations is the distribution of output. This would normally involve the dispatch of hard-copy output to the authorized recipients, control over spool files to networked printers as well as within the information processing facility itself, and the destruction of confidential scrap resulting as a byproduct from computer operations.

TECHNICAL SERVICES

Technical services include the provision of reliable computing resources at acceptable costs as a basis on which to run the appropriate application systems. These services may include:

- Operating system support
- Network support
- Technical database support
- Hardware support

In all cases, a higher degree of technical expertise is required in order to ensure the effectiveness and efficiency of the overall IT architecture. These functions are covered in more detail in Part Four of this book.

PERFORMANCE MEASUREMENT AND REPORTING

Performance measurement can be looked at in several ways:

- It is an environment in which strategic, tactical, and operational plans are linked via a feedback process whereby performance measurement systems provide the information needed to determine whether top management strategies have been effectively translated into tactical and operational decisions. This information is essential to improve decision making and enable proactive problem correction. It is a methodology in which the course of the organization toward its vision is steered by using feedback to make ongoing adjustments, thus ensuring continued quality of programs and services despite changes in both the internal and external environments.
- It is an iterative process consisting of: the setting of objectives, the development of strategies/plans to achieve those objectives, and the development of performance measures to assess progress toward those objectives.

One popular way of measuring overall performance is the *balanced scorecard* approach, which was developed by Robert S. Kaplan and David P. Norton.[6] This approach builds upon the traditional performance focus on *financial measures* by emphasizing *client satisfaction, internal business processes,* and *innovation/learning.* Each of these has, in its own way, a place in ensuring that performance is optimized.

These focuses can be mapped onto the traditional organizational vision, mission, and strategy as seen through the eyes of business owners, customers and other stakeholders, managers and process owners, and employees. The owners of the business are represented by the financial focus, customers and stakeholders are represented by the client satisfaction focus, managers and process owners by the business processes focus, and employees and infrastructure by the innovation and learning focus.

The financial measures deal with the measurement of the level of financial performance provided by programs and services. Examples of the financial impact of programs and services within IT can be measured through such indicators as budget versus actual expenditure, degree of cost recovery, achievement of cost budgets in systems development, and achieving the financial benefits anticipated in systems feasibility studies.

Within the IT area, the client-satisfaction measurement is concerned with the degree to which the IT services provided meet the needs of the users of such services and the organization as a whole. Such measures could include the achievement of performance and availability targets, satisfying users' functionality and information needs, flexibility of systems, and degree of user confidence in systems.

The measurement of the internal business generally relates to the quality of those processes used to provide the systems and services that satisfy user needs. Generic internal business performance indicators for information systems could include the achievement of time-related budgets on systems implementation; response times on operational requests; and frequency and duration of system failures including hardware, software, and communications.

One other critical performance area for an effective IT function is that of innovation and learning. The dynamic nature of IT directly impacts the ability of an organization to sustain innovation and growth. Continuous improvement and innovation is required in its use of all organizational resources including its human resources, technology, products, and services. In many cases information systems can be the drivers for such innovation. Performance indicators in this area would typically include the improvements in business processes facilitated by innovation in the use of information systems, degree of management and user interaction in the modification and improvement of systems, involvement of information systems in re-engineering initiatives, and amount of leverage obtained from the use of the organizational data warehouse.

Obviously, any framework for measuring organizational performance must be based on the strategic objectives of the organization. Nevertheless the unique role of IT has a dramatic impact and the organization's ability to allocate resources, utilize management information for decision making, and deliver products and services. Many organizations have no formal measurement program as yet and have still to develop and implement a balanced approach to measuring IT performance. Performance measurement must be carried out from the top down. IT goals and objectives cannot be determined until business objectives have been determined and communicated so that the appropriate strategies and goals can be established and plans implemented to achieve these.

 ## MEASUREMENT IMPLEMENTATION

In order to be universally accepted, implemented performance measurement criteria must be seen as quantifiable in the development and objective of the application. In order to achieve this, the organizational culture must support accurate, comprehensive, and balanced feedback in order to facilitate effective decision making by providing the information necessary. The resources required to implement this should not be underestimated because it takes time and effort to be introduced and maintained. A *"one size fits all"* approach cannot be used due to the extreme variations in architectures, methodologies, and approaches undertaken in developing and utilizing information systems.

Prior to implementation an impact analysis will be required in order to determine the ability of the organizational IT area to implement such an approach as well as both financial and functional impact of such implementation. Based upon the results of this analysis a controlled pilot project would normally be launched within one of the operational areas of the IT function. The area chosen should be one in which performance measurement points can be readily determined and the life cycle of improvement is comparatively short. The starting point, as ever, is the long-term business objective of the area to be improved. This may seem obvious but determining agreed-on objectives with a common interpretation can be problematic. Once the objectives have been agreed on, an appropriate measurement architecture can be developed to assess the performance area from the four perspectives mentioned earlier. Once the architecture has been agreed on, a strategy of transition to the new measurement approach must be developed. The pilot project will be used to adapt and streamline the performance measurement architecture prior to implementation of the full IT area.

The use of a balanced scorecard helps to create a Strategy-Focused Organization (SFO), rather than a Metrics-Focused Organization (MFO), which thus facilitates the alignment of its daily activities to strategy, and communicates that strategy throughout the organization. This is critical because many organizations utilize key performance indicators, which are tactical in nature rather than strategic. Because the balanced scorecard is designed to ensure achievement of strategic objectives, a strategic focus is essential. Many of the benefits of information systems are intangible in nature making it difficult to measure their relative contribution to overall business performance. There is a tendency to conduct project management at a technical level while ignoring the original business proposition that created the project in the first place. Many IT benefits such as improved customer service and increased flexibility are difficult to interpret into financial benefits. It has been suggested[7] that as many as 75 percent of IT interventions offer no demonstrable business value. The key word in this situation is *demonstrable* because traditional financial evaluation methods may not tell the whole story in an IT environment.

In order to adequately express measurement criteria within the balanced scorecard, the starting point must always be the statement of business intent or mission for the entity being evaluated. In such a case the *customer orientation* intent may be *"to deliver customer response times superior to competitors."* This could then be translated into measurement criteria by reducing the intent into measurable objectives such as customer satisfaction, acquisition of new customers from competitors, or retention of existing customers, leading to measurements such as numbers and severity of customer complaints, percentage of repeat customers, number of new customers acquired from competitors, and so forth. These are not the traditional financial measures but nevertheless express the strategic content of the information system. In a similar manner measurement criteria may be established for the other balanced scorecard perspectives. Internal business processes could, for example, be measured by percentage availability of systems, frequency of system crashes, response times, downtime, and so on. Innovation and learning could be measured by determining skills acquisitions or independence from consultants. Critically, the IT balanced scorecard measurement criteria should be able to indicate cause and effect of performance drivers rather than solely business outcomes. Kaplan and Norton recently released a follow-up to The Balanced Scorecard,[8] in which they noted:

> The Balanced Scorecard approach retained measures of financial performance, the lagging indicators, but supplemented them with the measures on the drivers, the lead indicators, of future financial performance. But what were the appropriate measures of financial performance? If financial measures were causing organizations to do wrong things, what measures would prompt them to do the right things? The answer turned out to be obvious: Measure the strategy! Thus all of the objectives and measures on a Balanced Scorecard—financial and nonfinancial—should be derived from the organization's vision and strategy.

Control Risks and Outsourcing

Outsourcing of IT services is a route chosen when: An organization determines that it does not have sufficient competence to tackle the work itself, where the costs of in-house processing are determined to be greater than the cost of outsourcing the activity, or where the risks associated with the executor function is determined to be too high to retain in-house. IT areas frequently considered for outsourcing include:

- Project functions such as systems analysis, design, and programming
- Running of selected application systems such as payroll
- Data capture or transformation prior to processing
- Operation of the IT facility

In all cases measurement and performance criteria must be developed prior to evaluation of the most appropriate process. Considerations such as the scope of services, level of service requirements, quality measurements, and cost must be taken into account in advance because choosing to outsource such services can be a higher risk intervention and the decision may be difficult to reverse.

Whether or not the outsourcing partner retains the organization's original staff as part of the outsourcing agreement, there may be insufficient skills and abilities retained to rebuild an internal IT service if required.

The selection of an outsourcer is a critical part of the process requiring that checks be made on both the quality of service received by the existing customer base as well as their market stability and track record.

A common mistake is approaching a selected number of outsourcers to inquire as to the variety and level of services they can offer. As with any project, business and technical requirement specifications should be designed with evaluation criteria before outsourcing agencies are approached.

Outsourcing contracts for information services will typically involve a longer duration than normal commercial contracts due to the longer duration of systems development and a higher cost in setup of specific architectures. As such, it is essential to ensure their contracts clearly spell out the variety of services to be provided, measurement criteria, and penalties for unacceptable performance. This would normally take the form of a service level agreement (SLA), which, in an outsourcing contract, would typically involve more detail than those in normal internal use. Performance areas such as security, right of inspection by audit, and contingency planning arrangements must be incorporated within the SLA.

As with any partnering agreement the intention and the belief is that all will go well. Nevertheless, a fundamental reason for the contract is to prepare for the eventuality that things do not go well and therefore options and remedies in the event of a partial or complete failure of the agreement need to be decided in advance. This is particularly true where IT services are involved because the technical nature of such services can result in lengthy court cases regarding performance measurement and contract terms. In cases of disputes many users of such services attempt resolution by arbitration in order to avoid costly and drawn-out court battles.

Where software is involved, escrow may be required for the protection of software interests. This involves the lodging of a copy of the software with an independent third party so that, in the event of the software provider failing to comply with the terms of contract or ceasing to exist, software service can be continued legally by obtaining the software from the third party.

Managing in a Cloud Environment

We will cover cloud computing at greater depth in Chapter 16. but it is worthwhile noting at this point some of the issues governing the management of computing within a cloud environment. This begs the question, what is cloud computing? One common definition refers to "a style of computing where massively scalable IT-enabled capabilities are delivered 'as a service' to external customers using Internet technologies"[9] with the emphasis on scalable, service, and the Internet.

In order to reduce infrastructure costs and address scalability concerns, some organizations are taking the position that they do not wish to own the assets or operate the systems within their own data centers. In such a scenario, the third-party—the cloud provider—provides the infrastructure, servers, networking, and storage capacity required to ensure the availability and scalability of applications to the cloud user.

A variation on this is the concept of the private cloud, which involves a proprietary architecture leased or owned by an individual organization to provide hosted services to internal customers of the organization. This architecture issue and increasing signs of attraction to large organizations means, however, that effective implementation requires that the corporate data center be capable of provisioning new environments, boosting computing power, and adding storage capacity at very short notice to facilitate the scalability of a cloud environment. It is possible to implement a hybrid combining the scalability advantages of a standard cloud environment for lower-risk applications while maintaining a private cloud behind an adequate firewall for mission-critical or sensitive systems.

One critical management aspect in deciding on a cloud environment is the difficulty involved in migrating existing applications to a cloud platform. Selection of a cloud provider will inevitably impose complications in application architectures since the existing enterprise solutions will typically involve dissimilar architectures. Switching over from internal databases serving large user bases and involving highly variable access rights can prove a stumbling block to effective cloud migration. In many complex environments this will mean that an organization that adopts cloud computing will typically end up doing so utilizing new applications.

Auditing IT Management

In reviewing a typical IT function, the auditor will use a standard set of indicators to determine whether management is performing at an acceptable level. These indicators could include:

- Operational
  - Degree of end-user acceptance of performance levels
  - Actual to budget comparisons
  - Frequency of hardware and software problems
  - Acceptability of computer response time
  - Frequency of unauthorized purchases of hardware and software
  - Frequency of upgrades of hardware and software
  - Degree of capacity planning
  - Adequacy of business-continuity planning
- Systems development
  - Cost and budget comparisons
  - Achievement of deadlines
  - Achievement of end-user objectives
  - Number of uncompleted development projects
- General management
  - Experience and training of staff
  - Staff turnover
  - Staff motivation
  - Reliance and key individuals

Such indicators would be examined using the conventional audit techniques of documentation review, observation, and interviewing in order to determine management's intent as compared to actual performance.

 NOTES

1 Project Management Institute (PMI) Standards Committee. *A Guide to the Project Management Body of Knowledge (PMBOK® Guide)*, Third Edition. Sylva, North Carolina: PMI Publishing, 2000.

2 R. D. Archibald. *Managing High-Technology Programs and Projects*. New York: John Wiley & Sons, p. 19.

3 B. Boehm. "A Spiral Model of Software Development and Enhancement." *IEEE Computer*. (May 1988): 61–72.

4 E. Fish. An Improved Project Lifecycle Model, Pandora Consulting, http://www.max-wideman.com/guests/plc/intro.htm (Guest Department), 2002, updated 2003.

5 International Organization of Standardization, ISO 8402: 1986.

6 Robert S. Kaplan and David P. Norton. The *Balanced Scorecard*. Boston: Harvard Business School Press, 1996. "Using the Balanced Scorecard as a Strategic Management System," *Harvard Business Review* (January-February 1996): 75–85

7 M. Raisinghani, "A Balanced Analytic Approach to Strategic Electronic Commerce Decisions: A Framework of the Evaluation Method," in W. Van Grembergen, *Information Technology Evaluation Methods and Management*. Hershey, PA: Idea Group Publishing, 2001, pp. 185–197.

8 Robert S. Kaplan and David P. Norton. *The Strategy-Focused Organization: How Balanced Scorecard Companies Thrive in the New Business Environment*. Cambridge, MA: Harvard Business Press, 2000.

9 *Cloud Computing Confusion Leads to Opportunity*, Gartner, Inc. (NYSE: IT), 2008.

CHAPTER TWELVE

Strategic Planning

T HIS CHAPTER EXAMINES INFORMATION TECHNOLOGY (IT) strategic planning and looks at competitive strategies and business intelligence and their link to corporate strategy. These, in turn, influence the development of strategic IT frameworks and applications. Strategic planning also includes the management of IT human resources, employee policies, agreements, contracts, segregation of duties within IT, and the implementation of effective IT training and education.

 STRATEGIC MANAGEMENT PROCESS

The strategic management process uses qualitative and quantitative information under conditions of uncertainty in order to integrate both intuition and analysis. Management intuition is based on judgment, past experiences, and feelings and is used in conditions of great uncertainty or conditions where there is no precedent to assist management in making decisions. At all levels within the organization, management must make decisions under conditions of uncertainty on a daily basis and it is their intuition which influences that interpretation of analyses that affects the strategic decisions taken. A key attribute of the strategic management process is adaptability to change, and organizations must monitor internal and external events as an iterative process in order to ensure timely adaptation is affected.

Over the past 20 years, the magnitude of the rate of change in information technology as well as its acceleration, combined with increased access to global marketplaces and increased national and international regulation, have forced change upon organizations at a rate never before seen. This increased the pressure on management to develop adaptive strategies in order to stay in competition and even to stay in existence. Strategies, overall, are the means by which long-term objectives are intended to be achieved and could include geographic diversification, product development, service differentiation, acquisition of other organizations, divestitures, retrenchments, or even liquidation.

Strategic management is an attempt to utilize *existing knowledge to forecast* the outcomes of events and the degree to which they can be influenced by management actions.

STRATEGIC DRIVERS

The start of the new millennium has been typified in the computer industry by a "merger mania" with the old practice of single portfolio suppliers giving way to problem and solution-based vendors. Information vending is becoming the future direction for all.

As far as the technology itself is concerned, it may be classified as:

- Hardware getting cheaper
- Communication bandwidth getting wider
- Software getting more powerful
- Advent of cloud computing
- Users getting more confused

Storage capacity is rocketing and network costs are reducing to virtually nil while PC operating systems have become mainframe-like in their sophistication. This combined with business's eagerness to embrace technology as an enabling tool resulted in the fundamental shifting of the manner in which business is done. Thus we saw the advent of corporate structuring of data warehouses to gain strategic advantage by being the best around at converting data to information and information to insight. In addition, technology such as electronic data interchange (EDI) has shortened the business cycle beyond previous comprehension. E-commerce is another such revolution that has, over the past few years, had much the same impact on conventional business as supermarkets had on the corner shop.

At the same time, in an environment of tightened funding, scarce resources, heightened corporate governance, and intensified global competition, an undisciplined approach to portfolio analysis is no longer viable. Most organizations are balancing dozens, in some cases, hundreds, of projects in progress at any given point. More than ever it becomes crucial to prioritize and resource only those initiatives with a close alignment with strategic objectives.

Without the prioritization of competing initiatives, an organization can be on time and on budget but remain drastically off target. Companies must accurately measure their projects' strategic value in order to optimize combinations of projects given risks, costs, and other dependencies.

NEW AUDIT REVOLUTION

In the same way that business is embracing the new technologies, audit has no choice but to follow suit and utilize technology to develop innovative ways to make information out of the vast resources of data available and so proceed to the development of risk and control insights.

Advanced systems include such components as *Communication Networks* including the Internet, intranets, and extranets. Integral to such systems are concepts such as EDI, EFTS (Electronic Funds Transfer Systems), EFTPOS (Electronic Funds Transfer at Point Of Sale), JIT (Just-in-Time), and MRP (Material Requirements Planning).

Such systems will typically integrate concepts such as real-time processing with relational database management systems (DBMS) and Integrated Data Warehouses to arrive at total integrated systems for the whole organization. This will include the use of EIS (Executive Information Systems) and SIS (Strategic Information Systems). Extensive use of teleprocessing and client/server environments will also typically be found.

LEVERAGING IT

Innovating new technologies and applying existing ones in new ways involves a major creative process. The Chief Information Officer, in advising management, must look at not only tactical issues, but big-picture and long-term issues as well. Any new project or system change will require a scan of existing modules and processes. However, because these existing products must also serve a strategic need or goal of the company, it is IT's responsibility to ensure the support of the strategic goals throughout alignment and to provide insight into the action plans and tactical efforts that are necessary to ensure alignment. When this involves the changeover to new technologies, the alignment effort becomes mission-critical. For example, when the World Wide Web was comparatively new, the introduction of interactive Web applications had the potential to give a leading-edge deployer a tremendous competitive advantage. Now that such applications are commonplace, the strategic impact is rather the prevention of competitive disadvantage by ensuring the competition cannot leverage your organization out of existence.

A major challenge leveraging IT is the temptation to overextend the organization's resources. Just because an application or service is feasible does not mean that it will necessarily meet the organization's strategic goals. After all, the leading-edge also known as the bleeding-edge. Additionally, ensuring the stability and reliability of new and amended systems may become a critical factor in achieving speed to market of IT solutions.

Traditionally, the IT function starts with the corporate strategic objectives for the year and translates these into a set of client-based IT priorities.

Internal audit can, on a periodic basis, conduct a comprehensive operational review in order to ensure IT resources are being used creatively to support the overall business objectives of the organization. In order for internal audit to be effective in intervening in this scenario, it is essential that the auditor understands the business processes and information flow within the organization. In addition, an auditor who has come from a background of compliance audit may actually be counterproductive and prevent the creation of a Culture of Innovation, which is a primary component of leveraging the IT resource for maximum business effect. A common failing involves overlooking existing systems that may be currently under-exploited in favor of a "new" solution. Again, internal audit is in a position to review proposals for new systems to ensure the business case dictates such development rather than, perhaps, enhancements to existing systems.

As corporations look toward leveraging IT with a view toward the re-engineering of the business as a result of changes and pressures in their business and competitive environment, it would only be sensible to examine the status of internal audit to determine whether it too requires some re-engineering.

Re-engineering as a process involves the fundamental rethinking and radical redesign of business processes to bring about dramatic improvements in performance. Improvement claimed includes:

- 48 percent reduction in cost
- 80 percent reduction in time
- 60 percent reduction in defects

As can be seen from the numbers, this is not tinkering with a few minor enhancements. At its best, it involves common sense reinvented (CSR).

 ## BUSINESS PROCESS RE-ENGINEERING MOTIVATION

There can be several motivations for any business process re-engineering (BPR). The motivation will affect the nature, focus, and probable success of the intervention.

Survival as a Motivation

- Indications for re-engineering
  - Outgrowing capacity
  - Value added versus revenue

Under this motivation the major success factor may be the speed of automation and the primary focus is the core operation of the organization with the intention being *"Don't Automate—Obliterate."*

Elimination of Competitive Disadvantage as a Motivation

- Indications for re-engineering
  - Losing market share
  - Performance lag

Within this scenario the most critical factor is probably an understanding of the original source of disadvantage and the primary focus is to lead the competition. This scenario is based on the concept that *"If you can't win at the game—change the rules."*

Generating Competitive Advantage as a Motivation

- ▪ Indications for re-engineering
  - ▪ Stable market share
  - ▪ Stable industry

Under these circumstances, the most critical success factor is the ambition of the leader of the process and the focus is clearly on customer-value drivers. This could be described as *"Cuddling up to the Customer."*

Creating a Breakthrough as a Motivation

- ▪ Indications for re-engineering
  - ▪ Declining market
  - ▪ New industry opportunities

Success factors here include both the vision of the leader as well as the communications capability throughout the organization. Here the focus will vary depending on the industry involved but can be typified as *"Breaking out of the Mold."*

Ultimately, such re-engineering is intended to lead to achieving client value that, in turn, requires a narrower focus for the organization in order to deliver superior client value. Client intimacy becomes essential in order to permit the segmenting and targeting of markets precisely, as well as the tailoring of services to meet these niches. Operational excellence is an imperative throughout the process and beyond. The organization must provide reliable service at a competitive price delivered with minimum inconvenience. The products themselves must be leading-edge products that consistently enhance the clients' use of the service. Success for such an organization means excelling at achieving client value while meeting competitive standards in operational excellence and leading-edge product delivery.

 ## IT AS AN ENABLER OF RE-ENGINEERING

Processes are about handling information and, if IT is used as an enabler, not as an end product, new audit possibilities allowing inductive problem seeking and international research on a massive scale are opened. As was the case, taking a mess and computerizing it simply creates a high-speed, expensive mess. Misuse of IT can seriously impede re-engineering by reinforcing old ways and stereotypes.

DANGERS OF CHANGE

All change involves risk to some degree. Change involves uncertainty and by disturbing the status quo we create a threat to vested interests, we disrupt harmony, and if this goes unchecked it can kill morale by creating emotional upheaval. This ultimately can cost a fortune in managerial time and effort and can cause loss of valuable people, talents, and skills, and change can thus become self-defeating. Change inspires resistance, which in turn can move from passive resistance to aggressive undermining. Fear of losing something, misunderstanding the transformation and its implications, or a belief that the change does not make sense can lead to a low tolerance for change. Hidebound infrastructures and top management misconceptions can lead to turf battles. Building around existing employees can lead to change in name only with no material effect.

Used properly, even resistance can become an energy to utilize. Resistance need not always be a roadblock. In order for it to become useful the transition process itself must be understood. Process transformation takes place in clearly defined and measurable phases. There is an *Ending Phase* involving letting go of old values and ideas—a disengagement and disenchantment with previously cherished beliefs. This is followed by a *Neutral Phase*. During this phase, disorientation may lead to disintegration of assumptions, discovery of new horizons, and a building of energy for transformation. The *Transformation Phase* itself allows the creation of those new horizons, new possibilities, and alignment of vision.

SYSTEM MODELS

Systems may take several forms. The most basic types of systems are those that are used on an ongoing basis to provide facilities for the day-to-day operations of the organization. These normally involve the processing of everyday business transactions.

Transaction processing systems include:

- Order processing
- Inventory
- Purchasing

In addition to these systems supporting our normal business processing, management requires information on an ongoing basis to inform them of the status of various parts of the organization. These Management Information Systems would include:

- Financial
- Manufacturing
- Marketing
- Personnel

A further categorization of systems comes when the information becomes used by a variety of decision makers to support business decisions. These Decision Support Systems are becoming more and more sophisticated and may be found in all business areas including:

- Financial
- Statistical analysis
- Project management

 ## INFORMATION RESOURCE MANAGEMENT

Information Resource Management is based on five fundamentals:

1. **Information Management.** Information is valuable and must be managed as such. In many organizations, information does not appear on the balance sheet or asset register and is thus seen as something that, while important, is not really *valuable*.
2. **Technology Management.** Technology Management addresses the whole aspect of the value of technology to the firm. This includes the impact and effect on other resources as well as the gaining of strategic advantage by judicious use of the appropriate technology.
3. **Distributed Management.** Where systems are located can have a significant impact on systems effectiveness as well as internal control and thought must be given to the maintaining of an adequate system of managerial control.
4. **Functional Management.** Like other functional areas, IT must be directed and controlled in order to ensure the effective, efficient, and economic use of what is, after all, an expensive resource.
5. **Strategic Management.** IT holds the potential to gain and maintain major competitive advantages for the organization. Used appropriately, IT can raise the barriers of entry to competition, gain exclusivity for the information holder, and generally keep the organization ahead of the pack.

 ## STRATEGIC PLANNING FOR IT

Strategic planning is a process of identifying long-term goals and objectives of any organization and then selecting the most appropriate approach for achieving those goals. In judging the impact that IT can have on the strategic planning process, the leveraging of the organization's information resources can make or break the process of achieving the strategic plan.

The corporate strategic plan, under the care of top management, represents the shared vision of corporate intent and provides an execution framework for a specific period of time. It sets an overall direction for the organization and lays the ground rules for the acceptance of new projects, products, and services. This facilitates the identification and selection of the best tactical and operational interventions in order to achieve strategic objectives. It allows prioritization of activities and expenditures in order to maximize the probability that successful outcomes will be achieved.

Strategic planning is therefore a broad-brush approach involving a statement of corporate intent. This then must be translated into tactical plans developed to meet the overall strategic objectives. This will typically involve a variety of individual operational objectives streamlined to ensure that all work undertaken will eventually assist in the achievement of the overall corporate goal.

From an IT perspective, the effectiveness of these tactical goals will depend largely on the clarity of the corporate vision being communicated to the operational managerial level. If misalignment takes place at this point, an organization can spend many years and many millions of dollars developing systems specifically designed to take the organization in the wrong direction. An IT strategy rests upon the comprehension of the corporate vision, which in turn leads to the development of an appropriate framework together with its management and control mechanisms through to its execution in the delivery of appropriate information processing systems. Development of an appropriate framework assists in achieving the vision by providing the structure within which results are measurable, repeatable, and sustainable. This is critical because IT strategy is a dynamic process as the corporate vision is dynamic dependent upon market circumstances. As with any other process it does not stand alone and must be integrated into the other business processes of the organization such as enterprise planning, budgetary control, product development, and delivery and marketing. Like all other business planning processes it must be both measurable and measured.

Management and control of the operational plans are fundamental to the overall success and achievement of the corporate strategic plan. An IT plan that looks good in theory can, under poor management conditions, lead the organization far away from its original strategic intent. Given the extended nature of the corporate IT investment whereby results may be seen only after several years, it is essential that *alignment of IT and organizational strategies* be achieved and maintained.

This alignment is one of the most difficult areas to achieve and control. If an IT project takes five years to develop, there is a strong possibility that, without appropriate change management, the strategic intent in developing the system may have changed radically in the intervening time. In addition, the project itself may produce a system that is intended to support the organization's business for the next 15 to 20 years. Without flexibility it is unlikely that the new system will maintain alignment with the overall corporate strategy.

Flexibility is fundamental both within the development process itself and within the execution phase after the project system has been developed. In today's business environments the only constant is change. It must be clearly understood by all concerned that the organization does not exist to run information systems. The information systems exist to support the organization and as it changes so must they. This involves a constant reassessment of the degree to which the overall IT strategy maintains its alignment with the overall organizational strategy, as well as the degree to which the IT operational planning is in line with its own strategic objectives. This requirement for flexibility in organizational operations has always existed; however, in the information-processing age the dynamics of change have become so complicated and so rapid that inflexibility can actually result in the total collapse of the organization.

A more difficult concept for many managers is that of *value for money* within an IT scenario. Information systems frequently produce an intangible benefit that accrues to client users rather than the information. Because most managers in the business arena have little conception of the costs of maintaining an appropriate IT infrastructure, information processing costs are commonly thought to be excessive and therefore frequently the *effectiveness* of the IT function itself is commonly measured by savings accrued and budgets achieved. These are in fact measurements of *efficiency* that can nevertheless result in the IT function maintaining a focus on simply keeping existing systems running at constantly reducing costs.

As a result, many managers of IT functions understand their objective to be the delivery of high-quality, reliable systems at the lowest possible cost. In a few organizations where this cost reduction imperative is not believed to have been achieved, complete decentralization of the IT function into business units can occur, which leads to a sacrifice of scale economies and an overall increase in costs. Taken to its extreme, this may even result in the outsourcing of the IT function because of the perception of excessive costs.

It should not be seen that all organizations are fixated on cost reduction. Many progressive firms see IT as being a fundamental driver toward achievement of their corporate strategy. Such firms seek innovative ways to leverage their information systems to gain and sustain competitive advantage. These firms face the danger that innovation becomes paramount and both cost and traditional quality measures may suffer as a result. It is the balance among alignment, flexibility, quality, reliability, and cost that achieves the accomplishment of the IT strategy.

It is understandable that, before IT can be accepted as a main driver of the execution of business strategy, it must first demonstrate its competency in cost control and quality. Only after competency is demonstrated can IT seek to participate in realizing organizational strategies, not just operational objectives.

 ## DECISION SUPPORT SYSTEMS

Another complication arises from the advent of Decision Support Systems. These systems, commonly combined with data warehousing, use databases in order to assist management in the making of fundamental business decisions. In such cases it is essential that management place reliance on the accuracy, completeness, integrity, confidentiality, and timeliness of such systems. These systems may, in turn, be extended into the concepts of EIS, which address those aspects of corporate governance that are of specific importance to executive management in deciding strategic direction in the first place.

STEERING COMMITTEES

In order to manage the process of achieving flexible, valuable systems many organizations delegate the responsibility and authority to a steering committee made up of managerial expertise in multiple functional areas of the business as well as IT itself. The concept is that each member of the committee can bring diverse skills and perspectives in order to ensure the alignment of the IT strategy with the corporate strategy and additionally to ensure that the information systems deliver the business requirements. In many committees it can be seen that individual members dominate and the synergy of differing perspectives is lost. Such committees become a "rubber stamp" for one or two individuals' decisions. Other steering committees have been known to devolve into "talk shops" where much is said but little is decided. In a worst-case scenario the committee can become a method for accountability evasion so that no decision ever becomes an individual's fault if it fails and therefore there is no incentive to get things right. Many individual managers express concern that the systems that are being delivered are simply re-hashes of existing systems with little improved benefit. Ultimately, systems alignment can only be dictated by those who fully understand the organization's business strategy, and in some extreme cases this strategy is seen to be a corporate secret and is not revealed to those making tactical and operational decisions.

 ## STRATEGIC FOCUS

Since its introduction in 1992, the Balanced Scorecard management framework (see Chapter 11) has been seen by many organizations as a key element in defining organizational strategy and as a facilitator in measuring strategic performance. It is not, however, the only means of achieving an IT strategic focus.

In 1995 Treacy and Wiersema[1] developed a model that can be used to guide the organization of IT internal activities. It uses the hypothesis that firms achieve competitive advantage by placing their emphasis on one of three *value disciplines*: operational excellence, customer intimacy, or product leadership. In order to maximize the value-added attention to its customers, IT must excel in all three disciplines. Once again, customer intimacy and understanding of the business unit's strategic and operation objectives can be seen as fundamental to the implementation of an effective IT strategy.

 ## AUDITING STRATEGIC PLANNING

As with any audit, the first stage is to obtain a business understanding of management's intentions. This may be complicated by the size and cross-function capability of such systems resulting in the business areas considered covering virtually the whole company. From this understanding, the business objectives and thus the control objectives may be derived. This permits the auditor to identify and evaluate critical controls/processes/apparent exposures within the overall systems and design the appropriate audit procedures. Once these have been agreed, the testing of the critical facets and evaluation of the results becomes routine.

As discussed earlier, another complication arises from the advent of Decision Support Systems. These systems, commonly combined with data warehousing, use the databases in order to assist management in the making of fundamental business decisions. In such cases it is essential that management can place reliance on the accuracy, completeness, integrity, confidentiality, and timeliness of such systems. These systems may, in turn, be extended into the concepts of EIS, which address those aspects of corporate governance that are of specific importance to executive management.

In auditing strategic planning there is a complexity multiplier factor at work where the vulnerability of the organization to inadequacies in internal controls in the development of strategic systems is limited only by the degree of corporate dependency on the system. This factor is normally unevaluated and commonly understated, but it could threaten the ongoing existence of the organization.

The involvement of internal audit in performing an audit of strategic IT planning provides internal audit with a vehicle for understanding the nature and effect of decisions in other function business areas of the firm.

Internal audit may be involved in the audit of the management processes involved in:

- *Planning*—within which strategy formulation becomes most critical
- *Organizing*—primarily concerned with the implementation of the strategy
- *Motivating*—primarily concerned with the implementation of the strategy
- *Staffing*—primarily concerned with the implementation of the strategy
- *Controlling*—primarily concerned with the evaluation of the effectiveness and efficiency of strategy implementation

In evaluating the planning aspects, audit would typically look at management's:

- Forecasting of needs and requirements
- Establishment of objectives
- Devising of strategies
- Development of policies
- Establishment of goals

In evaluating the organizing aspects, audit would typically look at management's:

- Organization design
- Job specifications
- Job descriptions
- Span of control
- Command structures
- Coordination

In evaluating the motivating aspects, audit would typically look at management's:

- Leadership quality
- Organizational structure

- Job enrichment
- Job enlargement
- Communication
- Employee morale
- Use of rewards and sanctions

In evaluating the staffing aspects, audit would typically look at management's:

- Employee acquisition
- Employee development
- Management development
- Employee safety
- Labor relations
- Disciplinary procedures
- Career development
- Termination procedures

In evaluating the controlling aspects, audit would typically look at management's:

- Quality control procedures
- Budgetary control
- Analysis of variance
- Project monitoring
- Timekeeping standards

All of these will give indicators as to the quality of management's strategic planning methodology and the degree to which it may be expected to be accomplished.

 ## DESIGN THE AUDIT PROCEDURES

In testing such planning the auditor cannot always test the actual control that management relies on. Many of these planning interventions have few controls or controls that report only if there is a problem. Where there is no problem, no evidence is retained. The auditor should be wary of relying on a lack of evidence to prove a control is effective and should rather seek ways of testing to obtain evidence. This means that the auditor should always know what to look for. Bear in mind that not all controls need to be tested. There may be common controls covering a variety of threats in a common manner. The auditor should try to identify the control structures and establish the degrees of control effectiveness before forming audit opinions.

 ## NOTE

1 Michael Treacy, Fred Wiersema. *The Discipline of Market Leaders*. Reading, MA: Perseus Books, 1995.

CHAPTER THIRTEEN

Management Issues

THIS CHAPTER LOOKS at the broader Information Systems/Information Technology (IS/IT) management issues including the legal issues relating to the introduction of IT to the enterprise, intellectual property issues in cyberspace, trademarks, copyrights, patents, as well as ethical issues, rights to privacy, and the implementation of effective IT governance.

The introduction of IT to organizations has had a dramatic impact on many aspects of their compliance with the law. Perhaps the most fundamental impact of IT on enterprises doing business has been the impact on the legal position of transactions. In order for business to continue taking place in a modern computerized environment, it must be enforceable that transactions concluded and performed in whole or in part by electronic means be regarded as legally binding. In addition, a variety of concerns regarding confidentiality, accuracy, and completeness of information, identity authenticity, and protection of intellectual property have required the rethinking of existing laws and legislation. The extent to which legislation has kept pace with advances in technology varies from country to country, although all face the same problems.

Business moving onto the Internet has created some of the greatest opportunities for fraud the world has ever known. *Cyberfraud* is a major international growth industry that has both the business and legal world struggling to keep pace. Fraud itself typically involves a false statement or omission made deliberately to induce an individual or organization to rely upon it to its prejudice. Prejudice itself may be actual or potential depending on the wording of the individual legislation. Electronic fraud, utilizing Internet technology, may come in the form of creating a false identity on the Internet, intercepting information sent over the Internet, using the Internet to spread false information, or using the Internet to access and manipulate information within the corporate information systems.

There is an old saying that *"on the Internet nobody knows you're a dog"* and identity misrepresentation or even identity theft have become a twenty-first century phenomenon. Such acts range from impersonation of an existing authorized user on a computer system, through *grooming* children on Internet chat rooms, to *phishing* for information by pretending to be a legitimate information seeker, to stealing an individual's identity via knowledge gained on the Internet. Creating a false identity is not a new phenomenon but it is considered more difficult to detect electronically. Acquisition of goods and services from a genuine dealer by assuming a false identity and using a false credit card number is comparatively common.

This is where Certification Authorities become critical. A Certification Authority is an organization that guarantees that the business or person is as claimed having checked their identity independently. This is not to say that all Certification Authorities are equal. Some merely check that a business exists and that the bank account is valid. Others go into considerably more detail and cost correspondingly more. One difficulty with the issuance of such certificates is that many customers do not have certificates and the cyber trader can either deny access to such potential customers and therefore lose business, or take a chance that the customer is legitimate even without the appropriate certificates. Given that the Internet appeals to customers who like to do things in an easy manner, as with most things, control is frequently seen to be an inconvenience.

One of the more common concerns about doing business electronically is that someone will intercept transaction and payment details in a form of *electronic eavesdropping* and use them to commit the kind of fraud described earlier. Although we have had the ability to encrypt information since information processing began, most of our communication remains in clear text, easily intercepted, read, amended, and retransmitted.

Circulating information over the Internet calls for little or no capital outlay and the information circulated may be erroneous, intentionally misleading, or even libelous. Misuse in this area ranges from falsely spreading rumors for financial gain, through character assassination, through the publication of propaganda for extremist groups of every sort. Much of this information sounds plausible, although factually it is false. Tracing the originations of such rumors is not impossible but does take effort, time, and money, which individuals and organizations may be unwilling to spend.

Deliberate penetration of an organization's systems with the intent to access and manipulate corporate information has become so common that it rarely warrants a mention in national newspapers. It has always been possible to break into any secure system, but the advent of e-commerce has effectively invited the world to have a go. Law-abiding citizens who would never consider larceny and burglary look on information larceny as a "bit of fun" and, in some cases, a challenge. The old laws regarding trespass were intended to prevent physical access and do not normally recognize logical access wherein nothing is physically damaged or removed.

New laws may be required to redefine these crimes should existing laws prove inadequate. Laws defining evidence, the nature of the signature, and proof may need to be reviewed in light of the advent of information processing.

 ## PRIVACY

Privacy itself is concerned with the collection and use or misuse of computer store data. Many information systems retained data on individuals, which has been collected, stored, and used without that individual's knowledge or consent. Although information databases are normally used correctly and justifiably, the potential for misuse is inherent in all information systems. Countries around the world and several states within the United States have enacted privacy legislation to provide safeguards for individuals against an invasion of personal privacy by facilitating:

- The individual determining which records have been collected, maintained, used, or distributed regarding themselves
- The prevention of records pertaining to the individual gathered for a specific purpose from being used or made available for another purpose without their consent
- The obtaining of by an individual of such information as has been held on the individual with the opportunity to correct or amend such records
- The determination that information held is current and accurate for its intended use and that adequate safeguards exist for the prevention of misuse of such information
- Civil suit for any damages incurred as a result of willful or intentional action violating the individual's rights under these acts

In April 2011 legislation, the Commercial Privacy Bill of Rights Act of 2011, was introduced in the United States to protect the "fundamental right of American citizens, that is the right to privacy"[1] and is currently in committee. Personally identifiable information was defined as including a first and last name, a residential mailing address, a Web cookie, an e-mail address, a telephone number, biometric data, and so on. *Sensitive* information is a subset and includes health records, religious information, or data that could lead to "economic or physical harm." One anomaly of this legislation was that it would regulate only commercial and nonprofit use of information that is personally identifiable. In addition, the legislation did not apply to government agencies including the Department of Health and Human Services, the Department of Veterans Affairs, the Social Security Administration, the Census Bureau, and the Internal Revenue Service (IRS), all of which collect vast amounts of data on U.S. citizens.

Many international regulations exist when the information, particularly financial information, crosses international borders and a control such as encryption is compulsory in some legislation and banned in others. Such *trans-border data flow* has become more complicated with the explosion of Internet traffic in an unregulated environment and in particular within a cloud-computing environment (see Chapter 19).

COPYRIGHTS, TRADEMARKS, AND PATENTS

Countries have, in the past, created enforceable rights in certain intangibles that have become known as intellectual property. This categorization includes copyrights, trademarks, patents, and trade secrets. As today's economy grows increasingly reliant on the current proliferation of computers and computer networks, the illegal reproduction and distribution of protected material has become considerably easier to accomplish.

Conventional wisdom is that copyright protection is important to protect the computer software industry. It should always be remembered because an organization's information itself may be as important to protect as the software it utilizes. Some of the most vital information and trade secrets are held on computers, connected into networks, and ultimately connected to the world at large. A trade secret may be defined as:

> any formula, pattern, device, or compilation of information used in a business to obtain an advantage over competitors who do not know or use it.[2]

A great deal of time and effort is now being spent in countries such as the United States in order to ensure that an organization's copyrights, trademarks, and patents have a legal protection within IT legislation. Obviously, the legal remedy is only of significance after a transgression has taken place, and the auditor's role may be to ensure that practical countermeasures have been put in place by management to prevent such transgressions from occurring. Countermeasures could include:

- Cryptography
- Effective access control
- Permissions management
- Biometric authentication
- Digital signatures and certification authorities

These technologies are discussed further in Chapter 27.

 ## ETHICAL ISSUES

Business ethics lay out the rules under which business takes place—fairness, honesty, integrity, and the opportunity for all participants to be winners. All stakeholders within an organization maintain an ethical responsibility to act in the best interests of the organization and all of its stakeholders.

An understanding of business ethics is essential for the IT auditor who will encounter ethical issues and dilemmas in his or her daily interaction with management and auditees in any organization. Thus it is useful to understand that the general dimensions of economic activity where management will be making decisions often present tensions between ethical and legal choices. Rossouw[3] identifies three main areas as including:

1. **Macro or systemic dimension.** The policy framework determined by the political power of the state that determines the basis for economic exchanges nationally and internationally between governments.
2. **Meso or institutional dimension.** The relations between economic organizations, such as public sector entities, private sector entities, and private individuals and those outside the organizations.
3. **Micro or intra-organizational dimension.** The economic actions and decisions of individuals within an organization.

Ethics are commonly confused with individual moral principles but in fact go far beyond them. They are designed to address issues from both practical and idealistic standpoints and as such the idealism may frequently be in conflict with the practical. From the professional's perspective they become a way of life. Wheelwright[4] defined three key elements in defining the impact of ethics on decision making:

1. Ethics involve questions requiring reflective choice
2. Ethics involve guides of right and wrong
3. Ethics are concerned with consequences of decisions

In respect to information systems, ethical issues commonly involve the use to which information is put and can be seen with and for specific areas of concern, namely, privacy, accuracy, intellectual property, and access.

As has been described earlier, *privacy* deals with the collection and use or abuse of computer store data. *Accuracy* and its risk equivalent *inaccuracy* can create havoc to individuals and organizations because the use of computerized systems involves an implicit trust in the accuracy and completeness of information provided. *Intellectual property* rights reflect the ownership and use of information including who has the right to buy or acquire the information as well as who determines the value of intellectual property. *Access*, as an ethical issue, is concerned with the ability of individuals to gain entry into information and information systems.

 CORPORATE CODES OF CONDUCT

One of the common controls in this area is the implementation of a *Corporate Code of Conduct.* Such codes are *directive* controls and do not enforce ethical behavior. Where they are combined with *detective* controls designed to identify breaches of the code and *corrective* controls designed to take effective action where such breaches are identified, they may serve as a means of expelling non-conforming members of a population.

Codes of conduct should be in place for all companies (recommended in 1987 by the Treadway Commission and confirmed by King II[5]) and should be enforced. They assist in setting an ethical tone at the top of the organization and must apply to all levels from the top down. They open channels of communications between management and employees and assist in the prevention of, for example, fraudulent reporting.

Codes of conduct are based upon a shared understanding of the values including but not limited to:

- **Honesty.** No intentional deception
- **Integrity.** One standard of conduct for all involved
- **Morality.** Acting in terms of accepted social norms
- **Equity.** Acting in a fair manner with equal treatment for all
- **Equality.** Provision of equal opportunities to compete and collaborate in business activities
- **Accountability.** To accurately record an individual's actions and to account to the stakeholders responsibly for those actions
- **Loyalty.** Trustworthy commitment to all those with whom an individual has dealings
- **Respect.** Recognition of the worth of superiors, subordinates, suppliers, and customers

These values are normally aligned to the values statement to form the basis for the agreed code of conduct.

Codes of conduct may typically take two forms:

1. Positive statement of honest intentions (all embracing but impossible to control)
2. Lists of improper behavior (easier to audit but difficult to keep comprehensive)

Codes that have been observed to be most effective contain a combination of positive generalizations and specific prohibitions. They include the basic rules of acceptable and unacceptable behavior and cover corporate positions and rules concerning:

- Acceptance of gifts
- Confidentiality
- Conflicts of interest
- Standards of corporate practice

It is inevitable that in the conduct of business ethical dilemmas will arise that have to be faced and resolved as a result of conflicting values among various stakeholders. There is often no way of telling which values are correct or incorrect because different people have different values that they pursue.

IT GOVERNANCE

The word "govern" is derived from the Latin word *gubenare*, referring to the steering of a ship, and the word "governor" is derived from *gubenator*, which refers to the captain of a ship or steersman. Business and corporate governance place the goal of business success within the context of honest business behavior and sound stakeholder relations. The purpose of good governance is to match business behavior and management conduct with the organizational intentions, mission, and objectives.

Following a variety of well-publicized breaches of the principles of good corporate governance, it was inevitable that IT governance would emerge as one of the more critical issues in the IT field. In well-managed companies IT governance was implemented in order to ensure the overall achievement of good management principles within the organization. In others it has become just another set of rules to be complied with. Governance responsibilities include setting the strategy, managing the risks, delivering perceived value, and measuring achieved performance.

These responsibilities, overall, have been driven by the need to demonstrate the transparency of risks to the enterprise, but the impact of IT and the organization as a whole has created a dependency requiring specific focus on IT governance. Risk management in these areas include the management of IT's impact and business continuity as well as reputational risk as a result of failures within IT itself. Generally then, IT governance is intended to facilitate the sustaining of organizational operations directed toward implementation of its general business strategies in the present and in the future.

IT governance itself has been defined as:

> . . . the responsibility of the Board of Directors and executive management. It is an integral part of enterprise governance and consists of the leadership and organizational structures and processes that ensure that the organization's IT sustains and extends the organization's strategy and objectives[6]

This indicates a clear difference between IT governance and IT management. Governance is concerned with IT achieving the current and future information needs of the organization in a controlled manner. Management focuses on ensuring an ongoing supply of quality services and products at an acceptable cost.

From a governance perspective, the ultimate responsibility lies with the board of directors or governing body of the particular institution. A critical part of the execution of this responsibility lies in ensuring that the managerial levels understand part of the play in achieving good governance and implement the appropriate control structures in order to achieve that. Overall, the primary responsibility for implementing the strategic plans and policies of the organization as laid down by the board rests on the Chief Executive Officer.

Given the critical role of information systems in achieving corporate strategies, the IT manager has a critical role to play in achieving good governance. The IT manager sets the operating objectives for the IT function ensuring alignment with the organizational strategic objectives in order to provide the initial goals for the IT function. Management control is achieved by creating a continuous feedback mechanism for measurement of performance, comparison to objectives, refinement of processes where necessary, and realignment of objectives where required.

One critical element of the government's process is the placement of the decision-making role for IT within the organization. Centralized versus decentralized was the traditional choice, but a more modern alternative is the Federal structure combining the efficiencies of the centralized structure with the flexibility of the decentralized.

Because IT governance occurs at different layers within the organization, Control Objectives for Information and Related Technology (COBIT©) addresses the governance issues via key goal indicators and key performance indicators. The *Board Briefing on IT Governance* includes IT governance checklists, a Board IT Governance toolkit, a management IT Governance toolkit, and detailed breakdowns of roles and responsibilities in achieving good IT governance.

Because both internal and external auditors are part of the conformance function of corporate governance, it is critical that IT auditors are familiar with the roles and responsibilities laid down in this document.

SARBANES-OXLEY ACT

The far-reaching Sarbanes-Oxley Act (2002)[7] in the United States provides stringent legal requirements to enforce sound corporate governance requirements on all U.S. Securities and Exchange Commission (SEC) registrants as well as their subsidiaries and associated entities, wherever established and operating in the world. All contain references to the important role of Audit Committees and Internal Audit in assisting management to ensure the effectiveness of the corporate governance processes.

The Act itself primarily focuses on what is required for acceptable financial reporting; however, the suggested internal control framework (Committee of Sponsoring Organizations [COSO]) to be used for compliance with the Sarbanes-Oxley Act, as recommended by the SEC, addresses the topic of IT controls, although it does not dictate requirements for such control objectives and related control activities, leaving such decisions to the discretion of each organization. Section 404 of the Act requires that the management of public companies specified within the Act assess the effectiveness of the internal control over financial reporting and report annually on the result of that assessment. Given that financial reporting in such companies is directly dependent on the establishment of a well-controlled IT environment, SEC registrants must provide assurance that their IT controls are effective within their financial reporting context.

In its document *"IT Control Objectives for Sarbanes Oxley,"*[8] the IT Governance Institute discusses the IT control objectives that might be considered by organizations for assessing their internal controls, as required by the Act.

PAYMENT CARD INDUSTRY DATA SECURITY STANDARDS[9]

With the increasing electronic commerce utilizing payment by electronic cards, the Payment Card Industry Security Standards Council developed a set of standards to encourage cardholder data security and facilitate the adoption of consistent data security measures on a global basis. The second version became effective in January 2011 and consists of 12 significant requirements and multiple sub-requirements that contain numerous directives against which businesses may measure their own payment card security policies, procedures, and guidelines.

The Standards encompass:

- Installing and maintaining a firewall configuration to protect cardholder data
- Changing vendor supply defaults for system passwords and other security parameters
- Protecting stored cardholder data
- Encrypting transmission of cardholder data across open, public networks
- Use of regularly updated antivirus software
- Development and maintenance of secure systems and applications
- Restriction of access to cardholder's data by business need-to-know
- Assignment of a unique ID to each person with computer access
- Restriction of physical access to cardholder data
- Tracking and monitoring of all access to network resources and cardholder data
- Regular testing of security systems and processes
- Maintenance of policies that address information security for all personnel

While the Standards have not yet been fully adopted on a worldwide basis, nevertheless in the United States some 46 states have implemented strict Security Breach Notification Laws with some states such as Nevada, Massachusetts, and Wisconsin specifically mentioning the Payment Card Industry Data Security Standard (PCI DSS) and/ or Information Security Policies.

 ## HOUSEKEEPING

Housekeeping procedures are intended to reduce the risk of loss or destruction of software and information and to ensure that sensitive output does not fall into unauthorized hands. Such procedures typically relate to the use of supplies, storage of software programs, handling of files including backups, distribution of outputs, and general care of the hardware itself.

In a centralized information processing facility, housekeeping controls and procedures are normally well established to ensure minimization of such risks. In a distributed, user-controlled environment, however, such controls may not be as obviously required, leading to food and beverage contamination of hardware; fire hazards caused by the use of multiple electrical adapters; data files and backups lost, stolen, or strayed; and confidential information either left lying around or sent to the wrong recipients.

The auditor must ensure that basic organizational controls are in place and effective in order to minimize such elementary risks.

 ## NOTES

1 Press conference in Washington, D.C. John McCain (R-Ariz.,) April 12, 2011.
2 David Goldstone. Prosecuting Intellectual Property Crimes, Office of Legal Education Executive Office for United States Attorneys, http://www.usdoj.gov/criminal/cybercrime/ipmanual.htm.

3 D. Rossouw. *Business Ethics in Africa*, 2nd Edition. Cape Town, Oxford University Press Southern Africa, 2002.

4 P. Wheelwright. *A Critical Introduction to Ethics*, 3rd Edition. New York: Odyssey Press, Inc., 1959, p 4.

5 The Institute of Directors (IOD), The King Report on Corporate Governance for South Africa, 2002.

6 IT Governance Institute, Board Briefing on IT Governance, 2nd Edition, www.itgi.org, 2003.

7 The Sarbanes-Oxley Act (2002), 107th Congress of the United States, Washington, January 2002.

8 IT Governance Institute, IT Control Objectives for Sarbanes-Oxley, www.itgi.org, 2004.

9 https://www.pcisecuritystandards.org/documents/pci_dss_v2.pdf.

CHAPTER FOURTEEN

Support Tools and Frameworks

T HIS CHAPTER INTRODUCES the reader to the need for support tools and frameworks such as Control Objectives for Information and related Technology (COBIT®): *Management Guidelines,* a framework for Information Technology/ Information Systems (IT/IS) managers and COBIT: audit's use in support of the business Support cycle. International standards and good practices such as ISO 17799, IT Infrastructure Library® (ITIL®), privacy standards, Committee of Sponsoring Organizations (COSO), Criteria of Control (CoCo), Cadbury, King, and Sarbanes-Oxley also play a vital role in ensuring the appropriate governance.

 GENERAL FRAMEWORKS

COBIT is one of the most widely accepted models of IT governance and control utilized to manage risks and implement controls within an IT environment in order to achieve business objectives.

COBIT was introduced to meld existing IT standards and best practices into one comprehensive structure designed to achieve international accepted governance standards. Working from the strategic requirements of the organization, COBIT encompasses the full range of IT activities focusing on the achievement of control objectives rather than the implementation of specific controls. As such, it integrates and aligns IT practices with organizational governance and strategic requirements. It is not the only set of standards in common use, but it integrates with other standards to achieve defined levels of control.

What may be classed as best practice for an organization must be appropriate to that organization based upon its needs and capabilities. Standards themselves do not achieve best practice but require careful selection, interpretation, and implementation in order to achieve an adequacy of control. At its highest level, COBIT presents a framework for overall control based upon a model of IT processes intended as a generic model upon which specific controls can be overlaid in order to achieve a unique system of internal controls specifically tailored to the business needs of the organization.

COBIT is designed to be utilized at different levels of management. Executive management can utilize it to ensure value is obtained from the significant investment in IT and to ensure that risk and control investment is appropriately balanced. From an operational management perspective, COBIT facilitates the gaining of assurance that the management and control of IT services, whether insourced or outsourced, is appropriate. IT management can use it as an operational tool to ensure the business strategy is supported in a controlled and appropriately managed manner in providing IT services. IT auditors can utilize COBIT to evaluate the adequacy of controls, design appropriate tests to determine the effectiveness of controls, and provide management with appropriate advice on the system of internal controls.

COBIT is based upon research into best practice within a variety of IT environments and is subject to continuous research and maintenance due to the dynamic nature of information technology. It is geared toward all aspects of IT governance unlike some other standards that are specific to, for example, security alone. Because of its close alignment with international accepted principles of good corporate governance, it is intrinsically acceptable to multiple layers of management as well as regulators.

COBIT utilizes a framework of domains and processes in order to create a logical structure of IT activities in a manner that can be easily subject to managerial controls. The process model divides IT into 34 processes covering:

- **Planning and organizing.** This domain covers all of the processes undertaken by management in order to ensure that the IT function is properly planned and controlled to provide assurance that corporate IT objectives will be achieved. Detailed processes include:

PO1	Define a Strategic IT Plan
PO2	Define the Information Architecture
PO3	Determine Technological Direction
PO4	Define the IT Processes, Organization and Relationships
PO5	Manage the IT Investment
PO6	Communicate Management Aims and Direction
PO7	Manage IT Human Resources
PO8	Manage Quality
PO9	Assess and Manage IT Risks
PO10	Manage Projects

▪ **Acquire and implement.** This domain covers the processes involved in identifying solutions through to installation and accreditation of solutions and changes. Detailed processes include:

AI1   Identify Automated Solutions
AI2   Acquire and Maintain Application Software
AI3   Acquire and Maintain Technology Infrastructure
AI4   Enable Operation and Use
AI5   Procure IT Resources
AI6   Manage Changes
AI7   Install and Accredit Solutions and Changes

▪ **Deliver and support.** This domain includes all of the processes required to deliver the appropriate service levels, manage information and operations, and ensure appropriate performance. Detailed processes include:

DS1   Define and Manage Service Levels
DS2   Manage Third-party Services
DS3   Manage Performance and Capacity
DS4   Ensure Continuous Service
DS5   Ensure Systems Security
DS6   Identify and Allocate Costs
DS7   Educate and Train Users
DS8   Manage Service Desk and Incidents
DS9   Manage the Configuration
DS10   Manage Problems
DS11   Manage Data
DS12   Manage the Physical Environment
DS13   Manage Operations

▪ **Monitor and evaluate.** This domain includes the processes required to monitor overall IT performance and ensure effective IT governance. Detailed processes include:

ME1   Monitor and Evaluate IT Performance
ME2   Monitor and Evaluate Internal Control
ME3   Ensure Regulatory Compliance
ME4   Provide IT Governance

Each of these is further subdivided into a variety of individual control objectives which, in turn, identify the control requirements, principal control structures, and measurement criteria. The measurement criteria are, perhaps, the most critical part of COBIT in terms of achieving corporate governance. Within each process, detailed control objectives are specified as a minimum level of managerial control. Roles and responsibilities for achieving these control objectives are spelled out and a maturity model for each process is given with measurement metrics under the headings:

- Nonexistent
- Initial/ad hoc
- Repeatable but intuitive
- Defined process
- Managed and measurable
- Optimized

These metrics facilitate management's and the auditors' judgment as to the degree of compliance achieved in each of the processes.

COBIT is based upon the understanding that the design and implementation of automated application controls is the responsibility of IT based upon the business needs as specified by the business-process owner. General IT controls are the direct responsibility of the IT function and are therefore also covered within COBIT.

Further Information

Further information is available from the IT Governance Institute (www.itgi.org). Details of direct interest to the IT auditor include the COBIT:

- Framework
- Control objectives
- Control practices
- IT assurance guide
- IT control objectives for Sarbanes-Oxley
- IT governance implementation guide

CobiT 5®, which was released in the third quarter of 2011, is a major revision, designed to meet the current and future needs of stakeholders and align with the latest thinking in enterprise governance and IT management techniques. It effectively merges with the existing Information Systems Audit and Control Association (ISACA) standards to provide an integrated Governance Framework. In addition, it facilitates the connectivity to the Information Technology Infrastructure Library (ITIL) and International Standards Organization (ISO) frameworks.

 ## COSO: INTERNAL CONTROL STANDARDS

As noted in Chapter 4, internal control was defined by COSO as a broadly defined process, affected by people, designed to provide reasonable assurance regarding the achievement of the three objectives that all businesses strive for, namely:

1. Economy and efficiency of operations, including achievement of performance goals and safeguarding of assets against loss
2. Reliable financial and operational data and reports
3. Compliance with laws and regulations

In order to achieve these objectives, COSO defined five components that would assist management in achieving these objectives, namely:

1. A sound control environment
2. A sound risk-assessment process
3. Sound operational-control activities
4. Sound information and communications systems
5. Effective monitoring

An internal control system would be judged to be effective if all five components were present and functioning effectively for operations, financial reporting, and compliance.

COBIT originally adapted its definition of control from COSO in that the policies, procedures, practices, and organizational structures are designed to provide reasonable assurance that business objectives will be achieved and that undesired events will be prevented or detected and corrected. COBIT emphasizes the role and impact of IT control as they relate to business processes, whereas COSO defined internal control, described its components, and provided criteria against which control systems could be evaluated.

The major goals of COSO were to establish a common definition of internal control in order to serve a variety of different parties and, at the same time, provide a standard against which organizations could assess their internal control systems and identify areas for improvement.

COSO emphasized that the internal control system is a tool of management, not a substitute, and that controls should be integral to operating activities rather than added on. Unlike COBIT, COSO defined internal control as a process in its own right and recommended that periodic evaluation of the effectiveness of internal control be carried out from time to time.

COSO also attempted to address the limitations of an internal control system including faulty human judgment, misunderstanding of instructions, management override, collusion, errors, and cost-benefit considerations, all of which can serve to undermine the effectiveness of the overall system of internal control.

COSO also stated that there should be separate and independent evaluations conducted of the system of internal control with the frequency and scope of such reviews dependent upon the assessment of risks and the effectiveness of management's monitoring procedures.

 OTHER STANDARDS

Security: BS 7799 and ISO 17799/27001/27002

As noted in Chapter 4, British Standard (BS) 7799 and ISO 17799 were both developed to assist companies by ensuring security and control within electronic trading systems. The 10 areas depicted within the standards facilitate the introduction of key controls as mandatory features and additional controls in higher risk organizations.

The ISO 27001™ standard was published in October 2005, essentially replacing the old BS7799-2™ standard and is the specification for an Information Security Management System (ISMS). It is intended as a certification standard, compliance with which can benefit an organization by providing proof of IT security management.

The process is predicated by an organization making the decision to embark on the exercise. This requires management commitment and the assignment of responsibilities for the certification project itself. Once commitment is made, an organizational top-level policy is normally developed and published, usually supported by subordinate policies.

This is followed by the scoping of the project in order to define which part(s) of the organization will be covered by the ISMS including the location, assets, and technology to be included.

At this stage a risk assessment is undertaken to determine the organization's IT risk exposure/profile, and identify the best potential routes to address this. The document produced will form the basis for the next stage, which is the management of those risks through the implementation of appropriate controls.

A part of this process will be the selection of appropriate controls with respect to those outlined in the standard (and ISO 27002™), with the justification for each decision recorded in a Statement of Applicability (SOA). The controls themselves should then be implemented as appropriate.

ISO 27002, itself, is a code of practice for information security. In essence, it outlines hundreds of potential controls and control mechanisms, which may theoretically be implemented, subject to the guidance provided within ISO 27001.

The standard is intended to establish both guidelines and general principles for initiating, implementing, maintaining, and improving information security management within an organization. The intention is that, following a formal risk assessment, actual controls may be selected from among those listed in the standard in order to address the specific requirements identified as a result of the risk analysis.

Overall the standard addresses the component areas of:

- Structure
- Risk Assessment and Treatment
- Security Policy
- Organization of Information Security
- Asset Management
- Human Resources Security
- Physical Security
- Communications and Ops Management
- Access Control
- Information Systems Acquisition, Development, Maintenance
- Information Security Incident Management
- Business Continuity
- Compliance

Once the risk architecture is identified, and the appropriate controls selected and implemented, the certification process itself can then be embarked upon via a suitable accredited independent third party.

Service Management: ITIL

ITIL® (www.itil.org) is intended to define the best practice in IT Service Management. It was developed by the Office of Government Commerce (OGC) and is supported by publications, qualifications, and an international user group. The approach is a top-down, business-driven approach to the management of IT, which is intended to address the need to deliver a high-quality IT service in order to deliver strategic business value. IT Service Management focuses on the people, processes, and technology issues that IT organizations face. ITIL, itself, attempts to assist organizations to develop a framework for IT Service Management by providing a cohesive set of best practices, drawn from both the public and private sectors. It offers a comprehensive qualifications scheme and accredited training organizations as well as specifically developed implementation and assessment tools.

Project Management: PRINCE

Projects in Controlled Environments (PRINCE®) is a widely used project-management method that navigates the user through all the essential elements for implementation of a successful project.

It was first developed in 1989 by the Central Computer and Telecommunications Agency (CCTA) as a U.K. government standard for IT project management. Since its introduction, PRINCE has become widely used in both the public and private sectors and is a widely recognized standard for project management both within IT as well for non-IT projects. It is designed to incorporate the requirements of existing users and to enhance the method toward a generic, best practice approach for the management of a variety of projects.

Criteria of Control: CoCo

CoCo, sponsored by the Canadian Institute of Chartered Accountants, is intended to translate COSO into practical, implementable activities and defines three major control objectives:

1. Effectiveness and efficiency of operations
2. Reliability of internal and external reporting
3. Compliance with applicable laws and regulations and internal policies

Within the CoCo framework, control is defined as encompassing:

▪ **Purpose,** which defines criteria that promote an understanding of the organization's direction. They use techniques such as vision and strategy, risks and opportunities, planning, policy development, and use of performance targets and indicators.

- **Commitment,** which defines criteria that promote a belief in the organization's identity and values. They impact ethical values, including integrity; human resource policies; responsibility and accountability; authority; and mutual trust.
- **Capability,** which defines criteria that address an organization's competence. They involve knowledge and competencies, skills and tools, information, use of appropriate communication processes, coordination, and control activities.
- **Monitoring and Learning,** which defines criteria that will facilitate the organization's evolution. They involve monitoring internal and external environments, monitoring performance, challenging assumptions, reassessing information needs and information systems, execution of follow-up procedures, and assessing the overall effectiveness of control.

CoCo promotes the treatment of risk through:

- Avoidance of risk
- Reducing the likelihood of risk occurring
- Reducing the impact should a risk occur
- Transferring the risk to a third party
- Accepting or retaining the risk

This is seen to be effected using controls of the five basic types, namely: *directive, preventative, detective, corrective,* and *recovery* controls.

 ## GOVERNANCE FRAMEWORKS

Three standards have become widely recognized as *IT governance* frameworks. While each has significant IT governance strengths, none may be looked on as a complete IT governance solution.

ITIL

ITIL, as mentioned previously, was developed by the United Kingdom's Office of Government Commerce. Although it is directed specifically toward service management, a part of that is, itself, directed toward the governance of service delivery.

CobiT

CobiT®, as mentioned previously in greater detail, is a generic IT governance framework.

CobiT regards IT governance as a balance between two primary areas:

1. Creation of corporate value
2. Minimizing IT risks

With overall objectives of:

- Ensuring strategic orientation, focusing on corporate solutions.
- Creation of benefits, focusing on optimizing the tasks and assessing the benefit of the IT.
- Implementation of risk management relating to the protection of the IT assets and taking account of disaster recovery and continuation of the corporate processes in the event of a crisis.
- Effective resource management in order to ensure the optimization of knowledge and infrastructure.
- Adequacy of performance measurement and the creation of the bases for continual improvement.

The CobiT approach to controlling is essentially a top-down approach where corporate objectives form the basis for defining the IT objectives that in turn define the IT architecture. This is intended to ensure that IT processes are appropriately defined and operated, ensure that information is processed, IT resources managed, and services delivered in a well-governed manner.

ISO/IEC 38508

ISO/IEC (International Organization for Standardization /International Electrotechnical Commission) 38508 was developed by the joint technical committee ISO/IEC JTC1, information technology, subcommittee SC 7, software and systems engineering. Designed as a worldwide formal international IT Governance Standard, ISO/IEC 38500 was published in June 2008 and sets out a clear framework for the Board's governance of information and communications.

The framework sets out six principles for good corporate governance of IT under the headings of:

1. Responsibility
2. Strategy
3. Acquisition
4. Performance
5. Conformance
6. Human behavior

As with all such frameworks, the difficulty comes in the implementation.

The CALDER-MOIR IT Governance Framework[1] is designed to facilitate the obtaining of maximum benefit from all these overlapping and competing frameworks and standards, and also to deploy best-practice guidance. The framework itself, is divided into six segments:

1. Business Strategy
2. Risk, Conformance, and Compliance
3. IT Strategy

4. Change
5. Information and Technology Balance Sheet
6. Operations

Each segment is then divided into three layers representing:

1. The board
2. Executive management
3. IT and IT-governance practitioners

Starting with the overall business strategy, each segment is then executed in clockwise order. In the first three segments the board establishes directions and business strategies. Depending on the nature of the organization, these need to be compliant with the overall corporate governance regimes and risk assessed. In the last three steps, architectures and plans are then developed to meet business strategies through use of the appropriate IT. After these plans are approved by the board, they are then implemented via a series of change projects.

The main tasks for directors in IT governance, evaluate, direct, and monitor, as per ISO/IEC 38500, are contained within the Calder-Moir framework. The board *evaluates* business conditions and strategies, *directs* using IT principles, and *monitors* all processes in the framework. Executive managers also evaluate, direct, and monitor processes carried out by IT practitioners.

 NOTE

1 Calder and S. Moir. *IT Governance*. IT Governance Publishing, 2009.

CHAPTER FIFTEEN

Governance Techniques

THIS CHAPTER COVERS the need for, and use of, techniques such as change-control reviews, operational reviews, and International Standards Organization (ISO) 9000 reviews.

CHANGE CONTROL

Periodically the necessity arises to modify an existing hardware and/or software configuration as a result of:

- Hardware changes as a result of performance improvements or reconfigurations caused by changes to other systems
- Hardware failures during normal operations
- The detection of a software error during normal operations
- Changes to legislation affecting the organization's business systems
- A change to the business operation of the organization requiring alterations within the information systems

As a result of these changes in the environment, the extent of change required within the existing system configuration must be determined and the change applied in a controlled manner so as to avoid any undue disruption to normal processing. It is critical that during periods of change, the production versions of software are protected against unauthorized changes, untested changes, or even malicious changes.

Change control's objective is to ensure risk is controlled, not introduced, during a change. This means ensuring that:

- All changes are authorized
- All authorized changes are made
- Only authorized changes are made
- All changes are as specified
- All changes are cost effective

This control requires a coordinated effort involving managers, users, information systems personnel, and IT auditors. An effective methodology for authorizing, testing, and implementing the change in a controlled manner is a prerequisite. In most organizations this will involve the use of a *Change Control Committee* involving members of all of the aforementioned disciplines. This committee is normally involved in evaluating change requests for corporate or control implications, authorizing those requests, ensuring that testing and documentation of the changes has been carried out, and finally authorizing the implementation of the change into the live environment.

All requests for amendments to production programs should be made in writing and include the business justification for the change requested. A full appraisal of the impacts, justification, and alternatives considered should be undertaken with more significant changes being subject to more stringent checks. If the change is of a major nature, a feasibility study may be required.

Once changes are approved by the committee, the work may be undertaken by such resources as the committee approves (normally IT with some user involvement) and, once the programmer involved is satisfied that the amended software is working as intended, independent testing should take place with the user participation prior to implementation in the production environment. Users, IT staff, and auditors should all sign off on the change to ensure that their individual needs have been satisfied. It should be stressed that when the Information Systems (IS) auditor signs off on a change, this is an indication that audit's control requirements have been met within the change system. It is not an indication of quality assurance of the system because this is the responsibility of both the users and IT management.

All changes to systems, whether hardware, software, or both, should be fully documented with the effects of all maintenance changes so that subsequent work on the relative systems can be expedited. With all possible care being taken there is still a chance that a change to a system will result in a production system failure. As such, operations recoverability procedures should be in place in the event of a system failure in the new configuration. This would typically involve securing the condition of the system and data prior to the change being implemented so that an unsuccessful change can be appropriately backed-out.

Within a mainframe environment it is common to separate the production and development versions of programs using completely segregated software libraries. Once implementation has been authorized, the change controller will normally copy the amended source code into the production library. For this to be effective, access to production libraries must be restricted to the change controller only. This access control is intended to prevent both accidental and malicious amendments to production software occurring without appropriate authorization.

Updating software on personal computers and local area networks would appear more straightforward because they normally involve installation of purchased packages. Unfortunately, not all purchased packages function immediately as intended. In the smaller environment of personal computers it is common that backups are not taken prior to system changes and that the introduction of a new version of software or even new software altogether may result in significant damage to the production environment.

Personal computers and local area networks also require careful control over changes made. The change-control processes may be different for the surrounding mainframe computers; nevertheless appropriate change-control procedures must be implemented.

 PROBLEM MANAGEMENT

The changes thus controlled are known and planned changes. The procedures involve ensuring prior authorization for all changes, supervision of the change process, adequate testing of all changes, and user sign-off on all changes.

Periodically things will go wrong with a system, which necessitates an urgent repair. Such changes are not known in advance and are commonly executed and permission sought retrospectively. Such changes are controlled using *Problem Management*. Problem Management's objective is to control systems during emergency situations arising from unforeseen changes. Typically this will involve bypassing normal control mechanisms and may require direct programmer access to live data. This must be controlled separately and must involve user authorization, even retrospectively.

 AUDITING CHANGE CONTROL

From an audit perspective, the IT auditor will seek assurance that change-control procedures are in place and effective over changes to hardware, software, telecommunications, or anything that affects the processing environment. Sources of evidence for the auditor would include minutes of change-control committee meetings, software movement reports, access-control logs, and system-failure records.

The auditor will typically seek to ensure that:

- Requests are recorded and stored for reference
- Each change is assessed prior to acceptance of the change, based on its projected effect to the computer system and business operations

- Unauthorized changes are limited by automated or manual controls
- A problem management change process is in place whereby the reasons for emergency changes and the authorization mechanisms are clearly defined
- Change documentation is kept up to date with all maintenance tasks and changes comprehensively recorded
- All new software releases pass through change control

 ## OPERATIONAL REVIEWS

Operational auditing involves first determining management's objectives followed by establishing which management controls exist leading to effectiveness, efficiency, and economy. The auditor must determine which key performance indicators are in use and their appropriateness as well as determining the achievement of control objectives.

The term *operational audit* is commonly used to cover a variety of audit types. An operational audit may cover the evaluation of some or all of the following:

- Internal controls
- Compliance with laws, regulations, and company policies
- Reliability and integrity of financial and operating information
- Effective and efficient use of resources

Operational auditors require standards against which current operations may be compared and evaluated. It is management's responsibility to devise and use appropriate standards to evaluate operating activities, and operational auditors will usually start with criteria that have been established by management (performance standards) or by some oversight board or agency.

In the absence of standards, the auditors may have to borrow from other sources or develop some type of criteria against which to compare performance. This is often a difficult task because frameworks such as Control Objectives for Information and related Technology (COBIT®) may not have been implemented in a sufficiently detailed manner and auditors should get management's reaction to the suitability of any criteria so developed. Reasonable criteria for evaluating performance are absolutely essential for successful operational auditing because no evaluation of operations is possible without a standard for comparison. While subjectivity cannot be completely avoided, objective criteria, which are considered appropriate and reasonable by both the internal auditors and IT, are essential for continuing success.

 ## PERFORMANCE MEASUREMENT

Performance measurement is a philosophy in which feedback is used to make ongoing adjustments to the course of the organization toward its vision. For example, the information derived from budgetary or client satisfaction measurements may provide the feedback used to assess the effectiveness of an organization from a variety of viewpoints. Using this feedback, it is possible to ensure continued excellence of programs and services in response to changes within both the internal and external environments.

The process commences with the setting of business objectives and the development of strategies and plans to achieve these objectives within an overall control framework. This is followed by the development of appropriate performance measures to assess progress toward the objectives.

Performance-measurement systems provide the feedback information required to determine if executive management strategies have been effectively converted into operational decisions.

Performance measurement provides a balanced, methodical attempt to assess the effectiveness of an organization's operations from multiple vantage points—financial, client satisfaction, internal business, and innovation/learning.

The Balanced Scorecard approach can give the auditor well-structured measurement criteria if it has been appropriately implemented. The mechanics of performance measurement are complex and the development and deployment of the process may be painful. Typically many measures will be evaluated before a key set will emerge. Many choices will involve industry best-practice measures so that a competitive benchmark can be established.

Improving performance measurement involves the development of integrated performance-measurement systems that are built around a strategic theme such as business strategy or value creation. They involve measuring those aspects of the IT structure that relate the activities of people and processes in the IT organization to the intended outcomes for the IT stakeholders.

Integrated performance measurement systems are a significant improvement over prior evaluation structures but still do not eliminate some of the basic difficulties of performance measurement. IT can be a complex organization offering considerably more opportunities for measurement than management can effectively employ. The difficulties lie in reducing the required number of measures to a significant few.

Managers generally understand how effective measurement provides key support in the pursuit of organizational goals when the consequences of performance results are communicated and understood. Within IT they tend to support the concept of performance measurement because their experience has shown it to be effective in helping to achieve success. Managers who use performance measurement on a regular basis understand the difficulties inherent in the process. Many measurement criteria form an imperfect definition of the underlying idea and can result in rewarding "bad" behavior and punishing "good" behavior.

Most IT managers understand the shortcomings of measurement systems. They are fully aware that distortions may be introduced through cost and asset allocations. They recognize that there may be an inclination to measure the things that are easy to measure, and to avoid measures that are more difficult with the subsequent distortions this creates.

ISO 9000 REVIEWS

The International Organization for Standardization (ISO) is the specialized international agency for standardization, comprising the national standards bodies of 91 countries. ISO is made up of approximately 180 technical committees, with each technical committee being responsible for one of many areas of specialization. In 1987, ISO published the original set of quality assurance standards commonly known as ISO 9000. The ISO Quality Management and Quality Assurance System Standards provide a set of requirements for quality-assurance systems. Compliance with ISO 9000 standards indicates that a producer has a basic quality assurance system in place.

Increasingly, customers expect organizations to have their quality systems reviewed and audited to one of the standards of the series. This involves having an accredited independent third party conduct an on-site audit of the company operations against the requirements of the appropriate standard.

Reviewing against a company's implementation of ISO 9000 involves reviewing:

▪ The methodology, including the philosophy, guidelines, policies, responsibilities, time line, and deliverables.
▪ The project/process, to ensure its compliance with the methodology and to identify reasons for any deviations.

An important role of such reviews is the establishment of quality objectives and reviewing of progress toward achieving the objectives and fulfilling the quality policy. IT quality objectives are established to improve performance and/or the quality system and thus fulfill the quality policy and other organizational goals and aspirations. This ties in closely to COBIT's use of control objectives.

Enacted in 1994, ISO 9001: *2000 Quality Management Systems* replaces the older ISO 9000, 9001, 9002, and 9003. These standards apply within every organization and can be either service or product oriented depending upon the orientation of the organization.

The standards themselves specify the quality levels desired and the organization is responsible for conducting a *gap analysis* in order to identify areas of noncompliance. This then facilitates the closure of these gaps in order to achieve compliance. At the organization's discretion, an external review can be carried out in order to determine compliance and, if achieved, an ISO certificate is issued and the organization recorded in the ISO registry. This registration is then valid until the next audit.

From an audit perspective, auditors are concerned with ensuring that the functions and processes of IT achieve their anticipated outcomes and that documented proof of this exists. Of critical importance to the auditor are specific clauses requiring full documentation of the quality procedures and processes, requiring competence on the part of personnel carrying out the work subject to quality assurance, and that acquisition of resources including hardware, software, and outsourced services meets stringent quality requirements.

PART THREE

Systems and Infrastructure
Lifecycle Management

CHAPTER SIXTEEN

Information Systems Planning

THIS CHAPTER COVERS the Information Systems (IS) planning and managing components and includes developing an understanding of stakeholders and their requirements together with IT planning methods such as system investigation, process integration/re-engineering opportunities, risk evaluation, cost-benefit analysis, risk assessment, object-oriented systems analysis, and design. Enterprise resource planning (ERP) software to facilitate enterprise applications integration is reviewed.

For most organizations, information resources are managed through the information technology (IT) department with three primary areas of responsibility, namely, operations, systems development, and technical support. These are not, however, the only *stakeholders* in the IT process.

 STAKEHOLDERS

Stakeholders are all of those individuals and organizations that have a direct or indirect connection to the Information Processing (IP) function of the organization. These include:

- **Management.** At all levels within the organization from general management to operational supervisors, management relies on the accuracy, completeness, and integrity of information processed through the computer systems.

- **Customers.** Customers wishing to do business with the organization require assurance that products and services provided will be of exceptional quality, timescales will be as promised, and building and account information will be accurately rendered. At the same time they require assurance that goods and services will be available when requested and that information held about the customer will be kept confidential.
- **Employees.** Requires assurance that the enterprise will continue to exist and function and for that the availability and integrity of information systems must be assured. They also must maintain confidence that information held upon the system about employees will be kept confidential.
- **Organizational functions.** Requires assurance that the IT services will deliver the functionality required in order to ensure that they are able to achieve their operational objectives.
- **Suppliers.** Requires assurance that the organization will continue to exist and will meet all debts.
- **External audit.** Requires assurance that the organization will continue to exist and that the financial and operational information, drawn from the information systems, upon which they place reliance in forming their opinion as to the fairness of presentation of the financial affairs of the organization do, indeed, reflect the actual situation.
- **Internal audit.** Seeks assurance that the controls function as intended in order that the organization may meet the strategic and operational goals.

In order to meet the diverse needs of this universe of stakeholders, IT management must plan appropriately each of their functional areas and implement appropriate control mechanisms.

 ## OPERATIONS

In a medium-sized to large organization the operations function is focused on the provision of IT services to the corporate or business unit. This includes the operation of all equipment associated with the computer systems including starting, stopping, and maintaining fully operating mainframe systems together with the peripherals as described in Chapter 1. Within the operations function a variety of roles exist including those of:

- **Operations management.** Responsible for the computer operations personnel including all staff involved in the effective running of the information processing facility (IPF).
- **Shift supervisors.** Responsible for the overall supervision of a group of operators running the day-to-day operations of the IPF.
- **Operators.** Responsible for handling the day-to-day operations of the IPF including starting and ending of jobs, loading the appropriate data files, aligning special stationery in printers, taking backups as specified, and general housekeeping tasks.

- **Control group.** Responsible in some larger organizations for the collection, data conversion, and control of input together with the distribution of output to the appropriate users.
- **Data librarian.** Responsible for the control and safeguarding of all program and data files maintained upon computer media by the IPF. In a large organization this may be a full-time employee dedicated to this function. In some installations this function has been taken over to a large extent by automated library-control software.
- **Data entry.** In most organizations today, data entry takes place within the user environment and under the control of user staff. There are, however, some organizations that have a requirement for high-volume data capturing of standardized inputs. In those organizations data entry typically falls under the control of the operations function. Where such central control exists the maintenance of the integrity of source documents from receipt to return to the appropriate user area is critical.

SYSTEMS DEVELOPMENT

With the advent of today's development tools, job titles and role functionality within this area are multiplying exponentially. Nevertheless, it is still possible to differentiate among the functions carried out by individuals.

The individuals associated with the development of computer systems include:

- **Project leaders.** Management specialists who control computer projects from planning, through assignment of tasks, through execution and monitoring, to final completion.
- **Systems analysis.** Business specialists who analyze information flow within the business environment in order to ensure that systems are designed based upon the business needs of the user.
- **System designers.** Technical specialists who take the business requirements and interpret them into detailed designs with sufficient information to ensure that programmers can encode the system as envisaged by the analysts.
- **Application programmers.** Responsible for both the development of new computer programs as well as the maintenance of existing application systems. They encode the programs that will eventually run the application system as specified by the user and as designed by the designer.

TECHNICAL SUPPORT

In order to achieve a smooth flow of information within the organization, certain technical requirements must be met to facilitate the uninterrupted operation and integration of all system components. The maintenance of these technical requirements lies in the hands of the technical specialists. Their focus is on providing user assistance in the areas of hardware and software acquisition and data administration. In today's complex IT world the degree of specialization is increasing but would typically contain:

- **Systems programmers.** Responsible for all maintenance on the system software, particularly the operating system. These individuals have ultimate power within an organization because the nature of the work requires unrestricted access to all facilities and structures to a technical level within the IT function. Because preventative controls cannot be used due to the nature of the systems programmers' job, it is critical that, in any site, the number of individuals with this degree of power is limited and that the work carried out is monitored appropriately.
- **Network management.** Responsible for the communication infrastructure and its components including:

  - **Multiplexers.** Permitting several telecommunications signals to be transmitted over a signal communications medium at the same time.
  - **Modems.** Translating data from digital to analog (modulation) and translating from analog to digital (demodulation).
  - **Switches.** Hardware devices allowing transmission devices and receiving devices to be connected.
  - **Routers.** An internetworking switch operating at the OSI level 3, the network layer.
  - **Firewalls.** A device installed at the point where networks connect into the site, which applies rules to control the type of network traffic flowing in and out.
  - **Gateways.** A major relay station that receives, switches, relays, and transmits traffic converting from one protocol to another where necessary and operating at any OSI layer above OSI layer 3, the network layer.
  - **Proxies.** Any facility that indirectly provides some service, for example, firewall proxies may provide access to Internet services on the other side of the firewall while controlling access to services in either direction.

    Network managers may also be responsible for administrative control over local area networks ensuring systems administration for hardware and software implementation is effective, and appropriate backups are taken.

- **Security administration.** Responsible for ensuring that users comply with the overall corporate security policy and that the controls designed and implemented effectively enforce adequate segregation of duties and prevention of unauthorized access to corporate assets.
- **Quality assurance.** Responsible for assisting in the design of quality standards for the IT area and ensuring that IT staff follow the quality procedures defined, and that software developed internally or purchased externally and installed locally meets user expectations and is free from significant errors.
- **Database administrator.** May be seen as part of the systems development team or as an independent technical specialist depending on the organization. The database administrator (DBA) defines the data structures used within the corporate database

system, both physical and logical. The DBA's role is to optimize the usage of and access to the database management system and includes:

- Controlling the physical and logical data definition
- Implementing database access controls, concurrency controls, and update controls
- Monitoring database usage in order to fine-tune performance
- Defining and controlling backup and recovery procedures
- Selecting and installing database tuning tools and utilities

Like the systems programmer, the DBA, in order to carry out his or her duties, has full and unrestricted access to all live data and data structures. As such the performance of the DBA's duties cannot be restricted by preventative controls and must be controlled by segregation of duties if possible and by supervisory review over activities and the use of the powerful database utilities.

OTHER SYSTEM USERS

In addition to these users, other individuals will have access to the computer systems, including end-users for whom the application systems were designed but who may also add their own user-written applications; and the help desk, who may either utilize in-house developed help desk software or who may use a propriety package and who frequently have administrative rights over user access.

SEGREGATION OF DUTIES

Staff members within IT have a great deal of power and authority within the computing environment. This creates the possibility that a single person could be responsible for incompatible functions such that errors, fraud, or sabotage could take place undetected. Due to the variety of job titles this may not be immediately obvious to the auditor but nevertheless segregation of duties must be enforced whenever possible.

The more powerful user authorities such as the systems programmer, network controller, or DBA should be available only to a restricted number of staff. For backup purposes, a single employee having such rights is too few but several are too many.

An incompatible duties matrix should be drawn up for each installation showing the individual job functionalities and where these are incompatible depending upon the nature of the organization and its IT function. As overall fundamentals, the auditor should seek to ensure that, where possible, access to live information including data and programs is restricted on a *need-to-have* basis. Where there is a genuine need, preventative controls cannot be used and therefore supervisory review is essential. Areas where the auditor should seek assurance that incompatible duties do not exist include:

▪ **Access to data.** Based upon organizational policy, access should be granted on a basis of least privilege. No user should have more authority than required to carry out their duties. Where additional authority is granted on a temporary basis, controls must exist to ensure that the authority is removed at the end of the temporary period.

▪ **Control over assets.** Based upon the organizational requirements, individuals with control over assets should not have access to manipulate records nor the authority to perform reconciliations. In today's environment it must be remembered that information itself is a corporate asset. The amount of money owed to an organization is largely determined by what the computer records say is owed to the organization and the assets owned by the organization are determined by what the asset register says is owned by the organization. Once again, where the organization is too small to enforce division of duties at an operational level, it cannot be enforced directly within the computer systems. Requiring two user IDs and passwords is of no benefit if it is the same individual who holds both. Under these circumstances it is more effective to use supervisory review, even after the event.

▪ **Authorization levels** come in various forms. Management is required to authorize user access to information and functionality within the Information Systems. In many cases there is no scrutiny of the access rights that management is authorized to grant and anything will be accepted as long as it comes in on the correct form with a signature that *could* be the manager's. At the transactional level authorization is normally seen as a user function granted to a more senior staff member with the knowledge, experience, and authority to authorize specific transactions. Once again, a common failing is the granting of such rights to individuals with insufficient experience who then authorize transactions that should not have been authorized.

 ## PERSONNEL PRACTICES

In a typical IT organization, staff turnover can be a major issue in ensuring continuity of well-designed and processed systems. As such, the acquisition, training, retention, and eventual termination of staff are critical control points. In large organizations an internal IT personnel function may exist, but even in smaller installations care must be taken in management of these areas because they have a direct correlation with the quality of staff used and systems produced. In all cases employment practices must comply with the relevant federal, state, and local labor legislation.

Acquisition

Different organizations follow different policies in staff recruitment. Some organizations seek to recruit inexperienced staff so that they may train them themselves to their own standards. Others prefer to seek fully trained and experienced staff so that they may be productive in a minimal timescale.

In recruiting staff the organization would normally seek to ensure that the new employee does, indeed, have the qualifications and experience claimed. It would also attempt to ensure that the new employee has no history that would make a person unsuitable for the position sought. In accomplishing this, background checks would normally be carried out and references checked, qualifications confirmed, and, where required, aptitude tests may be carried out.

A common mistake in recruitment is the bypassing of such controls in the case of temporary or contract staff. Temporary staff should undergo the same background checks as full-time permanent staff and contract staff, although covered legally by a contractual arrangement, may not be in a financial position to be held accountable should there be a breach of contract.

Once a new staff member has been selected the normal employment practices of the organization should ensure that conflict of interest agreements and confidentiality agreements are entered into. Where an employee is executing critical or sensitive functions *fidelity insurance* or *employee bonding* may be used to reduce the impact of losses caused by errors or intent.

Following the guidelines laid down in virtually all corporate governance reports, most organizations have a published code of conduct specifying each individual employee's responsibilities to the organization and the organization's responsibilities to the employee. This may be in the form of employee handbook or an actual agreement that the employee is required to sign on appointment.

Staff Training

It is incumbent upon IT management to ensure that employees are capable of undertaking the tasks allocated to them. This will involve maintaining the skills register for each employee so that, as part of work planning, skills shortages may be identified and appropriate training scheduled. A common mistake is for the IT function to train their staff solely in information-processing skills. An understanding of the nature of the business undertaken by the organization is critical to successful achievement of IT and corporate strategic objectives. In order to avoid dependency on a single individual, cross-training can provide backup skills, although care should be taken to avoid incompatible duties being vested in one individual.

Staff Retention

Staff turnover can be a problem in many IT organizations because expensive skills are lost and new recruits will have to go through a learning curve. In light of this, management must make a determined effort to retain their staff and implement the appropriate controls to monitor competitive salaries, staff morale, and alternative employment opportunities for their staff.

Once the appropriate staff has been obtained and trained, IT management must turn their attention to the planning of the systems.

OBJECT-ORIENTED SYSTEMS ANALYSIS

Object-oriented systems analysis (OSA) is a technique that involves the study of a specific domain of interacting objects for the purpose of understanding and documenting their essential characteristics. Within an IT context, it is concerned with developing software engineering requirements and specifications expressed as a system's object model composed of a population of interacting objects. This is in contrast to the traditional data or functional views of systems, which would involve techniques such as functional decomposition and structured analysis and design. Under OSA, an object is classed as any representation of a genuine entity or of an abstraction and OSA defines objects with data structures and behaviors together with events that trigger operations, or object behavior changes that change the state of objects. Numerous OSA techniques exist including Shlaer-Mellor, Jacobson, Coad-Yourdon, and Rumbaugh.[1]

Process-oriented analysis regards systems as being a network of interacting processes. By following this approach the analyst would focus on how the system might be designed rather than regarding the systems components and the inter-relationships. However, OSA organizes all knowledge about each system object so that information about a system object is easier to locate in object-oriented analysis than in other analysis methods. The techniques provide forms of abstraction including aggregation, generalization, and classification. As seen in Chapter 11, a method-driven approach consists of a fixed sequence of steps to follow, for example using the waterfall method or the spiral model. In practice, these steps cannot always be followed exactly. When problems occur in the development process adjustments may need to be made to the order of steps or the development processes.

An OSA model is structured with the intention that reality is represented in the way systems are perceived instead of being constrained by some particular programming language or methodology.

 ## ENTERPRISE RESOURCE PLANNING

ERP goes beyond OSA and is the term used to describe a broad range of business activities supported by modularized application software, which is intended to help an organization manage the important areas of its business. These areas can include product planning, materials purchasing, inventory control, servicing customers, tracking orders, and supplier interfacing as well as providing specific modules for the normal financial and human resources aspects of a business. It integrates the information across functions and provides a common set of tools for the planning and monitoring of those functions and processes.

Many suppliers offer an integrated suite of applications to meet the corporate needs and provide assistance in the implementation process. Used effectively they integrate all facets of the business, including planning, manufacturing, sales, and marketing. Used ineffectively they can jeopardize the survival of the complete organization. As such, any organization seeking to implement such a solution needs to be absolutely clear as to the reasoning, objective, and measurement criteria for the implementation, and audit's involvement at the planning stage is critical.

 CLOUD COMPUTING

As with many "new" technologies, cloud computing has its roots in many not-so-new technologies. One of the fundamental concepts of cloud computing is the sharing of computing resources among a community of users.

Many predecessors of the concept existed as far back as 1961 where the concept of "computing organized as a public utility" was introduced by Professor John McCarthy of the Massachusetts Institute of Technology (MIT) (now Professor Emeritus) in a speech given to celebrate MIT's centennial, that computer time-sharing technology might lead to a future in which computing power and even specific applications could be sold through the utility business model like water or electricity. This concept is fundamental to cloud computing as we now know it.

Cloud computing has been defined by the National Institute of Standards and Technology (NIST) in NIST Special Publication (SP) 800-145[2] as including five key characteristics:

1. On-demand self-service
2. Broad network access
3. Resource pooling
4. Rapid elasticity
5. Measured service

They noted three specific delivery models:

1. *SaaS* (Software as a Service)
2. *PaaS* (Platform as a Service)
3. *IaaS* (Infrastructure as a Service)

As well as four deployment models:

1. Public/Consumer
2. Private
3. Hybrid
4. Community

The overall concept is that the client computing should be a model to facilitate network access on a *convenient* and *on-demand* basis to a *shared pool* of computing resources that can be configured with *minimal management effort* or *interaction* with the service provider.

Cloud Advantages

From a strategic planning basis cloud computing may be seen to have several advantages.

▪ **Capacity Planning.** The *cloud provider* carries the responsibility of ensuring the needed resources are available on demand to the *cloud users*. Thus the management of resources to ensure the desired Quality of Service *(QoS)* is transferred to a third party, at a fee.

▪ **Variable Load Planning.** Prior to the implementation of cloud computing, capacity planning typically required allowance for maximum loads upon hardware and networks. In some cases, this could involve the acquisition of equipment two or three times the capacity required to handle the normal load. The service level for variable load handling can become part of the service agreement with the Cloud Computing Provider.

▪ **Pay as you go.** By utilizing cloud resources on an as-needed basis, companies avoid the capital expenditures involved in initial capital investments for hardware, software, facilities infrastructure, power, and networking capabilities. In addition, the operational costs involving hardware maintenance, software licensing, and personnel costs may be significantly reduced. The costs involved in system upgrades are also transferred to the Cloud Provider.

▪ **Response time.** As part of the service level agreement, both response time and availability can be predetermined and facilitated by the Cloud Provider due to their far larger infrastructure and ability to automatically shift resources to handle large workloads (e.g., by using virtual machines).

▪ **Time to market.** Because the user no longer needs to procure, install, and test operating system upgrades, application upgrades and middleware together with the need to train support staff on these changes, system upgrades and enhancements can be implemented and running live in minimal time.

Cloud Disadvantages

It should not be assumed that the implementation of cloud computing is all advantage. Several potential significant disadvantages exist and must be evaluated before the decision is made on the implementation. Among these, perhaps the most significant are:

▪ **Confidentiality and security.** The organization's most sensitive data will exist on, potentially, the same platforms as their competitors. In addition, the data may be exposed to the staff of the cloud-computing provider. In addition to their own competitive concerns, organizations may be bound by several types of national or international regulations regardless of their decision to delegate the responsibility for compliance to a third-party provider who may exist in a country covered by different national regulations.

▪ **Mission-critical applications.** These may now be the responsibility of a third party and, despite penalties for non-compliance within service-level agreements, when an application is deemed mission-critical, organizations may be reluctant to outsource the responsibility. This can result in hybrid systems as part within the cloud and part in-sourced. This can bring about the worst disadvantages of both systems while obviating many of the advantages.

- **Availability and contingency planning.** While the responsibility for ensuring adequate backup and disaster-recovery plans to protect the users activities in the event of natural or manmade disasters may rest with the service provider, some organizations may be unhappy to accept cloud providers' guarantees' without the ability to independently audit the effectiveness and testing of the plans.
- **Service-level agreement monitoring.** Where service providers have large client bases and no direct control over workload intensity across these clients, monitoring and enforcement of service level agreements at the client end may be problematic. Plans for monitoring and enforcement must be part of the initial negotiation of the service-level agreement.
- **Cost control.** Although the "pay-per-use" utility model of cloud computing may appear to provide an infinite supply of resource on demand, clients have to determine, plan, obtain, manage their computing budget, and pay for their own finite demand. Cloud computing enables consumers to pay for only what they use; however, consumers must diligently manage their demands so that they use only what they can pay for.

 NOTES

1 Claude Baudoin and Glenn Hollowell. *Realizing the Object-Oriented Lifecycle*. Upper Saddle River, NJ: Prentice Hall, 1996.
2 http://csrc.nist.gov/publications/drafts/800-145/Draft-SP-800-145_cloud-definition.pdf.

CHAPTER SEVENTEEN

Information Management and Usage

T HIS CHAPTER COVERS the areas of information management and usage monitoring. Measurement criteria such as evaluating service-level performance against service-level agreements, quality of service, availability, response time, security and controls, processing integrity, and privacy are examined. The analysis, evaluation, and design information together with data and application architecture are evaluated as tools for the auditor.

WHAT ARE ADVANCED SYSTEMS?

Since computer systems first came into being in the early 1950s they have been used to perform common business applications, thus automating many routine, labor-intensive business systems. Because these early systems handled and processed normal business transactions, they were called Transaction Processing Systems (TPS). These systems, in their latest forms, still play a critical role in the organization and management of today's enterprises. It was soon realized that the data stored within the computer system could be better utilized in helping management in decision making in their respective functional areas, thus creating the Management Information Systems (MIS) of the 1960s and 1970s. Such systems were characterized by the production of reports at a managerial level to assist managers in performing their duties. During the 1980s, improvements in technology resulted in systems that were considerably more powerful and considerably less expensive. Personal computers spread throughout organizations to handle a variety of tasks independently of the Information Technology (IT) department. At the same time, new systems are evolving to provide real-time assistance in solving complex managerial problems not handled by the traditional MIS. Such systems became known as Decision Support Systems (DSS).

Certain systems will always be developed or enhanced in order to achieve compliance with legislative changes; however, organizations today are seeking considerably higher returns for their investments in advanced systems.

A modern variation on such integrated systems is the enterprise-wide systems such as SAP and Oracle. These systems, when fully implemented, are used as an Enterprise Resource Planning (ERP) systems and come with their own organizational risks.

Unlike its predecessors, such a system crosses departmental and organizational boundaries and this is not without "political" implications. While bringing undeniable benefits to some areas of the organization, others may see the implementation as involving a great deal of work on their part for little local benefit. This can, if not adequately addressed, develop into significant resistance to change from those who do not see immediate benefits to themselves. In order to achieve successful implementation, users at all levels within the organization who are affected by the new system need to have their expectations built as to the performance levels and benefits to be expected.

This area is critical to the achievement of appropriate service-level agreements and system-quality expectations. The size and complexity of such projects ensures that, regardless of the management effort expended on pre-planning, problems will occur and resistance will be encountered. The best that can be achieved is to minimize anticipated problem areas and maximize organizational commitment by creating realistic expectations.

Measuring the Deliverables

When such systems-development projects are embarked upon in the full knowledge of the potential problems, the organization does so in the expectation of significant and quantifiable benefits to the organization. In order to fully achieve these benefits, metrics must be produced to indicate the progress toward quantifiable and beneficial objectives. In many cases anticipated benefits are expressed in general terms with significant difficulties encountered in measuring their attainment. This is not surprising given the history of IT in improving efficiencies by automating manual processes. Under such circumstances quantification of benefits was relatively simple. Today's modern complex systems are geared more toward enabling organizational *effectiveness* that can be considered more difficult to measure.

For IT to facilitate effectiveness, a clear understanding of the organizational value chain is required in order to optimize the business processes in that chain. Porter[1] identified five activities within a typical value chain, namely:

1. Inbound logistics
2. Operations
3. Outbound logistics
4. Marketing and sales
5. Service

At each stage of the value chain, IT can enable the organization to differentiate the value provided to its clients from its competition. IT can assist in driving down costs in order to create a low-cost differentiation or can be used to reconfigure the value chain to create a value-added of differentiation. The implementation of ERP packages to implement value chain changes requires tailoring of the systems to achieve an appropriate combination of interventions in order to facilitate the achievement of the organization's revised goals. Without a clear understanding of the goals in each of the five activities within the value chain for a specific organization, IT intervention can do more harm than good.

By examining the relative criticality of each activity within the value chain, the value of specific IT interventions may be quantified resulting in a metric specifically designed to measure the effectiveness of a given intervention. Such metrics are normally designed to indicate to management where improvements in performance against set objectives are being achieved on a consistent basis or not, as the case may be.

Since each organization's objectives are different, their strategy to achieve their objectives will be unique and therefore both the interventions and the measurement metrics must also be unique. The normal financial measurement metrics such as return on investment (ROI) are inappropriate given the pervasive effect such interventions have on organizational performance as a whole. By the same token, a pervasive effect should not be used as an excuse to avoid any form of measurement. Unless benefits can be quantified there can be no measurement of the cost of failing to achieve the benefits.

The Balanced Scorecard[2] previously discussed facilitates the measurement by monitoring for specific areas of activity linking intangible benefits to observable consequences. By dividing the organization into financial performance, customer relationships, operational excellence, and the ability to learn (all observable consequences), the scorecard allows a monitoring of improvements in the value chain.

 ## SERVICE DELIVERY AND MANAGEMENT

As integrated systems attempt to cater to the needs of all users, processes, and corporate objectives, the complexity itself introduces unexpected outcomes, errors, and an inability to achieve its desired objectives. In order for systems implemented to achieve the dramatic improvements in the achievement of organizational objectives, service delivery becomes critical to ensure that users' expectations are met consistently and that problems encountered are addressed swiftly and effectively. This is not simply a question of speedy resolution of problems but the implementation of good business practices to ensure that predictable problems are, indeed, predicted and overcome prior to significantly impacting the user or system.

Service management involves the provision and operation of services to the organization by IT. In recent years integrated frameworks for the delivery and management of IT services to the customer had been developed, principally International Standards Organization (ISO) 20000 and its forerunner British Standards (BS) 15000.

Implementation of ISO 20000 was intended to produce significant advantages to the organization including the alignment of the services provided by Information Technology with a strategic objective of the organization. By creating a formal framework for measuring current service-improvement projects, it is possible to benchmark against best practices across the industry. This is intended to lead to competitive gains through the promotion of cost-effective services delivered in a consistent manner. In achieving this, IT can undergo a paradigm shift from reactive processing to proactively driving.

ISO 20000 comprised two parts. Part One is a theoretical base intended to facilitate the effective delivery of managed services to meet the requirements of both the organization and specific customers. It comprised 10 sections, namely:

1. Scope
2. Terms and Definitions
3. Planning and Implementing Service Management
4. Requirements for a Management System
5. Planning and Implementing New or Changed Services
6. Service Delivery Process
7. Relationship Processes
8. Control Processes
9. Resolution Processes
10. Release Process

Part Two of ISO 20000 describes the best practices for service management and stands as a "code of practice" for the implementation of effective service management.

Part Three (scenario based advice) was published in 2009.

In April 2011 the second edition of ISO/IEC 20000-1 (Part 1) was published.[3]

Part Two is due in a few months. Part One is now a longer document with more requirements. In addition, there has been a rationalization of certain of the clauses. Clauses 3 and 4 in edition one have been merged into Clause 4, which now covers all of the general requirements for the Service Management System and has been aligned with ISO 9001 and ISO 27001 requirement statements.

Some of the recommendations that existed in Part Two are now compulsory within Part One (e.g., the requirement for service catalog). Clause 5 has been expanded to include requirements as part of the design and planning of new and changed services.

A new Clause, 4.2, has been included to require the service provider to demonstrate that they control their suppliers effectively. Part One classifies the "other parties" to include their control of processes operated by internal groups within the same organization as the service provider, but not under the service provider's direct control. This is most likely for an in-house service provider.

Auditing Service Delivery and Management

From an auditing perspective, IT service delivery can be seen as an operational audit within the areas of configuration and change management, capacity management, service-level agreement management, business-continuity management, and incident management. In each of these areas the auditor must clearly understand the objectives sought by the organization and the measurement criteria applied by management in order to judge the accomplishment of those objectives on an ongoing basis.

Configuration and Change Management

As we approached the year 2000, many organizations spent large amounts of money creating an inventory of assets specifically utilized to provide IT services to the organization. This was done in order to determine that all components were fully Y2K compliant. Since that time, however, many organizations have allowed this inventory to fall by the wayside. This resulted in many organizations losing track of what assets they own, where they are, and who is accepting responsibility for them. Configuration management involves the maintaining of a detailed inventory of the resources within the organization used in the provision of IT services. This goes beyond the traditional asset register because it must address hardware, software, networking, and knowledge. It must also include information regarding the existence, location, state of maintenance, problems encountered, and resolution action taken for each of the resources.

The IT auditor must evaluate the process by which configuration management is carried out in order to achieve a corporate objective.

In the absence of an effective change-management process, an "insignificant" change in an operating environment such as the implementation of a new service pack can cause disruption or even failure within a critical operational area. Change management ensures that all changes to all critical resources are implemented in a planned and authorized manner.

The auditor must ensure that, in addition to ensuring appropriate authorization of such changes, appropriate planning, testing, and implementation and, in case of a change failure, the development of a fallback plan take place.

Capacity Management

Every individual resource contributing toward the provision of IT services will have a limited capacity. This includes human resources as well as technical resources. Effective Information Systems assisting in the growth of the business inevitably increase the workload on all resources. Effective service management requires effective capacity management whereby the capacity of each individual component is known and monitored, and the load balanced in order to achieve optimal performance.

Once again, the auditor will seek to determine that appropriate processes exist to monitor resource utilization and to plan for the increasing capacity inevitably required.

Service-Level Agreement Management

Service-level agreements (SLA) are written commitments that the IT function will deliver a level of service acceptable to the user and are normally defined in terms of response time, uptime, hardware and software error rates, and problem-resolution time.

It is common for IT to utilize software solutions to record incidents and the resolution and the auditor must determine whether SLAs exist, are adequately monitored, provide meaningful management information, and are used by management to improve service delivery.

Business-Continuity Management

This area is fully discussed elsewhere within this book. The auditor would typically seek to determine that business-continuity management is carried out, has been assigned to a knowledgeable person with appropriate authorities, is tested regularly, and works.

Incident Management

Incident management involves the recording of all incidents as they happen including the quantification of the impact on the business (users impacted, customers affected, impact on corporate image, impact on revenues and cash flow). In addition the process also seeks to determine the actual cause and appropriate resolution of the problem.

The auditor must determine that an appropriate and effective incident-management process has been implemented within the organization and is monitored appropriately by management.

Auditing Information Management and Usage

Much of the evidence the auditor will seek in auditing the usage and management of information will exist in clerical records, procedures, and people's minds. As such the traditional audit techniques will come into play in order to obtain such evidence. In addition, however, much of the evidence regarding the effectiveness of management's controls in this area will reside within the computer and, as such, will require the appropriate tools and techniques to extract the evidence in a form usable by the auditor.

COMPUTER-ASSISTED AUDIT TOOLS AND TECHNIQUES

Computer-Assisted Audit Tools and Techniques (CAATs) used will include Test Data Generators for testing all or selected parts of the systems, and Flowcharting Packages to document data flows and controls. Certain of the more sophisticated systems may require the use of specialized audit software to carry out tasks that are unique to the audit of those systems and that, due to the nature of the systems, file structures, and so on, could not effectively be carried out by generalized audit software.

Generalized audit software is standard software produced for auditors to permit non-programmers to carry out a variety of normal audit procedures on a variety of systems. They are designed to be as flexible as possible while remaining as user-friendly as possible. Utility programs are those standard software products that handle everyday facilities such as sort, copy, print, backup, restore, and so on. They can be invaluable audit tools in a complicated systems environment. Non-audit-specific software includes those programs that were never designed as audit tools but may easily be utilized by auditors. They include report writers and general interrogation packages.

In addition to these tools, the auditor has available automated tools to assist in the areas of risk analysis and audit planning. Automated working papers are possible using certain software packages and, in an extensive audit of a complicated and integrated system, such a tool may be invaluable.

These tools and techniques are covered in more detail in Chapter 23.

 ## NOTES

1 M. E. Porter. "What is Strategy?" *Harvard Business Review*, vol. 74, no. 6, 1996.
2 W. Van Grembergen, R. Saull, S. De Haes; "Linking the IT Balanced Scorecard to the Business Objectives at a Major Canadian Financial Group," *Journal of Information Technology Cases and Applications*, 2003.
3 Lynda Cooper, *A Guide to the New ISO/IEC 20000-1: The differences between the 2005 and 2011 editions*, BSI British Standards Institution, 2011.

CHAPTER EIGHTEEN

Development, Acquisition, and Maintenance of Information Systems

T HIS CHAPTER INVESTIGATES the development, acquisition, and maintenance of Information Systems (IS) through Information Technology (IT) project
management involving the planning, organization, human resource deployment, project control, monitoring, and execution of the project plan. The traditional
methods for the system development life cycle (SDLC) (analysis, evaluation, and design
of an entity's SDLC phases and tasks) are examined, as are alternative approaches for
system development such as the use of software packages, prototyping, business process
reengineering, or computer-aided software engineering (CASE). In addition, system
maintenance and change-control procedures for system changes together with tools
to assess risk and control issues and to aid the analysis and evaluation of project characteristics and risks are discussed.

PROGRAMMING COMPUTERS

Computers are electronic adding machines that are told what to do and how to add up
by pre-defined instructions called programs. Commercial computers are programmed
in binary (base 2) mode, which consists of 1s and 0s as shown below. In the early days
of computers, programmers coded each instruction as a combination of 1s and 0s and
entered these directly into the computers. It took about six months to write a fairly basic
program. This was the first-generation language.

```
0110   1001   1110   0101
1101   1110   1011   1010
0001   0101   0101   0011
```

This was obviously slow and expensive and a better way to program had to be found. Early attempts used *Symbolic Code.* In these cases, programmers wrote in a cryptic code such as the following one. The use of such codes (Easycoder, Atlas Autocode, NEAT, Assembler, etc.) speeded up systems development considerably and a simple program could now be written in two weeks. These were the second-generation languages and many are still in use because of the efficiency of the programs produced by such a language.

```
PACK        RATE,RATE1

L           HRS,HRS1

MVC         REG,4
```

Attempts were made to make programming into a more programmer-friendly science by introducing languages that were more meaningful to a casual reader. This resulted in two separate streams of programming language coming into being, the scientific languages such as FORTRAN (FORmula TRANslator) and ALGOL (ALGOrithmic Language), and the business languages such as BASIC (Beginners All-purpose Symbolic Instruction Code), CLEO (Clear Language for Expressing Orders), and COBOL (COmmon Business-Oriented Language). These were third-generation languages.

FORTRAN

```
PAY:

REGPA=RATE*HOURS

CALL TXCAL

DED=WITTX+UIF+INS+PENS
```

COBOL

```
NET-PAY-CALC-ROUTINE.

MULTIPLY RATE BY HOURS-WORKED GIVING NORMAL-PAY
```

Fourth-generation languages such as Natural or ADS-On-Line do not follow the "first do that, then do this" approach of the previous generations. These "non-procedural" languages attempt to focus on the question "What do you actually want the computer to do?"

Periodically someone claims to have invented a fifth-generation language (LINC, etc.) and there are claims that, in the future, microchips will be so specialized that no languages will be required. Examples are cited that you do not have to be a programmer to drive a car whose engine is fully computer controlled. Artificial intelligence or expert systems also drive this belief.

PROGRAM CONVERSIONS

Although today's programming languages are more sophisticated than early versions, the computers themselves still operate in binary mode and somehow the programming language of choice must be converted to the 1s and 0s. This gives rise to two types of code. The *source code* the programmer writes and the *executable object code* the computer runs.

This conversion is achieved by means of *Compilers, Assemblers,* and *Interpreters.* Compilers are programs that take third-generation source code and create a permanent copy in binary form. Assemblers handle second-generation languages in the same manner. Interpreters behave in a different manner. They take third-generation source code and create an executable copy but they do *not* create a permanent version of the object code and they perform their function *line-by-line.*

From a control perspective, this split between source and object codes is critical because any person with access to the source code can change a program to make the computer do whatever he or she wants. A system that is written using interpretive code is thus highly susceptible to alteration and fraud.

Programs are written by computer programmers, end-users, systems designers, operators, auditors, and anybody else who feels like writing programs. This anarchy can rapidly lead to systems chaos if not properly controlled. Only authorized programmers and end-users should be permitted to write programs.

NO THANKS SYSTEMS DEVELOPMENT EXPOSURES

Failures of control during systems development can lead to a variety of business problems including:

- Erroneous management decisions
- Unacceptable accounting policies
- Inaccurate record keeping
- Business interruption
- Built-in fraud
- Violation of legal statutes
- Excessive operating cost
- Inflexibility
- Overrun budgets
- Unfulfilled objectives

These may prove to be minor annoyances or major business catastrophes to the business depending on the organization and the system concerned. The primary causes of development exposures may be summarized as:

- Incomplete economic evaluation
- Management abdication

- Inadequate specifications
- Systems design errors
- Incompetent personnel
- Technical self-gratification
- Poor communications
- No project "kill" points
- Temptations to commit computer abuse
- Incoherent direction

SYSTEMS DEVELOPMENT CONTROLS

In order to achieve controlled systems, the development process must itself be controlled. Major controls in this area are:

- Methodology (SDLC)
- Staff hiring policies
- Training
- Technical review and approval
- Management review and approval
- Audit participation
- Systems test phase
- Post-implementation review
- Checklists
- Documentation

Project management controls to assist the process involve periodic schedule reviews, work assignment, performance monitoring, progress monitoring, and status reporting and follow-up. In other words, an IT project is managed no differently than any other long-term, high-cost engineering project.

The project planning elements would include appropriate project guidelines, work breakdowns complete with start and completion dates, and an effective monitoring mechanism to measure against agreed schedules.

SYSTEMS DEVELOPMENT LIFECYCLE CONTROL: CONTROL OBJECTIVES

Control objectives for each stage of the SDLC would typically include:

- Methodology
  - Formalized, structured methodology will be followed
  - Roles and responsibilities will be clearly laid out and adhered to
  - Methodology will be kept up to date and in step with current developments

- Project Initiation
  - Each new project will be clearly scoped prior to commencement of work
  - The user department will be involved in the definition and authorization of new or modified systems
  - Team assignments will result in the use of appropriately skilled and qualified staff
  - Commencement of each phase will be preceded by the appropriate authorization
- Feasibility Study
  - Alternative courses of action will be evaluated in order that an appropriate solution be selected
  - Technological feasibility of the recommended solution will be assured
  - All relevant costs will be included in the cost/benefit analysis
  - All relevant risks will have been identified and quantified
  - Project approval will be given by the appropriate management based on knowledge
  - Project will be capable of being monitored through its existence
- Systems Design
  - Design methodology is appropriate to the proposed system:
    - Life cycle
    - Structured
    - Database
    - Skeletal
    - Prototype
  - Documentation will be created to standard
  - Input validation requirements will be appropriate
  - File structures will be as per departmental standards
  - All requisite processing steps will be identified and designed into the system
  - All programs will be fully specified as per departmental standards
  - All sources of data required for the system will be identified and approved
  - Security requirements of the system will be fully defined and approved
  - Audit trails will be appropriate and approved
  - Documentation of the system design will adhere to departmental standards
  - Overall design shall include the design of appropriate testing and verification plans
  - Design approval will be obtained from the appropriate levels of management
- Development and Implementation
  - Written narratives of all programs in the system will be available and up to date
  - Commercial packages selected will be compatible with existing operations and departmental policies
  - Use of contracted programming staff will be approved and the quality of their work will be contracted for
  - Operational documentation will be produced according to departmental standards
  - Training plans will be produced for all users of the system
  - Program testing will be comprehensive and effective

- System testing will test both for functional capability as well as operational efficiency
- Conversion planning will ensure smooth conversion to the new system
- Acceptance testing will be comprehensive and carried out by the appropriate staff
- System Operations
  - All organizational controls will operate as designed and intended
  - Cost monitoring will ensure efficient operation of the system
  - Modifications to the system will only be permitted via the departmentally authorized route

 ## MICRO-BASED SYSTEMS

In-house developed micro-based systems should be subject to the same controls but often are not. They are frequently substituted for IT-developed systems and suffer the same SDLC problems but, in addition, they fall under nobody's control, and may be developed by amateurs with no specifications, documentation, controls, cost/benefit analysis, or backups.

 ## CLOUD COMPUTING APPLICATIONS

With the surge of interest in cloud computing, many organizations are going through the process of deciding if they should move to a cloud environment or not. Should the strategic decision be made to make such a migration, specific operational decisions are required to facilitate the move.

Before an application can be migrated into the cloud, it needs to be a web application. This may seem like common sense but it can trip up the unwary. It is important that before migration the organization understands the technological aspects of what is being transferred. Differing cloud environments support differing technologies including the database management system as well as management and monitoring tools.

Ensuring the application will run in an adequate security environment means that the organization must understand its own internal security requirements and determined the Cloud Provider's trust level in delivering security against these criteria.

In choosing the specific cloud platform on which to run the application, transferability may become a significant determinant. If the application system requires modification to fit the specifications of a specific cloud platform, it may lock the organization into one specific architecture thus restricting the ability to transfer to another Cloud platform should it be deemed desirable.

In a *Thought Leadership White Paper* published in April 2011, IBM defined three basic principles governing the detailed components of each application module:[1]

1. **Efficiency principle**. Systems to be designed with a view to cloud-scale efficiencies and time-to-deliver/time-to-change metrics while ensuring elasticity, self-service access, and flexible sourcing. The overall objective being to drive down costs per service instance hour and time to response.
2. **Lightweight principle**. Utilizing an eliminate-standardize-optimize evolutionary approach in order to support lightweight service management policies, processes, and technologies. In this principle, the objective is to ensure radical exploitation of standardization in cloud environments in order to reduce management costs.
3. **Economies-of-scale principle**. By leveraging the identifiable commonality in cloud service design, management components and infrastructures can be optimized across cloud services in order to drive down both capital expenses and operating expenses while reducing the time to market.

Considerations for Cloud Computing Applications ultimately depend on whether the organization intends to implement as:

- Software as a Service (SaaS) where the intention is to use the provider's applications running on a cloud infrastructure. The applications are then accessed via various client devices through a thin client interface such as a web browser.
- Business Process as a Service (BPaaS) where business-process services may be any business process delivered through the Cloud Service Model via the Internet with access attained via web-centric interfaces and exploiting web-oriented cloud architecture (see Cloud Computing in Chapter 16).

 NOTE

1 http://public.dhe.ibm.com/common/ssi/ecm/en/ciw03078usen/CIW03078USEN.PDF.

CHAPTER NINETEEN

Impact of Information Technology on the Business Processes and Solutions

T HIS CHAPTER EXAMINES the impact of Information Technology (IT) on the business processes and solutions, business process outsourcing (BPO), and applications of e-business issues and trends.

 IMPACT

In recent years, IT has changed with the business world as well as the rules and conditions under which business is transacted. The introduction of concepts such as globalization, e-commerce, Internet technology, and cloud computing, and the rapid changes in global market demographics have made flexibility and reliability survival attributes of the corporation. External opportunities and threats, including economic, social, and cultural, may dramatically change the organization's need for processing information in the future.

Given that the basic tenet of strategy formulation is to take advantage of external opportunities while avoiding or reducing the impact of external threats, revisiting business processes in order to make best use of corporate information becomes a survival issue. Accordingly, auditors and accountants must be fully up to date on how technology impacts their business, their industry and related industries, the legal and regulatory environment, and their profession.

The appropriate uses of IT impact management strategies as well as the roles and relationships within organizations; the skills, tools, and methods of implementing strategies; and the cost structures. These, in turn, invoke new rules for competitive advantage and require new training and skills. The traditional view of separation of duties changes with the elimination of many of the control structures caused by computerization. New economies of scale are possible and price/performance ratios are changing dramatically. Such changes have introduced continuous control monitoring (CCM) and continuous auditing.

CONTINUOUS MONITORING

The concept of continuous monitoring and auditing has been known for many years with little progress being made on the implementation. With the arrival of Sarbanes-Oxley's section 404, an imperative has arisen to be able to determine, on a timely basis, when control deficiencies have occurred. A need now exists to be able to quantify the impact of potential control deficiencies and gain assurance over the ongoing effectiveness of controls. Traditionally, transactional data analysis has been used to test internal controls for exceptions to control procedures. In a modern system, such analysis frequently occurs too late to be of any practical value.

One solution is to independently test all transactions' compliance with controls at the point at which they occur. This model requires the identification of the individual control points for each business process area using an appropriate control framework, the establishing of tests to validate specific controls in order to identify suspect transactions, execute the tests on an ongoing basis, and notify the appropriate personnel of any transactional failures so that both the individual transaction and the control problem can be rectified.

This continuous monitoring model is intended to provide a method of determining the effectiveness of control structures in a timely manner in high-volume systems.

At a more advanced level, transactions can be scanned to seek patterns of abnormalities in order to raise alerts with known abnormalities being updated in the same way as virus definitions.

The value of continuously monitoring and auditing controls has been discussed and experimented with extensively over recent years but it is only now, with the advent of sophisticated computer models, that it is technically feasible and desired. It should be noted that continuous audits are viable only when there is a high degree of automation of the business processes together with adequate staff training and acceptance by management of this revised approach to the traditional annual audit.

Depending on the objective of the exercise, continuous monitoring can fulfill a variety of needs. According to Gartner:

> Within the governance, risk, and compliance (GRC) marketplace, continuous controls monitoring (CCM) is a set of technologies that assist the business in reducing business losses from fraud or failure to follow rules governing financial transactions, and improving performance through continuous monitoring (CM) and reducing the cost of auditing through continuous audit (CA) of the

automated controls in ERP systems or other financial applications. CCM contributes value to risk management and compliance initiatives in three ways:

1. Lowering compliance costs—A CCM solution can reduce the cost of audits by eliminating much manual sampling and minimizing the time it takes to gather documentation.
2. Improving financial governance—CCM can increase the reliability of transactional controls, improve auditor trust, and increase the effectiveness of antifraud controls.
3. Improving operational performance—CCM controls, such as those that monitor duplicate payments, incorrect discounts, or misapplied warranties, go beyond what most people consider compliance. By preventing these violations of business rules, CCM can improve key financial processes and increase the availability of working capital.[1]

From a purely security perspective, within their overall risk management framework, National Institute of Standards and Technology (NIST) takes a different viewpoint on continuous monitoring. It defines the objective of continuous monitoring to be the determination of whether the complete set of planned, required, and deployed security controls within an information system will continue to be effective over time in light of the inevitable changes that will occur. Continuous monitoring is therefore seen as a key activity in assessing the security impacts on an information system resulting from planned and unplanned changes.[2]

The framework calls for a six-step process:

Step 1.   Categorization of Information System
Step 2.   Selection of Security Controls
Step 3.   Implementation of Security Controls
Step 4.   Assessment of Security Controls
Step 5.   Authorization of Information Systems
Step 6.   Monitoring of Security Controls

In either event, continuous monitoring does not provide a comprehensive, enterprise-wide risk-management approach. It does, however, provide a key component in the risk-management process. Over-emphasis on continuous monitoring at the expense of a comprehensive risk management approach can significantly reduce the effectiveness of the overall management of risk.

To be effective, the risk management strategy requires the active involvement of information system owners as well as the suppliers of common controls all operating within the overall mission and strategic objectives of the organization. Generically, continuous monitoring as well as continuous auditing can play a significant role in fraud prevention and detection as well as ensuring compliance with policies, plans, procedures, laws, and regulations and generally monitoring both risk compliance and effective risk management. They therefore become significant factors in ensuring corporate risk oversight and transparency.

From an audit perspective, many of the computerized tools currently in use by IT audit can be readily adapted for continuous monitoring/continuous auditing purposes. Generalized audit software such as IDEA and ACL may easily fulfill this purpose.

 ## BUSINESS PROCESS OUTSOURCING

BPO involves the contracting of a specific business task, such as accounts payable or call center support, to a third-party service provider. In most cases BPO is intended to be a cost-saving measure for non-core tasks that an organization requires but does not depend upon. Using technology, it has become increasingly easy to contract to a third-party service provider outside of the organization's own country (i.e., *offshore outsourcing*).

There is a difference between BPO and the outsourcing of IT itself. BPO involves handing over a function that may be dependent upon IT but is a distinct business function separate from core IT operations. It becomes critical that an organization can recognize a core competency (a function that *must* be done well) and differentiate this from an activity that will not "make or break" the organization and which could be handled more efficiently or effectively by a third party. Companies frequently choose to outsource where there is a lack of in-house strength or in order to streamline business processes. In smaller organizations many back-office functions may be outsourced so that limited management time may be devoted to the core business of the company. Larger organizations typically choose the outsourcing route in order to improve their efficiencies.

Outsourcing of a specific business process may be a critical component within a larger business strategy such that the process itself becomes re-engineered to more closely fit the organization's requirements rather than simply changing who is performing the function.

BPO should not be confused with "contracting out," which involves the organization purchasing goods or services from another organization. In this scenario, the purchaser still controls the process by defining exactly what is required and how it should be supplied. An outsourced process transfers control of the process to a supplier such that the only thing specified by the purchaser of the service is the outcome desired. The purchaser of the service determines the scope and performance levels desired from the supplier of the service with predefined measurement criteria. If this is not done specifically and precisely, it can lead to the supplier providing a service that was not agreed upon and is less than the buyer understood would be provided for the price paid. In seeking a service provider, companies must decide whether they require a niche provider or a provider of general services.

Outsourcing tends to be unaffected by fluctuations in economic performance. Cutting costs in times of poor economic performance or rapid expansion in times of good performance can both create a desire in organizations seeking alternatives to in-sourcing of non-core operations.

In all cases, poor governance of the process combined with poor communication can have a major negative impact on the organization leading to increased costs, inefficiencies, and ultimately business collapse. In addition, leakage of confidential information from the outsourced service provider may prove catastrophic without adequate safeguards.

Outsourcing can lead to staff apprehension regarding job retention and resentment over job losses of friends. This, in turn, can lead to a decline in commitment and to possible reputational risks to the organization.

In addition, the IT auditor should be aware of the risks potentially facing a supplier of the BPO service. In order to ensure continuity of service, the purchasing entity will require assurances that sufficient controls exist and are effective within the service supplier.

Risks faced could include changes to the legal environment under which the service provider operates and which potentially could affect the conditions under which services are provided, costs of such services, or the legal rights of the purchaser within the applicable legislation.

Changes of control within the service provider as a result of management changes, restructurings, mergers, and acquisitions could potentially have significant impact on the terms and conditions under which services are provided. In order to satisfy the requirements of multiple users, the service provider may decide to change the processes by means of which the service is provided. While this is normally done to enhance the service level to clients, for some clients it may mean unacceptable changes to the manner in which the service is delivered. This could be as a result of technology changes or changes in the regulations governing the provision of such services.

Once again the IT auditor must seek advance confirmation of the contractual terms under which the services are provided and under what circumstances the provider can unilaterally change such processes together with the termination rights of the service purchaser.

 ## E-BUSINESS

E-business is a wide-ranging phenomenon utilizing the greater level of connectivity among organizations and people to create opportunities that did not previously exist. At its most basic, companies can make their products and services directly available to enormous, untapped markets. At a more advanced level, e-business incorporates the use of customer relationship management systems and enterprise systems to create a vehicle for radical reforms to business concepts.

These opportunities are typically seen as covering business-to-business (B2B), business-to-consumer (B2C), or consumer-to-consumer (C2C). In addition, the opportunities for the integration of web-based technology into the supply chain of the core business processes abound. Alternatively, web-based technology can be used to achieve strategic change through direct interaction with the customer or through a distribution channel. Providers of such services may be existing organizations utilizing new technology to achieve a more effective delivery of existing goods and services, or new entrants to the market providing products and services that did not exist prior to the advent of the Internet. The third category is the creation of new business ideas involving the generation of a new set of services based upon analysis of perceived needs rather than delivery of hard products from a portfolio available to the organization.

There are many potential opportunities within the implementation of e-business. The obvious one is a conversion to low-cost administration systems in order to streamline the workplace. Additionally, the advent of such technology facilitates the re-engineering of the core business process of the organization leading to potential improvements in cost structures, servicing of service requests, and turnaround of customer orders. Within a B2B environment electronic data interchange can be used to streamline procurements electronically and ultimately the creation of a virtual vertically integrated business for closer ties with suppliers and better supply-chain management.

E-marketing is a rich source of new customers reachable globally in a manner hitherto unimagined. In addition to the new customers, the potential to influence buyer behavior via electronic marketing by leveraging the information base of existing purchasing behavior is enormous.

Social Media, one of the most culture-changing trends in e-business, is the integration of social media across all activities. The use of social media strategies for marketing, sales, and service across the enterprise not only increases market awareness of an organization's products and services but can also provide valuable feedback on customer experience and branding. The use of technology such as Twitter is now fully recognized as a means of rapid deployment of information to consumers in matters ranging from one-day price reductions to early warning of severe weather, depending on the nature of the organization.

Mobile Applications, smartphone applications facilitating self-service mobile transactions, allow existing customers access to organizational functionality while non-customers can obtain insurance quotes or prices from comparison shopping sites, as well as locate shopping venues and restaurants. This can permit the organization to effectively gain competitive advantage by the placement, flexibility, consumer appeal, and prioritization of the applications.

In addition to interfacing with consumers and customers, increasingly employees are seeking mobile support from the organization in order to achieve cost and performance objectives. With increasing numbers of employees working away from the head office environment, mobile connections via laptops, personal digital assistants (PDAs), mobile phones, and tablets can give flexible access to business processes.

Naturally, in this environment, one of the IT auditor's key concerns is the adequate protection of information both on mobile devices as well as in communication transit to ensure confidential business information is not lost or stolen. In addition, the consistency and accuracy of information held on mobile devices would require effective real-time synchronization.

NOTES

1 French Caldwell and Paul E. Proctor, *Magic Quadrant for Continuous Controls Monitoring*, Gartner Research Publication ID Number: G00174594, March 2010.
2 Special Publication 800-37, Revision 1, Applying the Risk Management Framework to Federal Information Systems (February 2010).

CHAPTER TWENTY

Software Development

THIS CHAPTER LOOKS at the software development design process and covers the separation of specification and implementation in programming, requirements-specification methodologies, and technical process design. In addition, database creation and manipulation, principles of good screen and report design, and program language alignment are covered.

 ## DEVELOPING A SYSTEM

The process of developing a new computer system is commonly known as the Systems Development Life Cycle (SDLC) and consists of a finite and predefined number of tasks, which include:

- Analyze
- Design
- Code
- Test
- Retest
- Redesign
- Retest
- Run
- Audit

As seen in Chapter 11, the SDLC can come in a variety of forms including the *water-fall, iterative spiral,* or *vee,* to name but three. Regardless of the model taken SDLC will split these tasks into:

- **Feasibility study** to decide if the project is worthwhile
- **Outline design,** which involves analyzing and designing the new business system
- **Detailed design,** where computer programs are specified, file layouts designed, and access rules laid out
- **Code, test, and implement,** where programs are written, tested, and signed-off
- **Conversion,** which involves acquiring data and converting it into the new formats
- **Installation** and live running
- **Post-implementation review** to determine what went wrong with the SDLC process itself

Feasibility Study

Systems proposals come from a variety of sources and for a variety of reasons. They may come from the Board of Directors as a result of a business change. They may come from the government in the form of legislative changes. They may be intended to improve business effectiveness or efficiencies. They may come because technology itself has changed. They may be required as a response to competitive forces. In all cases, the feasibility of the change and cost-desirability of the change must be assessed. This requires that the outline systems design be known. This outline design expresses the business requirements of the proposed system in terms of user-requirement specifications.

Outline Design

These user specifications identify:

- Business functionality required of the system
- Actions the user is to take
- Decision rules to apply
- Services required of Information Technology (IT)
- Methods and timescales for user/IT interaction
- Assignments of responsibility

Detailed Design

Once the outline design has been agreed, the detailed design must be defined. This involves taking the business design and interpreting it into "computerese" by defining:

- File and record layouts
- Operational constraints
- Processing logic definitions
- Access rules

Problems at the specification stage include:

- **Availability of user staff** whereby the IT staff may be left in isolation to develop the system as they see fit.
- **Access to the right level of staff.** In many cases the user staff available are not of the right authority level or lack the required knowledge base to carry out the appropriate liaison.
- **"Technology lust,"** which results in a constant search for the latest technology regardless of whether it is genuinely required.
- **Over-extended timescales** with no measurement points in between. To allow effective project planning, timescales should be short with measurement milestones at frequent intervals. In addition, over-extended timescales can mean that key staff change in the meantime, business objectives change, costs will escalate, and hardware/software may become obsolete.
- **Inexperienced staff** can cause complications because many organizations increase staff for large-scale projects with staff who may be technically competent but have no understanding of the organization, its objectives, or standards.

Acquiring, Testing, and Implementation Planning

Once the system has been designed successfully, it must be implemented. This involves reviewing the scope and objectives to ensure they are still appropriate, reassessing the timescales/budgets/benefits based on the fuller understanding of the system now available, drawing up implementation timescales based upon the full detailed design, allocating responsibilities for the development of the various parts of the system, and conducting a pre-implementation review to ensure that problems encountered in the past do not recur.

Implementation itself typically involves:

- Programming
- Coding
- Prototyping
- Unit testing
- Test linking to other modules
- Documentation
- Installation
- User acceptance testing
- Parallel running
- User training
- File conversion
- Live running

Some of these activities may be conducted simultaneously, but that, again, is a factor of the effectiveness of the project planning process.

Conversion Activities

Conversion activities are, perhaps, the most crucial for the ongoing success of systems implementation. If the auditor is not involved at any other stage of systems development, it is critical that they be involved here. Once the system has been developed and adequately tested, conversion from the previous manual/computer system must take place. This will typically involve:

- Acquisition of data
- Identification of sources
- Development of conversion programs
- Sanitization of input data
- File conversion

System conversion is a major task and requires that strict control be enforced. Poor conversion may jeopardize the whole project on a "rubbish in— rubbish out" basis. Audit involvement is essential. Care should be taken to ensure that audit's role does not become one of IT quality assurance. The auditor's role is to ensure that management has adequate controls to ensure that conversion was effective.

While all this is going on, maintenance must continue on the current systems.

Given the limited resources available to the IT auditor, the focus must obviously rest on the highest-risk project areas. Ideally, auditees should be involved throughout a project's life cycle and not solely post-implementation. System conversion becomes one of the more critical focus areas for the IT auditor. This area is further covered in Chapter 22.

Installation

Once all of the previous stages have been completed, the new software must be migrated into the production environment and immediately falls under the organization's normal access-control procedures regarding live systems.

Post-Implementation Review

The final stage of the SDLC is the post-implementation review. This is used to determine what went/is going wrong with the development process as well as what went/is going right. Its objective is not to determine flaws in the developed system but to refine the SDLC itself by identifying skill shortcomings and improving control techniques.

From this point onward the system will be subject to ongoing maintenance for the normal business reasons such as design corrections and "bugs," mandatory changes, enhancements as the business changes, or accommodation of technology changes.

The SDLC is used to control the generation of programmed systems with the objective being to produce a quality system, as specified, on time, within budget.

CHANGE CONTROL

Once the system has been created, it is essential that it remain intact and impossible to change in an unauthorized or uncontrolled manner. The process of achieving this is called *Change Control.* Change control's objective is to ensure risk is controlled, not introduced, during a change. This means ensuring that:

- All changes are authorized
- All authorized changes are made
- Only authorized changes are made
- All changes are as specified
- All changes are cost effective

The changes thus controlled are known and planned changes. The procedures involve ensuring prior authorization for all changes, supervision of the change process, adequate testing of all changes, and user sign-off on all changes.

Normal systems maintenance involves checking, changing, and enhancing the system to make it more useful in obtaining user and organizational goals. Major causes of program maintenance include:

- New requests from users and managers
- Bugs or errors in the program
- Technical and hardware problems
- Corporate mergers and acquisitions
- Governmental regulations that require changes in the program

In addition, many application systems are more than 15 years old, and some are as old as 25 years. Maintenance may take the form of a patch, a new release, or even a new version. The cost of maintenance can be staggering. For older programs, the total cost of maintenance can be up to five times greater than the original cost of development. The average programmer can spend between 50 and 75 percent of his or her time on maintaining existing programs as opposed to developing new ones.

Periodically things will go wrong with a system that require a repair urgently. Such changes are not known in advance and are commonly executed and permission sought retrospectively. Such changes are controlled using *Problem Management.* Problem Management's objective is to control systems during emergency situations arising from unforeseen changes. Typically this will involve bypassing normal control mechanisms and may require direct programmer access to live data. This must be controlled separately and must involve user authorization, even retrospectively.

 WHY DO SYSTEMS FAIL?

It is an unfortunate fact that computer systems do fail from time to time. The distance between these times or *mean time between failures* is, to a large extent, governed by events that took place during systems development. The most common of these problematic events are:

- **Poor support from top management.** Top management, even today, is content in many cases to leave the development of new and strategic systems to computer staff rather than being actively involved. This means that, commonly, IT staff develop systems blind and the systems become the IT staff's interpretation of what they believe management should be looking for. This interpretation is not always accurate.
- **Poor staff attitude.** Taking their lead from top management, the users whose system it is from inception will also sit back in many cases and leave the detail to the IT staff. An attitude of non-ownership of the development process becomes prevalent.
- **Unclear business objectives.** In many systems, the development was triggered by a senior manager deciding "wouldn't it be a good idea if we had a system which would. . ." The system is then developed to meet the requirements of a single manager rather that the needs of the organization.
- **Management and users unsure of their needs.** It is a common occurrence that, when asked to express their needs for IT support, management and users are unable to clearly articulate what they require. Auditors find the same problem in asking managers to explain how control is achieved. Think how difficult it would be to explain to someone exactly how you breathe. You have done it all your life, but you would find it difficult to explain it. It is part of the job of the IT staff to uncover the users' business needs and translate these into potential computer support areas.
- **IT personnel unfamiliar with user needs.** In many cases the IT staff assigned to a given project have no fundamental understanding of the actual business process to be computerized. Once again this leads to misinterpretation of users' wants and needs.
- **Additional user requirements not previously specified.** A common complaint of users is that "the system can't do. . ." while the IT response is "you never told me you wanted to. . ." One of the most difficult areas of systems analysis is ensuring that your understanding is fully comprehensive and that all requirements are known.
- **Changes in user requirements.** Many systems are developed over a number of years. During that time the business needs of the final user will change due to a changing business environment, new technology requirements, and changes in managerial personnel and style. Systems must be developed with as much flexibility as possible both during development and in the final product.
- **Organizational changes during the project.** Given the life of many IT projects, it would be unusual for a project to reach completion without staff changes. At either the IT or user end, loss of a key member of the development team can create havoc and seriously jeopardize the project's viability.
- **Failure to understand interrelationships between parts of the organization.** In today's environment, most systems implemented are designed to be integrated systems treating the business needs of a disparate group of corporate

functions. In many cases management, even at the director level, are so specialized that they have no in-depth understanding of how other areas of the business function. As a result many integrated systems do not adequately map onto the business functionality required.

▪ **Over-optimistic file conversions.** Acquiring data and converting from previous systems is a critical task and should be treated as such. This does not happen overnight and of its own accord. It must be planned for and appropriate resources committed.

▪ **Poor quality input for file conversions.** In many cases the source of the data to be converted for the new system is suspect and such data must be "sanitized" or cleaned up prior to systems implementation.

▪ **Poor documentation.** Many systems development projects work on the basis that the documentation will be completed at the end of the project after the new system has stabilized. This is a source of two distinct types of problems. First, the time when documentation is most needed is at the design and coding stage to ensure the final system is what was intended. Second, completion of documentation at the end results in rushed and scanty documentation, and occasionally no documentation because project time has run out.

▪ **Inadequate system and program testing.** Testing of systems is a complex business involving programmers, systems analysts, users, and internal auditors. The first three must satisfy themselves that the system performs as desired in that it does everything it is supposed to and conversely does *not* do the things it is not supposed to. The auditor's role is to satisfy himself that the testing has, in fact, been done and been done to acceptable standards.

Appropriate controls to ensure the development process is an overall success have already been covered in Chapter 18.

 ## AUDITOR'S ROLE IN SOFTWARE DEVELOPMENT

The auditor's traditional role is to evaluate whether the controls within the project management are adequate to provide assurance that the system will be delivered as required and whether business-control processes have been incorporated in the design of the new or amended system. The auditor's objectives are thus twofold, namely, to ensure that the controls over a substantial corporate investment in the development of systems will produce value-for-money and, at the same time, to ensure that systems developed meet the internal control requirements of the business.

In achieving the latter, the auditor may undertake the role of being a part of the systems-development process. This is frequently seen as a hindrance to auditor independence but should rather be regarded as the most appropriate person undertaking the role of internal control consultant. The individual auditor's independence may be compromised, but another auditor, auditing independently, should find a system with well-designed controls incorporated. This means that during the development process, the auditor will typically be required to participate in selected project-management meetings in addition to risk-assessment, systems-design, development, and systems-delivery meetings in order to provide ongoing, proactive control recommendations.

An alternate role for the auditor is the review of end-stage deliverables throughout the development process without becoming a part of the process. In this role, the auditor will review each stage's deliverables in order to ensure that what was planned from the previous stage has been accomplished and that the planning of the next stage has been refined appropriately.

In either case, the auditor requires an in-depth understanding of both the overall IT development processes adopted and the business process being computerized. The audit will result in the production of formal audit reports to the appropriate business managers including an overall assessment of the controlled progress of the project as well as areas requiring improvement in order to complete the project, as specified, within budget and at an appropriate quality level.

CHAPTER TWENTY-ONE

Audit and Control of Purchased Packages and Services

THIS CHAPTER LOOKS at the audit and control of purchased packages to intro-duce those elements critical to the decision taken to make or buy software. This includes a knowledge of the systems-development process and an understanding of the user's role in training required so that the outsource decision on the factors sur-rounding it may be made to best effect.

Application software may come from a variety of sources including external soft-ware suppliers as well as internal development, and in today's environment as many as 60 percent of implemented systems are packages.

At the conclusion of the system-design stage, the organization possesses complete specifications for both the logical and physical design of the proposed information sys-tem and should have selected the business design that best meets the organization's needs. The make-or-buy decision must now be made depending on a variety of criteria including time constraints, skills availability, costs, and support capabilities. Vendors of possible systems will be furnished with a request for proposal (RFP) detailing the functional and performance requirements of the business system so that an alternative may be costed and evaluated. Sometimes, during this stage, as proposals from vendors are solicited and evaluated, new information becomes available to the organization that modifies its criteria for system selection.

In many cases, a standard package, combined with interface programs written to meet specific corporate needs, can be utilized at a significantly lower cost.

IT audit should be involved in the process of any systems acquisition in order to pro-vide advice and assistance in the control aspects of identification of systems and vendors.

In order to facilitate this, it is critical that IT audit be informed of all systems development projects at the initial stage of project proposal and that IT audit then liaise with the appropriate project management to assure IT audit's involvement during each subsequent phase.

 ## IT VENDORS

Systems acquisition often requires purchasing, leasing, or renting computer resources from an IT vendor, which could include:

- General computer manufacturers
- Small computer manufacturers
- Peripheral equipment manufacturers
- Computer dealers and distributors
- Leasing companies
- Time-sharing companies
- Software companies

In general, software can be purchased as a package and tailored for the organization or developed specifically to meet the unique needs of the purchaser.

Purchasing or leasing software from a software company or vendor, as opposed to developing it in-house, is an attractive alternative for many organizations and offers a number of advantages, including:

- Lower costs
- Less risk
- High quality
- Less time
- Fewer resources needed

It should not be imagined that acquisition of a packaged solution completely removes the need for corporate involvement in the process. Using an externally developed, purchased program involves more than just paying for the package. Certain acts are still needed and the following steps are suggested:

Step 1. Review needs and requirements
Step 2. Acquire software
Step 3. Modify or customize software
Step 4. Acquire software interfaces
Step 5. User testing and acceptance
Step 6. Maintenance and modifications

Care should be taken to ensure that the organization is not defining requirements for features that will never be used but that could significantly add to the costs and time schedule. Installation and tuning of most standard packages take time and effort and should not be underestimated. By the same token future modifications will undoubtedly be required and the cost and ease of maintenance must be considered. The initial stage within the systems acquisition is the issuing of a Request for Information (RFI).

REQUEST FOR INFORMATION

An RFI is normally issued at an early stage in the overall development process in order to gather information on the currently available products when the acquisition of an external package is being considered.

Information about potential vendor products may already be available but, by using a formal RFI, data can be gathered not only on the product but on the overall desirability of doing business with this particular vendor.

At this stage detailed analysis of the intended functional capabilities would not normally have been performed and may eventually include information drawn as a result of the RFI document. In order for a supplier to adequately complete an RFI, certain information must be provided:

- An overview of the organization, the outline functionality desired, and the operational environment (hardware and systems software) currently in place.
- Existing application systems with which interfaces must be developed.

Once responses have been received from potential suppliers, these must be reviewed against evaluation criteria predetermined for acceptance. This review would normally entail the project team and possibly the user's representative. IT may be involved either in their own right or as the user's representative. A danger in this approach is that the subsequent detailed requirements definition may be colored by the project team's awareness of the functional capabilities of specific packages, which could potentially bias selection.

Once the team is fully aware of purchase alternatives, the detailed Requirements Definition (RD) stage begins.

REQUIREMENTS DEFINITION

The detailed RD phase defines the functional requirements of the proposed system in sufficient detail to facilitate selection of the appropriate vendor package. User involvement at this stage is critical as is that of the IT auditor. This document defines the business requirements of the proposed system together with the business controls to be effected within the new system. At this stage, technical specifications may or may not be included. Where there are known technical constraints it would be expected that these be detailed within the RD, particularly if there are predetermined hardware and/or software requirements.

It should be noted that the adequacy and quality of the RD will have a major impact on the degree to which the packaged solution will meet the business requirements of the organization. Quality assurance of this document rests within the IT function and within the user area. Audit involvement at this stage is to ensure that both of these functional areas have completed their appropriate tasks prior to sign off. The user function must determine that the requirements definition accurately and completely reflects the functional requirements for the proposed system. IT must ensure that the requirements definition is feasible within the technical infrastructure in place or envisioned. Audit must always remember that any proposed system will, eventually, require an audit and IT audit may have its own functional requirements to be included within the definition document. Once the requirements definition has been satisfactorily completed, a RFP document is drawn up.

 ## REQUEST FOR PROPOSAL

Where one or more packages meet the requirements defined within the RD document, an RFP will be sent to the vendor to elicit bids for any or all of: delivery, tailoring, and implementation of the packaged solution. This document is based upon the RD document but should also include information on the user base to be supported by the system and a description of the operational environment within which the system will operate. Deadlines for submission and implementation schedules would also be laid out at this point together with the standard corporate terms and conditions relating to normal acquisition procedures. The access control and hardware/software constraints within which the selected package must operate will be detailed for proposed vendors as will the support requirements both during the installation process and from an ongoing support perspective. The supplier will be required to provide details on the nature and level of support provided together with associated costs including the level and experience of support staff to be assigned.

The responsibility and costs of future upgrades can also be determined within this RFP because these can contribute a significant cost over the lifetime of the package. The manner in which upgrades are implemented (new releases, patches, or service packs) should also be specified in this stage. If maintenance of the proposed package remains the responsibility of the supplier, then information regarding the ongoing viability of the supplier company may also be requested. Such information would typically include the number of years the vendor has provided the services and software, client references, financial status, and size of the installed package base.

Once supplier proposals have been received they must be evaluated against predetermined criteria in order for selection to take place. In selecting among package alternatives, the team must evaluate the vendor's track record in completing or installing similar applications as well as the degree to which the package itself matches the business requirements. The financial stability of the vendor must be determined and, if required, financial statements can be requested. Client lists can be used to determine the current level of satisfaction within the installed base of the vendor's packaged solutions. Care should be taken not to simply contact reference sites selected by the supplier in order to present the best possible image.

Where ongoing support post-implementation is to be provided, the proposal will be evaluated against criteria such as the degree of support available within the organization's geographical area including numbers and expertise of support staff. Response times must be specified in the event of a problem identification and costs of ongoing support as well as new releases must be predetermined.

It should be clearly understood by all concerned that, even at this stage, the decision to go ahead has not yet been taken and it may be determined from supplier proposals that the envisioned system is no longer desirable or feasible. IT audit should ensure that a positive decision to go ahead or not is taken and that the system does not proceed by default.

Once the decision to proceed has been made and the supplier selected, the contract is normally negotiated and completed. The terms and conditions of this contract are critical, particularly if the relationship was intended to be an ongoing one. Like any contract, it is drawn up in the honeymoon period where everyone intends and hopes that the relationship will prove mutually beneficial. Like any contract, it is needed most when relationships deteriorate and the terms and conditions become major matters of contention.

 ## INSTALLATION

Once the contracts have been agreed to and signed, the expectation is that the package will be delivered and the installation will happen as a matter of course. The reality is that the installation, even of a package solution, must be planned carefully in order to ensure a smooth implementation. The installation of packages frequently requires some programming of interfaces and customization of the package. As with any other programming this must follow the traditional life cycle including the appropriate analysis, design, programming, and testing phases. Data acquisition and conversion programs must also be planned and, where necessary, data must be sanitized (cleaned up) prior to conversion into the new system.

 ## SYSTEMS MAINTENANCE

As previously stated, systems maintenance involves checking, changing, and enhancing the system to make it more useful in obtaining user and organization goals. Major causes of program maintenance include:

- New requests from users and managers
- Bugs or errors in the program
- Technical and hardware problems
- Corporate mergers and acquisitions
- Governmental regulations that require changes in the program

In addition, many application packages are more than 15 years old, and some are as old as 25 years. Maintenance may take the form of a patch, a new release, or even a new version. The cost of maintenance can be staggering. For older programs, the total cost of maintenance can be up to five times greater than the original cost of development. The average programmer can spend between 50 and 75 percent of his or her time on maintaining existing programs as opposed to developing new ones.

 ## SYSTEMS MAINTENANCE REVIEW

Systems maintenance review is the process of analyzing existing systems to ensure they are operating as intended and may be event or time driven. Factors to be considered in conducting systems reviews include:

- Response time
- Training
- Reliability
- Mission
- Goals and objectives
- Procedures
- Communications
- Hardware and software
- IT personnel
- IT budgets
- Efficiency
- Documentation

Such reviews involve critical evaluation of all systems components. This would include not only the software but also any databases, telecommunications, personnel, and procedures.

 ## OUTSOURCING

Instead of having its IT employees complete systems implementation, an organization can choose to outsource this activity. That is, the organization can hire outside companies to do some or all of the implementation work in the same manner as any other outsourcing of a business process (see Chapter 19).

 ## SAS 70 REPORTS

In the United States, the selection of an outsourcing vendor will typically fall within the remit of the Statement on Internal Auditing Standards (SAS) 70 developed by the American Institute of Certified Public Accountants (AICPA) to provide an auditing standard to deal with service organizations. This is intended to give customers of such service providers an indicator of the effectiveness of the internal controls of the service provider without having to conduct their own audit of the service provider. In practice, the service provider would employ a certified independent service auditor to perform an SAS 70 audit and issue a report that can then be used to demonstrate the effectiveness of the service organization's internal controls to potential customers.

Again, within the United States, the Sarbanes-Oxley Act of 2002, within section 404, requires proof of the effectiveness of internal controls over any aspect of financial reporting including aspects that have been outsourced. SAS 70 reports may be used as acceptable evidence to satisfy the requirements of section 404.

The auditor should be aware that there are two forms of an SAS 70 report:

- *Type 1* reports provide a description of the system of internal controls and an opinion on their design but no indication of testing of the controls by the independent service auditor to determine the effectiveness during the period under review is provided.
- *Type 2* reports cover both the description and opinion as well as the results of the independent service auditor's tests to measure effectiveness of the control structures during the period under review. Obviously, this type of report gives the IT auditor the appropriate degree of satisfaction of the measurement of the adequacy and effectiveness of the system of internal controls at that point in time.

The auditor should also be aware of the requirement to determine the time period during which the SAS 70 audit took place in order to determine the currency of positive findings.

Once again, this may extend to cloud computing (see Chapter 16).

CHAPTER TWENTY-TWO

Audit Role in Feasibility Studies and Conversions

T HIS CHAPTER LOOKS at the auditor's role in feasibility studies and conversions. These are perhaps the most critical areas of systems implementation, and audit involvement should be compulsory.

In considering the auditor's role in feasibility studies and conversions, we must consider where they fall in the Systems Development Life Cycle (SDLC). The typical SDLC comprises:

- Problem definition and feasibility study
- Analysis and design
- Language selection
- Coding
- Testing and debugging
- Documentation
- Conversion
- Implementation

FEASIBILITY SUCCESS FACTORS

As previously noted, acquisition of information systems involves, first, definition of a computer strategy including evaluation of the organizational requirements. Second, establishment of the requirements including a thorough examination and evaluation of potential alternative courses of action. Third, the precise specification of the requirements including interfacing all future systems with existing hardware and software constraints, conditions of supply, and future modification. Fourth, evaluation of alternative sources of supply, and finally, the acquisition and installation of the systems. The second stage is typically carried out via a *feasibility study.*

Factors to be considered in audit involvement in feasibility studies are those surrounding the probability of a successful outcome. These usually focus on the overall desirability of a system from a corporate perspective, as well as the likelihood of successful implementation. Where the system is to be developed in-house as an option, the skills required to develop it must be considered and in any event the skill levels required to run the system will be an obvious factor. Both the cost of development/ acquisition of the systems and the cost of eventual running must be considered. If the degree of integration with existing systems and with existing hardware is low, there may be a requirement for special bridges into these systems. This commonly means that significant parts of the systems being replaced end up being retained indefinitely, and much of the cost advantage is lost. It is part of the auditor's role to ensure that such hidden costs have been considered and that the critical success factors have been correctly identified.

In order to ensure that internal controls over the process are both efficient and effective, the auditor must determine that an effective structure exists to ensure that a proper analysis of the IT requirements can be made and that the acquisition or development procedures can be effective in ensuring the selection and acquisition of appropriate hardware and software. The auditor must determine that the appropriate evaluation criteria have been established in advance of the feasibility decision and the feasibility process has proceeded in an unbiased manner in order to ensure that the IT requirements of the organization are met in the most efficient and effective way.

The feasibility study must cover points such as a clear statement of the business and information processing requirements that the new or amended system is intended to cover. In addition, the integration of the new or amended system into the existing information technology (IT) architecture must be spelled out in order to maximize the probability of success of the developed or acquired system. Where system alternatives have been considered, the feasibility study must demonstrate the strengths and weaknesses of each alternative considered so that the final decision to proceed or not to proceed can be clearly understood. Where an in-house-developed solution is decided upon, the feasibility study may be incorporated into the overall systems definition document but should nevertheless include sections on:

- Overview of the proposed system in business functionality terms
- Technological alternatives considered together with the cost-benefit analysis of each
- Analysis of the alternative courses of actions compared to the selection criteria
- Analysis of the costs and benefits associated with each alternative

- Operational, security, and control risks associated with each alternative together with the control structures considered for risk minimization of each
- Availability of resources internally and externally to carry out the appropriate development or implementation
- SDLC methodology to be applied under each alternative including the monitoring mechanisms to ensure systems delivery on time and within budget

At this stage the auditor must determine that the detailed requirements of the user area have been properly identified and agreed on, and the costs and benefit estimates used in the feasibility study are reasonable and have been derived from the appropriate sources. Time, resource, and cost budgets must be complete and structured in detail so that ongoing monitoring and project control can be effected. The auditor should be alert for information that may be incomplete or inaccurate in selecting among alternatives or, indeed, for selected alternatives that are not supported by the information provided. Where inadequate details have been included regarding the planning, control, and project management of the system, the auditor must draw this to management's attention. While it is not the role of the auditor, at this stage, to evaluate IT skills availability, nevertheless it is part of the role of the auditor to ensure that such an evaluation has taken place in order to ensure the required skills are available both from a technical and business perspective to ensure a successful implementation of the project as well as the ongoing maintainability of the future system.

As can be seen, the feasibility study document is a critical part of the development process in order to ensure a high probability of successful implementation. Insufficient attention paid to this stage can result in the development or acquisition of expensive, inappropriate systems that do not fully address the IT requirements of the organization. At this stage little expenditure has been made but a wrong decision here can lead to many millions being invested to little effect as well as the loss of significant amounts of time in gaining strategic advantages. Too many feasibility studies are conducted as a matter of course, although the go-ahead decision has already been made and the feasibility study is simply intended to support this decision whether or not there are clear benefits, tangible or intangible, and whether or not there are unacceptable risks in either the development process or the implementation of the intended system. *It must be clearly understood by all concerned that an acceptable finding of the feasibility study could be not to proceed with any systems development or acquisition.*

The typical structure of a feasibility study would normally include:

- Executive summary of the business objectives, anticipated costs, expected benefits, and possible risks of the proposed investment
- Business background and needs or opportunities leading to the desire for intervention in this area including any statutory requirements
- The service delivery requirements and impacts on existing IT processing as well as other user functional areas

- Business disruptions anticipated as a result of the development, conversion, and implementation process including the acquisition or training of staff within the user area
- Evaluation criteria used to select among alternatives
- Alternatives considered as specified previously
- Proposed solution in terms of specific deliverables, technical tools required to support the solution, changes to business processes and organizational structures required to support the implementation of the eventual system
- Project management roles and responsibilities as well as the proposed project organization; controls; quality assurance strategies; estimated time frame; and the major project phases, roles, and responsibilities
- Cost-benefit analysis proving the viability and desirability of the proposed solution
- Ongoing maintenance plan together with costs and resource requirements once the system has been fully implemented

Once a decision has been made to go ahead based on the feasibility study, systems development may proceed as detailed in Chapter 18. Once the system is ready to implement, *conversion* to the new system must take place. Again, this is a critical phase that can make or break the successful use and long-term viability of the new system. Audit involvement at this stage is essential.

 ## CONVERSION SUCCESS FACTORS

Successful systems conversion is not a matter of chance. The roles in the conversion process must be defined at an early stage so that those responsible may identify the existing sources of data that will be used as well as identifying any new sources of data required.

An assessment must be done of the quality of data available and any conversion routines required must be identified and specified. Given the one-time nature of such conversion routines, there is a temptation to minimize the system testing. These conversion routines will require their own testing cycle to ensure their effectiveness, but once again this will largely be a factor of the quality of the input data. Rubbish in—rubbish out!

The auditor must ensure that this has been taken into account and any data-sanitation programs required have been developed and implemented. The measuring of the effectiveness of sanitation programs is a management function that may also require auditor evaluation. The overall conversion effectiveness must ultimately be evaluated and conversion signoff must be confirmed.

It is critical that the auditor determine how the conversion process will be verified to ensure the accuracy, completeness, and validity of the data converted.

Conversion audit activities will typically focus on both the planning and implementation of the operational changes required within the organization as well as the data conversions of the IT system itself. The conversion project will already have identified the various operational and system changes to be implemented and the auditor will typically review and assess the overall project plan as well as a project management approach. Tasks for the IT auditor will include:

- Evaluating management's project plan as well as the control and measurement models
- Evaluating the overall systems and data structure design including access control
- Reviewing testing plans and evaluating the effectiveness of actual testing carried out including user-acceptance testing
- Reviewing data-conversion plans and ensuring the accuracy and completeness of data converted
- Reviewing the design of back-out plans intended to recover to current status should problems be encountered on commencement of the new systems
- Reviewing management's control of the actual startup process of the new systems

CHAPTER TWENTY-THREE

Audit and Development of Application Controls

THIS CHAPTER LOOKS at the audit and development of application-level controls including input/origination controls, processing control procedures, output controls, application system documentation, and the appropriate use of audit trails.

 WHAT ARE SYSTEMS?

Systems may be defined as a set of elements or components that interact to accomplish goals and objectives. These systems may take the form of systems that perform business-related activities *(application systems)* or systems that help the computer itself function *(operating systems).* In this chapter, we will concentrate on the auditing of application systems.

Characteristics of good systems include all of the following attributes:

- Accuracy
- Completeness
- Economy
- Reliability
- Relevance
- Simplicity
- Timeliness
- Verifiability

CLASSIFYING SYSTEMS

Systems themselves come in all shapes and sizes and may be categorized into:

- **Simple versus complex.** Simple and complex systems face the normal risks of inaccuracies, incompleteness, and so forth, but complex systems, by their very nature, are more likely to experience these problems because the more complex a system becomes, the harder it is to adequately test and the easier it is for a systematic error to go undetected.
- **Open versus closed.** Open systems are more vulnerable to both errors and attempted penetration. This is a factor of the number of sources of input and output as well as the degree of systems interactivity.
- **Stable versus dynamic.** The higher the degree of instability of a system, the more likely it is that changes will be made to the system that are not clearly thought through with all of the side effects taken into account. Additionally there is a greater probability of rushed and inadequate testing in highly dynamic systems.
- **Adaptive versus non-adaptive.** Adaptive systems are designed to be flexible and all things to all people. As such it is comparatively easy to tailor these systems erroneously. By the same token, non-adaptive systems may be run in an inappropriate manner and be supplemented with unofficial add-on sub-systems with all of their inherent error opportunities.
- **Permanent versus temporary.** Permanent systems are designed, implemented, and maintained within a controlled environment. Temporary systems may fall outside of this system of internal control and may be undertested, undocumented, open for all to change, and generally out of control. They also have a habit of becoming semi-permanent unintentionally.

These categorizations affect the way we approach the audit because the varying categories face different types and levels of risk.

In all cases systems are expected to perform efficiently, effectively, and economically.

 CONTROLLING SYSTEMS

Application systems may be controlled in several ways and by several individuals. At a macro level, system variables will be determined by the business decision maker to cover such items as:

- Will the payroll be daily, weekly, or monthly?
- Will the financial ledger be produced monthly or in 13 four-week periods?

On a day-to-day basis the system parameters, controllable by the system operator, will be used to alter variables that require amendment such as report dates, file control dates, and so on.

CONTROL STAGES

Control over applications is exercised at every stage and begins at the start of the development of the system. This takes two basic forms: control over the development process itself and ensuring adequate business controls are built into the finished product. Major control stages would include:

- System design
- System development
- System operation
- System utilization

 CONTROL OBJECTIVES OF BUSINESS SYSTEMS

In order to achieve the potential benefits of properly managed information systems, they must themselves be generated and operated in order to achieve specific control objectives. These would include the general control objectives of:

- Accuracy
- Completeness
- Validity
- Integrity
- Confidentiality

In addition the differing system types may have additional control objectives as well as differing priorities within the general control objectives. System types could include:

- Order processing
- Invoicing
- Inventory control
- Accounts receivable
- Accounts payable
- Purchasing
- Shipping
- Receiving
- Payroll
- General ledger
- Specialized systems
  - Banking systems
  - Retail systems
  - Manufacturing systems
  - Electronic data interchange (EDI)

GENERAL CONTROL OBJECTIVES

In addition to the overall objectives for information processing of:

- Integrity of information
- Security
- Compliance

there are specific control objectives at every stage of processing, for example:

- Input control objectives
  - All transactions are initially and completely recorded
  - All transactions are completely and accurately entered into the system
  - All transactions are entered only once
- Controls in this area may include:
  - Pre-numbered documents
  - Control total reconciliation
  - Data validation
  - Activity logging
  - Document scanning
  - Access authorization
  - Document cancellation
- Processing control objectives
  - Approved transactions are accepted by the system and processed
  - All rejected transactions are reported, corrected, and re-input
  - All accepted transactions are processed only once
  - All transactions are accurately processed
  - All transactions are completely processed
- Controls over processing may include
  - Control totals
  - Programmed balancing
  - Segregation of duties
  - Restricted access
  - File labels
  - Exception reports
  - Error logs
  - Reasonableness tests
  - Concurrent update control
- Output control objectives over hardcopy, file outputs, and on-line inquiry files
  - Assurance that the results of input and processing are output
  - Output is available only to authorized personnel
- Typical controls here could include:
  - Complete audit trail
  - Output distribution logs

- Program Control Objectives
  - Integrity of programs and processing
  - Prevention of unwanted changes
- Typical controls here could include:
  - Ensuring adequate design and development control
  - Ensuring adequate testing
  - Controlled program transfer
  - Ongoing maintainability of systems
  - Use of a formal Systems Development Life Cycle (SDLC)
  - User involvement
  - Adequate documentation
  - Formalized testing plan
  - Planned conversion
  - Use of post-implementation reviews
  - Establishment of a quality assurance (QA) function
  - Involvement of internal auditors

Testing of these controls will require the auditors to seek evidence regarding their adequacy and effectiveness as detailed in Chapter 9. Where such evidence resides within the information system itself, computer assisted audit tools (CAATs) will probably be required.

 ## CAATS AND THEIR ROLE IN BUSINESS SYSTEMS AUDITING

In order for the auditor to successfully draw conclusions about the effectiveness of the control environment within which applications operate, automated tools (CAATs) will normally be required. These may include:

- **Test Data Generators.** Automatic producers of data for systems testing. These take away the drudgery of preparing test data to try out the various pathways through systems as well as ensuring that all desired avenues of testing are carried out.
- **Flowcharting Packages.** This audit tool is becoming increasingly popular with auditors who wish to document information flow, control points, and operational procedures. Such packages allow the maintaining of up-to-date records with a minimum of re-work.
- **Specialized Audit Software.** Specialized audit software is software written explicitly to achieve some desired audit objective. It may be utilized for any purpose the auditor chooses but, because it was designed to achieve specific ends, it may prove inflexible where audit objectives and sources of evidence are rapidly changing. In addition, such software is typically expensive to develop because there is a limited market.
- **Generalized Audit Software.** This is some of the most common software in use by auditors today. It incorporates general interrogation routines as well as statistical

sampling and prefabricated audit tests. This is seen to be the major growth area for CAATs over the next few years.

■ **Utility Programs.** This software, supplied with the hardware or systems software, is designed to perform common and repetitive tasks such as sorting files, printing, copying, and comparing files. As such these can be powerful tools for the auditor to employ. Because of the power of some of these utilities, special authorization may be required to access the requested data.

Determining which of these tools would be appropriate depends to a large extent on the audit objective and selected technique. These techniques are normally performed for one of two objectives: either to verify processing operations or to verify the results of processing. No single technique is infallible and none tells the whole story so the auditor will typically choose a variety of techniques in order to satisfy multiple objectives. Typical techniques would include:

■ **Source code review.** In this technique, no specific tool is needed, although a utility may be used to produce a printout of the appropriate program source code (the English-like coding for the program). Once printed, the auditor may "play computer" to determine what is actually happening within an application. Source code review can be time-consuming and tedious and may, in the end, prove little. Program source code tends to be voluminous and may be poorly annotated so that the auditor may have a problem in even deciding where to start. Nevertheless it can be a powerful technique to examine the logic within limited parts of a program. This always presupposes that the auditor is satisfied that the source code matches the live running program.

■ **Confirmation of Results.** This technique involves the interrogation of systems containing information about a third party (debtors, creditors, etc.), selecting a representative sample of that data, and requesting confirmation from the third party of the accuracy and completeness of the data. This technique, while it may be the only way to obtain such confirmation, suffers from several drawbacks. It is slow and replies may arrive up to one year later. It is uncertain and in many cases produces a less than 10 percent return. It may be biased in that replies tend to predominantly favor the third party. Few will contact the auditor to insist that their debt has been understated.

■ **Test Data.** This technique involves transacting data through the system in order to achieve predetermined results. Because this affects the files transacted against it, it is normal to use a copy of the live programs and test versions of files. This has its own problems in that the auditor must be satisfied that the program tested is, in fact, a copy of the live program. In addition the volume of test data passed through the system is normally limited and tests must be selected to test both correct data as well as a variety of erroneous data. This is problematic because the auditor may be biased in the selection of test data by his or her expectations of the system.

■ **Integrated Test Facility.** This technique is a variation on the test data technique. In this test the live system and data files are used and a dummy entity, for example, a department, is established on the live file. Test data is then processed along with live data to transact against the dummy department. This has the advantage of testing the live system in the environment under which it normally operates. It also has several disadvantages, among which is the prime disadvantage that the live data is being affected and any unwanted, adverse effects will impact this data. A system error detected thus may, in fact, crash the live system and the auditor will have some explaining to do. Even if this does not happen, the auditor must ensure that the test transactions are removed before live figures, payments, control totals, or even tax records are interfered with. This may not always be possible. Some systems, in order to preserve the integrity of the audit trail, deliberately prevent the removal of transactions.

- **Snapshot Technique.** This technique takes a known transaction and follows it through the processing logic of a program taking "snapshots" at pre-specified places within the program. These snapshots take the form of memory and data dumps. This is a highly specialized technique and requires a relatively high level of computer expertise to interpret the results. It is commonly used by programmers to localize and trace fault areas within programs.
- **Sampling.** Audit sampling is a technique whereby an auditor can examine large volumes of data by looking at a smaller sample in a specific manner that allows the auditor to predict the condition of the larger mass of data with a known level of accuracy and confidence. Prior to computerized techniques being available, many sample tests were discredited due to poor knowledge of sampling theory on the part of the auditor, poor selection technique, and poor interpretation of the results. With today's powerful Generalized Audit Software as well as with the more sophisticated statistical software, such misapplication should be a rarity and statistical sampling is becoming an easy and effective technique.
- **Parallel Simulation.** This technique is used to determine the accuracy and completeness of processing. It involves taking live transaction data and reprocessing it through a program that is not the live program but that theoretically duplicates the functionality of the live program. The results of processing, live and test, are then compared and any discrepancies are investigated. This is most commonly used to test the accuracy of programmed calculations and it is essential that the parallel program originate from a source other than that of the original program.

COMMON PROBLEMS

As pointed out previously, no CAAT is perfect and problems will be encountered with each. Common problems the auditor will encounter include:

- Getting the wrong files
- Getting the wrong layout
- Documentation is out of date
- Prejudging results

The auditor's first rule of thumb should be to never believe what the first printout tells you, particularly if you wrote the program yourself. In any application system the auditor should attempt to identify the controls the user relies on. Bear in mind that documentation is often misleading and that not everything needs to be audited. Program logic should mirror the business logic so that if the auditor understands the business needs and controls, system testing becomes much easier.

AUDIT PROCEDURES

In carrying out an audit of a business system a predefined generic audit program can be followed, namely:

- Identification of users' control concerns
- Identification of system components
- Identification of system processes
- Identification of known controls
- Identification of known control weaknesses
- Verification of controls
- Evaluation of control environment

CAAT USE IN NON-COMPUTERIZED AREAS

Not all CAATs are applicable only in computerized areas. Computerized tools may assist the auditor in:

- Risk analysis
- Sample selection
- Operation modeling
- Analytical review
- Regression analysis
- Trend analysis

Not all of these need to happen on computerized information. By the same token, computerizing the audit does not necessarily mean computerizing the old techniques. New audit approaches are possible and innovative automation can make internal auditing more attractive as a career and thus improve staff stability.

DESIGNING AN APPROPRIATE AUDIT PROGRAM

As with any audit program we start with the *Business Objectives* of the application area under review. Based on those we may, together with the user of the system, define the *Control Objectives.* Having established these we may determine the *Audit Evidence* required to prove or disprove the control objectives. At the same time we will identify the *Source* of such evidence. This will dictate the *Manner* of obtaining the evidence, that is, the *Technique*. Once this has been established the *Extraction* of the required evidence becomes a matter of using the correct tool to apply the appropriate technique. If these steps are properly followed, the *Evaluation* of the results becomes simple because the auditor knows what evidence was sought to prove which control objectives and whether such evidence was indeed found. *Reporting* then follows as per any other audit.

IV

Information Technology Service Delivery and Support

CHAPTER TWENTY-FOUR

Technical Infrastructure

THIS CHAPTER EXAMINES the complex area of the Information Systems/ Information Technology (IS/IT) technical infrastructure (planning, implementation, and operational practices). IT architecture/standards over hardware, including mainframe, minicomputers, client-servers, routers, switches, communications, and personal computers (PCs), as well as software, including operating systems, utility software, and database systems, are revealed.

Network components including communications equipment and services rendered to provide networks, network-related hardware, network-related software, and the use of service providers are covered as are security/testing and validation, performance monitoring and evaluation tools, and IT control monitoring and evaluation tools, such as access-control-systems monitoring and intrusion-detection-systems monitoring tools.

In addition, the role of managing information resources and information infrastructure through enterprise management software and the implementation of service-center management and operations standards/guidelines within Control Objectives for Information and related Technology (COBIT), IT Infrastructure Library®(ITIL®), and International Standards Organization (ISO) 17799, together with the issues and considerations of service center versus proprietary technical infrastructures, are explored.

Effective and efficient information systems are the cornerstones of most enterprises today. For the systems to be capable of adaptation to the variations in business-processes and the introduction of new products and services, an appropriate technical infrastructure is required. The infrastructure is the skeleton upon which the systems supporting the business are overlaid, and the achievement of an application portfolio that effectively supports the business unit in a cost-competitive manner requires an IT architecture carefully designed and tailored for the specific organization.

To properly support the business, this infrastructure must be carefully planned in advance. In the late twentieth century many systems expanded and diversified into an uncontrollable mess of diverse technologies and systems. The challenge for many organizations is the integration of these existing structures into one cohesive, appropriately designed architecture.

An appropriately designed architecture can assist businesses in achieving the correct balance between the strategic needs of business innovation and the requirement for stability within information systems.

Flexibility is the key because business needs and technological advancement enforce a rapidly changing infrastructure requirement. The infrastructure architect has now become an accepted role in the overall IT strategic-planning process and the advent of electronic commerce has considerably increased the complexity of this role.

The balancing of the IS/IT infrastructure into an effective architecture requires expertise in a variety of disciplines in order to seek solutions to business problems through the selection and implementation of appropriate information technology. This architectural design involves the integration of a wide variety of technologies, operating environments, products and services, application environments and networks, as well as a diverse array of hardware and software.

When Y2K occurred, many organizations began an exercise to identify and locate the various components of that infrastructure in order to ensure that they were all year-2000 compliant. For many, this was the first attempt at a consolidated asset register and organizations were shocked to see the networks of incompatibility that had built up over the years. Making sense of this plethora of divergent architectures became critical in achieving a smooth transition to modern, effective information processing. This goes beyond the role of a traditional asset register and seeks to determine environments; problem management; maintenance and release levels of all hardware; system software; communications components; and application software at the mainframe, network, and PC level. This information is fundamental to the implementation of effective *configuration management*.

For configuration management to be effective, four specific functions must take place:

1. **Identification.** The technical specification, location, and identification of all individual components within the technical infrastructure
2. **Control.** The human element with authority to maintain and modify each individual component
3. **Status.** The monitoring of the operational status, versions, release level, patches, and options selected
4. **Verification.** The scrutiny and review of all component information to ensure its accuracy, completeness, and integrity, without which integration cannot be designed

It is critical that all components are fully and accurately recorded so that appropriate combinations can be selected to provide specific services at an agreed-on control level with the knowledge that such combinations can be integrated effectively. In addition, should one component fail, such information will be essential for swift replacement. Where standardization is possible the technical infrastructure can be rationalized and simplified, thus minimizing systems destruction in the event of a failure.

From a systems-development perspective a clear architecture covering the technical infrastructure simplifies the development process and permits the modularization of the application systems. Maintenance may be reduced and reliability enhanced due to the use of standardized components.

ITIL[1] is an internationally accepted approach to IT service management that provides a cohesive set of best practices, drawn from the public and private sectors internationally and supported by the British Standards Institution's standard for IT Service Management (BS15000). It comprises a series of documents used to facilitate the implementation of a framework for IT Service Management (ITSM). This framework defines how service management can be applied within specific organizations. Because it is a framework, it is designed to be totally customizable for use within any form of business or organization that has a reliance on an IT infrastructure. In addition, extensive support for the development of a common manageability infrastructure can be found within the *Enterprise Management Forum*, which "works to develop a common manageability infrastructure that can be used by both applications developers and management system vendors to create an open management environment in which complex solutions can be constructed without artificial barriers to their management"[2] and which is independent of software and systems vendors.

 ## AUDITING THE TECHNICAL INFRASTRUCTURE

With the increasing stress laid upon regulations and standards such as Control Objectives for Information and related Technology (COBIT), ISO 17799, and Sarbanes-Oxley, the requirement to prove adequacy of control over key information processes is now of critical importance. One critical component of such process control is the technical infrastructure and architecture itself. The technical complexity and flexibility of the infrastructure is such that the periodic manual audit may prove ineffectual in providing adequate assurance of the ongoing control effectiveness. Because each individual component has its own internal control processes that may add to, or detract from, the overall system of controls, a simple security review has now become a complex operation involving assessing the adequacy of the security systems deployed including firewall rules, server privilege settings, access control lists, authentication procedures, bypass limitation, and the interaction of all of these. As a result, the concept of *continuous auditing* using the appropriate computer-assisted audit tools (CAATs) comes into its own in this area.

A continuous audit permits auditors to monitor an organization's systems using appropriate sensors and digital agents. Rules of procedure are defined within the digital agents and corporate systems are continuously monitored against the standards with any discrepancies being immediately flagged and reported to the auditor. Such monitoring is done electronically and automatically with the audit routines executing as required in real time, 24 hours a day, 7 days a week and could include technical areas such as:

▪ Monitoring network file shares to ensure that no system offers full access permissions to default, anonymous, or guest logins
▪ Monitoring access control lists to ensure that no changes are made to the individuals or groups authorized to have specific levels of access into live databases

One constraint is the impact such monitoring has on the performance of the organization's systems and the relevancy of such monitoring must be carefully considered prior to implementation. Executing multiple audit routines on high-volume, transaction-based systems in real time could be significantly detrimental to normal business processes. In standard audit operations such as file interrogations, data extraction and analysis can be performed using a generalized audit software package such as the IDEA system downloadable with this book. Depending on the complexity, however, the requirement for immediate reporting in complex areas may require that the audit tools be highly integrated with the organization's systems and operate continuously using embedded audit modules (EAMs) or System Collection Audit Review Files (SCARFs).

One of the most critical considerations in implementing a continuous audit protocol is that auditors require the proficiency to implement and understand the various aspects of information technology at an in-depth level. Continuous auditing can only be implemented if the auditors fully understand the critical control points, rules, and exceptions. The use of specialist IT technical auditors may be required in establishing a continuous audit in such a manner that it can be monitored and maintained by the conventional IT auditor.

It should be noted that there is a distinct difference between continuous monitoring and continuous auditing. Continuous monitoring is designed to obtain information about the ongoing performance of a process or system and is the responsibility of management. Continuous auditing has an audit objective of accumulating sufficient evidence to communicate to management their current status regarding the risk-control objectives of the standardized audit report.[3]

In the absence of continuous auditing, the auditor can still gain satisfaction as to the adequacy of controls over the infrastructure by ensuring that management:

▪ Maintains an activity audit trail with real-time monitoring particularly of those powerful entities within IT who have virtually unrestricted access and who can change the infrastructure at will.
▪ Enforces access-control standards and operator level with particular emphasis on role-based access control to network infrastructures. Once again, monitoring via the activity audit trail should detect and alert the appropriate personnel.

- Bans the use of standardized administrator passwords shared by multiple operators, administrators, and superusers.
- Enforces change management on all infrastructure changes as well as changes to application systems.
- Facilitates independent inspection of infrastructure-management records on demand and independently produced.

The auditor's role in this arena is a highly technical one and will require continuous professional development in order to stay abreast of changes to technology and the control implications to a particular organization's infrastructure.

 ## INFRASTRUCTURE CHANGES

In addition to the purely technical infrastructure, the IT auditor would seek to ensure that appropriate safeguards existed to avoid potential business impacts or change-related incidents associated with developing, implementing, or changing the IT infrastructure. Key controls around the risks inherent in the changing of the IT infrastructure due to ongoing development or maintenance would include:

- The development of an IT strategic plan that needs to be accepted and understood by the user community and that ensures the alignment of IT infrastructure investments and resource allocations with the strategic direction and business priorities of the organization.
- Definition of any organizational-specific need for unique IT infrastructure equipment and services that require effective approval and certification of new technology to meet operational requirements.
- Employment of both business and IT continuity plans in order to ensure that critical operations continue to be available during any period of disruption.
- Implementation of the appropriate general controls surrounding the management and life-cycle of IT assets.
- The implementation of appropriate internal control practices to avoid potential negative impacts on the organization due to change-related incidents associated with the IT infrastructure.
- Up-to-date definition of the roles and responsibilities for the management of IT infrastructure assets are required in order to facilitate the planning and management of infrastructure costs and the realization of benefits.
- In general terms, the IT auditor would review all current aspects of:
  - Corporate technology standards
  - IT infrastructure planning procedures and controls
  - Overall IT architecture governance
  - IT infrastructure investment management
  - IT infrastructure asset life-cycle management

- IT infrastructure change management
- Infrastructure roles and responsibilities

Change management controls for the procurement and upgrade of IT infrastructure items are intended to ensure that change initiatives are implemented in a controlled manner in order to minimize production issues and achieve greater system reliability. It is the responsibility of IT management to ensure that adequate resources exist to support overall IT operations in an efficient and effective manner.

The IT auditor must determine that controls within the overall procurement process are designed and implemented to ensure overall compliance with installation technology standards and that purchase approvals are justified.

COMPUTER OPERATIONS CONTROLS

The structure of the IT department will vary considerably among organizations. The structure of the individual department will obviously depend on constraints such as workload and size but will typically involve an operations function, a project-based or programming function, and technical services.

The computer operations department is the location of the staff involved in the day-to-day operation of the Information Processing Facility. This may be a large mainframe environment or a small local area network. The operations function is responsible for many of the routine tasks associated with the effective and efficient running of an installation including:

- Mounting and dismounting data files
- Loading paper into printers
- Aligning special forms
- Scheduling runs
- Loading programs
- Balancing run priorities
- Responding to operating-system prompts
- Responding to application-system prompts
- Maintaining incident logs
- Performing routine housekeeping tasks
- Responding to equipment failures
- Production of backup copies as defined
- Restoration from backup when authorized
- Handling "unpredictable" conditions

The operations department may itself be subdivided into a control section responsible for monitoring information passing into, through, and out of the computer operations area. In addition, a data-preparation section may exist separately, although considerable progress has been made in moving this function into the user area. Computer operators remain responsible for the accurate and efficient operation of the scheduled jobs on the computer and reporting to the chief operator or shift supervisor. Some organizations additionally utilize a separate tape librarian to handle the vast quantity of physical tapes, disks, and other backup media.

The operation department is responsible for maintaining physical security over the computer, peripherals, magnetic media, and the data stored. This includes the various measures designed to minimize the impact of such disasters as flood, fire, malicious damage, and so on.

Data must be secured against accidental or deliberate disclosure, modification, or destruction. Processing controls must exist to ensure the organization receives complete, accurate, timely, and secure processing of data. This includes on-site and off-site file and program libraries. Included in these libraries will be safety copies of data as well as program source and object codes. Automated library software can assist in ensuring the library is maintained in an appropriate form. Ensuring segregation of duties, handling the distribution of output, and dispatch of hard copy as well as controlling access to spool files and networked printers are usually functions of the operations department.

OPERATIONS EXPOSURES

These include the normal range of exposures including human error, hardware failure, software failure, and computer abuse as well as potential disasters. The prime error areas in daily operation are the data-entry procedures as well as operator commands entered from the control console. Using wrong generations of files or wrong versions of programs can be catastrophic should they occur and an ever-present danger is simple media damage in handling.

OPERATIONS CONTROLS

Controls within the operational area are primarily performance and compliance controls associated with the running of computer jobs. These would typically include the use of:

- Predefined run schedules
- Computer and manual run logs
- System-performance statistics
- Budgetary controls
- Supervision

PERSONNEL CONTROLS

Because operations departments are so heavily dependent upon people, it becomes critical to ensure that the personnel aspects are adequately controlled. This includes segregation of duties where typically we would seek controls to ensure:

- IT cannot initiate transactions
- Systems and programming are independent from operations
- Programmers cannot operate the machine
- Operators cannot access file libraries
- Electronic data processing (EDP) librarian is an independent function
- Data-processing staff have no control over corporate assets

In addition we would seek to ensure that operations staff are rotated, must take holidays, and do NOT attempt to correct programs.

SUPERVISORY CONTROLS

The nature of the operations function makes it very easy to implement effective supervisory controls. Such controls would include the approval of run schedules, the monitoring of operations, the scrutinizing of the daily console log, the reviewing of the manual reports, and continuous observation.

Generally 80 percent of machine utilization can be predicted—but there will always be additional user demands, program reruns, reprocessing of files, and the handling of unforeseen problems.

Machine usage can itself be categorized into machine time spent in:

- Compilation
- Test
- Rerun
- Maintenance
- Production

This allows operational efficiency and effectiveness to be determined. Reruns will always be required from time to time because of machine failure, operator failure, application failure, operating system failure, or simply high volume or critical input errors.

INFORMATION SECURITY

Information Security's role within IT is to ensure that confidentiality, integrity, and availability of data is maintained. In a typical installation, this would include:

- Ongoing and continuous monitoring of the overall environment and security of the facility.
- Ensuring that up-to-date security patches are identified and installed.
- Ensuring that physical and logical vulnerabilities are identified and resolved in a timely manner.

- Limiting logical and physical access to IT resources to those who require access and are authorized to access it. These may appear to be the same thing, but in practice authority is frequently granted where no access is required from a job-function perspective.

OPERATIONS AUDITS

Reviewing an operations area involves initially obtaining an organization chart of the function together with job descriptions of the staff. These would then be reviewed to ensure proper segregation of duties particularly in smaller departments. In addition lists of equipment, networks, system software, and running applications will be required.

Personnel of the operations section have hands-on access to the hardware, software, and networks of the organization. As such, it is imperative that the personnel practices utilized in this section be above reproach. The personnel policies of the operating department must be reviewed with respect to delegation of duties when staff are absent because of illness, vacation, or for any other reasons. Termination procedures must be scrutinized in order to ensure that no weakness occurs when staff leaves.

The view of the operations function itself would include scrutiny of computer room access in order to determine the following:

- Who is permitted access to the computer room?
- Under what circumstances will outsiders be permitted access?
- How is control over computer room access enforced?

Operation of computer equipment would include scrutiny to determine who is authorized to operate such equipment. The auditor must examine operating instructions to ensure that installation standards exist and are followed for operating system software, application software, restart and recovery procedures, and handling disposition of inputs and outputs. Operator actions will be scrutinized to determine whether controls exist in areas where operators have discretion, such as amending parameters while systems are running.

This would also include scrutiny of incident logs covering reporting of system failures, restart and recovery, emergencies, and any other unusual situations. It should be noted that logs will include both manual and automated logs and that comparisons may be done between the two in order to determine that management is informed of all deviations from normal procedures.

From time to time operators may have to cope with emergency circumstances that could involve making urgent modifications to production programs, job control language, and procedure libraries bypassing the normal procedures. In these circumstances it is critical that adequate documentation is maintained of all operator actions and the reasons for these actions. Operators have access to powerful utilities that can typically dump data, production programs, or even memory at execution time. Such access must be monitored closely by management in order to ensure that no unauthorized procedures are carried out. Evidence must be sought of adequate supervision of operators including management or shift supervisor sign-off of logs.

 NOTES

1 OGC—IT Infrastructure Library (ITIL): http://www.itil.co.uk/.
2 The Open Group Enterprise Management Forum: http://www.opengroup.org/management/.
3 Further information on continuous auditing may be obtained from the Institute of Internal Auditors in their Global Technology Audit Guide 3. Institute of Internal Auditors: http://www.theiia.org/download.cfm?file=19897.

CHAPTER TWENTY-FIVE

Service-Center Management

THIS CHAPTER INTRODUCES service-center management and the maintenance of information systems and technical infrastructures. These involve the use of appropriate tools designed to control the introduction of new and changed products into the service center environment and includes such aspects as security management, resource/configuration management, and problem and incident management.

In addition, the administration of release and versions of automated systems as well as the achievement of service-level management through capacity planning and management of the distribution of automated systems and contingency/backup and recovery management are examined.

The key management principles involved in management of operations of the infrastructure (central and distributed), network management, and risk management are outlined as are both the need for customer liaison as well as the management of suppliers.

Before we can examine the issues and service-center management, a clear definition is required of what constitutes service delivery. Service delivery involves the ongoing management of the Information Technology (IT) services in order to ensure that they are in line with the agreement between the service provider and the customer.

Service delivery is generally taken to be the sum total of a variety of individual tasks to be undertaken by IT management.

PRIVATE SECTOR PREPAREDNESS (PS PREP)

Following the events of September 11, 2001, the USA Patriot Act identified specific components of the critical infrastructure in the United States. In addition, it drew attention to the importance of protecting those key resources that are essential to the minimum operations of both the economy and government whether controlled privately or publicly.

As a result of this, the United States developed the National Infrastructure Protection Plan (NIPP) to improve the protection and resilience of the key resources of critical infrastructure components.

In 2007, a report entitled *Implementing Recommendations of the 9/11 Commission 2007 Act—Comprehensive Summary of Public Law 110-53*[1] was enacted into law. Part of this law (Title IX) identifies a program for encouraging the private sector to be voluntarily certified that they are prepared to manage risks appropriately and that the resilience of the organization has been increased.

In June 2010 three specific standards were accepted for compliance, namely:

1. British Standard 25999-2:2007—Business Continuity Management[2]
2. ASIS SPC. 1-2009—Organizational Resilience: Security Preparedness, and Continuity Management Systems-Requirements with Guidance for Use[3]
3. National Fire Protection Association 1600-2010—Standard on Disaster/Emergency Management and Business Continuity Programs[4]

The intention of the standards is to provide private-sector partners with the tools required to enhance readiness and resiliency.

Not all of these standards are applicable to all businesses. The organization must decide which of the standards would be best aligned to the resilience programs already in place.

 ## CONTINUITY MANAGEMENT AND DISASTER RECOVERY

Continuity management is covered in more detail in Chapter 30, but must be seen within a service-center management context as the process by which plans are designed and implemented to ensure the ongoing availability of information-processing services in the event of a serious incident or accident. Continuity is too critical a component for reliance to be placed on purely reactive measures, and a proactive approach to reduce the probability of serious disruption is a critical part. Information processing has now become so integral to achievement of the business objectives of organizations that non-availability of the services can seriously jeopardize the ongoing viability of many organizations and a variety of business sectors. Recent international studies have indicated that organizations suffering a computer disaster without an effective contingency plan in place stand a good chance of being out of business within the next 12 months. The length of time before business collapse is dependent upon the nature of the information services provided and the criticality of availability to the primary business functions.

One common failure in the way in which continuity management is approached is to see it as a purely IT function. This approach removes continuity management from the governance framework of the organization as a whole and regards it as a technical problem to be managed within a technical department. IT-continuity management must be seen as an integral part of *Business Continuity Planning* with information-processing being seen as a critical resource, but not the sole resource, for the ongoing survival of the organization. From this aspect, continuity management can be seen as a partially technical solution to a business problem.

The cornerstone of continuity management is the *Business Impact Analysis*, which identifies the critical processes within the organization and, from an IT perspective, identifies the data flow and support structures provided by information systems. Based upon this, critical systems—both manual and computerized—can be prioritized together with the inter-relationships among them. Once prioritized, risk analysis can be carried out for each of the service areas in order to identify specific threats and vulnerabilities to information and other assets at risk in order to determine the appropriate control structures to balance these threats and vulnerabilities. In some cases, countermeasures may be as simple as reverting to manual procedures or utilizing backup copies of data files. In many threat scenarios this would be insufficient in order to assure recovery and continuity and a full-blown *contingency plan* may be required. The contingency plan must include recovery options for a variety of scenarios from partial interruption to total loss and must be tested and reviewed frequently in order to match the changing circumstances of the organization both in terms of business protocols and IT usage. This should not be seen as an inexpensive exercise because properly done, contingency planning will involve a variety of resources and consume considerable time. Nevertheless, the cost must be viewed in the light of the cost of doing nothing, which could be the cost of bankruptcy.

Having ensured the ongoing availability of information processing resources, the next question that arises is whether the information processing resources provided have sufficient *capacity* to deliver the agreed level of service, in the agreed place, at the agreed time, and at the agreed cost. In order to ensure the appropriate capacity management, workload and performance levels must be monitored over a period of time so that resource forecasting can be based upon demand forecasting and application sizing. Capacity planning is not simply a question of throwing more resources at the problem, but improving process efficiency by systems tuning and elimination of redundant files and processes can significantly reduce systems overheads and lower the capacity levels required to maintain adequate performance levels.

Once it has been established that the information systems will probably survive (continuity management) with sufficient resources (capacity management) to carry out the work, the question of individual *systems availability* must be addressed. Availability does not simply address whether or not an application system exists but also includes the *resilience* of the total system including all components (to withstand failure), the ease with which it can be maintained, the *reliability*, which is normally taken as the average time between failure of a particular system, the ability of the system to withstand internal or external attack with intent to breach *security*, and the ease of *recoverability* in the event of a component failing.

The *financial* aspects of service-center management involve the acquisition of the whole infrastructure and the most cost-effective price to the organization. This does not necessarily mean that the price of acquisition will always be the lowest because the aforementioned aspects such as reliability and availability must be taken into consideration. Only when costs are fully known and attributable to individual business functionality can cost benefit be truly and accurately identified.

The IT auditor needs to be familiar with the many terms encountered in costing service-center management. Most important of these is the distinction among:

- *Direct costs,* which are related to the specific item or function and can be attributed to it in a feasible way.
- *Indirect costs,* which are related to the specific item or function but cannot be attributed to it in a feasible way. Indirect costs are then allocated or assigned using an appropriate cost-allocation method.
- *Variable costs,* which change in direct proportion to the volume of outputs.
- *Fixed costs,* which do not vary with volumes produced, but are fixed, for example, equipment rentals, payable irrespective of usage.

Different costing approaches are used by different organizations with varying implications. These are typically determined not only by the specific business processes or services provided, but also by the types of costing systems generally in use in the sector that the organization is engaged in, such as manufacturing, service, or merchandising sectors.

An IT auditor may become involved in operational audits of the service center to determine the reasonableness of costs attributable to individual user areas. Disagreements commonly arise regarding the assignment of fixed and variable overhead costs to individual users of services particularly in a mainframe environment where the majority of hardware costs cannot be related to individual users using direct costing. In such environments, system usage is a commonly used alternative. Such allocations of cost may directly affect the remuneration of user managers who may seek to have IT costs transferred to other users in order to defend bonuses or departmental profitability.

One final area of cost within a service center is the overall *cost of quality,* which can impact both performance evaluation and customer satisfaction. Specific costs within these areas include *prevention costs* to ensure delivery at the service level specified, *appraisal costs* incurred in monitoring service delivery, *internal failure costs* where costs are incurred as a result of failures within the service center itself, and *external failure costs,* which involve failures detected only after they reach the user and where a service has to be re-performed.

Overall, *Service-Level Management* involves ensuring that the services requested and agreed on with functional user management are delivered on an ongoing basis as and how they have been committed to be delivered. Achieving service-level management is dependent upon the achievement of all the other areas of service delivery previously mentioned, thus providing a framework upon which an effective and efficient range of services can be delivered in a secure manner. This management is normally measured against a *Service-Level Agreement*, which is the formal document specifying the level and cost of services in all of the performance areas of the individual service center. This is a contractual document entered into between IT and the user business areas to which services are supplied. This document specifies the performance criteria, security levels agreed, and cost structures to be applied in delivery of service.

 ## MANAGING SERVICE-CENTER CHANGE

It is well understood that most service-center problems occur when changes are made either as a result of upgrading of system components or as a result of failure in a single component. Managing of change within the server center refers to the making of changes in a planned and managed fashion in order to effectively implement new hardware, software, networks, and security in an ongoing manner within the organization. The variety of change management best known within IT circles is probably the version control or release levels of operating systems and this is commonly used for the distribution of new and changed products into a distributed environment. In addition to these, however, changes within the service center can be triggered by failure of infrastructure or the desire to improve infrastructure and can be hardware based as well as software based.

Software products are available that can assist management in controlling and managing both planned changes and unexpected problems and also handling software bugs and reporting such incidents.

 ## NOTES

1. Downloadable from: http://intelligence.senate.gov/laws/pl11053.pdf.
2. Download at cost from: http://www.bsiamerica.com/en-us/Standards-and-Publications/Available-Management-systems-standards
3. Download free of charge at http://webstore.ansi.org/RecordDetail.aspx?sku=ASIS+SPC.1-2009
4. Download free of charge at: http://www.nfpa.org/assets/files/PDF/NFPA16002010.pdf

Protection of Information Assets

PART FIVE

Protection of
Information Assets

CHAPTER TWENTY-SIX

Information Assets Security Management

THE ADMINISTRATION of security focusing on information as an asset is commonly problematic and may frequently be observed as a patchwork of physical and logical security techniques with little thought to the application and implementation of an integrated approach designed to lead to the achievement of specific control objectives.

This chapter examines Information Assets Security Management and covers Information Technology (IT) and security basics as well as the fundamental concepts of Information Systems (IS) security.

WHAT IS INFORMATION SYSTEMS SECURITY?

IS security may be defined as security around and within the computer and associated equipment as well as the people using it.

The U.S. Federal Information Security Management Act (FISMA) of 2002 defines information security as:

> The term "information security" means protecting information and Information Systems from unauthorized access, use, disclosure, disruption, modification, or destruction in order to provide—

    (A) integrity, which means guarding against improper information modification or destruction, and includes ensuring information nonrepudiation and authenticity;

    (B) confidentiality, which means preserving authorized restrictions on access and disclosure, including means for protecting personal privacy and proprietary information;

and

    (C) availability, which means ensuring timely and reliable access to and use of information.[1]

This includes attempts at authorized access and the use of data-processing resources for unauthorized purposes.

The scope of computer security includes:

- Physical security
- Personnel security
- Data security
- Application software security
- Systems software security
- Telecommunications security
- Computer operations security
- Vital records retention
- IS insurance
- Outside contract services
- Disaster-recovery plans
- Computer crime and fraud

From this it may be seen that the scope of computer security is virtually all-embracing and covers just about everything that could go wrong. One of the most significant aspects of computer security is its capacity to protect us from the effects of our own mistakes.

Implementing effective computer security is complicated by the myths that surround it such as:

- Computer security is a technical problem
- Security breakdowns only happen to other firms
- The major threat is the data processing staff
- The major threat is outsiders
- Only a computer wizard can perpetrate a computer fraud
- Computer security is physical security
- It is not my problem

In all of these myths, the major impetus is toward a situation where nothing needs to be done or, if something must be done, it must be done by someone else. In fact, computer security is the responsibility of all employees from management down.

Management concerns regarding security focus on the effects of a breakdown in security rather than the technical implementations of a security system.

These concerns would typically include that:

- Accounting, financial, and operating records may be falsified
- Unauthorized employees may access confidential data
- Authorized employees may prove to be risk agents
- Employees may sell confidential data to competitors or others
- Computer facilities, hardware, and software may be subject to damage by disgruntled employees
- Unauthorized outsiders may attempt to break in
- Data integrity could be undermined by inadequacies in security
- Computer software that is not secured, is obsolete, or is inappropriate will lose its competitive edge
- Business viability could be jeopardized in a disaster situation
- Insurance coverage on IT equipment may be inadequate
- Self-insurance may be too risky and/or too expensive
- Gap between computer technology and computer security is widening
- Erroneous management decisions based on altered or manipulated data may occur
- Data inadequacies and transaction-processing delays may disrupt business activities
- Data-processing departments' security goals and objectives may not be compatible with the organization's information security goals and objectives resulting in inefficiencies and ineffective security
- Employees may sell software developed internally to outsiders for money

From these it can be seen that the emphasis is on business problems associated with the interruption of effective security measures rather than on the effective implementation of appropriate control techniques. The responsibility for such implementation falls on IT management together with user management. IT audit has a responsibility to examine the technical implementation in order to determine whether executive management's business control objectives are being attained on a continuous basis.

It can also be seen that information assets security management can be reduced to three basic principles, namely, *integrity, confidentiality,* and *availability.*

Integrity of information is the fundamental basis for trust in computer systems. Integrity can be seen as the property that information remains unchanged unless there is a specific intention to change it in an authorized manner. Integrity can be threatened either at a logical level where information can be changed programmatically or its physical level by corruption of the media containing the information. Computer viruses and other malware can corrupt information to the extent that the users of the information may have no choice but to scrap all of the information and start again.

Failure to maintain confidentiality in commercial enterprises could result in problems ranging from minor embarrassment and inconvenience through to disclosure of an organization's results from a multimillion dollar research project and anything in between. At a governmental level, such failure could cost lives in a terrorist situation and could even, alternately, lead to war.

The consequences of denial of availability can be seen on a daily basis at a minor level. Ranging from an automated teller machine (ATM) being offline to a web site being unavailable, we have all been inconvenienced to a greater or lesser extent. At the corporate level, however, extended unavailability and an inability to service customers can be life threatening to many organizations.

Selection of appropriate control techniques will depend upon management's perceptions of the vulnerabilities and threats in the environment and the consequent risk exposure faced. Some risk is desirable because it is normally not cost effective to attempt to eliminate all risk, and management must strike a cost-effective balance in mitigating risk. Risk will be assessed by:

- Assessing the impact of losses or damage to the assets in question
- Identification of vulnerabilities
- Identification of sources of threat
- Selection of the appropriate control techniques
- Assessment of the residual risk after the control techniques have been applied

 ## CONTROL TECHNIQUES

Information asset security can be enhanced by a variety of techniques including preventative controls, access controls, and use of appropriate technology.

Procedural controls will be implemented within both the IT area as well as the user operating environment. It is the combination of specific control elements that overall achieve an adequate security architecture. This would typically include the elements of workstation security, communications security including both encryption and message authentication, as well as reconciliations and general business controls such as segregation of duties and use of authorizations.

 ## WORKSTATION SECURITY

At the physical level we would seek that the workstation be located in a secure area with limited access and be hazard protected against threats such as fire, dust, electrical surge, or even theft.

At the logical level, controls such as restricting the number of users and restricting authority levels, when coupled with adequate user authentication, would be sought.

 ## PHYSICAL SECURITY

Physical security itself goes beyond simple protection against workplace hazards and includes unauthorized access to hardware, software, and documentation. Authorization procedures must be protected to prevent abuse as must originating transactions and outputs. In many organizations physical security falls below acceptable standards.

LOGICAL SECURITY

Logical security involves determining *who* can go *where* and whether they are *authorized*. This means that identification of users as well as authentication of users is a prerequisite for any subsequent security measures such as determining the authority level of users. User access should be granted on a strict need-to-have basis and access rights must be kept current at all times. This includes both local and remote users and involves ensuring that a highly effective mechanism exists for both original authorization as well as the authorization for changes of users.

USER AUTHENTICATION

User authentication involves gaining assurance that a user is who he says he is. Users may be authenticated by a variety of techniques as detailed in Chapter 27.

Unfortunately, user authentication remains vulnerable to identity theft. As long as authentication takes place by means of something the user knows or something the user has, it is possible that the user's identity may be usurped by a third party. Since the computer has no direct knowledge of the user at the other end of the communication, it uses such techniques to confirm that the user is who she claims to be. If this falls into unauthorized hands, then the computer may have no separate preventative mechanism. The organization then falls back on the use of detective controls such as Intrusion Detection Systems (IDSs) to detect potential compromise. This risk increases in an outsourced model particularly in cloud computing and dedicated hosting due to the shared infrastructure whereby an authentication failure in one customer could result in compromise of the system's integrity in other customers.

COMMUNICATIONS SECURITY

Data that is communicated between two computers or between a workstation and a computer must be secured against eavesdropping or even manipulation. This means a combination of securing the communication medium, which could be cables, fiber optics, or even satellite; securing the message, commonly encrypted; and message authentication.

ENCRYPTION

Cryptography is the name given to the use of mathematical algorithms to transform data. Its primary use is the protection of information and it is a fundamental tool used in underpinning many aspects of computer security including data confidentiality, data integrity, user authentication, and electronic signatures. Under this heading, we may see that encryption is a technique whereby a message is rendered unreadable by scrambling the data (*encrypting* it) in such a way that the legitimate recipient can unscramble or *decrypt* the message easily, but an unauthorized recipient would only see garbage. Encryption is probably the most common form of protection and conceals the content of the message. It also makes undetected message corruption difficult.

It should be noted that it may be illegal in certain countries to encrypt data on the normal telephone lines, or Public Switched Networks, to give them their correct title. In such cases, encryption may be permitted subject to the decryption keys having been provided to *escrow agents* where, with the application of the appropriate law or court order, law enforcement officers can gain access to decrypt if required. To avoid abuse, keys may be split and given to several escrow agents.

Many common commercial encryption products are based on *DES* (Data Encryption Standard, a U.S.-licensed product), although many Internet encryption products are based on the two-key or *public key* system.

Encryption does not prevent message destruction/loss or knowledge of the fact that there *was* a message. Nor does it have any effect on message inaccuracy, incompleteness, or untimeliness. Encryption, therefore, must be seen as only one of a variety of control techniques required.

 ## HOW ENCRYPTION WORKS

There are two essential components in encryption, namely, an *algorithm* (mathematical formula) and a *key* (randomizer).

There are many techniques that are used in combination in order to achieve effective encryption. Perhaps the simplest is the Caesar shift attributed to Julius Caesar. In this technique, the alphabet is written down. Beneath it a second alphabet is written but offset left or right by a specific number of characters. The letters to be converted are located on the top alphabet and read off of the underneath alphabet. In the following example the word *BEd* on the top line translates to *EHG* on the bottom line.

A B C D E F G H ..... X Y Z

D E F G H I J K ...... A B C

As long as the recipient knows which direction to move the second alphabet and by how many letters, the message can be decrypted by reversing the process.

The second common technique is the use of a transposition cypher. In this case the message is split into five-letter groups and the order of the letters in each group switched. Again if the recipient knows the order of switching, decryption is simple. Other techniques such as railfence cyphers exist but are not commonly used.

Unfortunately, this simplistic form of cryptography is vulnerable to *letter-frequency analysis* because each letter in a piece of text has a known frequency of use in every language. In addition letter combinations can also be detected and decrypted. As a result a methodology is required to randomize the output of the encryption in such a manner that it is easy to decrypt but difficult to crack. This is done using a secret key as a randomizer into the algorithm.

There are two primary types of key systems. *Single key systems* (symmetric encryption) use one single key to encrypt and decrypt. In this type of system both the encryptor and decryptor must know the key because it is the same key. Where, for example, the file is encrypted on a computer disk, this form of encryption can be highly effective. Probably the best known single key system is the *Data Encryption Standard* (DES), published by National Institute of Standards and Technology (NIST) as Federal Information Processing Standard (FIPS) 46-2 (1993). DES remains the most widely accepted symmetric encryption system and is the standard against which other single key systems are measured.

Where the purpose of encryption is to conceal the contents of a message sent between two individuals, this is less satisfactory because knowing the key in two places doubles the chance of an unauthorized outsider gaining access to the key. In this situation, the *two key* or *public key system* (asymmetric system) is normally more effective.

Using this methodology, one key (A) is used to encrypt the message and the other (B) to decrypt it. The process may be reversed using key (B) to encrypt and key (A) to decrypt. It is impossible in a public key system to encrypt and decrypt the same message with either (A) or (B). Using this technique, an individual or organization can place one key in the public domain while retaining the second key as a secret key. Any message sent to the individual would be encrypted using the public key but only the individual could decrypt it using the private key. By reversing the process, an individual can encrypt using the private key, attach his or her identification and send the encrypted message to a second party. The second party can read the identification of the sender, look up the public key, and decrypt. Any individual intercepting the message could do the same but only the originator could have sent it. Using combinations of single and double public key systems, end-to-end authentication can be achieved such that only one person could have sent the message and only one person could receive it.

 ## ENCRYPTION WEAKNESSES

While it is an important control mechanism, it should not be assumed that encryption automatically gives acceptable levels of security. Encryption techniques suffer from several potential weaknesses including the length of key. The key must be long enough to be difficult to guess, but short enough to be efficient in use. Management of a key may be a problem, particularly in a single key system where both communicating parties must know the key. Despite popular belief, the availability of published algorithms makes secure encryption difficult in today's environment. By applying distributed processing power from a variety of IT sources, many popular encryption algorithms that are already published and available may be readily cracked. The latest high-security algorithms are classified as highly confidential and, in the United States, there are severe penalties for leaking such information. The reversibility of cyphertext is a balancing act between efficient encryption and effective encryption. Easily reversed cyphertext is highly efficient but not very effective, and vice versa. Another problem of a management nature is the use of common words as encrypted passwords. This makes the encryption breakable not by guessing the word, but by repeating the process with a dictionary and seeking matching encrypted results.

 ## POTENTIAL ENCRYPTION

Encryption is used to protect data inside as well as outside the boundaries of a specific computer environment. While it remains within the organization, the data is directly under its control and a variety of control techniques will be used. Once it is placed on communication lines, however, logical and physical access controls cease to be effective and data encryption may be the only choice. It should be noted that encryption is not a technique used exclusively for communication. Sensitive data on disk may be encrypted as well as communications from terminal to modem, modem to carrier, and carrier onward.

 ## DATA INTEGRITY

Within a conventional computer system, it is bordering on the impossible to recognize whether data has been changed, added, or erased without first taking precautions to ensure that such modification would be detected. For example, "problems were found in purchasing" in an audit report could be modified to "no problems were found in purchasing." Controls do exist to detect such eventualities (cyclic redundancy checks and the like) but cryptography can be an effective control to prevent undetected modification. It cannot prevent the modification from occurring but, should it occur, the data will not decrypt and therefore it will be immediately recognized that modification has taken place. Where cryptography fails in maintaining data integrity is where a data file has been completely removed. Under these circumstances, other control mechanisms to verify the integrity of complete disks or disk volumes may be required.

When the integrity relates to transmitted messages, cryptography can be used to derive a *message authentication code* (MAC) from the clear text itself and appended to the data. This may be for all transmitted data or it may involve key fields only. At the other end, the MAC can be re-derived and compared to the one sent. If the two codes are identical, end-to-end message integrity can be assured. A variation on this is the use of public key cryptography to verify the integrity by creating a *secure hash* or *message digest.* The hash is an abbreviated form of the message in encrypted format, which is then signed with a private key. Anyone receiving the message can recalculate the hash and then use the appropriate public key to verify the integrity of the message. If the two values match, the recipient can have a degree of confidence that the message arrived uncorrupted, although not necessarily unread.

 ## DOUBLE PUBLIC KEY ENCRYPTION

This is a more advanced form of a two-key crypto system that is used where the highest levels of communications security are desired. In this form, the plain text is encrypted with the sender's private key (only the sender could have encrypted and sent). The sender then attaches his or her identification. The whole message is then re-encrypted using the receiver's public key and transmitted. When received, the receiver decrypts using his private key (only the receiver could decrypt). The receiver now sees the original message still encrypted with the sender's key, but also sees the sender's identification in clear. With this information, the receiver can identify the sender and look up the public key. The receiver can then decrypt the sender's message using his public key. This gives assurance that only the sender could have sent, only the receiver could receive. This is known as *end-to-end message authentication*.

 ## STEGANOGRAPHY

Steganography has been defined as "the art and science of writing hidden messages in such a way that no one apart from the intended recipient knows of the existence of the message; this is in contrast to cryptography, where the existence of the message itself is not disguised, but the content is obscured."[2]

This involves the hiding of information by embedding messages within other, seemingly harmless messages. Steganography works by replacing bits of useless or unused data in regular computer files with bits of different, invisible information. This hidden information can be plain text, cipher text, or even images. Thus, it is possible to hide a confidential, encrypted message within an innocuous photograph and send that as an e-mail attachment to a third party. Without knowledge that the photograph contains the message, it is unlikely that an interceptor would even know that such a message existed. The genuine recipient would be in a position to extract the message and, using the appropriate key, to decrypt it. This has the added advantage over cryptography that there is no knowledge that the confidential message exists and therefore no attempt will be made to break into the message. Among its uses is the creation of digital watermarks to be used in electronic copyright protection. These "electronic fingerprints" are then hidden in files so that they appear to be part of the original file and are not easily detected. Should the copyrighted material then appear in an unauthorized place, steps can be taken to prove ownership of the copyright. Alternatively, steganography can be used simply to maintain the confidentiality of valuable information. It is becoming a common technique in countries where encryption is illegal or where the authorities have the legal right to demand the decryption key. Steganography can, however, also be used for unauthorized or illegal purposes. Confidential corporate data could be copied and concealed within a legitimate message and then transmitted in a normal e-mail where a firewall could have identified an unauthorized attachment. In addition, pirate software, pirate music downloads, and unauthorized applications or images can be concealed on corporate information resources.

The detection of steganographically encoded packages is not impossible and the simplest method of detecting modified files is to compare them to the originals. This, however, requires that clean copies of the files are available for comparison purposes. If the files containing the packages are not standard files, readily available, it is unlikely that they will have been retained for comparison purposes.

 ## INFORMATION SECURITY POLICY

In order to have effective and integrated assets security management, an *information security policy* is required to provide the fundamental guidelines used in assessing the value of the information assets and the impact should an untoward event occur. At the same time, management can express the level of risk they are willing to accept. The corporate policy must spell out in detail:

- That information is seen to be an important asset of the organization and must be protected as such
- That in protecting its information assets, the organization will comply with all applicable laws and regulations and will ensure that its employees will do so also
- That access to information will be granted to individuals as required to perform their business function
- That the confidentiality of information be maintained whether it concerns personal information on individuals, classified or sensitive information, copyright or intellectual property
- That information must be appropriately protected against unauthorized modification either on computer systems or in communication
- That information be available as and when required to support the authorized and judgment business functions of the organization
- That appropriate control structures will be implemented to ensure the integrity, confidentiality, and availability of information

For such a policy to be effective, organizational commitment to enforcement is critical from the highest level to the lowest and enforcement must be seen to be effective.

 ## NOTES

1 National Institute of Standards and Technology: http://csrc.nist.gov/policies/FISMA-final.pdf.
2 Wikipedia, the free encyclopedia: http://en.wikipedia.org/wiki/Steganography.

CHAPTER TWENTY-SEVEN

Logical Information Technology Security

I N THIS CHAPTER, logical access control issues and exposures are explored together with access-control software. The auditing of logical access to ensure the adequate control of logical security risks using the appropriate logical security features, tools, and procedures are also detailed.

COMPUTER OPERATING SYSTEMS

In the early days of computers, a single group of individuals designed, manufactured, programmed, and operated unique machines. Programming was commonly executed by using *plugboards* where wires were connected to control the basic functions of the computer. Each individual plugboard was a single program that operated on its own to carry out numerical calculations. By the early 1960s, computers were being manufactured as standard machines to be operated in a standard manner and individual job roles became apparent for operators, systems designers, and programmers. It now became a requirement that computers operate, on an ongoing basis, from application program to application program with minimal operator intervention. Computers were becoming more complex with capabilities such as multiprogramming, time-sharing, virtual memory, and spooling, all of which caused complexities in the normal operations of mainframe computers. To simplify the process, software was written to manage the basic functionality of the computer in a standard format and provide an easier interface to the user-written application systems.

In today's networking environment, networked operation systems and distributed operating systems are commonplace and auditors face a confusing array of operating environments and technologies.

Operating systems can be classified into:

- **Mainframe operating systems.** Handling batch processing, transaction processing, and time-sharing
- **Server operating systems.** Serving multiple users at once over a network facilitating the sharing of hardware and software resources
- **Multiprocessor operating systems.** Also known as parallel computers or multi computers, these are variations on the server operating systems
- **PC operating systems.** Intended to provide an easy interface for one single user
- **Embedded operating systems.** Designed for palmtop computers and personal digital assistants (PDAs) as well as controlling single devices such as mobile telephones or microwave ovens
- **Smart card operating systems.** Primitive operating systems normally handling one single function

 ## TAILORING THE OPERATING SYSTEM

Operating systems are, by their nature, designed to be all things to all people. In order for them to perform as desired for a specific user they must be tailored to the needs of that user. This is normally done by selecting among potential alternatives using *parameters*. These parameters can drastically affect the manner in which security is implemented, or is not implemented, within a given operating environment. To a large extent these parameters may be unknown to the user until something goes wrong within the environment. Tailoring the operating system specifically for security goes beyond the scope of this book and is specific to each individual operating environment. Nevertheless, some common fundamentals apply in all operating systems:

- Only authorized personnel should be capable of changing operating parameters and such changes should be independently scrutinized by a knowledgeable third party.
- Powerful utilities that run under the control of the operating system should be accessed by a limited number of individuals because these can, in some cases, bypass other security features of the operating system or even amend the operating system itself directly.
- Critical directories should have access restricted in a similar manner.
- Default users and accounts should either be removed or have their passwords changed immediately upon installation.
- Certain rights can be granted to individuals that go well beyond the normal scope of user rights and can affect internal functionality of the operating system. Once again, the number of users with these rights should be limited.
- Appropriate log files should be created and retained to record security events and these log files must be scrutinized on a regular basis.

- Share permissions granting users and programs access into remote volumes or servers should be restricted on a need-to-have basis.
- Trust relationships between domains should be minimized to as low a level as possible taking into consideration the practicalities of trusts required.
- System integrity should be monitored on an ongoing and frequent basis using appropriate software to verify that system configuration parameters, ownerships, permissions, and application software have not been changed maliciously or accidentally.
- Firewalls should be in place to ensure that only authorized access is permitted and user access outward is controlled.
- Antivirus and malware protection should be utilized to protect the operating system itself against malicious damage.

 ## AUDITING THE OPERATING SYSTEM

In truth it is unlikely that the auditor will ever actually audit the operating system itself. Rather the auditor will examine the *operating environment* and the way in which it has been implemented and controlled in order to ensure that the internal controls within that environment function as intended. Appendices D and E give sample audit programs for auditing typical operating environments.

With no computer assistance available, the auditor can still look for normal controls such as segregation of duties, authorization of work, and so forth. It is also possible to seek abnormalities such as excessive machine usage, regular late hours, and the like. A more effective audit will involve using the computer to audit the computer. This will typically involve the use of Computer-Assisted Audit Tools (CAATs) using generalized audit software such as IDEA, specialized audit software, or utilities.

Prior to the use of such CAATs it is essential that the auditor knows what he or she wants to do. General browsing is expensive, does not inspire confidence and, worst of all, usually does not work. From your manual audit you should know what you want to look at, where to find it, how to get it, and what you will do with it.

Using CAATs in interrogation of files can be highly effective if:

- You know they have not been doctored
- You have the right files
- You know what you are looking at

The auditor should always bear in mind the axiom that, to be wise, never believe what the first printout tells you. Ultimately, the auditor is not there to exercise control, the manager is, and the auditor should check the controls the manager relies on.

From the IT auditors' perspective, the operating system, regardless of which system is being dealt with, comes with a set of security features that may be turned on or off as mentioned previously. In many cases the operating system as it is initially configured is not set for a high security environment. It is at the user's discretion that the security features will be enabled to raise the security level to the one desired for the installation. In auditing the operating environment therefore, the IT auditor seeks to determine which of the security features have been enabled and whether the controlling parameters have been set to the appropriate values to implement the security policies of the organization. To conduct this kind of audit the IT auditor will need a good knowledge of the security features and options within the particular operating system under review. Typically the audit itself will involve the interrogation of the system in order to determine the values of security parameters. In many cases the operating system itself will be supplied with utilities that the auditor may use in order to determine the values of the most common security parameters such as:

- Password rules
- Password history
- Password aging
- Login time restrictions
- Login station restrictions
- Event logging parameters
- Operating-system-access control

Where the auditor seeks to go beyond the capabilities of standardized utilities, specialized audit tools are generally available for individual operating systems.

 ## SECURITY

Access to computer systems consists of both logical and physical access aspects and must, in general, provide support for:

- Management
- Users
- Data processing
- Internal audit
- External auditors

and all parties concerned who have an interest.

 ## CRITERIA

Hardware, firmware, and software co-exist and the auditor cannot regard one aspect in isolation. It is the interaction of these components that provides complexity and the auditor should look upon access control as a complex exercise in risk management technology. This exercise may be aided by utilizing the features within the operating system itself as well as security software. Packages such as Resources Access Control Facility (RACF), Access Control Facility 2 (ACF2), Top Secret, and the like, exist within the IBM Z/OS operating environment but even librarian packages controlling access to source libraries such as LIBRARIAN or PANVALET may assist.

The overall objective is to ensure control over access to data files. This includes the prevention of unauthorized amendments or disclosures and means that access to on-line data files as well as authorization of data file usage and physical security over data files become essential. The usage of standard utility programs to directly access such data files must be controlled whether by authorized users or by the members of the Information Technology (IT) function itself. Functional capabilities within application systems must be segregated, which, in turn, means that there must be highly effective user authentication. If there is not a high degree of certainty that a user is who he or she claims to be, then the use of user profiles defining access authorities becomes ineffective.

 ## SECURITY SYSTEMS: RESOURCE ACCESS CONTROL FACILITY

This IBM-supplied product is designed to run under the control of large-scale operating systems such as Z/OS or Z/VM. The RACF components include the:

- User profile detailing what resources the user can access
- User password (hidden)
- User attributes and authorities
- Group option to protect all new data sets

In addition, there are Connect Profiles and Group Profiles showing what grouping of users exist, who are the members of such groups, and their authorities. Resource profiles also exist containing the resource details, owner-user/groups, Universal Access Code (UACC), and authorized users/groups together with their access authorities.

RACF profiles may be maintained by the person(s) so authorized in user/group profiles. In these contexts, users represent individuals, while Connect Profiles associates users and groups and groups consist of one or more users.

Resources that can be protected by RACF include:

- DASD data set
- DASD or tape volume
- TSO or IMS terminals
- IMS and CICS transactions
- Groups of IMS transactions
- Specific applications
- Installation-defined resource (e.g., "Fetch")

User attributes that may be assigned include:

- **Special.** Full control over RACF profiles
- **Auditor.** Full responsibility for auditing security including logging options and auditing options
- **Operations.** Any maintenance operation on RACF-protected resources such as copy, reorganize, catalog, or scratch
- **CLAUTH.** User defined profiles for specified class of resource (user, dataset, tapevol, etc.)
- **GRPACC.** Group access to data set created by user
- **ADSP.** All permanent DASD data sets automatically defined to RACF
- **REVOKE.** Excludes RACF-defined users from accessing

Given the power associated with these attributes, Special, Auditor, and Operations should be restricted to a minimum number of persons within the site.

 ## AUDITING RACF

Bearing in mind that the purpose of auditing is to ensure that the appropriate controls are in place and not to enforce access patterns or implement security, an audit of RACF may provide the forensic information used to analyze the activities of users after the access occurs.

An audit program to investigate RACF implementation would involve the auditor in several ways:

- Identify RACF-protected resources using printouts from security officer in order to obtain details of:
    - RACF options (e.g., security, console, SETROPS, etc.)
    - Logging options
- Record administration procedures for modification, revoking, emergency procedures
- Identify whether resources subject to audit are protected (e.g., certain data files)
- Analyze resource profile
- Identify users/groups of above resources
- Obtain their attributes/group authorities
- Evaluate adequacy of security and perform tests
- Identify who can control the security (e.g., RVARY, SETROPS, new profiles)

Other RACF considerations for the auditor to bear in mind are that RACF protection can be "zapped" using powerful utilities available within the operating environment. RACF "migrates" among multiple central processing units (CPUs) and user-access authorities may not be transferable. RACF data sets must be backed up and recovered in order to maintain integrity during recovery. User exits may be present that may reduce RACF's effectiveness.

A starting point for an audit program for auditing RACF would include such items as:

- Checking the current attributes for the IBMUSER account (default)
- Determining which RACF users have SPECIAL/AUDITOR/OPERATIONS attributes assigned
- Determining which RACF users have CLAUTH(USER), CONNECT, JOIN, or GROUP-SPECIAL attributes
- Examining the PASSWORD PROCESSING OPTIONS including COMPLEXITY, HISTORY, LENGTH, and ACCOUNT LOCKOUTS to ensure they are in line with installation standards
- Ensuring users have non-expiring passwords unless separately authorized
- Ensuring RACF's own RVARY SWITCH and STATUS passwords have been changed from their original default
- Ensuring that the JES-ATTRIBUTES configuration is set to SAUDIT, CMDVIOL, and OPERAUDIT
- Ensuring that none of the program entries are defined to bypass the password protection (NOPASS)
- Ensuring SMF (Systems Management Facility) logging files are RACF protected
- Examining the SMF parameter definitions to determine appropriate logging is being done
- Evaluating the list of installation defined Supervisory Calls (SVCs) and ensuring none of the SVCs is defined as APF (Authorized Program Facility)=NO
- Determining which datasets have the selection criteria as APF along with the UACC
- Ensuring none of the APF-assigned datasets have UACC=ALTER/UPDATE

ACCESS CONTROL FACILITY 2

An alternative security product is Access Control Facility 2 (CA ACF2), supplied by Computer Associates. ACF2 is intended to prevent accidental or deliberate modification, corruption, mutilation, deletion, or viral infection of files. Within this software all resources are protected by default when it has been fully installed. ACF2 can run in five separate modes of operation controlled by parameter. These Global Systems Option (GSO) mode options include:

- **Quiet Mode.** Disables ACF2 data set rules only
- **Log Mode.** Permits access but records the fact
- **Warn Mode.** Issues warning but allows access
- **Abort Mode.** Logs, issues messages, bars access (default)
- **Rule Mode.** Individual access rules are defined

When run in Rule Mode, by default, ACF2 users may only access data if granted authorization utilizing a rule by the security administrator or the owner of that data.

Rules are used to specify both Access Rules and Resource Rules, which determine user access to specific resources.

Such access rules may be made up of portions of:

- Data set names
- User ID string
- Volume number
- Accessing program name
- Accessing program library name
- Expiration date of temporary rule

Users accessing via ACF2 can be granted more than one privilege. The fundamental privileges that maybe granted to system users include:

- **ACCOUNT.** Allows a user to create, delete, modify, and display logonid records within the limits of the user's scope.
- **SECURITY.** Allows access to all resources, data set, and protected programs.
- **AUDIT.** Displays loginid records, infostorage records, as well as resource and access rules. While a user can display ACF2 system controls a user cannot modify any logonid records or access any resources unless he or she is authorized to.
- **CONSULT.** Displays most fields of loginid records, but only updates nonsecurity-related fields pertaining to TSO. The fields permissible to be modified and displayed by the user are installation defined.
- **LEADER.** Displays most logonid records but with increased authority for updating fields within these records as specified by the installation.

From the IT auditor's perspective, these privileges would be examined to determine the appropriateness and control over their maintenance.

TOP SECRET

Yet another alternative security product is Top Secret, also supplied by Computer Associates. Within this software all resources are also protected by default when it has been fully installed. Top Secret can run in four separate modes of operation controlled by parameter:

- **Dormant Mode.** The system is active but no security checking is done
- **Warn Mode.** Checks violations and logs them but does not prevent them
- **Implement Mode.** Operates as in Fail for defined users and as in Warn if undefined
- **Fail Mode.** All users must be defined and all resources are protected

As with the other two security packages, Top Secret provides system-entry validation, individual accountability, auditing, resource access control, and security administrator control.

Top Secret is user oriented with the authorities held in an encrypted database. Resource access is by ACID (ACcessor ID) and each user has an ACID. Under Top Secret all resources must be owned and there can only be one owner. When operating in full (Fail) mode protection is by default for all methods of access to all DASD data sets. All other resources are protected on an exception basis.

ACIDs are not restricted only to user IDs. They can also be zones, divisions, departments, groups, and profiles. The zone, division, and department ACIDs are the foundation for the hierarchical Top Secret setup. The groups, profiles, and users are the foundation for the functional setup.

From these it can be seen that a security package, while assisting in increasing security levels, is not a universal panacea for all security problems. In order for such a package to be even minimally effective, there is a need for security administration procedures for the establishment/modification/bypassing/emergencies/revoking of protection and the security profiles must themselves be protected.

 USER AUTHENTICATION

User authentication involves gaining assurance that a user is who he or she claims to be. This is fundamental to any internal control because the segregation of incompatible duties relies upon knowing who the persons performing those duties are. While no authentication method is foolproof, in general terms, users may be authenticated by:

- **Something they know.** Authentication based upon knowledge commonly involves the use of Personal Identity Numbers (PINs), which are normally short and frequently written down. Passwords are probably still the most common form of knowledge-based authentication used within computer systems today. Passwords may be any combination of letters, digits, or special characters but should in general be:
  - Hard to guess
  - Easy to remember
  - Well guarded
  - Frequently changed
    Passwords are the most common form of user authentication but suffer from some major drawbacks:
  - The initial password assignment can be a problem in that, if users are not forced to change the initial password, the password will commonly remain unchanged and therefore be known to the security administrator.
  - The system must hold a password file somewhere within itself. If this password file is not adequately protected, it becomes a separate source of vulnerability within the system.
  - Users must remember their passwords and this leads to short, easily guessed passwords. Longer or more difficult passwords are commonly written down and kept near the terminal where they are needed.

- Passwords must be changed periodically to be an effective control. Passwords that remain unchanged for an excessive period of time will frequently become common knowledge.
- Users must enter their password into the system and these passwords can be obtained through the simple expedient of looking over the password holder's shoulder as it is entered.
- In a well-designed password system the default password must be changed by the user before it can be used. Password changes must be system enforced and must exclude previous passwords. Passwords over communication lines must always be encrypted. Passwords must be of a minimum length, contain at least one alpha and one numeric character, and never be displayed on the screen.
- **Something they have.** These are typically hand-held devices such as Smartcards, Microchip cards, or Laser cards, which contain User Identification parameters. These operate in challenge and response mode in that they are used to establish an interactive session with additional random challenges being issued and requiring that a response be keyed into the device. To be effective, the device must be secured at the user end. It should be emphasized that such authentication will not protect privacy and will not prevent the taking over of a session.
- **Something they are.** Biometric measurement is based on physical characteristics of the computer user and may include the use of techniques such as:
  - Fingerprint scanning
  - Voice recognition
  - Optical scanning
  - Holographic recognition
  - Signature recognition
  - Password entry rhythm

  Biometrics are highly effective as an authentication technique, particularly when combined with other authentication techniques, but have a significant drawback in that, should the biometric authentication be compromised, the user may have no way of modifying the authentication.

In the early 1990s Distributed Computing became popular across organizations. In this architecture, each individual user was required to track their ID and password on multiple systems. This resulted in a variety of problems such as inconsistent password control and different systems, failure to remove excess when no longer required, users granted excess of access rights, and even employees sharing their accounts. Because of a lack of centralized control structures, overall governance was ineffectual. In response to this many organizations utilized enterprise IDs to grant access into all systems based on the user profile.

With the advent of cloud computing (particularly Software as a Service [SaaS] and dedicated hosting) the potential exists for the recurrence of the same problems faced in the early days of distributed computing. In such an environment, the IT auditor must seek confirmation that the appropriate governance mechanisms will function within the cloud environment.

BYPASS MECHANISMS

User authentication is intended to gain assurance that a user is who he or she claims to be. Such security controls may be circumvented by mechanisms such as trapdoors/backdoors.

These software loopholes are deliberately left in systems to permit entry in an unauthorized manner. They are normally hidden and used when needed; however, anyone can use them if they are aware of them and know how to activate them. Such bypass mechanisms are very popular in mainframe environments and are normally introduced by insiders. Several reasons are given for needing trapdoors. The systems programmers may claim to need to modify the operating system without restarting the computer. They may want to issue operator commands from a user or programmer terminal or even require unlimited access at 3 A.M.

Generally these are not a good idea for several reasons. Backdoors may be found by the wrong persons who trip over them and, because there is usually no built-in security, all access controls may be bypassed. Under normal circumstances, all systems maintenance should, at all times, go through change control as normal. In addition, the machine should be operated by the operators and no one else, and the security system should not be bypassed at will.

SECURITY TESTING METHODOLOGIES

A variety of security testing methodology exists and are designed to facilitate the assessment of technical controls. Probably the most commonly used are:

- Open Source Security Testing Methodology Manual (OSSTMM)
- National Institute of Standards and Technology (NIST) 800-115
- Information Systems Security Assessment Framework (ISSAF)
- Open Web Application Security Project (OWASP)

Each of these methodologies has been constructed to service specific needs and should be used by the auditor as a guide and a starting point rather than as a Standardized Audit Program.

OSSTMM

Open Source Security Testing Methodology Manual is a peer-reviewed methodology for performing security tests and metrics. It is designed to provide an audit that is an accurate measurement of security at an operational level. The current version, version 3 (version 4 is in beta test at the time of publication) encompasses tests over human, physical, wireless, telecommunications, and data networks. It has been designed to suit the testing of cloud computing as well as virtual infrastructures and mobile communication infrastructures. The conversion is downloadable from the Institute for Security and Open Methodologies (ISECOM).[1]

NIST 800-115

Technical Guide to Information Security Testing and Assessment was published in 2008 and is designed to be a repeatable and documented security assessment methodology that can:

- Provide consistency and structure to security testing
- Minimize testing risks
- Expedite the transition of new assessment staff
- Address resource constraints associated with security assessments.

Overall, it is intended to provide guidance on:

- Management role
- Security testing policies
- Testing methods
- Review techniques
- Identification and analysis of systems
- Vulnerability assessment
- Penetration testing
- Security testing planning
- Security-testing execution
- Post-test activities

The latest version NIST sp 800-115 is also downloadable.[2]

ISSAF

Information Systems Security Assessment Framework, developed by the Open Information Systems Security Group[3], is an older methodology that is nonetheless an enormous body of work at an extreme level of detail. It covers both the business aspects of security as well as providing a penetration test framework. Although some of the material is out of date, it can be effective in providing an overall structure for security testing.

OWASP

Open Web Application Security Project is a 501(c)(3) not-for-profit worldwide charitable organization focused on improving the security of application software. It has created a number of tools, guides, and testing methodologies that are free for anyone to download and use. The OWASP testing guide has become the de-facto standard for web application testing. The Testing Guide is currently available as version 3 (2008)[4], although version 4 is currently under development.

NOTES

1 http://www.isecom.org/osstmm.
2 http://csrc.nist.gov/publications/nistpubs/800-115/SP800-115.pdf.
3 http://www.oissg.org/issaf.
4 http://www.owasp.org/images/5/56/OWASP_Testing_Guide_v3.pdf.

CHAPTER TWENTY-EIGHT

Applied Information Technology Security

THIS CHAPTER looks at the application of Information Technology (IT) security including communications and network security. The principles of network security, client-server, Internet and web-based services, and firewall security systems are all detailed together with connectivity protection resources such as cryptography, digital signatures, digital certificates, and key management policies. IT security also encompasses the use of intrusion-detection systems and the proper implementation of mainframe security facilities.

COMMUNICATIONS AND NETWORK SECURITY

In considering how network security should be implemented, one of the most difficult areas to establish is exactly where the network starts and ends. For many organizations, this is where primary security is established with a "peripheral" defense. In the same manner as a peripheral defense over the physical building, network peripheral defenses work on the basis of having a limited number of entry points, each securely guarded. Unfortunately not all networks work in the same manner and most have considerably more entry points than a normal building. In addition, this form of defense suffers from the same deficiencies as a peripheral defense around a building in that, once inside the building, it is assumed that the intruder has a right to be there and, in many cases, no further security checks are done. Another parallel can be found between the security checkpoint at the entrance to a building and the firewall on the network. In both cases it is commonly assumed that they are 100 percent effective and that all who manage to pass this point have a right to be wherever they are. It is also assumed that all threats are external in origin and that there are no significant security threats originating from an internal source. Before any such assumption can be made a security risk analysis is required.

As with all controls, the control objectives and risks faced must be clearly understood prior to the design of an effective control environment. Assets at risk must be identified and the sources of risk understood so that a *structure* of controls can be developed to specifically address both the likelihood and impact of potential vulnerabilities. As discussed in Chapter 6, risk management can take a variety of forms and utilize different techniques and can never be 100 percent effective in identifying all possible risks. Nevertheless an effective security risk assessment can go a long way toward identifying significant security risks and assisting in the development of appropriate control structures. Common risks organizations may face from failures of network security include:

- Loss of reputation
- Loss of confidentiality
- Loss of information integrity
- User authentication failure
- System unavailability

These risks, considered at a detailed level and rated based on the organizational criticality of the assets, are risks that can be used to identify the appropriate control mechanisms to secure communications and networks.

After individual risks have been identified and classified according to their nature and threat potential, security strategies can be developed to ensure that the assets required to support the business functionality of the organization are adequately protected.

Solutions can be implemented that test individual workstations (the organization's own as well as those employed by outsiders including those connected via wireless connection and employees' home computers) for compliance with the organization's security policies including the use of firewalls, operating system patches, security settings, antivirus software, and malware protection software. Workstations that satisfy the security requirements are initially granted access to the network but may be re-tested during the connection to ensure ongoing compliance. Workstations that fail security testing may be quarantined from the network.

 ## NETWORK PROTECTION

In the early days of networking, computer networks involved the connection of several computers into one single network. In today's environment, networking encompasses networks of networks encompassing hundreds or even thousands of individual workstations. In order to avoid requiring each individual user to sign on to each individual workstation in the network, systems of *trust zones* have developed whereby large networks can be subdivided into logical zones based upon the degree of control that the organization can directly exert on that specific zone. As a result, individual parts of networks can be classified as:

- Network areas containing sensitive systems with all accesses falling under the direct control of the organization where users and systems can be validated and authenticated to the degree specified by the organization with authority levels and access rights also being under direct control. Unauthorized access in such an area could be highly detrimental to the organization and, as such, this area of the network would be seen as *hostile* zones.
- Network areas that contain information resources which are open to the public but which require user identification and authentication would be seen as *untrusted* zones.
- Network areas that contain information resources which are open to a restricted number of authorized outside users who are identified and authenticated would be seen as *semitrusted* zones.
- Network areas with no outside access containing systems requiring full access by internal users and systems who can be validated and controlled directly under the authority of the organization would normally be seen as *trusted* zones.

Within the individual zones, security requirements can be well defined and appropriate controls implemented but it is in the intermixing of trust zones that network security starts to take on an enormous degree of complexity. Wherever there is a doubt regarding the interfacing of zones, the safe assumption is that the zone from where a connection originates is of a lower security level and the zone being connected to the security must be enforced with this in mind. It should always be borne in mind that any network security is as strong as its weakest link and that all workstations on a network should utilize a secure operating system. Many operating systems are intrinsically insecure and even those that can be secured are frequently implemented in an insecure manner. In those network areas exposed to greater threats the operating environment may require further strengthening to make them operating environments.

Generically, networks may be seen as vulnerable in three primary areas, namely, *Interception of Data, Availability of Communications,* and *Unauthorized Access* via the entry points.

The IT auditor would typically seek controls over the physical security of the network as well as the use of data encryption and digital certificates. The availability of the communications has as its primary control an effective network architecture combined with appropriate monitoring within the network management software. Such software will typically allow for the monitoring of the utilization of bandwidth in order to prevent bottlenecking across the network. As with any other computer system, network access should be restricted to facilitate traffic only from those systems with known addresses by means of access control lists within the routers and the use of an appropriate firewall.

 ## HARDENING THE OPERATING ENVIRONMENT

Where high-value information assets are at risk or where there is a high degree of unrestricted access, attention should be paid to the degree of insecurities commonly found in standard operating environments.

Modern operating systems come complete with a variety of sophisticated security capabilities but initially that is all they are, capabilities. For these to become effective controls, thought must be given to those services and network ports actually required and all those not required should either be eliminated at the workstation or filtered at the firewall. Many of these services permit the use of unencrypted protocols such as *FTP* or *NELNET, which can, if uncontrolled, facilitate "sniffer" attacks for electronic eavesdropping* on network traffic. In addition, the use of *Anonymous FTP* can enable an unknown outsider to download confidential information from a server and its use should be discontinued wherever possible.

Today's operating systems are continually upgraded by the vendors of the software in the form of service packs and software patches available online. Where such updates are security related, it is the responsibility of the network administrator to decide whether a given patch is appropriate for the network and to ensure that it is applied within the appropriate operating systems.

Default system accounts and passwords should either be renamed, disabled if not in use, or removed where possible. Default passwords should always be changed and no account should be accessible without the use of a password. Where guest accounts are specifically desired without password control, care should be taken to ensure that network access permissions are kept to a minimum.

The easiest way to share resources on a network is simply to give everyone access to everything, which completely eliminates any security protection the organization thought it could rely on. All directory and file permissions on each machine should be reviewed periodically and the permissions granted adjusted according to the criticality and sensitivity of information held at the particular machine. Access should be granted on a "need-to-have" or "least privilege" basis where users are granted access only to those assets and functions actually required in order to perform the activities authorized by the organization. In order to effectively implement such access control, the users' functional requirements within the business itself must be subject to a segregation of duties analysis in order to ensure that one individual cannot carry out incompatible duties. It is not possible to enforce an appropriate least privilege environment within the computer where segregation of duties does not exist within the business.

Antivirus and malware protection software is generally available on most networked computer systems but not all systems are kept up to date with the latest virus and malware definitions. Additionally, many systems have the software installed but not in active use, with the usage being at the discretion of the workstation user who may or may not be security aware.

Detective controls involving the use of system log files can facilitate intrusion detection as well as network recovery after an untoward event. For such log files to be effective they must be scrutinized on a regular basis for any abnormalities and retained for sufficient time for such abnormalities to become apparent. Access to these logs must be restricted to the individuals authorized to scrutinize them and update access should be barred to all users.

 ## CLIENT SERVER AND OTHER ENVIRONMENTS

Client server is an architecture in which the functionality and processing of a system are split between the client workstation and a database server. The client and the server are separated both physically and logically and it is the client-server system that coordinates the work of both of these components to complete assigned functions. This separation facilitates the mixture of hardware and operating environments. It is the distribution of functionality in client-server systems that increases the vulnerability of the systems to viruses, fraud, and misuse, with the cost of security being balanced against the cost to the organization in system corruption. In many client-server environments, the network component remains largely insecure on the assumption that identification and authentication take place at the workstation and logical access restrictions takes place at the client with no possible security implications on the network. The problem is compounded when a single login is used to access all servers on the network. This is commonly done for customer convenience but, once again, electronic eavesdropping on the network can occur using packet sniffers to breach confidentiality or to gain passwords so that direct access into the server may be obtained. As with many intra-network communications, encryption is a badly neglected control that could obviate many of these risks.

A common risk in client-server environments is that management places reliance on a single individual in charge of administrating the security of the environment. This reliance may put the organization at risk of loss of a key individual should the person move on to another organization or at risk to potential incompetence or dishonesty on the part of the administrator.

 ## FIREWALLS AND OTHER PROTECTION RESOURCES

Firewalls are designed to control access to and from a given network and ensure the old connections pass through the firewall where they can be examined and evaluated against a network's access policies.

A firewall provides an organization with a mechanism for implementing and enforcing network access security policies by providing access to control both users and services. It is therefore an enforcement mechanism transforming *directive* but discretionary controls into *preventative* controls.

Used correctly, firewalls can greatly enhance network security by filtering those services that are inherently insecure in order to prevent services from being exploited by unauthorized outsiders while still enabling the authorized use of such services. This can significantly enhance privacy by preventing outsiders from obtaining information about the site or the uses of the site using services such as *finger*, which can be used to display information about users within a site. They can also control access in both directions in order to bar inward access to unknown outsiders or to bar outward access to unauthorized sites.

In addition, firewalls can record information regarding accesses, invalid access attempts, and statistics on network usage. Depending on the firewall selected, intruder detection of probes or attacks can trigger alarms to the security administrator.

From this it should not be assumed that firewalls are the ultimate in protection and no other mechanisms are required. Many organizations have a network structure that is not conducive to the implementation of a firewall. Under these circumstances, implementation of an appropriate file may require significant restructuring at considerable cost and inconvenience. In this instance the organization may decide to select a control mechanism other than the standard firewall implementation. In addition, where a firewall is used as a funnel for all access to the Internet, there is a temptation to assume that all accesses are now protected. In reality, any user with an available modem port can connect to an outside telephone line and connect directly to the Internet thus allowing access into the network behind the firewall. Where an organization uses a solitary firewall access route there is no protection from insider threats behind the firewall. To control these problems, individual firewalls are required on each workstation on the network with appropriate security levels being set. On many networks this is seen to be a major inconvenience to the administrators, potentially preventing them from accessing workstations at will.

As with any other protection mechanism, one disadvantage of a firewall that will eventually be felt is that it can block a service that, sooner or later, the user will wish to use.

For a firewall to be truly effective, authentication beyond a simple password is required and organizations are increasingly looking toward the use of *digital signatures* and *digital certificates.*

Digital Signatures

A digital signature uses similar technology to asymmetric encryption in that the "signature" is a mathematical summary (*hash*) of the information encrypted using the equivalent of the signer's private key. Once received, the message is rehashed by the receiver. The attached message hash is then decrypted using the sender's public key and, should the two hashes match, the receiver can accept that only the sender could have sent the message and it has not been tampered with. Digital signatures do not conceal the content of messages because the message itself is not encrypted but nevertheless, where assurance is required that the message came from an authenticated source, digital signatures can be an effective enhancement of communication authentication. Within internal networks, digital signatures can be used as a stronger authentication method than handwritten signatures. Documents with signatures written on them can be photocopied or scanned and the message altered. With digital signatures such alteration would be immediately noticeable because the two hashes would not match.

Digital Certificates

A digital certificate is an electronic verification issued and digitally signed by a *certification authority* (CA). These certification authorities utilize *public key infrastructures* (PKIs) and issue digital certificates indicating the certification of an organization's or individual's public key together with the privileges for which the certificate's holder has been certified. In order for a public key to be certified, the prospective subscriber registers his or her public key with the certification authority and requests a certificate. After approval, a certificate is generated and issued to the subscriber. This means that, within an electronic commerce environment, all parties participating in transactions are able to positively identify the other parties with whom they are dealing. When transactions involving millions of dollars occur via the Internet it is critical that the authenticity of identities claimed be confirmed. Use of the certificates is not, however, limited to Internet transactions of an e-commerce nature. Any electronic communication where the authenticity of the transmitter is critical can make use of digital certificates. Within the internal network they can be used to control logical access while digital certificates stored on smart cards can be used to restrict physical access to controlled areas.

 ## INTRUSION-DETECTION SYSTEMS

Notwithstanding all of the controls previously noted, from time to time attempts may be made to breach network security and these can be detected using an appropriate intrusion-detection system (IDS). Early versions of these generally functioned in a similar manner to antivirus software in that they retained a database of common attack patterns and monitored the network seeking these patterns. This method of pattern seeking has a fundamental flaw in that, should the attack be indistinguishable from conventional network traffic, it may be overlooked.

More advanced IDSs are based on anomaly-detection-seeking network activity that is different from the normal pattern. As far back as 1987 Dorothy Denning described a "model of a real-time intrusion-detection expert system capable of detecting break-ins, penetrations, and other forms of computer abuse."[1] Where an earlier IDS would typically use a predefined set of rules or filters designed to trap a specific, malicious event, an IDS with anomaly works from a baseline of "normal" activity. Any behavior that deviates from the baseline is identified and reported. Denning's original model used statistical analysis to identify deviant behavior. Other models attempt to use a logic-based description of expected behavior to identify "normal" activity identified in a rules database. These intrusion-detection systems and anomaly detection systems, used in conjunction with firewalls, can create effective defense mechanisms for both networks and hosts.

Without the use of appropriate intrusion detection and prevention techniques, both systems and data are potentially at risk of compromise. Once again, in an outsourced model or a cloud model, the risk may be increased because of the shared infrastructure.

From the IT auditor's perspective, infrastructure and systems located at third-party sites would lead the auditor to seek proof of effective *Intrusion Prevention Systems* (IPSs) that, when used effectively, can cut off potential attacks on a proactive basics. In addition, proof of the usage and monitoring of *Intrusion-Detection Systems* will be sought in order to detect potential attacks on both the systems and the integrity checking tools. Proof of appropriate *Incident Response* would give the auditor confidence that processes exist and are effective in responding to actual or potential security incidents.

 NOTE

1 Dorothy Denning, An Intrusion-Detection Model, IEEE Symposium on Security and Privacy, February 1987.

CHAPTER TWENTY-NINE

Physical and Environmental Security

I N THIS CHAPTER, we will examine physical security with respect to Information Technology (IT), which refers to the safeguarding of the hardware, buildings, and media containing the data and programs, as well as the infrastructure used to support the processing of data. Physical security encompasses control measures to mitigate the risks of *natural* events (e.g., flood, earthquake, severe weather conditions) as well as man-made problems (e.g., fire, destruction, theft, civil unrest). Environmental security encompasses the support structures that are the foundations of the physical environment including power, air conditioning, heating, and lighting.

Controls must be appropriate to the threats faced and therefore physical security becomes dictated by the risks in the environment. These can be broadly categorized into:

- **Physical damage and destruction.** This type of damage could be temporary or permanent and may require repair or replacement of the system components affected. As in any control environment, a combination of preventative, detective, and corrective controls will be required to adequately offset the impact of physical damage and destruction. Damage could be accidental as a result of a natural event and could range from minor (such as physical damage to a data medium where a backup is available) to catastrophic (such as physical damage to the whole installation and its personnel with no hope of an immediate recovery). Alternatively, physical damage can come about as a result of direct malicious activity either from insiders or from individuals outside the organization. A common result of physical damage may be short- or long-term *disruption of the delivery of information services.* The extent of potential losses, and therefore the degree of control desirable, will be dependent upon the duration of the interruption as well as the criticality of the service interrupted.

- **Theft of equipment.** It is not unheard of for mainframe computers to go missing over the weekend from a secured corporate building, but theft of network servers, workstations, and notebook computers are commonplace as are thefts of individual components such as hard disks, computer memory, and even the humble mouse. As with any corporate asset, computer equipment must be protected against direct physical theft.
- **Loss of data confidentiality.** Confidentiality may be lost when physical control over confidential outputs becomes degraded. Information outputs that may be classified as confidential or even corporate critical can frequently be found thrown out with the trash or even donated to a local children's play group so that the reverse side can be used as scrap paper.

With the advent of portable, lightweight computers, theft, not only of the information but of the computer containing it, has become common. In many cases where laptop computers have been stolen it is assumed that the thief was after the computer itself. This may indeed be the case but as a byproduct the thief has also acquired a rich source of potentially damaging and confidential information.

The days in which theft of information meant the theft of filing cabinets are long gone and today's information thief can obtain all that is required using a DVD burner or even a memory stick. All that is then required is physical access to the network on which the required information is stored. Again, a common source for loss of data confidentiality is theft of backup copies of media. Even communication lines are vulnerable to attack if physical access can be gained.

When problems are encountered in the use of computer equipment, it is common to either call in the experts or hand over the offending system to them. This is effectively placing physical control of the hardware containing sensitive corporate information in the hands of strangers with little or no way of knowing whether confidentiality is breached and sensitive information viewed or even copied.

In all cases the design of an appropriate control system will depend upon management's perceptions of where the losses are most likely to occur and which would involve most corporate pain.

With the coming together of IT and communications as an integrated "backbone" for the business, the availability of physical housing, cabling, security, power, cooling, and fire protection is looked on as a network-critical physical infrastructure. In a modern environment the modularity and standardization of the infrastructure becomes critical in increasing the liability and improving the availability.

 ## CONTROL MECHANISMS

Physical Access Control

Physical access controls are intended to manage the movements of personnel, media, and hardware in and out of a controlled area as well as within that area. Controls may include:

- Identification of the risk areas within the computer environment that require higher levels of access control so that access may be granted, once again, on a need-to-have basis.
- Adequate peripheral protection in the form of fences and walls with restricted points of access and control measures such as scanning for undesirable items being taken in, including explosives and firearms, as well as computer hardware not belonging to, and therefore not under the control of, the organization. Card or biometric access systems and closed circuit television monitoring would typically be used.
- Locks on doors normally take the form of the traditional key locks, card locks, combination locks, or biometric locks. Both key and card locks are dependent upon the physical security and restricted number of the keys and cards, respectively, that have been issued. Card locks are also vulnerable to the individual entering through some form of turnstile and passing the card to a second person who then reuses it to gain entry. Combination locks, while seeming more secure, are vulnerable to simple observation. In some instances it has been noted that closed circuit television cameras have been directed at the locks and are recording all combinations entered. Biometric locks, such as those containing thumbprint scanners, provide a higher level of access security but even they, in common with all locked doors, suffer from the problem of one person opening the door and three people entering.
- A formal identity card system in use with strangers in an area challenged by staff members to produce identification.
- Identification and access restrictions within those areas containing the support infrastructure such as communication lines, electrical power conduits, source documents, and pre-printed outputs such as checks.
- Within the area being protected physically, there may be additional areas of even higher security where access can be gained more readily because of being within the outer peripheral defense. In modern office blocks it is common to find prefabricated interior wall panels that can be moved around to suit the office environment but that provide little protection against physical assaults and, in many cases, only go as high as a suspended ceiling. In such a case it is comparatively simple to remove a ceiling tile and go over the wall into the "secure" area. In similar fashion, raised floors are also vulnerable should they extend beyond the peripheral wall.
- Motion detectors may be used in "lights-out" computer rooms where there is normally no human movement to detect as soon as the periphery is breached.
- Use of shredders of the appropriate type can ensure that scrap leaving the secured area is not vulnerable to an outsider searching the trash cans. Even DVDs can be passed through the modern shredder, although care must be taken where microfilm or microfiche is used to ensure that the shredder reduces the material to a small enough size to be effective as a confidentiality control.
- Disposal of outdated or obsolete equipment commonly carries with it the risk that the equipment will contain components or information that is confidential to the organization. In the case of disposal of hard disks and other storage media, destruction may be a safer option.

■ When equipment is sent for repair, sensitive media should be removed whenever possible and, if this is not possible, security should be taken into consideration in deciding whether the equipment should in fact be repaired or whether it should be scrapped and replaced. This may seem wasteful but the replacement cost of a hard disk is low while the cost of lost confidentiality could be high.

■ Use of scanners, de-gaussers (which can wipe magnetic media clean), and physical searches may be required to prevent the removal of corporate assets from these closed areas.

Environmental Controls

The criticality of information systems for today's business environment places an enormous burden on data centers to remain interruption-free. In the event of a data center catastrophe, an organization may lose not only equipment but also the ability to continue in business. Recent studies indicate that organizations closed by a fire will fail to reopen in 40 percent of cases. Even those that do manage to reopen can suffer ongoing corporate pain and almost 30 percent of those will fail within the first three years after the fire.

In addition to controls governing physical access, controls around the security of the environment to prevent losses due to fires and other hazards are therefore required due to the potential for total destruction of the information processing facility as well as the threat to human life. Heat, smoke, noxious gases, and even damage from fire extinguishers and hoses can all play a role in destroying Information Systems.

Fires require three things, namely:

1. **Heat.** Fire starts when sufficient heat exists to cause a fuel source to burn. Heat can come from a variety of sources such as overloaded electrical systems, poorly stored combustible material, human carelessness, or deliberate intent.
2. **Fuel source.** With an adequate supply of oxygen, even steel will burn and in most office environments fuel in the form of combustible material such as paper, wooden desks, plastic, and the like, are almost inexhaustible.
3. **Oxygen.** Fires require a replenishing source of oxygen in order to maintain flame. Office air conditioning and open windows can accelerate the flames while automatically shutting down systems and the use of fire retardant materials can slow down the progress of a fire. One area of concern is that many materials within an office environment contain their own source of chemical oxygen so that simply smothering it to remove the oxygen supply is ineffective.

Fires within Data Centers are commonly caused by power problems in concealed areas such as raised floors and cable conduits frequently due to lightning and power surges or simple overload. Over and above such "natural" causes the potential, of course, exists for corporate sabotage in the form of arson.

Ideally, the primary control mechanism will be preventative to stop such fires from occurring; however, in the event of an actual fire, the next most effective control will be rapid detection and ability to bring the fire under control without disrupting either the ongoing information processing or the safety of the personnel within the data center.

Fire prevention works by denying the fire any or all of the three requirements for combustion. Most fire extinguishers work by denying the fire access to oxygen as well as by removing the heat (e.g., water, carbon dioxide, and halon fire extinguishing systems). The fuel source can be denied, in many cases, simply by keeping the environment clean and removing threats from multiple electrical adapters and carelessly stored scrap paper. Where chemical fires are involved, denial of oxygen is more difficult because it requires breaking the chemical chain reaction inducing combustion.

The more quickly a fire is detected, the greater the probability that it can be extinguished before significant damage to property or personnel is done. Fire can spread with a speed that astounds most people and early detection, combined with some basic firefighting knowledge, can quickly extinguish a small fire before it becomes a large fire.

In designing fire control and prevention systems, care should be taken to ensure that the extinguishing of the fire does not create more damage than the fire itself. Water damage from sprinkler systems and use of inappropriate dry-powder fire extinguishing systems on electrical fires may reduce the fire damage overall but may create local problems in the area where the fire originated. Nevertheless, such systems are highly effective in limiting the spread of a fire and protecting human lives.

Physical Environmental Controls

Information Systems are, to a large extent, dependent upon the physical environment within which they run. Loss of power and inadequate temperature and humidity control can be highly disruptive if appropriate care is not taken. Because computers, by their nature, require electricity to function, an uninterruptible supply of electricity at a constant voltage and amperage is a prerequisite to smooth functioning of the Information Systems. This can be assured using a variety of techniques, including use of dedicated power supplies, uninterruptible power supplies (UPS), use of chokes on the power lines to ensure constant voltages, and the use of standby generators in the event of a prolonged power outage.

Many modern desktop and notebook computers will run happily in a typical office environment but mainframe computers and more critical servers will require an environment where the temperature is kept within acceptable tolerances and humidity is adequately controlled. Should these systems fail, the information processing will, at best, shut down and, at worst, may suffer significant permanent damage.

Building Collapse

Following the events at the World Trade Center on 9/11, structural collapse has come to the fore as a physical threat to computer systems. In reality it has long been a threat due to a variety of causes both natural and manmade. Earth tremors, severe weather conditions such as tornadoes, poorly built structures, and even impacts at ground level have been known to cause a structural collapse of offices containing computer centers. This is before the threat of explosion and terrorism is even considered. As preventative measures, physical security combined with the proper design and construction of buildings remain the strongest defenses while, from a corrective perspective, in the event of a catastrophic collapse the contingency plans (see Chapter 30) come into their own.

 ## IMPLEMENTING THE CONTROLS

As with all other controls, physical and environmental security controls do not exist in a vacuum. They coexist with, influence, and are influenced by logical security controls and controls surrounding the effectiveness and efficiency of information processing. As with any other control, they consume resources in the forms of labor, machinery, and money. As such, controls in this environment are frequently implemented after a breach of physical and environmental security has occurred when the cost of control can be seen to be justified. Some controls in this environment are required by legislation, in particular where human life is at risk, so that fire exits, fire escapes, fire detectors, and extinguishing systems are all typically required by law. Other controls are implemented where the cost of not implementing them could prove highly expensive, publicly embarrassing, or even life-threatening to the organization. In most cases controls are implemented where the impact is seen to be cost beneficial, that is, where the cost, whether high or low, is significantly offset by the benefit accrued.

PART SIX

VI

Business Continuity and Disaster Recovery

Protection of the Information Technology Architecture and Assets: Disaster-Recovery Planning

F OR MANY YEARS, business continuity has been recognized as a fundamental component of management's role in achieving good corporate governance. This has frequently been confused with the concept of computer Disaster-Recovery Planning (DRP) resulting in the responsibility of being seen as belonging to the Information Systems (IS) processing function instead of where it belongs, at the top. It is a management responsibility to ensure that an organization's business processes that deliver value to its stakeholders will continue to function despite the occurrence of unforeseen circumstances. The Business-Continuity Plan (BCP) therefore refers to those activities intended to ensure the ongoing running of the organization during a period of disruption of normal operation Information Technology (IT). DRP refers to those activities required to minimize the disruption on the organization of a loss, short to long term, of information-processing facilities.

With the complex integration of IT as enabling and driving mechanisms for those business processes, it has become apparent that an organization's Information Systems are a critical resource, although not the only resource required to ensure business continuity and even corporate survival. Thus the computer disaster recovery plan is a critical component of the overall business continuity plan and sufficient care is required in the production of the DRP to ensure that the risks associated (see Chapter 6) with the IT process are appropriately mitigated. As previously stated, preventative controls are never 100 percent effective and therefore controls must exist to mitigate the effects once an untoward event has occurred.

The original concept of the DRP was to maintain a standby hardware platform that could be utilized in the event of something critical happening to the normal site. The standby site could be provided and maintained either by the organization itself or by a third party who would lease time on the site in the event of a disaster. In the days when mainframe computers dominated the business environment, this was seen as an adequate response and degrees of "warmth" of such a site indicated the degrees of readiness.

In such a scenario a "hot" site was seen to be one in which the hardware, communications capability, and systems software were all available instantaneously with only the current version of the data files to be restored. The hot site was typically situated close enough to the main site to be of immediate use but far enough away not to be vulnerable to the same physical threats (e.g., flood, earthquake, and the like).

A "warm" site consisted of a computer room and computer, perhaps shared, where a disaster would result in the loading of the appropriate operating environment, application systems, and data files so that recovery could take place in an acceptable time frame.

A "cold" site consisted of an empty computer room with an agreement contracted with the hardware vendor that, in the event of an emergency, a computer could be supplied quickly and configured appropriately for the organization.

Obviously there were degrees of "warmth" between hot and cold that could be tailored to suit the individual requirements of specific organizations. In many cases, combination plans required immediate access to a hot site (expensive) with medium term transfer to a warm or even cold site (considerably cheaper).

The proliferation of local area networks (LANs) and client-server environments brought an awareness that the DRP had to cater to not only the mainframe architecture but also the distributed environment increasingly fundamental to the IT viability of an organization. This transition also had to cater to the fact that the hardware itself was increasingly the easiest and quickest item to replace while the communication links and the people to utilize the systems were increasingly more difficult to back up.

The increasing awareness of the vulnerability of information processing to natural disasters such as tsunamis and floods as well as disasters caused by human beings such as terrorist attacks have caused organizations to rethink the appropriateness of the established solutions and, in some cases, to realize that one DRP may not be enough to cater for all eventualities.

 ## RISK REASSESSMENT

The foundation of any BCP or DRP is a risk assessment involving the identification and analysis of potential vulnerabilities and threats. As usual, risk assessment begins with the identification and evaluation of the assets and information at risk together with a threat analysis and an evaluation of the effectiveness of the controls intended to mitigate the risk. This results in an identified list of potential threats, the probable likelihood and anticipated exposure, as well as the controls required to mitigate the threats including those corrective controls that will become part of the DRP. From an IT perspective, it also includes the establishment of the impact on the individual parts of the organization of the short-, medium-, and long-term unavailability of any IS resource. This study facilitates the prioritization of the recovery process and the identifications of systems'

inter-relationships including the relationship between clerical systems and computerized systems.

Overall, the business continuity plan will require elements addressing the organizational risks and will typically include sections on:

- Security
- Business Continuity and Disaster Recovery
- Software, Hardware, Programming, and Purchases
- Internal and External Audit
- Contracting with Vendors
- Computer Operations
- Microcomputers
- Acceptable Use
- Home Computer Use and Connectivity
- E-Mail
- Local and Wide Area Networks
- Data Processing Management
- Compliance
- Electronic Imaging
- Remote Access
- Firewall
- Intrusion-Detection Systems

 ## DISASTER—BEFORE AND AFTER

Perhaps the best prepared organizations are the ones who have lived through a calamity. Among the threats faced by an organization are:

- Fire
- Flood
- Building collapse
- Explosion
- Industrial failure
- Power failure
- Viruses
- Deliberate sabotage
- Computer abuse
- Deliberate action by staff
- "Hacking" into systems
- Internet penetration
- Terrorism

As can be seen, many of these risks have nothing to do with computer systems but remain for the enterprise as a whole. There is a tendency to focus upon the Information

Systems to the exclusion of all else within the organization, and this is as dangerous as not looking at contingency planning at all.

Disasters may be looked at in four basic categories:

1. **DISASTER A**

LOSS OF	CAUSES
People	Explosion
Building	Aircraft crash
Factories	Total fire
Finance	Flood
Credibility	Industrial action
Materials	Earthquake
Computers	Terrorism and sabotage
(Permanent loss)	Economic sanctions

2. **DISASTER B**

LOSS OF	CAUSES
Hardware	Explosion
Software	Fire
In-house data	Flood
(Temporary loss)	Industrial action

3. **DISASTER C**

LOSS OF	CAUSES
Software and the ability to recover in-house data	Explosion
	Fire
	Freak atmospheric force
	Flood
	Poor operating standards
	Deliberate destruction
	Bad systems design

4. **DISASTER D**

LOSS OF	CAUSES
Software: Partial loss only and the inability to recover	Poor operating standards
	Computer operational error
	Deliberate destruction
	Bad systems design

In all these cases a different approach to recovery planning is required. The plan for evacuation of the building to a new location is inappropriate if the disaster involves the loss of a small but vital file.

As such a DRP must be capable of responding to a variety of "disasters" and provide optimal solutions for each.

 ## CONSEQUENCES OF DISRUPTION

Should disruption occur the consequences may include any or all of:

- Loss of revenues
- Delays in invoicing
- Lost interest
- Lost sales
- Lost future business
- Incurred costs
- Extra manpower
- Increased interest on loans
- Loss of discounts
- Inefficiency

From a production-control perspective in a manufacturing company, problems would typically include lost production and schedule disruption, while, from a legal perspective, penalty clauses could jeopardize the whole enterprise.

At a minimum there will be ill will generated among customers, shareholders, and staff.

Preparedness for a disaster may be categorized as:

- **Poor.** Organization highly vulnerable to damage to its data processing capability; could jeopardize corporate survival.
- **Weak.** Disaster would result in conspicuous interruption of IT services; could result in loss of business.
- **Adequate.** Organization could recover from the loss of computer capabilities at some cost and public embarrassment.
- **Good.** Organization could recover from the loss of computing capability with some cost but little embarrassment.
- **Very Good.** Organization is ready for virtually any eventuality. Disaster should have no material effect on the business.

 ## WHERE TO START

As part of an overall comprehensive policy for sound physical and internal controls within the Data Processing and IT Department, a business continuity and emergency disaster recovery policy will be required to provide for the continuation of data processing operations to minimize risk to the organization. The purpose of this policy would be to protect personnel and property during emergencies and to provide procedures to continue or recover operations should an emergency render any part the organization's IT department or infrastructure unusable.

The goals of such a policy would include the establishment of authorities and responsibility in the development, implementation, and maintenance of an emergency and disaster recovery policy and plan; the documentation of backup plans for hardware, software, communication, documentation, and data files; the outlining of strategies to ensure business continuity and disaster recovery planning; and the establishment of requirements for periodic testing of the plans.

As with any other form of business analysis, the beginning involves understanding the business. In DRP terms this means modeling the business, identifying data flow and dependencies, and identifying the critical systems as well as any dependent systems (including manual systems).

Computer systems may be identified by types, for example:

- By operating objectives
- Centralized
- Stand-alone
- Distributed
- Real time
- On-line
- Batch

These can then be assigned degrees of priority. Priorities include:

- Business loss rating
- Alternative service level required
- Maximum down time tolerable

Systems may be categorized by the effect of stoppage and by identifying any essential interfacing systems identified (computer and manual).

Once systems have been prioritized, all systems, including manual systems, must be documented. Relationships must be identified and the effect of stoppage quantified.

A commonly omitted consideration is ensuring that alternative:

- Accommodation
- People
- Stationery supplies
- Office equipment
- Control procedures

have been identified and that work in progress has also been considered.

Data used within each system needs to be graded by application and therefore by strategic importance as well as by alternate methods of sourcing and degree of pain in loss. In a comprehensive plan data may even be rated by disruption period.

Each application is therefore graded, although not all of its data is of the same importance. Where unique software has been produced by a third party specifically for the organization, escrow copies may be required to be lodged in case of emergencies.

For recovery purposes it is important to establish:

- The minimum configuration required
- Whether continuity agreements with vendors exist
- If backup procedures have been agreed to
- If there is compatibility of equipment
- If there is compatibility of firmware
- If security arrangements have been agreed
- If testing of hardware backup arrangements is carried out regularly (and successfully)

In addition controls such as redundant hardware, that is, hardware in excess of current requirements, dual controllers for peripheral devices, switchable communications capabilities, and duplicated communication lines, should be considered. Uninterruptible Power Supply (UPS) systems and standby generators may assist in preventing power problems from becoming full-fledged disasters.

 ## TESTING THE PLAN

In order to carry out a successful test of the plan, management needs must be fully defined and approved. The plan must cover all in-house and third-party risks and define all "retained" risks, and testing should be as realistic as possible. A full-scale test would normally involve management and the users as well as IT personnel.

Effective recovery does not simply mean getting initial systems up and running on the day of the disaster but the achievement of full recovery back to normal working conditions. Certain fundamentals are required to perform any form of recovery, such as:

- Appropriate backups retained for appropriate lengths of time
- An appropriate hardware configuration including communications
- An appropriate venue for users in the event of the loss of their normal accommodation
- Appropriate procedure manuals in sufficient detail for inexperienced staff to carry out recovery
- Supplies of pre-printed stationery if required including negotiable documents such as checks

AUDITING THE PLAN

The BCP and DRP will both require reviews by the IT auditor in order to ensure that management has implemented controls to a reasonable level and thus ensure successful continuity and recovery. As with any other audit, planning of the assignment is critical to successful implementation and, as usual, starts with the business objectives of the function to be reviewed.

The audit involves investigating and evaluating the policies, application systems covered, user data defined, hardware required, systems software needed, and the realism of the testing. Overall the auditor must evaluate the probability of successful business continuity. In addition, the confidentiality and integrity of information must be assured throughout the recovery process.

There are three main phases within such an audit:

1. Verifying the adequacy of the plan
2. Determining the effectiveness of the implementation of the plan
3. Determining the mechanisms by which the plan is kept up to date and in line with corporate requirements

Verification of the adequacy of the plan is dependent upon the IS auditor's familiarity with the business requirements of the organization and the Information Systems in use to support those business requirements. The degree of dependence on information processing of the individual business areas is used to determine the prioritization of the recovery process. The auditor's objective is to determine whether the plan, as formulated, should give the organization the capability of short-term recovery and eventual return to full operational capability under a variety of circumstances, within a reasonable time scale, and at an acceptable cost. This involves identifying management's evaluation criteria used in developing the plan and matching this against the auditor's own knowledge of the business and Information Systems requirements. One of the more critical areas is the assignment of responsibility for control during the process of recovery coupled with the authority to declare an emergency and invoke the plan. Where multiple versions of recovery sites are used, the plan should include procedures to switch from one site to the next as recovery progresses.

In most organizations, plans are time dependent with events and actions required within a 12-hour period, a 24-hour period, and a three-day period in the short term. These actions may themselves be calendar dependent because priorities at the start of a financial month may differ from those at the end of the financial month.

The effectiveness of the implementation can be measured by examining management's records of the testing of the plan to ensure its operability and to ensure that the testing has been carried out for a variety of categories of disaster ranging from minimal disruption to full-scale unavailability in as close to a realistic setting as possible. If possible, the auditor should participate in such a test to observe the general effectiveness of testing and how accurately it simulates a genuine disaster.

Disaster recovery planning is a dynamic undertaking because the business, the Information Systems, the corporate procedures, and the staff are all changing simultaneously and the plan must be updated with this in mind. As such, management must take great pains to ensure that the plan reflects the current business and Information Technology status and the testing is amended to take this into consideration. The auditor will typically check management's control mechanisms to ensure that such changes are fully reflected in both the plan itself and the testing of the plan. Overall, the auditor must also be satisfied that the plan itself will be kept up to date and appropriate. This means that the auditor must:

- Ensure responsibility for plan maintenance
- Ensure management is kept informed
- Ensure the master copy of the plan is secure
- Ensure distributed copies are kept up to date and secure

Although the plan is intended as a last resort in the event of a system catastrophe occurring, it should not be seen as the only control over business continuity. Preventative controls to minimize the likelihood of system catastrophe occurring should be a priority with management.

CHAPTER THIRTY-ONE

Displacement Control

T HE ULTIMATE CONTROL in any event of something untoward happening is the displacement control involving transfer of the risk to a third party through insurance. In many cases this control can cover a variety of threats such as data corruption, viral attack, system crashes, and even strike action.

 INSURANCE

For most organizations, risk management is classed as relative and risks are managed depending on the *risk appetite* or willingness to accept risk of the parties involved. This is in contrast to the typical IT approach to risk where control is commonly viewed as an absolute. That is, either full control or no control and risk is seen as something to be avoided at almost any cost.

With the realization that absolute control is neither possible nor even desirable because it is generally within the areas of risk that an organization makes its profits, risk avoidance has given way to risk management where risks are divided into those that are appropriate to control; those that cannot be avoided and must be accepted; and those that remain unacceptable and can be transferred to a third party, normally via an insurance policy.

In order for the insurance to be effective, however, the right type of coverage must be obtained. Most insurance policies do not cover maintenance costs or normal wear and tear, but insurance can be sought for losses caused by electrical or mechanical breakdown, fraud and dishonesty, consequential losses, or damage caused through civil unrest.

Some insurance policies cover only the hardware and thus if a computer gets stolen or destroyed in a fire, the insured can claim for the damages up to the amount detailed in the policy either on a replacement basis or on a depreciated value basis. Unfortunately, the cost of hardware replacement may be the lowest of the costs faced in an emergency situation.

In the case of laptops and desktop computers, the opportunist thief looks on the computer as ready money, easily removed, and sometimes difficult to trace. This is a common problem in business environments, buildings with public access, and increasingly, while mobile computers are in transit. In addition to the risk of theft, users who travel with a laptop to business meetings stand a substantial risk of accidental damage in transit. As a result of this increase in portability, key features for insurance over mobile computers include "all risks" covered worldwide with no excess on the policy and no exclusions. Where coverage is required for fraud or consequential lost this must be specifically stated in the policy and an additional premium will normally be charged.

For mainframe computers, too, insurance is a critical component of the overall control structure. It is tempting to believe that the traditional controls such as firewalls and antivirus software can prevent the logical threats from hackers and viruses, but no such protection is 100 percent foolproof and a long-stop displacement control is critical in the event of problems. Subject to certain safeguards, organizations such as Lloyd's of London will offer insurance coverage running into hundreds of millions of dollars in the event of catastrophic breaches of security or availability.

Despite all of management's attempts to ensure computer security, businesses are increasingly reporting deliberate and successful attacks including denial of service attacks, outside penetration of secured systems, data network sabotage, and insider financial fraud. While computer insurance is not cheap, the cost to the organization of such a successful attack without adequate insurance coverage could threaten the ongoing viability of the company.

Some non-specialized insurance policies pay for computer losses under standard commercial loss-of-business or act-of-vandalism clauses, but to address specific risks policies must be written to specifically cover those risks and can attract premiums that may range from $100,000 to $5 million based on an assessment of risk probability, damage expectation, and the amount of excess negotiated on the policy.

One specialized area for e-insurance is the transfer of the risks associated with unauthorized or malicious access to an organization's information assets. Around the world, privacy legislation is being enacted with severe penalties for organizations whose confidentiality is breached either on their own computer or while it is in transit. The possibilities of civil or criminal action taken against companies involving fines, penalties, and consequential liabilities as a result of breach of privacy has brought such insurance to the forefront of management's attention.

Insurance can be obtained from reputable underwriters that includes those impacts caused by fraudulent and malicious acts committed by employees or third parties against an insured's computer systems, the computer programs themselves, or the electronic information and records as well as computer virus attacks that hinder or close down the operations of the insured. Direct or indirect financial losses as a result of fraudulent input into computer systems can be covered, as can losses resulting from accidental alteration or destruction to electronic information and records.

Other insurance can cover such risks as:

- Business interruption and extra expense incurred in the event of a computer virus causing malicious destruction of the contents of a computer system
- Computer systems liability such as failure to prevent authorized access, denial of service, damage to a third party's computer system, theft of information, and breach of duty in provision of outsourcing services
- Loss of intellectual property should trade secrets be copied or recorded
- Extortion as a result of threats to divulge or utilize information held on the computer systems or even threats to introduce a computer virus or malware into the system
- Third-party liability such as libel, slander, invasion of privacy, infringement of copyright, plagiarism, and false advertising
- Expenses for legal fees in defense of a claim
- Expenses incurred to re-establish corporate reputation and market share in the event of a loss or claim

In some market sectors such as banking, specific insurance policies such as *Banker's Blanket Bond* exist to cover professional liability, directors' and officers' liability, electronic funds transfer, errors and omissions from trust departments, as well as consultants' errors and omissions.

In addition to the premium, organizations are normally obliged to pay upfront to have their IT environment assessed. In deciding the premium, insurance companies normally rely upon actuarial data that may take many years to collect. In the fast-moving world of information processing, such data does not exist for new products and may well be obsolete for old products. The first stage is therefore the evaluation of potential risks based upon known exposures and the existing security and control environment. This would normally take into consideration management's controls as well as the extent of IT auditing carried out both internally and externally and the turnover rate in management itself and is normally carried out using an independent external assessor for potential customers. For many businesses this is preceded by a process of self-evaluation in order to bring the security practices up to a standard acceptable for insurance purposes. In some cases it has been found that the evaluation process itself is of sufficient value that, even should the organization decide not to purchase coverage, the gains in confidence regarding the areas considered for potential insurance are sufficient to justify the cost of the evaluation. Today's corporate governance increasingly requires individuals and organizations to demonstrate that they are exercising appropriate financial oversight by protecting the information resources as part of their fiduciary duty. Where the placing of insurance is the final outcome, lower insurance premiums can normally be negotiated based on the increased security and concomitantly lower risk.

In order to be eligible for appropriate insurance coverage, a business must be able to demonstrate the serious intent to control risks internally with insurance claims being a last resort.

In the event of a claim, a similar exercise may have to be carried out in order to assess the extent of actual loss and to ensure that the controls specified at the time of risk evaluation were still operating as intended.

From an audit perspective, the IT auditor must understand the organization's existing insurance policies. Close scrutiny should be made of inclusions and exclusions to ensure that the coverage is as management intends. Such scrutiny has, in the past, revealed that logical damage to information may not be covered under traditional asset insurance because, without physical damage, information may not be recognized as an asset of the organization. Because of their spread through the Internet, there is an increasing trend toward insurance companies expressly excluding or severely limiting the coverage offered for losses caused by computer viruses, Trojan horses, and other malware. Technologies that are known to be of specific vulnerability, such as wireless networking, are commonly excluded from some types of insurance and specific protocols may be required when the organization connects to the outside world.

As with any insurance product, care must be taken to ensure that the vendor possesses the appropriate infrastructure to back up the policies sold. These policies tend to involve low-frequency/high-value claims and again care must be taken to ensure that the companies offering the insurance products have sufficient underwriting talent and industry credibility to substantiate the coverage they offer.

When facing IT risks specifically, multiple categories of insurance may be looked at in order to ensure adequacy of cover.

IT systems typically have high concentrations of electronic data processing (EDP) equipment: development/designer workstations, data communications equipment, servers, manufacturing equipment, scientific devices, and so on. It is important that the organization ensure that such items are adequately covered in the event of a loss since many general-purpose insurance policies exclude coverage or limit the coverage on certain types of electronic equipment.

In the unfortunate event of a loss, insurance coverage for Business Income & Extra Expense will cover ongoing expenses as well as the use of an alternate facility and equipment until the original business facility is fully restored. This may be critical for the business where servicing the client's needs in a time-critical manner is essential either to the ongoing survival of the business or to the prevention of substantial penalty clauses in service delivery contracts. In examining the contract, the auditor should determine that not only the software, hardware, and media are covered, but also laptops, notepads, and other mobile equipment used by the organization's staff.

As part of the overall comprehensive IT insurance solution, the organization may wish to consider professional liability coverage as well as errors and omissions insurance. Depending on the nature of the business, organizations supplying technical services to clients will typically be responsible for meeting particular client requirements and deadlines. Improper handling of client data or misinforming potential customers of a client, perhaps through inaccurate web site publications, can lead to significant penalties on the uninsured. If the organization has an obligation to control access to the client's private information, such as a cloud services provider may, a failure in this area could potentially lead to the closure of the business. Professional liability insurance is commonly used to mitigate risks associated with technology projects having lawsuit potential.

 ## SELF-INSURANCE

The organization may choose to retain the risk on the basis that it is more cost effective to absorb internally any losses incurred as a result of problems of an IT nature. This is a valid decision as long as it is a conscious decision and not arrived at by default. Based on the organization's assessment of its own risk-avoidance controls it may decide that the cost of offsetting the risk to a third party outweighs the benefits to be accrued. For some, the cost of insurance may be prohibitive and beyond their financial capability and therefore they choose to mitigate the risk using the appropriate managerial and technical controls. An organization that takes this approach must be confident of not only the adequacy but the effectiveness of such controls in mitigating risk.

In reality, the selection of insurance coverage normally involves the retention of some specific elements of risk and the transfer to a third party of those risks that could threaten the existence of the organization or which are simply more cost-effective to transfer. One alternative to insurance in this area is the use of outsourcing of specific IT functions to a third party in order to transfer the risks associated with those functions.

PART SEVEN

VII

Advanced IT Auditing

CHAPTER THIRTY-TWO

Auditing E-commerce Systems

ELECTRONIC COMMERCE (E-COMMERCE) includes all commercial activities performed through various electronic sources such as the Internet, Information Technology (IT) networks, ATM machines, electronic funds transfer (EFT), and electronic data interchange (EDI). One of its distinct characteristics is the use of computers to perform the transactions.

E-COMMERCE AND ELECTRONIC DATA INTERCHANGE: WHAT IS IT?

E-commerce involves the real-time processing of business transactions with full contractual liability either on a business-to-business (B2B) or business-to-customer (B2C) basis. This normally involves an individual entering data directly into another individual's or organization's computer systems. This is in contrast to electronic data interchange (EDI) where it may be considered as the computer-to-computer, application-to-application exchange of business data in a structured format. Effectively it replaces business forms such as invoices, purchase orders, checks, and so forth, with electronic transmissions.

Degrees of implementation may vary from the basic reception of a transmission on a micro computer and printing it, to a complex management of "distribution pipelines" integrating accounting and operational systems and effectively replacing paper audit trails with electronic signals.

EDI is not electronic mail, fax, or video text, although all of these may have a part in the overall network. To function effectively, EDI requires three primary components:

1. A standard format of a common language spoken between trading partners
2. Translation software performing file conversions from internal application formats to a standard format and back
3. A data communications link providing information-transport capabilities

EDI is now in use by a wide variety of companies worldwide covering all market sectors including:

▪ Manufacturing
▪ Shipping
▪ Construction
▪ Transport
▪ Finance
▪ Retail

OPPORTUNITIES AND THREATS

The benefits of successful e-commerce implementation in an organization include:

▪ Reduced transaction costs and greater productivity
▪ Service availability 24 hours a day, 7 days a week
▪ Opportunities for fundamental reform of how organizations and their supply chains communicate and work with business
▪ Opportunities for local business to grow and compete in the global marketplace

Despite the many benefits of e-commerce, an even greater number of risks pose concern for management.

Because e-commerce means global trading, the quantity and range of parties that can attempt to access the systems create a new challenge in protecting critical activities. By streamlining approvals, this may remove control steps that in turn increase risk compared with paper-based trading while, at the same time, the actual paper trail is greatly diminished.

Fraud in E-commerce

Fraud is a highly publicized risk in an e-commerce environment. Because of its global impact, fraud can be perpetrated either by a staff member within the firewalls or by anonymous parties in a foreign country using the Web as a tool and includes such activities as:

- Unauthorized movement of money such as payment to fictitious suppliers located in jurisdictions where recovery of money will be difficult
- Corruption of electronic ordering or invoicing
- Duplication of payment
- Repudiation of a transaction at either end
- Invalid contracts
- Suppliers not being paid for goods and services delivered
- Agencies not receiving services/goods already paid for
- Denying receipt of goods

Loss of Privacy/Confidentiality

For e-commerce to be successful, information about an organization or individual needs to be made available to other participants in the trading community. This can put information at risk such as:

- Services and prices, which are not normally provided to the general public
- Cost structures—particularly relating to tenders
- Catalogs of technical details, prices, or discounts offered
- Individuals' information such as name, address, contact details, previous purchase, services provided, and activity (such as criminal or medical). This, in turn, may lead to inadvertent breaches of privacy legislation.

Public confidence may be adversely impacted if information is accessed without due authorization.

The risks themselves may arise as a result of malicious activity from a virus attack or hacking and interception of transactions by unauthorized persons.

Lack of Authentication

Lack of authentication refers to unauthorized persons/parties performing a transaction. Proper authentication is a critical component of an e-commerce transaction because, once the party has been accepted in the system, a legally binding transaction process has begun. The risk will therefore involve creating liability for a party by, for example:

- Creation of fictitious suppliers ("masquerade"); for example, an agency believes it is dealing with its supplier when in fact it is dealing with a hacker in a foreign jurisdiction
- Unauthorized ordering or approving of a transaction
- Corruption of list of agreed suppliers

Corruption of Data

Corruption of data refers to issues of data integrity. The commonly held view is that risks involve activities that can be performed remotely through Web resources. The reality, however, is that almost all corruptions are conducted within the system.

Corruption may be accidental or malicious and could result in:

- Amending catalogs without authorization (advertising, reporting, approval)
- Destruction of audit trail
- Tampering with the ordering process
- Interrupting the recording of transactions
- Disrupting online tendering

Business Interruption

Business interruption is considered a key risk; if companies cannot promptly and adequately resume business after a crisis, there may be legal liabilities because services/goods were not delivered or payments were not made. Risks within this area would include denial of service attacks where high-volume, spurious transactions may stop the systems or slow it down to unacceptable levels.

Risk assessment will therefore be a critical tool for the internal auditor to assist in determining audit objectives and building an audit program.

Benefits of EDI as reported by Hansen and Hill[1] include quick response and access to information, cost efficiency, and the effect of EDI on paperwork. Benefits of EDI, anticipated as being the most important, include improved customer service and improved control of data as well as reduced clerical error and decreased administrative costs. Interestingly respondents did not report that these had been achieved as a major benefit so far.

With the increased interdependence comes increased vulnerabilities of computer-using companies. With a large number of partners, an upstream and downstream impact can be anticipated should anything go wrong and the domino effect makes trading partners vulnerable.

From an auditability point of view the way in which we must approach our audit of these systems changes dramatically because the loss of source documents removes a large part of the auditors' evidence of:

- Authorization and execution
- Completeness
- Single processing of transactions
- Capability of batching transactions

In addition, the altered transaction audit trail to an electronic form may result in the full trail existing for only a short time. This trail in itself may be vulnerable to alteration and loss.

Electronic Payments

At present, payment transmission as a form of EDI is one of the major growth areas and utilization of this form of EDI involves a mutual trust in systems between trading partners as well as a comprehensive data security policy, because failure of security in one partner may lead to uncontrolled risks in others. One future trend may well be that participation in an EDI network will require trading partners to demonstrate systems integrity on an ongoing basis.

Third-party service providers are also a new source of potential risk, including risks such as:

- Disclosure of confidential information
- Loss of transactions en-route
- Loss of the network at the service provider's site
- Loss of audit trails when going intra-network

Due to the risk of the domino effect, failures of applications can have a major impact not only on the host site but on all trading partners. As a result of this, the need for contingency planning becomes paramount. Contractual liability may be limited within the legal agreements; however, outage tolerances must be determined.

 ## RISK FACTORS

Risk factors may be unique to each organization and must be determined by a risk assessment. This must cover:

- Inherent risk. The gross risk of a specific threat ignoring risk-reduction elements. It becomes an informed, subjective evaluation of maximum risk.
- Control risk. That portion of inherent risk not covered by a single control element. That is the net exposure after a given control is accounted for.
- Control structure risk. An informed, subjective evaluation of the maximum potential net exposure after assessing the full control structure.

In identifying threats, a threat itself is an event that will result in direct damage unless averted or mitigated by controls. These should be identified by mixed discipline teams consisting of:

- System users
- Information System staff
- Auditors

 ## THREAT LIST

The initial threat list should be developed by the design team at the system-proposal stage and modified constantly during systems design. Typical threats could include (although not be limited to):

- Manipulation of input by an authorized user
- Outsider accessing messages in transit and amending them
- Message adulteration resulting in an overstatement of transaction
- Loss of transaction
- Duplication of transaction

Indicators are therefore required to detect:

- Circumstances leading to new threats
- Elimination of previously identified threats
- Conditions influencing the severity of previously identified threats (inherent risk)
- Conditions influencing the control-structure risk associated with the threat

 ## SECURITY TECHNOLOGY

The overall need for security technology and the application thereof will be determined largely by the nature of risks to the system itself. These normally take the form of authenticity of messages and confidentiality.

 ## "LAYER" CONCEPT

As noted previously, in EDI each message will have within it a number of header messages to route it across the networks. The most common model used for EDI is probably the ISO/OSI Seven Layer model:

1. **Physical.** Specifies the mechanical and electrical circuits
2. **Data Link.** Specification to move through physical links
3. **Network.** Routing and relaying through the data links
4. **Transport.** End-to-end data-transfer services
5. **Session.** Specification for orderly data exchange
6. **Presentation.** Specification of syntax used to represent data
7. **Application.** Interface to allow interaction to lower layers

 ## AUTHENTICATION

Two U.S. standards apply. ANSI X 12.58 covers message authentication and encryption while ANSI X 12.42 covers the rules governing exchanges of keys. In 1997 these merged with EDIFACT,[2] the global standard in EDI transactions.

Message authentication involves the prevention of undetected modification of the message content. This may involve key fields or the whole message. Typically this is affected by use of Message Authentication Code (MAC), which is calculated from the readable text and re-derived at the receiving end to be compared to the transmitted value. It is required of all electronic funds transfers in the United States.

In order for MACs to be effective, they must be secured in the same way as encryption algorithms are secured, they must be transparent to the user, and they must be automatically invoked.

 ## ENCRYPTION

Encryption has already been extensively covered in previous chapters but, within an EDI environment, special techniques are used to manage the encryption keys governing the four primary functions:

1. Key definition
2. Key generation
3. Key distribution
4. Key initialization

EDI keys are most frequently defined using a three-level hierarchy:

A *Master Key*, unique to each network node, is used to protect the other keys and the cryptograms. These Master Keys must be kept confidential within each organization.

Key Exchange Keys (KEK) are unique to each link in the network. Their function is to protect data keys during exchange when establishing communication between nodes.

The *Data Key* or *Working Key* is used for both data encryption and message authentication.

Security violations on the EDI network may be in the form of known or suspected violations, typically:

▪ MAC failure
▪ Compromise of keys
▪ Key counters out of step

In addition to security over keys, normal node security architectures are expected. These include items such as:

▪ Access control
▪ Accuracy and completeness controls
▪ Validity controls
▪ Software change control
▪ Auditability
▪ Timeliness controls
▪ Recoverability
▪ Legal issues

The legal issues may depend on the transaction types and whether international transactions are taking place but must address questions such as:

- Do the transactions form a contract?
- Is it enforceable?
- What terms and conditions are implied? Do governmental regulations apply?
- Is there a general contract between partners? What terms and conditions apply?
- Is the third-party network supplier covered by contract?
- Would a claim be enforceable?
- Which country's laws will apply?

 ## TRADING PARTNER AGREEMENTS

At present no mandatory standard is in place internationally and each country has its own recommended model for trading partner agreements. Generally, specialized legal advice should be sought over the wording of the contract. Contracts typically take two parts: EDI terms and general trading terms.

EDI terms and conditions include:

- Which laws will govern
- What is the definition of a signature
- When is the contract "received"

General trading terms are similar to those terms found on the back of standard business documents such as invoices. Disputes normally are over trading disputes rather than EDI disputes and may include:

- Quantities delivered
- Quality of goods
- Timeliness

The acceptance of evidence within the "structures" varies from country to country and should be stated in the trading agreement.

The primary factor may be the "reliability" of evidence and may involve "trusted" evidence sources such as full electronic logs and non-erasable optical disks. In order to comply with legal requirements, attention should also be given to record-retention policies, which should comply with corporate policies as well as legal requirements.

 ## RISKS AND CONTROLS WITHIN EDI AND E-COMMERCE

Authenticity

Once again, organizations doing business electronically are faced with the difficulty of determining that the person or system conducting business is, indeed, the entity it claims to be. Authentication for electronic business may be partially achieved using digital signatures whereby, for every transaction an authenticating party is enabled to check the signer's digital certificate in order to determine whether it has expired or is included in a certificate revocation list (CRL). If the certificate is still authentic and valid (confirmed with the public key), then the authenticity of the signer is accepted.

Nonrepudiation

Repudiation involves a denial of one or both parties that all or part of the transaction took place. Use of the digital signature and digital certificate make it extremely difficult for the signer of a transaction to repudiate the transaction or deny the contents of that transaction. With a digital signature in place, the sender's authenticity is confirmed and the hashing ensures that the data has not been corrupted en-route.

Timing

Where the timing of a transaction is critical, for example, where currency exchange rates apply, a transaction may be automatically time stamped to prove the authenticity of the exchange rates claimed.

Data Integrity

As with any business transaction it is critical that the receiver have some degree of certainty that the transaction has not been tampered with prior to its receipt. It is common in manual systems to require original documentation rather than accept copies and, in electronic form, digital signatures can include a hash value (mathematical summarization), which is unique to the digitally signed transaction. With this defense mechanism in place a digital signature can be seen as unique to the transaction that has just been signed rather than to the signer. When the transaction has been received the recipient will recalculate the hash value and compare it to determine whether the integrity of the transaction remains intact.

Interception of Data

Regardless of ensuring the authenticity of the originator and the validity of the data, there may still be an organizational risk if the data is intercepted and examined or even blocked. Data may be intercepted at its origin, prior to its introduction on the system, by simple observation of the data-collection process. In today's high security environment this can even be done by the closed circuit television cameras intended to enhance security. Due to the fact that such transactions are normally transmitted electronically (as opposed to fiber optics) for at least part of their journey, electromagnetic signals will be generated that can, in some instances, be detected using radio-receiving equipment or using transducer microphones, which can detect such signals without penetrating the cables. If an unauthorized individual can gain access to the data communication network, packet sniffers, designed to enhance network security by monitoring transmissions, can be used to intercept and copy messages or possibly even introduce their own spurious messages. As such, once again, encryption comes to the fore as the major control mechanism to obviate these risks.

Identity Theft

One risk that has arisen as a result of e-commerce is that of identity theft whereby a stranger gains access to authentication mechanisms permitting the assumption of an individual's identity in a provable fashion in order to carry out electronic transactions. Even if the individual whose identity has been "stolen" does not participate in any form of electronic transaction they may be vulnerable to this form of impersonation. Identity theft is discussed in detail in Chapter 36.

E-COMMERCE AND AUDITABILITY

Auditability implies the capability of substantiation of transactions coupled with the traceability of transactions from origin to final disposition or, in reverse, from final disposition back to origin. With the speed of e-commerce transactions, responding in retrospect to detective controls may prove too late to be of operational use. As such, the pre-verification of controls within systems becomes the option of choice coupled with the ongoing monitoring of transactions in real time through the process of continuous auditing as previously discussed. The sheer volumes involved in commercial e-commerce systems make substantial testing impractical and exception auditing becomes the only economic alternative. Tracing of transactions involves the electronic authentication of signals, the verification of electronic signals, and the maintenance of adequate audit trails. With these in place the tracing of transactions backward to source and forward to effect is possible.

Pre-verification of controls implies the testing of controls within the system on-line and in real time using techniques such as test decks, integrated test facilities (ITFs), embedded audit collection modules, and the like.

It is up to the auditor to determine the adequacy, functionality, and time of testing but this must include testing user profiles, passwords, and so on. On-line monitoring should be automated as far as possible due to the multiplicity of partners and low manual intervention levels. In addition the lack of paper audit trails and high transaction volumes in many cases preclude any other form of monitoring.

COMPLIANCE AUDITING

Compliance auditing to generally accepted standards must be agreed upon in advance by trading partners and should be formalized in the trading partner agreement. This may become, in the future, a legal prerequisite for participation in an EDI network and would be required to be conducted by a qualified auditor specializing in EDI security.

Retention of information for auditability is normally less than that for paper audit trails due to the faster reaction cycle required in which response needs to be virtually instantaneous. Legal statutes may still apply, however, and records may need to be retained for specific periods. Security-related data sets should be retained to match the general data retained including profiles, incident logs, and maintenance logs.

E-COMMERCE AUDIT APPROACH

As with any other audit, the audit approach in an e-commerce environment involves the standard six basic steps, namely:

1. Preliminary survey
2. Documenting the environment
3. Audit planning
4. Program development
5. Audit fieldwork
6. Audit reporting

The overall audit objective is to determine by evaluation and testing that control objectives have been achieved, are being achieved, and will continue to be achieved. The auditor seeks to determine that the appropriate controls exist and perform as expected and that standards and policies are appropriate and are being achieved.

This environment will normally involve the auditor in extensive use of computer-assisted audit techniques (CAATs) to determine the effectiveness of these controls. The auditor will need a mixture of skills including both mainframe and micro experience as well as network and communication experience, an understanding of access and security controls, and the corporate EDI and e-commerce business cycles. Not all auditors need all skills; however, the use of multidisciplinary teams and outside experts may give the auditor access to the appropriate knowledge, skills, and disciplines.

The preliminary survey involves a review of general background of business operations allowing the auditor to develop threat categories and identify controls mitigating those threats. This in turn leads to the development of overall control structures and allows the auditor to observe the operations. All assessments of inherent risk should be agreed with the users, IS, and management.

Steps in reviewing the general business objectives include observing the activities of the system and evolution of the system as well as determining any known weaknesses from these evaluations. At this stage legal contracts may also be reviewed together with contingency plans.

AUDIT TOOLS AND TECHNIQUES

Audit tools available for identifying controls and determining their effectiveness include the standard audit tools of internal control questionnaires, interviews, observation, and document review. At this stage no evaluation of effectiveness would be performed. Perhaps one of the most difficult audit techniques to learn is observation. "Looking with a purpose" is an acquired skill bringing corroboration of understanding and should provide the first evidence of control operation environments.

Network documentation derives from the business needs governing items such as:

- Reliability and performance
- Costs
- Security
- Control structures
- Responsibility structure

An evaluation of network reliability will typically involve the auditor seeking answers to such questions as:

- Who monitors performance?
- Who corrects problems?
- Who examines the network periodically?
- What problems have occurred?
- What action was taken?
- How is the network kept up to date?

At the same time, the costs of such systems would cause the auditor to seek to determine who accounts for the costs, whether EDI suppliers and vendors accounted for costs appropriately, and what controls management relies on to ensure accuracy and completeness of EDI charges.

From a legal perspective the auditor will seek evidence that legal contracts exist, have been validated with competent legal authorities, and are valid within appropriate laws and jurisdiction.

Network security will be assured by determining what controls exist in order to ensure that the system will be available when required, that both sender and recipient can be authenticated, and that both disclosure and transaction modification can be adequately prevented.

 ## AUDITING SECURITY CONTROL STRUCTURES

In auditing security control structures, as with any other audit, the major steps involve identification of key control points and those controls relied upon to cover primary control concerns. Once controls have been identified, they can be documented as they are intended to operate, and measurement criteria may be designed to identify and measure their effectiveness.

In auditing the EDI and e-commerce structures, auditors must pay particular attention to:

- Management and organization
- Accuracy and completeness controls
- Security
- Auditability
- Timeliness
- Recoverability of the system
- Electronic funds transfer systems

 ## COMPUTER-ASSISTED AUDIT TECHNIQUES

Implementation of the audit program will, in all probability, involve use of CAATs in all the varieties previously discussed. Where generalized audit software is required, the auditors must be capable of using the organization software as comfortably as they currently use a calculator. To this end, the latest version of IDEA (demonstration version) is included with this book. The demonstration version includes a full tutorial on the use of the software. The software is downloadable as per the instructions at the end of the book.

As always, in utilizing CAATs, the auditor should beware of the common pitfalls of obtaining the wrong files or the wrong layouts, of using out-of-date documentation, or prejudging results.

 ## NOTES

1 James V. Hansen, and Ned C. Hill. "Control and Audit of Electronic Data Interchange," *MIS Quarterly*. December 1989, pp. 403–414.
2 http://www.unece.org/etrades/download/downmain.htm#edifact.

COMPUTER-ASSISTED AUDIT TECHNIQUES

NOTES

CHAPTER THIRTY-THREE

Auditing UNIX/Linux

T HE UNIX OPERATING SYSTEM, although now in widespread use in environments concerned about security, was not really designed with security in mind. This does not mean that UNIX does not provide any security mechanisms; indeed, several very good ones are available. However, most "out of the box" installation procedures still install the operating system with little or no security enabled.

HISTORY

UNIX was originally designed by technical programmers as an operating system for use by other programmers. The environment in which it was used was one of open cooperation, not one of privacy. Programmers typically collaborated with each other on projects, and hence preferred to share their files with each other without having to climb over security hurdles.

By the early 1980s, many universities began to move their UNIX systems out of the research laboratories and into the computer centers, enabling their user population as a whole to use this new and wonderful system. Many businesses and government sites began to install UNIX systems as well, particularly as desktop workstations became more powerful and affordable. In these environments the UNIX operating system was no longer being used where open collaboration was the goal.

Universities required their students to use the system for class assignments, yet they did not want the students to be able to copy from each other. Businesses used their UNIX systems for confidential tasks such as bookkeeping and payroll. And national governments used UNIX systems for various unclassified yet sensitive purposes.

To complicate matters, new features have been added to UNIX over the years, making security even more difficult to control. Perhaps the most problematic features are those relating to networking: remote login, remote command execution, network file systems, diskless workstations, electronic mail, and the Internet.

All of these features have increased the utility and usability of UNIX by untold amounts. However, these same features, along with the widespread connection of UNIX systems to the Internet and other networks, have opened up many new areas of vulnerability to unauthorized abuse of the system.

UNIX has been available for PCs for some time, but you had to pay nearly as much for fully configured commercial PC UNIX operating system as was budgeted for the PC hardware itself. This situation changed, however, when Linus Torvalds of the University of Helsinki, Finland, decided to build a UNIX-like operating system for the PC. Many programmers around the world contributed and collaborated to bring Linux to its current state.

Version 1 of Linux was released in 1994. Linux proved to be the exception to the rule that "you get what you pay for" in that the source code was available free of cost to anyone. Since 1994 many developers around the world have collaborated over the Internet to add features and functionality. Incremental versions have continually been downloaded by users and tested in a variety of system configurations. This means the Linux revisions ultimately go through much more rigorous beta-testing than any commercial software.

Over the past few years Linux has matured into a full-fledged 32-bit and 64-bit operating system with features that rival those of commercial UNIX systems and with graphical user interfaces that enable it to compete directly with Microsoft Windows environments. The current version at the time of publication uses LINUX kernel v 3.0.

Microsoft has responded to the UNIX challenge through Windows. The late 1990s saw vendor after vendor abandoning the UNIX server platform in favor of Windows 2000 while concurrently software suppliers who traditionally service the Windows sector have been climbing on the Linux bandwagon.

Unlike many freely available software programs, Linux comes with extensive online information on topics such as installing and configuring the operating system for the wide varieties of PCs and peripherals possible. A large number of Linux users use the system at home and increasingly Linux is finding a home in the business market.

Today, Linux is first and foremost a server operating system. Many applications are now appearing that allow Linux to be a user's primary workstation desktop system and projects are underway to enable Linux to run applications software designed for the Windows environment. Linux performs as well as (if not better than) other operating systems running on identical hardware. Most of the popular database packages are available in Linux-native versions, including products from Oracle, Informix, Sybase, IBM, and Computer Associates. Personal productivity software such as Corel WordPerfect, StarOffice, and Applixware are all making it possible for Linux to be the primary system for many users.

Several software houses have come forward introducing tailored versions of Linux and the suppliers charge for the value-added component of their version. Ultimately control of Linux is based around the control of UNIX because that is the core of the operating environment.

For Linux, or any other operating system for that matter, to achieve all-around success as the standard operating system in multi-user computing, there must be a reliable method of preventing unauthorized users from accessing information. UNIX/Linux systems are a favorite target for hackers and crackers, often because they used UNIX in schools and universities and can still apply that knowledge to literally thousands of sites. Internet usage has popularized UNIX features such as anonymous logins, still used by many UNIX sites, and the relatively easy to use FTP (file transfer protocol) to copy files from one remote site to another. These facilities also allow casual users access into some systems.

In order for an operating environment to provide an acceptable level of security, the system should be hard for unauthorized persons to break into. That is, the value of the work necessary for unauthorized persons to break in should exceed the value of the protected data.

In order to achieve adequate control in a UNIX/Linux environment, it is essential that all users, data, and system components can be uniquely identified. Authentication (confirmation of identity) must be achieved for individual users as they enter the system. Access rights and permissions for users, systems, and processes must be granted on a need-to-have basis only with proper authorization. Assurance must be provided that all systems operations are correct, reliable, and authentic in order to ensure the integrity of processes and data. It must be possible to trace all significant events including successful events and unsuccessful events.

SECURITY AND CONTROL IN A UNIX/LINUX SYSTEM

In order to implement effective security, a full risk assessment will be required in order to:

- Identify and categorize systems and information which could be a risk if not adequately secured
- Identify threats which could have a negative impact on UNIX data assets including both the value and probability of such threats
- Quantify the criticality and sensitivity of sensitive data assets and prioritize them in terms of vulnerabilities and need for security
- Identify those actions relied upon to mitigate or reduce the risk, including operational controls as well as technical controls

The basic elements of security and control cover are:

- Identification and authentication
- Access control

- System, or file and process integrity
- Recoverability
- Flexibility

 ARCHITECTURE

The basic architecture of a UNIX/Linux system follows a strict hierarchy starting with the hardware on which the operating system resides, through the channel (often a UNIX system) that interacts directly with computer hardware and provides the basic functions of input, output, scheduling, memory management, security protection, interrupt error handling, and system accounting.

The *file system* provides a hierarchical structure of directories and files with the capability of file level security.

The UNIX *shell* is *the* most frequently used utility program controlling the initial interaction with any given user once login has been successful. The shell is a command interpreter that prompts the user for commands and acts as primary user interface. In the Linux environment the shell will typically be a graphical user interface to give a Windows lookalike environment.

Tools and *utilities* are standard programs provided with the operating system. These range in use from common tasks such as printing, copying files, editing text, and developing software through graphics and communications support. Utilities in any form are typically very powerful and may prove a significant security threat to standard operating environments.

At the application level, *user programs*—either in-house developed, or developed by third parties—may be written in a variety of programming languages to create standard business applications.

 UNIX SECURITY

Access to UNIX is achieved by logging into the system using an account. The user recognizes an account as a name and the system recognizes the account as a number. To UNIX, any account with the user ID (UID) of zero (0) is known as root or superuser and has unrestricted access to all other account passwords and files.

Login accounts may be protected by passwords, which are used to authenticate users before granting access to the system. In most, although not all, UNIX installations, passwords are stored encrypted in a password file providing fundamental protection against casual browsers. Initially, this was thought to be a highly secure environment; however, hacker tools, which are readily available on the Internet, make the breaking of these passwords less problematic. Tools such as *crack* work by comparing encrypted password file entries with dictionary lists that are encrypted using the same algorithms. This type of attack is not unique to UNIX. Password length, composition, and change restrictions are possible and users can be restricted to specific shells to limit further access.

In should be noted at this point that many of these facilities are optional and, although they can be highly effective, in many installations they are not properly used.

Once users have logged in they are given an operating environment or *shell*, which allows them to interact with the system prior to file access. At the times files are created they belong to the *owner* who typically can configure the access control. The types of ownership recognized within UNIX include the direct *owner* of the file; the *group*, which is a set of people given common access rights; and *world* or *public*, which is granted to all users. Access to files is then based on "permissions" that are granted uniquely for owner, group, or world access. Each individual file may permit read access, write access, or execute access.

 ## SERVICES

As part of the standard UNIX network package, numerous network services are provided, all of which contain security risks and must be balanced against the business needs. Examples of the most common network services include:

- **File transfer protocol (FTP),** which allows transfers of files between systems. Anonymous ftp allows anyone on a network to deposit or retrieve files from another machine on the network. This is commonly used on the Internet as a low-cost method to distribute information but, if not adequately controlled, it represents a major security threat.
- **Trivial file transfer protocol (TFTP)** is a server similar to FTP except that there is no security. *This program should never be permitted in production environments.*
- **Telnet** is a service that permits users to log in to remote computers as if they were on a directly connected line. However, user IDs and passwords are transmitted unencrypted and are therefore vulnerable. Few sites continue to use Telnet; however, in many sites the facility remains enabled and open to abuse.
- **rlogin** provides similar remote user services to Telnet and may also prove a security threat.
- **Trusted Host** permits any user to migrate from one system to another without providing a password as long as the user name exists on the second host.
- **Trusted User** provides similar services but permits the user to log in to a given account without requiring password entry.
- **Finger** is a program permitting identification of the user ID, name, location, and other semi-confidential information for every user connected.
- **Network Information System (NIS)** permits multiple computers to share password and other system files over the network. If badly configured, this can lead to potential vulnerabilities.
- **Network File System (NFS)** allows computers to share files over networks by permitting the user, once logged in, to *mount* file disks and access them as if the files were stored locally. No additional logging in to the other system is required.

- **Hypertext Transport Protocol (HTTP)** permits users to communicate with other Internet users on the World Wide Web using a set of tools built around *HTML* (Hypertext Markup Language).
- **Simple Mail Transport Protocol (SMTP)** is used commonly with mail programs that do not provide adequate security by themselves.
- **Network News Transport Protocol (NNTP)** is used to facilitate access to news-groups in much the same way that *mail* collects mail.
- **UNIX to UNIX Communication Protocol (UUCP)** is a communication mechanism used by UNIX machines to exchange files including mail. Although this has been largely replaced by *HTTP*, the facility is still possible and in many cases unprotected due to its perceived lack of use.

 ## DAEMONS

UNIX uses a variety of special programs to support the Kernel (the central part of the operating system). These programs, called daemons, stay resident within the memory of the machine and operate in conjunction with the Kernel. Given the comprehensive nature of these programs, modification access should be severely restricted to systems administrators. Daemons include *init* (the initial process after putting), *logind* (the login daemons in some UNIX systems), *cron* (submits other jobs based on time request), and *sendmail* (handles SMTP processes), among others.

 ## AUDITING UNIX

The primary objectives of a UNIX security audit are:

- Evaluation of the adequacy of controls over physical and logical access to the UNIX environment.
- Evaluation of the adequacy of procedural controls designed to reduce the above risks to acceptable levels.
- Evaluate and test the security and audit features of the operating environment to ensure their effectiveness and the appropriateness of the monitoring of such controls.

One of the critical aspects of maintaining computer security is the monitoring of the system. Auditors must ensure that this monitoring is carried out on a regular basis.

- **Daily.** On a daily basis, checks must be made for:
  - Inappropriate access permissions to sensitive files
  - Login failures
  - Failed access to sensitive files
  - Successful logins from unknown hosts
  - User activity after hours

- Unexpectedly mounted file systems
- Unexpected changes in permissions and ownerships
- System reboots and shutdowns
- Changes to the system date and/or clock
- Existence of a valid password file
- Owned by *root*
- Read permissions for *other*
- Password field for every account
- Only *root* having the UID of 0
- **Monthly.** On a monthly basis, checks should be made for:
  - System usage totaled by user
  - Unusual messages from system daemons
  - Account and activity
  - Error messages and the system log files
- **Random.** From time to time the systems administrator should examine the systems for potential problem areas by checking for:
  - Unexpected users logged on
  - Unexpected hosts access
  - Normal users logged on at unexpected times
  - Unexpected system processes running
  - Normal system processes not running

SCRUTINY OF LOGS

Log files are commonly kept of user access, incidents, file access attempts, and so on. Maintaining these logs is an overhead on the machine and worthless unless they are frequently and regularly scrutinized and the appropriate action taken based on the contents.

AUDIT TOOLS IN THE PUBLIC DOMAIN

Many tools have been written to examine the security of UNIX systems. While some of these have been written with security administrators in mind, some have been written by hackers and crackers to determine system vulnerabilities. They still may be used by auditors for the same reason, but care should be taken that the programs do not contain unauthorized coding inserted by the hackers. Some of these tools are:

- **COPS.** *Computer Oracle and Password System* is a public-domain assessment tool for a single UNIX system. This program identifies suspected problems and recommends fixes.

- **Tiger.** Similar to *COPS* but enhanced and more common than *COPS* in addressing security issues. Many sites use both.
- **Crack.** The crack utility uses a dictionary and rules to make password guesses. In many sites the use of common words as passwords can lead to some 60 percent of all passwords being broken with one pass of *crack*. Crack should be used with care because broken passwords are stored in plain text and can therefore be scrutinized by unauthorized users.
- **Npasswd.** Npasswd is a public domain password checker that replaces the standard password command and prevents users from selecting easily guessed passwords.
- **Satan.** *Security Administrators Tool for Analyzing Networks* searches for vulnerabilities by recognizing several common network-related security problems and reporting on them. For each type of problem found, Satan offers an explanation of the problem and what the impact could be. It also explains what can be done about a problem to fix it.
- **Swatch.** *Simple Watcher* helps monitor daemons.
- **Tripwire.** Tripwire is a file integrity checker that compares a designated set of files against information stored in a previously generated database. Differences are flagged and logged so that critical system files with unauthorized changes can be quickly identified and corrected.

 ## UNIX PASSWORD FILE

The normal location for the UNIX password file is within/etc/passwd; however, on a UNIX system with either *NIS* or password shadowing, the password data may be stored elsewhere. *NIS* (Network Information System) is used to permit many machines on a network to share configuration information, including password data. Password shadowing is a feature whereby the encrypted password field of /etc/passwd is replaced with a special token where the actual encrypted password is stored separately and is not readable by normal system users. The exact location of the shadow password file is dependent on the version of UNIX or Linux implemented.

An entry in the UNIX password file consists of seven colon-delimited fields consisting of a username: the encrypted UNIX password with optional password aging data: the user number: the group number: GECOS information: the home directory: the shell. Thus,

    robert:3fh65ghF5f3fg:2302:10:Robert
    Jones:/home/robert:/bin/bash

This would then interpret as:

Username	Robert
UNIX password	3fh65ghF5f3fg

User number	2302
Group Number	10
GECOS Information	Robert Jones
Home directory	/home/robert
Shell	/bin/bash

 ## AUDITING UNIX PASSWORDS

UNIX passwords are encrypted with a one-way function and cannot be decrypted. At the time of log on, UNIX accepts the text entered at the Password: prompt and passes it through the standard UNIX encryption algorithm with the encrypted version being compared to the version stored in the passwd file.

In order to audit UNIX passwords, each encrypted password in the UNIX password file is compared to a set of potential encrypted passwords. These potential encrypted passwords may be created by encrypting every password in a list of plain text passwords. This is an example of a dictionary attack. Alternatively, every possible combination of letters, numbers, and special characters may be encrypted systematically and compared to the encrypted passwords. This is an example of a brute force attack.

UNIX password auditing software such as that listed previously uses word lists to implement either a dictionary attack or a brute force attack

A sample UNIX audit program is included as Appendix D.

CHAPTER THIRTY-FOUR

Auditing Windows VISTA and Windows 7

THE PHENOMENAL SUCCESS of Windows from the time of the release of Version 3.0 surprised many people. The success did not surprise the engineers and evangelists at Microsoft, who had praised Windows since the beginning, and it did not surprise users who had preferred the benefits of a graphical interface, multitasking, and connectivity between applications for years. As a result, Windows has steadily become the operating system of choice in the corporate environment.

 HISTORY

In 1981, IBM introduced to the marketplace the IBM personal computer (PC) based on the Intel 8088 chip. This PC arrived bundled with a 16-bit, single-user, command-line operating system called PC-DOS 1.0. The operating system was produced by a relatively new company called Microsoft, better known for its BASIC interpreter. The operating system was based around a functionality of the much smaller operating system, CP/M, which had been used on home computers prior to that date. Microsoft also introduced its own proprietary version of the operating system, which was known as MS-DOS.

In 1983, Microsoft released the more powerful MS-DOS version 2, which contained a number of more powerful features derived from UNIX. In 1986 MS-DOS 3.0 was produced to coincide with the introduction of the new IBM PC/AT, but DOS continued to be a single-user, command-line-oriented operating system.

In 1990, partially in response to the graphical user interfaces utilized in Apple computers, Microsoft released a graphical shell called Windows 3.0. Windows had originally entered into the marketplace in 1985 in competition with Software Carousel, both of which were intended to facilitate multitasking in a graphical environment and neither of which was particularly successful in the marketplace. With the advent of Windows 3.0, 3.1, and 3.11 (Windows for Workgroups), Windows was fully adopted into the workplace and came to dominate single-user PCs. These versions of Windows were effectively graphical user interfaces overlaid on top of the MS-DOS operating system, which still controlled both a machine and the structuring of the file system. All application programs ran in the same address space and any problems would typically stop the system in its tracks with a *General Protection Fault* error message.

In autumn 1995, Windows 95 was released with the new graphical interface and the latest MS-DOS 7.0, and incorporated many of the features found in many mainframe operating systems including true multiprogramming, process management, and virtual memory management. As it was delivered, however, Windows 95 retained much of the old 16-bit code from the earlier versions and was still subject to the limitations of the MS-DOS file system.

The arrival of Windows 98 in June of that year still did not resolve the MS-DOS problems. Once again, the user interface changed to integrate the networking functionality and the desktop more closely and, although it could now handle larger disks, Windows 98 still retained some of the old code, which caused performance problems in multiprogramming. Its memory sharing could still permit programs to interfere with each other, resulting in system crashes.

To coincide with the millennium, Windows Me was released with more support for entertainment and Internet features; however, the base was still Windows 98.

NT AND ITS DERIVATIVES

While all this was going on in the home and, largely, in single-user environments, Microsoft developed a brand new 32-bit operating system called Windows New Technology or, as it became popularly known, Windows NT. This operating system was intended primarily for the business market because, by the time it was introduced in 1993, the first indications were appearing that networked microcomputers could prove a significant supplement to mainframe computing in the workplace. The initial version of this operating system was known as Windows NT 3.1 in order to align it numerically with the popular Windows 3.1 16-bit operating system, although, even at this early stage, MS-DOS had disappeared with only a command-line interface remaining. In the early 1990s memory was still comparatively expensive and NT utilized much more memory than 3.1 and initially NT languished in the marketplace.

In 1996 NT 4.0 was introduced with a similar interface to Windows 95 but with the power, reliability, and security potential of the NT operating environment. With this version of the operating system Microsoft began to dominate the office automation side of computing and even to challenge mainframes with large networks of integrated PCs. NT was seen as a stable operating platform with the opportunities to create a highly secure environment, which had not been achievable under the DOS-based systems. Under DOS, files and directories utilized FAT (File Allocation Table) and could be protected only to the extent that they were either shared or not shared, hidden or not hidden, and read-only or not read-only. NT introduced a new file system, NTFS, which could now offer restrictions by user and by a group of users to modify, read, write, as well as read and execute files and programs.

Windows 2000 (originally codenamed NT 5.0) was a true multiprogramming operating system with each individual process running in a private demand-page protected virtual address space. Processes were able to have multiple threads under the control of the operating system. NTFS was extended to support encrypted files, mounted volumes, linked files, and quotas while many of the facilities of Windows 98, which had been missing in NT 4.0, such as support for Plug-and-Play devices, USB bus, and FireWire, were incorporated together with Kerberos security, system monitoring tools, and active directory. *Active Directory* is a set of directory services for locating and accessing resources over the network. This includes information regarding accounts, organizational units (OUs), security policies, files, services, and domains. Active directory can be shared across LANs and even WANs. Like the parameters held within the *registry*, the active directory is protected by access control lists (ACLs), which limit access.

Windows XP (Experienced) was the next operating system introduced in late 2001 with the intention of merging the two fundamental Windows product lines. Windows XP included a new interface with the ability to change its appearance and functionality largely based on the Windows NT 5.1 kernel. It did, however, move strongly toward the home market in its support of entertainment and Internet-based systems.

Windows Server 2003 was offered in April 2003 as an update to Windows Server 2000 with enhanced security and management features.

The next client operating system, Windows Vista, was released in November 2006. It had enhanced security introduced by a new restricted user mode called User Account Control, replacing the "administrator-by-default" philosophy of Windows XP. Windows 7 is the current release after Windows Vista and was released in late 2009. Windows 8 is the next scheduled version of Microsoft Windows, scheduled for release in fall 2012.

For purposes of this book, security and auditing will be looked at from a Vista/Windows 7 perspective.

 ## AUDITING WINDOWS VISTA/WINDOWS 7

Windows VISTA/Windows 7 are network operating systems designed for enterprises, servers, and workstations. Networks running Windows VISTA/Windows 7 are designed to share key information and resources throughout an organization.

VISTA/Windows 7 manages a number of security policy issues. It also makes provision for the concept that each user might need a different environment. It has a comprehensive auditing function that enables the administrator to determine which events will be recorded, and then to audit these events at a later date.

Although the subject of securing and auditing a Windows VISTA/Windows 7 network is worthy of a manual in its own right, and several excellent guides have been written, nevertheless the fundamental approach remains the same as any other operating environment. The first stage of the audit is to identify hardware, software, network, people, and administrative issues within the operating environment.

This involves identifying and locating the VISTA/Windows 7 hardware and checking to ensure that:

- All devices are identifiable and incorporated in an inventory.
- All devices belong to you and are within your control.
- There is adequate physical security, particularly over servers and over locations that produce sensitive or valuable output.
- There are written procedures covering administrative and operational practices, system roles, routine maintenance, and housekeeping functions.

The second stage is to determine the uses to which the system is put:

- What systems are being run?
- What communications networking takes place?
- What sensitive data exists and how does management intend that it be protected?
- What protection mechanisms have been put in place and how is their effectiveness monitored?

The third stage is to match the users of functionality within the systems against the requirements of their jobs to ensure:

- Adequate segregation of duties
- Enforcement of appropriate levels of confidentiality
- The maintenance of integrity of systems, data, communications, and the operating environment itself

It should always be borne in mind that, while enforcement takes place at a technical level, the control objectives remain business objectives. If these do not adequately support the business, the best that can be hoped for is strict enforcement of sloppy control.

The latest Windows 7 comes with more than 300 diagnostic tools, many of which are extremely useful for IT audit purposes. It also has numerous security settings that enable it to meet compliance regulations, including U.S. government regulations. It should be noted, that, although Windows 7 is fairly secure out of the box, it is not sufficiently secure for environments requiring high levels of security. Like any operating system, Windows 7 needs configuration changes and other measures to reach its full security potential.

 ## PASSWORD PROTECTION

As with UNIX, passwords within VISTA/Windows 7 are one-way encrypted, although they use a different hashing algorithm. In order to ensure backward compatibility with

Microsoft LAN manager software, it also stores the passwords redundantly as a DES hash. Because of the poor design of this algorithm, Windows network security can be detrimentally impacted and can be vulnerable to a similar dictionary or brute force attack that UNIX is.

As with UNIX, password audit (cracking) software exists including *John the Ripper* (http://www.openwall.com/john/) and *Cain & Abel* (http://www.oxid.it/cain.html). John the Ripper is a fast password cracker, currently available for many flavors of UNIX (11 are officially supported, not counting different architectures), Windows, DOS, BeOS, and OpenVMS. Its primary purpose is to detect weak passwords. Cain & Abel is a password recovery tool for Microsoft Operating Systems. It allows easy recovery of various kinds of passwords by sniffing the network; auditing encrypted passwords using dictionary, brute force, and cryptanalysis attacks; decoding scrambled passwords; revealing password boxes; uncovering cached passwords; and analyzing routing protocols.

 ## VISTA/WINDOWS 7

There are some significant differences in the ways in which VISTA/Windows 7 handles file sharing over previous versions.

The default workgroup name in Windows VISTA has been changed to WORK-GROUP. New computers running Windows VISTA can have a different workgroup name than the other computers on your network. Using different workgroups gives more flexibility; however, from an audit perspective it takes more time and effort to view all of the computers on the network. It is worth noting that where an older operating system had a workgroup name of MSHOME, this will be retained unless changed by the user. This can cause confusion when networking computers with upgraded operating systems (MSHOME) and new systems (WORKGROUP) and file sharing appear not to work. Both systems must share the same workgroup name before file sharing can be effective.

Unlike previous versions of Windows in which the Shared Documents folder was used to simplify file sharing, VISTA uses the Public folder. With Public folder sharing enabled, the public folders and all of the folders within the Public folder are automatically shared, with the name Public removing the need to configure file sharing on separate folders. Sharing can be achieved by either moving or copying the file or folder you want to share on the network to the Public folder.

By default, VISTA does not allow simple file sharing. Access to shared folders, including the public folder (if shared), requires a user name and password.

 ## SECURITY CHECKLIST

From an audit perspective, the auditor must determine that:

- NTFS is in use in all partitions
- Simple file sharing is disabled whenever possible

- *Guest* user accounts have been disabled
- Unnecessary user accounts have been eliminated
- All user accounts use passwords, particularly the Administrator account and any users with Administrator privileges
- The Administrator user account has been renamed
- Passwords are not "remembered" by Windows
- A minimum number of users have been added to the Administrator group
- Firewalls are used for network as well as Internet connection
- Antivirus and anti-spyware software is installed and up to date on all workstations
- Microsoft service packs and hotfixes are kept up to date, particularly for security fixes
- Wireless network connections are fully secured against unauthorized access
- All backups on tape, CD, DVD, or memory stick are adequately secured
- An effective password-security policy has been implemented by the administrator
- The last logged in username is not automatically displayed in the login dialog box
- The ability to boot from a floppy, CD-ROM, USB device, or the network is disabled and physically secured systems are used
- Autorun is disabled on all CD/DVD drives
- The page file is automatically cleared on system shutdown
- Backup and restore features exist in both VISTA and Windows 7. Ensure that this has been used because certain forms of hardware failure or corruption may block access to disk files
- BitLocker Drive Encryption is a facility that is available in the Enterprise and Ultimate editions of both VISTA and Windows 7. It is designed to protect data by providing encryption for entire volumes. It can also be used to protect all files on your external or USB flash drives.
- User Account Control (UAC) attempts to improve the security of Microsoft Windows by limiting application software to standard user privileges until an administrator authorizes an increase or elevation. In this way, only applications trusted by the user may receive administrative privileges.

Many books have been written specifically on the securing and control of Windows VISTA/Windows 7 for auditors who seek to specialize in this area.

A sample Windows/VISTA/Windows 7 audit program is included as Appendix E.

CHAPTER THIRTY-FIVE

Foiling the System Hackers

H ACKING HAS BEEN DESCRIBED as the electronic equivalent of breaking and entering. It is the deliberate gaining of unauthorized access to a computer system, usually through the use of communication facilities.

Consider how we protect our homes from breaking and entering. We restrict access by keeping doors and windows shut, by locking and bolting doors—especially if the house is empty or it is night—and by use of alarm systems. These are all defense stratagems designed to deter or detect intruders. The level of deterrence depends on the degree to which we enforce our defenses (not leaving doors open or unlocked), the quality of those defenses (flimsy door or armor-plated door), and the desirability of entry (how valuable the known contents of the house are to the would-be intruder). Beyond these security deterrents are deterrents imposed by society through legislation. Thus if someone breaks into our house he or she is liable to be prosecuted in the criminal courts and may be sued for damages in the civil courts.

Having gained access to our houses the intruder may just browse through the contents of the house, or may steal assets (both tangible and intangible), or may cause malicious damage (either at the time or at a future time by use of a time bomb). This is exactly the same with intruders (hackers) in our computer systems.

There has been much written and said on the subject of hacking, much of which has concentrated upon whether or not such activities should be criminalized. There has been a case made that hackers provide a useful service in that they help to identify weaknesses in computer systems and that to criminalize their activities would be to drive them even further underground and into the arms of organized crime. This is the same argument that would legalize petty theft to stop petty thieves from becoming large-scale thieves. There is also an argument that suggests that hackers are benign and that they are harmless browsers. This position would justify the total abolition of all business and personal privacy, leading to an unlimited "Big Brother" scenario.

Any company may be a target from anywhere in the world and the world's most spectacular "hack" has not yet been caught.

In order to break into a system from outside the established network, the system must either have dial-up line connections, or be connected to a networking service such as the Internet. There are a number of reasons why a computer might have such a link. Commonly, the computer manufacturer's technical-support staff can dial in and review diagnostic and breakdown records, which the machine automatically accumulates, and may even initiate changes to systems software on the machine. This may be true for both application systems and operating systems. Some applications require input from third parties such as customers or sales representatives, but the access is required relatively infrequently and therefore a leased (i.e., a permanently rented) telephone line would not be appropriate.

Another danger has arisen. Networks are linked together, via gateways, to allow legitimate communication to take place between organizations. However, when a link is made into another network without stringently controlling access via the gateway, anyone with access to the other network now has access to your network. That person can then try to access any resources that are not properly protected on the network. This includes users who, to avoid detection at the corporate firewall, connect a modem directly to their personal computer (PC) and enter the Internet. If they are simultaneously on-line to the network so, potentially, is the whole Internet.

With the introduction of e-commerce these threats have multiplied.

To access many computer systems, a hacker must have a dial-up number or network address. These can be easier to obtain than may at first be thought. Hackers sometimes try to bluff, and call the computer department on its published voice number and pretend to be a confused user requesting information. In many cases computer departments have a *help desk* whose job it is to help just such users. It should never be forgotten that many system hackers are internal hackers employed by the company. In addition hackers may be ex-employees or their associates.

If entering via dial-up, once the hacker manages to obtain a dial-up number, he then must discover the protocol that the machine he is attempting to log onto uses. However, identifying the correct protocol is not usually difficult. Most computer publications will publish information that, with a little research on the part of the hacker, will yield the required information. Even recruitment advertisements can provide a wealth of information on hardware and software environments.

Assuming a hacker managed to obtain a sign-on screen display of the target computer on his terminal, he will be asked for a valid user ID and password. It is not particularly difficult to obtain a valid user ID because commonly this is not thought to be confidential. This can be done by:

- Trying standard user-IDs that comes with the system and will be published in the manufacturer's literature describing the system.
- Trial and error. Badly controlled systems may accept an unlimited number of attempts to input the correct user ID, without generating a warning or shutting down the terminal. User names are commonly used as user IDs.
- From some knowledge of the installation. User IDs are not normally treated as confidential and are often displayed on printouts, for example.

Assuming a hacker manages to get this far, he must then enter a valid password for the system. Hackers often gain access to systems by using standard passwords. Many systems are distributed with certain standard user IDs and passwords, such as the systems manager's user IDs (SYSMAN, ADMIN, or SPECIAL) and the chief operator's user IDs (OPS, OPERATIONS, etc.), and a user ID for the manufacturer's systems engineer. When the system is supplied to the installation, it often has these standard user IDs set up with an initial password, often the same as the user ID or PASSWORD. These user IDs may have more power than any other user of the system and are therefore the hacker's first choice.

All this information is commonly provided with the supplier's documentation provided with every system and is also sold independently by the supplier.

The auditor should review the standard user IDs supplied and ensure that they have been deleted if possible or, at minimum, the passwords have been changed from their original settings.

If a user ID is known but not the password, the easiest way to discover the password may simply be to ask the user. Used in the context of checking the system, a question such as "We're checking for commonly used passwords, what's yours?" will frequently yield results and no questions asked. Users should be trained to treat their passwords as highly confidential.

If a hacker wishes to break in without assistance, the next procedure would be to try likely passwords such as common names. Months of the year, pop stars' names, or even the name of the pin-up girl of the month in a well-known calendar may be used.

Many hacking programs will perform such a *brute force* attack in the background, trying thousands of common words in rapid succession, leaving the hacker free to pursue other interests. This is only one of a variety of types of hacker tools commonly available on the Internet. They include war dialers, password guessers, sniffers, key loggers, flooders, spoofers, and a variety of other nefarious styles of unauthorized software. These tools make it easy for unsophisticated hackers to exploit known security weaknesses.

Common causes include:

- Use of "standard" passwords
- Non-changed passwords
- No password required
- Poor security awareness
- No corporate policy

- No user education
- Poor personnel policies
- Poor operating environment
- Redundant security files
- Poor change control
- Lack of security enforcement

In short, hackers gain entry by poor internal controls, commonly as a result of no risk analysis being done.

Common threats in today's environment include the impact of economic recession whereby many outsiders used to be insiders who have now lost their employment and may hold a grudge against the ex-employers. In many cases these individuals understand not only the technology but also the structure of internal controls in place within the organization.

Social media has given rise to a new generation of social engineering in order to obtain access rights based on knowledge of the individual under attack. Social networks involve structures of individuals, business partners, friends, and organizations connected via technology using devices including computers, notepads, smart phones, personal digital assistants (PDAs), and even digital televisions.

Many mobile devices are nowadays small, easily portable, and contain vast quantities of confidential information including user IDs, passwords, and access codes into the individual's and the organization's computer systems.

Removable media in the form of high-capacity DVDs and thumb drives combined with direct communication via wireless connections has opened up the opportunity for, in many cases, and detected copying of confidential information directly from the source.

In addition to these, the older, standard weaknesses such as poor destruction of confidential scrap and poor access control from over-powerful users with inadequate authentication remain.

Additionally, new generations of browser-based attacks and techniques such as cross-site scripting (XSS) are facilitating access-control bypass. We have already seen phishing migrate from simple email attacks into social networks, use of *Botnets* to create *Zombie Computers,* and *Rootnets* being used to take control of the system without authorization by the system's owner.

Mobile agents in the form of mobile code acting autonomously on behalf of the user to achieve continuous collecting and processing of information can be used in the form of web applets, dynamic email, and so forth, to visit any number of sites before returning to the originator.

Threats in the cloud environment multiply based on the types of cloud used ranging, as previously mentioned, through:

- SaaS (*Software as a Service*). Network-hosted application
- DaaS (*Data as a Service*). Customer *queries against* provider's database
- PaaS *(Platform as a Service).* Network-hosted software development platform

- IaaS *(Infrastructure as a Service).* Provider *hosts customer VMs* or provides network storage
- IPMaaS *(Identity and Policy Management as a Service).* Provider *manages identity and/or access control policy* for customer
- NaaS *(Network as a Service).* Provider *offers virtual networks* (e.g., virtual private networks [VPNs])

All of this has been facilitated by a combination of increasingly open technology combined with a security outlook based on the threats of years gone by. Impacts range from destruction and denial of service attacks through disclosure of confidential information to the potential for fraud on a major scale due to modification of data in an unauthorized manner.

Protection against such attacks involves a complex combination of training of both technical staff and users, combined with a more robust approach to logical security within our Information Technology (IT) systems. This includes use of one-time passwords and compartmentalization of accesses and privileges combined with effective hardball implementation, adequate monitoring of access, and hardening of operating systems.

Quantum Cryptography is a technique using *Conjugate Coding* to produce and distribute encryption keys and includes the ability of the two communicating users to detect the presence of any third party trying to gain knowledge of the key.

All of these techniques remain ineffectual unless there's an understanding on the part of the user of the computer systems and the threats faced and of their responsibility to implement the appropriate control mechanisms.

CHAPTER THIRTY-SIX

Preventing and Investigating Information Technology Fraud

I N RECENT YEARS, an enormous amount of publicity has been given to the threat of computer crime, which has led to a greater awareness at the executive level of the vulnerability faced within information technology (IT) functions. The growth of organized fraud in the computer world in conjunction with the comparatively new threat of organized terrorism or politically motivated penetration of computer systems makes this awareness essential.

Advances in computer science have come at a staggering pace and computer crime has remained in step with them. Unfortunately, computer crimes happen in real time and the crime is completed in microseconds. Only a tiny percentage of such crimes were found in time to perform any form of meaningful investigation unless care had been taken beforehand to create an appropriate detective environment.

 ## PREVENTING FRAUD

In order to prevent IT fraud, it is necessary to understand how such fraud can be carried out. Generally speaking, the online criminal requires access to your personal information before he can do anything. Many fraud schemes make use of a type of program called spyware. Spyware is software that, once installed, will collect information about you and return to its source. In many cases spyware manipulates technology such as

ActiveX to remotely install malicious software on the computer. This can happen simply by visiting a nonsecure web site.

Once stolen, this information can be used either to commit a fraud directly or to steal the identity of the legitimate user. ID theft comes in a variety of forms including, among others:

- Phishing
- Email fraud
- Browser hijacking

Phishing

This is a form of fraud in which the fraudster will fake the identity of a known and trusted entity by appearing to be a genuine communication from the trusted entity in order to steal sensitive information from unsuspecting victims. Although such scams have received a great deal of publicity in news media and television, nevertheless they remained relatively effective in deceiving unsuspecting users. Many such scam attempts arrive in the form of emails attempting to lure the recipient into disclosing personal information such as credit card numbers or Social Security numbers as well as account usernames and passwords. Some are easily spotted as they contain spelling errors or awkward grammar or purport to be from a financial institution claiming that your account has been compromised. In more sophisticated phishing attacks, the attacker will have gone to the trouble of making the email look like an official email from the appropriate financial institution with the correct email as a sender's address and incorporating its logo. Skepticism is the recipient's friend in such cases and any such email should be confirmed by telephone (not to any telephone number given in the e-mail) before any response is given. If in doubt, the safest response is no response.

Email Fraud

Email fraud is one of the biggest problems on the Internet today and fraudulent emails are becoming harder and harder to identify. The major intent of email fraud is to elicit some form of response. Some emails will promise you a large return on a small investment, while others try to convince you that you are donating to a humanitarian organization, particularly after a major catastrophe. These emails typically look highly professional and generally elicit a high volume of response from well-intending people. Unfortunately, in many cases, the transfers of funds take place electronically and the money is gone and the trail gone cold almost instantaneously. In addition, the user should beware of any email from an unknown source containing attachments. Such attachments may be used to install spyware or malware on your computer without your knowledge.

Browser Hijacking

This is a form of malware that modifies the settings of Internet browsers without the user's permission in order to redirect users to web sites they would not normally visit.

The user may find this a minor nuisance, and the intent of the fraudster is to artificially inflate traffic to their own sites in order to increase their advertising revenue. Once in the site it can be difficult to leave without inadvertently triggering multiple additional hijacks. Frequently, hijackware will attack the browser by modifying its settings within the registry so that a typical, nontechnical, user may find it impossible to change the Internet options manually. In some cases, even fixing the registry will, upon restart, revert to the hijacked addresses once again

 INVESTGATION

Where investigation is commenced, few will actually go to court, and for all those prosecuted even fewer will be convicted. In many of these cases it is the fear of failure of prosecution and of exposing the corporation to ridicule that reduces the likelihood of prosecution. The failure of successful convictions is frequently due to a lack of proper care or methodical approach by the investigator. Frequently the evidence obtained is improper, inconclusive, and not legally gathered or maintained.

In addition, business moving onto the Internet has created the greatest opportunity for widespread and methodical fraud the world has ever known.

The most common computer crimes are those that merely involve the computer as a tool to implement the crime. In addition, the computer may be the victim of the attack resulting in the theft of information, disclosure of confidential data, vandalism, sabotage, or viruses.

Given that activities within a computer environment consist of three main elements—input, processing, and output—it is no surprise that IT fraud can be classified in the same manner.

Input frauds normally take the form of amended or forged transactions, but entered into the computer so that the normal system processes can continue and valuable assets, normally cash, may be obtained. This type of fraud does not require any specific expertise within IT and is a common form of user-level data-entry fraud.

Throughput frauds typically involve modifications to live programs in order to enter unauthorized code for improper purposes. Viruses, trapdoors, and Trojan horses are all examples of such coding.

Output frauds commonly occur when correct and valid outputs are intercepted and amended prior to use. This may take the form of altered payments or breach of confidentiality.

Once more, with the advent of the Internet, computer hacking has become a widely known source of risk to computer systems. Fortunately, hacking for fraudulent purposes is not yet widespread.

Many investigators have a fundamental fear that computers are being used to investigate computer-related crime and are happy to leave such investigations to specialist auditors or outside consultants. This fear has built up over the years as a result of the air of secrecy surrounding IT and the technical jargon associated with it. Once the technical jargon has been gotten out of the way, understanding the risks and controls within computer systems and a means of investigating an IT fraud become clear.

IT fraud frequently comes to light because of the impact upon the organization. However, the most common manner in which computer crime is uncovered is by a tip from another person who may or may not be an employee.

When an IT fraud is suspected, the first objective of the IT auditor or security personnel is to confirm whether an incident actually occurred. If there appears to be a case for believing such an occurrence happened, all subsequent steps must be specifically designed to promote the accumulation of accurate information and establish control for retrieval/handling of evidence.

This can cause complications because of the need to protect the privacy rights of both the suspected perpetrator as well as the defrauded organization. There is little point in recovering stolen assets by destroying corporate confidentiality.

The investigation must minimize business disruption. Gathering of forensically acceptable evidence will commonly involve isolating the information source to prevent contamination. In the case of Information Systems, such isolation—if extended over a period of time—could result in considerably more damage to the organization than the original fraud.

Once gathered, the evidence must be such that would allow for legal recriminations. This means that the evidence must be capable of standing up to public scrutiny and challenge.

Mandia and Prosise[1] define an incident response methodology as incorporating:

- Pre-incident preparation
- Detection of incidents
- Initial response
- Response-strategy formulation
- Duplication (forensic backups)
- Investigation
- Security measure implementation
- Network monitoring
- Recovery
- Reporting
- Follow-up

Pre-Incident Preparation

The objectives of pre-incident preparation are to ensure that, should an incident occur, the organization is in a position to identify what exactly happened and to what systems. From this it may be determined what information was compromised, what files were created/modified, and who may have caused the incident. It is also useful to determine, in advance, who should be notified and what steps will be required to return to normal.

Major steps in the process would include identifying the vital assets in advance and conducting a risk analysis to determine what would be the most likely nature of exposure faced. Individual hosts could then be prepared to detect incidents by producing cryptographic checksums of critical files and enabling secure logging. Preventative measures would include hardening the hosts' defenses in a variety of ways. Back-ups of critical data stored securely can help protect against the threat of non-availability leading to fraud. And directive controls would include comprehensive user education about host-based security.

Networks should be prepared by installing firewalls and Intrusion Detection Systems (IDSs) as well as by the use of access-control lists on routers. Companies can create a topography conducive to monitoring, encrypt network traffic, and require authentication beyond the password level.

At the user end, preparations would include determining an appropriate corporate-response stance. This could be to ignore the incident, to defend against further attacks, to prosecute, or to simply perform surveillance and gather data of the incident for future use. The appropriate response may, in fact, vary based on the circumstances of the incident. If, for example, a hacker is detected, it may be more beneficial to the organization to allow the hacker to believe the system penetration is successful and let him in. This would allow time to gather forensically acceptable evidence for his future prosecution as well as facilitate tracing the hacker to his lair. Obviously such a policy would require a very high level of confidence that the activities of the hacker could be traced and limited.

From the audit and investigation perspective, preparation could include the building of a *forensic response toolkit.* Such a toolkit would normally consist of a hardware/software combination to promote the demonstrably non-corrupting nature of the investigation. It would typically consist of hardware in the shape of a high-end processor with a large memory capacity, and a large capacity empty drive. A DVD-RW drive, a high-capacity tape drive, and cables galore for connecting everything to anything would be needed for the interchange of information. An uninterruptible power supply is needed to prove no corruption took place during the investigation phase because of power outages. DVD/Rs and labels together with external hard disks and a high-capacity memory stick will also prove essential. In addition, the standard tools for forensic examination including folders and labels for evidence, a digital camera so that evidence may be captured directly into the system, lockable evidence storage containers, a printer and paper, and finally burn bags to securely dispose of evidence when approval is given by legal counsel would all be required.

On the software side, response software would include two to three native operating systems (e.g., Windows 2000/LINUX), forensic duplication tools (e.g., EnCase or Expert Witness), all the drivers for all your hardware on all platforms, a file viewer (e.g., Quickview plus or Handy Vue) capable of handling a variety of file structures and formats, as well as disk-write blocking routines.

With this toolkit, the auditor should be able to conduct forensically acceptable examinations.

An Incident Response Team should be established to respond to all security incidents and conduct a complete investigation free from bias. The team must confirm or dispel an incident quickly and assess the damage and scope. A 24/7 hotline should be established to allow the team early notification so that they can control and contain the incident. The team's job is to collect and document all evidence while maintaining a chain of custody, to protect privacy rights and to provide expert testimony.

Detection of Incidents

Incidents may be detected via IDS, firewalls, suspicious account activity, malfunctioning services, or even defaced web sites. In all cases it is essential that the discoverer note the critical details such as:

- Current date and time
- Who/what is reporting
- Nature of the incident
- When the incident occurred
- Hardware and software affected
- Contacts for involved personnel

Initial Response

The initial response should be directed toward determining what probably happened and determining what is the best response strategy. At all times the investigator must be mindful of the legalities and must ensure that all searches are carried out within the letter of the law. This will typically involve an examination of network topologies; verifying policies; and investigating the incident by conducting personnel interviews, systems administrator interviews, management interviews, and interviews of end-users. Only then should hands-on actions be taken.

All actions to be taken must follow the fundamental rules and everything the investigator does must be documented with every care taken to ensure that the evidence itself is not compromised during the investigation.

Acquiring the evidence will first involve securing the physical area. Before anything is disturbed, photographic evidence should be gathered of the system, the monitor, and all cable interfaces. Photographs should also be taken of the surrounding area, and all papers and disks should be inventoried and collected.

The system should be shut down by unplugging directly from the power supply. Under no circumstances should the keyboard be touched or the power switch used to power down the machine. Shutting down the machine in a normal manner may activate software traps to encrypt or delete sensitive data. At a minimum it will alter the data held in virtual memory.

Before the computer itself is moved, it should be sealed and all cables and connectors clearly labeled. Once the computer is in the physical location in which it is to be examined, the case may be opened and, once again, photographs should be taken of the inside before anything is touched. All hard drives should be isolated by disconnecting the power leads prior to starting the system.

The system can then be started so that the date and time may be collected from the setup menu. This will be used in later examination to compare to date and time stamps and other evidence. It is at this stage that it is recommended the BIOS be changed to ensure that the system boots from a floppy drive only.

The machine may then be switched off once more. An unused hard drive will be connected to the system to be the target drive for the forensic backup. This drive should become drive 0, with the original drive classed as drive 1. This prevents the system from attempting to boot from the original drive. A bootable diskette containing the forensic copying software should be placed in the diskette drive and the system restarted.

The forensic copy of the hard disk may then be made. All drives should then be removed from the system and placed into antistatic bags and sealed. The sealed disks should be dated and signed and placed in a secure environment.

Duplication (Forensic Backups)

By preference, forensic examinations should never be performed on the original media. An exact clone of the media should be made and the original evidence must then be stored securely. Care must be taken to ensure that the cloned media is in fact a complete copy of the original evidence. Most back-up software available on the market today does not copy information in a manner that would be acceptable for further investigation. In the normal course of events, data that has been deleted still remains on the magnetic media until overwritten. This data can be a rich source of forensic evidence. Most copying, cloning, and backup software will copy only current files from the media. To be acceptable, the copy must be made on a bit-by-bit, sector-by-sector basis. Only in this manner can the investigator assert that the working copy was a true reflection of the original evidence.

In addition, encryption technology should be used so that the investigator in court may avow that the working copy could not be adulterated in an undetectable manner or even read by an individual without personal supervision of the investigator.

When the copy is made, the media being copied to should be forensically sterile. By preference, the target media should be brand new and unused or, alternatively, scrubbed clean to internationally acceptable standards prior to use. The investigator must understand that the examination must be carried out in a manner that ensures that the evidence remains unmodified. Even looking at a file on computer modifies the attributes of the file. Where such data modifications are not preventable, the maintenance of an investigation log detailing all access becomes critical.

As with any forensic examination, the chain of custody must be maintained at all times.

Common mistakes at this stage include the failure to maintain proper documentation throughout the investigation process. Failure to notify decision makers within the organization may jeopardize the legality of any evidence gathered. If digital evidence is not properly controlled and secured, its forensic acceptability may also be challenged.

Failure to report the incident in a timely manner may lead to problems with authorities where such reporting is a matter of law. Such failure may confuse the issue and allow the perpetrators of the wrongdoing sufficient time to defeat the ends of the investigation.

One of the most common mistakes involves simply underestimating the scope of the incident. If too narrow a focus is taken, some evidence may be omitted or even destroyed during the course of the investigation.

At the technical level, altering date and time stamps on evidence systems before recording them can inadvertently destroy the forensic nature of the evidence. Failure to record the commands used, or the use of untrustworthy commands and tools can also raise questions about the validity of any evidence gathered. Even the very act of installing the tools, if done incorrectly, can overwrite significant evidence and cast doubt on the remaining evidence.

Conducting the Investigation

Once a working copy of the data is available, the investigator must decide what evidence is to be sought. Depending on the nature of the investigation, files accessed, email sent and received, Internet sites visited, programs executed, and graphic files accessed may all be of interest to the investigator.

In its simplest form, an investigator seeking evidence of the presence on the computer of illicit or illegal files or software may simply have to do a search for a specific file name or file type. Even this may be complicated if the files concerned have been deleted and the investigator may have to resurrect such deleted files prior to examination.

Where fraud has occurred, the files accessed, date and time of access, network paths taken, and software executed may be critical. Most modern operating systems have the capacity to record such accesses. Log files and registry entries can contain such information as user names, passwords, recently accessed files, and network connections used. Unfortunately, having the capacity does not necessarily mean that such records are created and retained. Once again the investigator will have to search for such files, possibly now deleted, before they can be interrogated.

Network Monitoring

In the course of the investigation of an ongoing fraud, the investigator may have to monitor traffic flowing over the communication network. This will typically involve using packet sniffers to monitor traffic flow. Such activity is purely detective and is designed to confirm or dispel suspicions. The accumulated evidence may be used to verify the scope and extent of the system compromise by identifying compromised systems, user accounts, and passwords. It may be possible to identify source addresses on the network as well as to intercept stolen files, pornography, or downloaded hacker tools.

At its best, such monitoring can identify the parties involved, determine the timelines of an event, and possibly even assess the skill level or numbers of individuals involved in the illicit activity.

In a covert investigation into the activities on a specific machine, monitoring software may be placed upon the machine to record all email sent and received, keystrokes, images on screen, mouse clicks on the screen, and Internet and intranet sites visited. Such software would run in stealth mode and gather the information for subsequent retrieval. The software can be used to automatically send the information gathered to the investigator's machine. In all cases, care should be taken to ensure that the evidence gathered is restored in an acceptably secure manner both on the target's machine and while in transit to the investigator.

The investigator should be aware that many antivirus and spyware detectors can detect such monitoring and care should be taken to ensure the specific software cannot be detected on the target's computer.

Security-Measure Implementation

Security-measure implementation is largely dependent on the results of the investigation stage. By examining verified information and network logs, a response plan can be established in order to ensure that the appropriate security remedies are selected and enforced in order to prevent a repetition of the exposure. These remedies must support the goal of the overall computer security as well as the business practices of the organization within both its administrative and legal policies. The selected security measures must be simple to implement and effective in impact. In order to be forensically acceptable, evidence must be provided by the selected controls to support administrative as well as civil and/or criminal action.

Network Monitoring

Network monitoring on a selective basis can be used as a continuous monitoring process on the network logs to ensure early detection of future incidents. Once again, over-logging places a load on the operation performance of the computer systems and therefore the appropriate logging needs to be selected in order to ensure adequacy of detection without over-monitoring.

Recovery

Recovery involves the restoration of the computer systems to an acceptable security level and may involve resorting to backups, hardening of the operating environment, and increased user education.

Reporting

Reporting may be external or internal. External reporting is typically intended to support criminal actions against perpetrators. Internal reporting is generally intended to communicate lessons learned and amendments required to prevent repetitive incidents. External reporting will typically require organization from senior-level management unless the audit charter already specifies a requirement for external reporting. The level of internal reporting will be dependent on the identification of any internal collusion with the perpetrator.

Follow-Up

In all cases, follow-up is a prerequisite in order to ensure action, external or internal, has been taken and will be effective. It should be noted by the auditor that follow-up does not involve a repeat of the audit. Where recommendations have been made and security remedies have been selected, the follow-up is a measurement of the effectiveness of their implementation and utilization, including the ongoing monitoring of vulnerabilities.

IDENTITY THEFT

One common form of fraud that is associated with network monitoring is identity theft. Probably the most common form of this is simple unauthorized use of a credit card account without the owner's knowledge or permission. Such a fraud would normally come to light as soon as the owner checks the next statement. With the advent of e-commerce via the Internet, this crime has escalated and the source of the information on customers' credit cards can result in significant reputation damage to an organization that has been penetrated. One of the more common uses of such information is to obtain access to pornographic sites, resulting in large charges for the individual and significant embarrassment when the identity of the recipient becomes known. Identity theft at a corporate level can permit a thief to order goods and services charged to the company that can also facilitate the conducting of industrial espionage, resulting in a loss of competitive or marketing advantage, or sabotage, including breaches of criminal law in the company name.

It should be noted that network surveillance is not the only method of identity theft. *Phishing* has recently become a significant threat whereby computer users are simply asked for their information in a plausible manner and it is provided willingly to unknown inquirers. Also, dumpster diving can be a major source of confidential information leading to identity theft including the targeting of wastepaper from home, where shredders are seldom used and confidential information included on bills, bank statements, and letters—including signatures—are carelessly thrown away.

Over and above the use of credit card information, identity theft achieved by obtaining confidential information on individuals via computer systems can enable the criminal to impersonate the individual in a variety of manners including accessing and downloading confidential information, opening bank accounts, entering into legally binding contracts, falsification of emails, destruction of creditworthiness, and access to online banking facilities. Increasingly, mobile devices such as Personal Digital Assistants (PDAs) are utilized for storing passwords, access codes, and a variety of confidential information. Because of their portable nature such devices are easy to steal, but, in addition, many of them are used to connect wirelessly to communication networks with little or no security implemented. Encryption and even password protection are used rarely.

Overall, the major control to prevent identity theft is *awareness* on the part of each individual that there are criminals out there who will exploit any weakness or exposure left by an individual or organization and that common sense must prevail to prevent such exploitation.

 NOTE

1 Kevin Mandia and Chris Prosise. *Incident Response: Investigating Computer Crime.* Berkeley, California: Osborne/McGraw-Hill, 2001, pp. 16–17.

Ethics and Standards for the IS Auditor[1]

ISACA CODE OF PROFESSIONAL ETHICS

The Information Systems Audit and Control Association®, Inc. (ISACA) sets forth this Code of Professional Ethics, including standards, guidelines, and procedures, to guide the professional and personal conduct of members of the Association and/or its certification holders.

Members and ISACA Certification holders shall:

- Support the implementation of, and encourage compliance with, appropriate standards and procedures for the effective governance and management of enterprise information systems and technology, including: audit, control, security, and risk management.
- Perform their duties with due diligence and professional care, in accordance with professional standards.
- Serve in the interest of stakeholders in a lawful and honest manner, while maintaining high standards of conduct and character, and not discrediting the profession or the Association.
- Maintain the privacy and confidentiality of information obtained in the course of their duties unless disclosure is required by legal authority. Such information shall not be used for personal benefit or released to inappropriate parties.
- Maintain competency in their respective fields and agree to undertake only those activities that they can reasonably expect to complete with professional competence.

- Inform appropriate parties of the results of work performed; revealing all significant facts known to them.
- Support the professional education of stakeholders in enhancing their understanding of the governance and management of enterprise information systems and technology, including: audit, control, security, and risk management.

Failure to comply with the *Code of Professional Ethics* can result in an investigation into a member's or certification holder's conduct and, ultimately, in disciplinary measures.

RELATIONSHIP OF STANDARDS TO GUIDELINES AND PROCEDURES

Information Systems (IS) Auditing Standards are mandatory requirements for certification holders' reports on the audit and its findings. IS Auditing Guidelines and Procedures are detailed guidance on how to follow those standards. The IS Auditing Guidelines are guidance an IS Auditor will normally follow with the understanding that there may be situations where the auditor will not follow that guidance. In this case, it will be the IS Auditor's responsibility to justify the way in which the work is done. The procedure examples show the steps performed by an IS Auditor and are more informative than IS Auditing Guidelines. The examples are constructed to follow the IS Auditing Standards and the IS Auditing Guidelines and provide information on following the IS Auditing Standards. To some extent, they also establish best practices for procedures to be followed.

Codification

Standards are numbered consecutively as they are issued, beginning with S1. Guidelines are numbered consecutively as they are issued, beginning with G1. Procedures are numbered consecutively as they are issued, beginning with P1.

Use

It is suggested that during the annual audit program, as well as individual reviews throughout the year, the IS Auditor should review the standards to ensure compliance with them. The IS Auditor may refer to the ISACA standards in the report, stating that the review was conducted in compliance with the laws of the country, applicable audit regulations, and ISACA standards.

Electronic Copies

All ISACA standards, guidelines, and procedures are posted on the ISACA web site at www.isaca.org/standards.

Glossary

A full glossary of terms can be found on the ISACA web site at www.isaca.org/glossary.

Audit Program for Application Systems Auditing

THE BUSINESS SYSTEM is an integral element of the business function. Therefore the application and functional risks and the related controls must be considered together.

The approach selected to review business systems must address all relevant risks, management and general controls, and manual controls that are part of the business function under review.

There is a definite trend toward the migration of controls from the application to the general environment. For example, the database management system features may be used to restrict access to critical functions across applications.

An audit of general information technology (IT) control functions provides information on the reliability of the control structure, which could significantly impact the level of testing required during application-system audits.

Auditors need to have a full understanding of the technology platform that supports the application: database management systems, networks, security provisions, hardware, software, and operating systems.

To determine the effectiveness of access controls, the auditor should understand the capabilities and characteristics of the software, the manner in which the software is implemented from a technical point of view, the interrelationship of the application with other applications, systems software in use and conditions that allow overrides of controls, and the administrative controls related to the use of the access control software.

Application controls are dependent on the general controls in the IT environment. The general controls environment must be reviewed to ensure that controls resident in an application system cannot be circumvented by non-application system components.

General IT controls include, but are not limited to, data and program security, program-change control, system-development controls, and computer-operations controls.

Of major importance is the segregation of duties in terms of functional responsibilities as well as access to application system processing capabilities.

GENERAL AUDIT PROGRAMS FOR APPLICATION SYSTEMS

Questions	Yes	No	N/A	COMMENTS
Input Controls:				
Determine that appropriate input controls are used to ensure accuracy and completeness of data. Evaluate the effectiveness of various input controls in fulfilling their objectives.				
Audit Procedures:				
Check digit verification ensures accuracy of the data entered. The check digit is created as the result of a calculation routine.				
• Review the source code to ensure that the defined edits are included and are coded properly to achieve the desired result.				
• Review test results performed by the auditor as the system is being developed or modified.				
• Input test transactions with invalid numbers into an audit copy of the production software used to perform the check digit verification. The testing should be done in the test environment separate from the production environment.				
• Review error reports produced by the application to verify that errors are being detected.				
Reasonableness and data validity edits ensure that the data is reasonable for the purpose intended. Some examples of edits include alphanumeric check, range of values check, and so on.				
• Review the source code to ensure that the defined edits are included and are coded properly to achieve the desired result.				
• Review test results performed by the auditor as the system is being developed or modified.				
• Create test transactions to test edits of control significance.				
• Review edit reports from the production-processing system to verify that input errors are being detected.				
Hash total verification verifies accuracy for non-amount or non-numeric data.				
• Independent testing of a copy of the production software using copies of production data files as input to the test. The test should include steps to ensure that added, deleted, and/or modified records are properly detected by the verification routines.				
• Simulation of a hash total routine using independent audit software. Copies of production data files should be used as the test input.				

Questions	Yes	No	N/A	COMMENTS
• Manually re-foot hash totals from printouts of input data files produced by utilities program.				
Batch balancing verifies input to pre-established control total and item counts. *Note: Many applications provide manual override capabilities that allow for bypassing batch-balancing errors. It is necessary to review control over the use of this capability.* • Independent testing of a copy of the production software using copies of production data files as input to the test. The test should include steps to ensure that added, deleted, and/ or modified records are properly detected by the verification routines. • Simulation of the routine using independent audit software. Copies of production data files should be used as the test input. • Manually re-foot totals from printouts of input data files. The printout can be obtained through standard utilities. • Observe balancing procedures.				
Observe data-entry operation to determine if screen masking is used to prevent confidential data from being displayed on a terminal screen during the inputting process.				
Review a sample of the transactions on the log to determine that a record is kept showing the individuals who input the data.				
Input verification can be performed by having a second individual review the data entered. Proper implementation of this control in conjunction with access controls can provide for the necessary separation of duties between the input and verification process. • Review access control rules for access to the input and verification transactions to ensure proper separation of duties. • Review control over the capability to override or bypass verification. Determine how the capability is installed and what authorization is required to use it.				
Call-back and dial-back to a predefined phone number. Verify the accuracy of the source attempting to initiate a transaction. • Initiate test transactions from an unauthorized location in the test environment. • Observe the call-back/dial-back procedures. • Analyze application software and hardware. • Review call-back/dial-back records.				
Input source verification provides assurance that data is only being modified by, or disclosed to, authorized individuals at known locations during approved time frames. Many applications provide this type of control by defining users, terminals, and printers in a security table that is embedded in the application software or data and is maintained by the application owner.				

Questions	Yes	No	N/A	COMMENTS
• Review on-line copy of the security table for propriety.				
Observe the operation to determine if the data-encryption method is used to prevent unauthorized disclosure and modification of data.				
A transaction log provides an audit trail for transactions processed. It may be a stand-alone log or it may be included as part of an overall system log. The log should be accurate and complete. • Use audit software developed specifically to read the log to get a report listing the totals and details of all transactions processed for the day. The totals can be matched to accounting entries. Differences between the records indicate potential problems.				
Run-to-run reconciliation ensures that the established control is maintained each time the data file is used for processing. • Use an independent software test. • Review outputs. • If the override capability is provided, additional review must be performed to ensure that the use of this capability is properly restricted and recorded on an audit trail.				
Reject re-entry data verification ensures correction and re-entry of rejected transactions. When items are rejected, a record or log of these items should be created so that correction and processing can be monitored. Records of outstanding rejected data and suspense items are reviewed regularly and followed up so that timely corrective action is taken and transactions are recorded in the correct period. • Observe reject re-entry operation. • Use an independent software test. • Review aging report of outstanding rejected items.				
Is there a complete and current set of documented procedures? • Interview employees. • Observe compliance with procedures. • Review documentation. • Review the procedures for updating documentation.				
A review of software modification controls could be performed as part of a business area audit if it is directed at reviewing user involvement in the software-modification process. The review could be used to assess user involvement in: • Authorization and approval of software-modification requests. • Providing user acceptance testing of software modifications. • Establishment of communications between the users and developers.				
Provisions for the backup and recovery of application data protect against unnecessary delays in providing required services.				

Questions	Yes	No	N/A	COMMENTS
• Review audit work performed by auditors conducting the system-development review to determine the extent of reliance that can be placed on the work.				
• Execute an independent test of backup and recovery of the application data.				
• Determine the extent of backup and recovery testing that was performed through a review of or participation in the implementation testing performed. If sufficient testing was performed to satisfy current audit objectives and assurances can be made that backup and recovery process has not changed since it was tested, reliance can be placed on the implementation testing rather than conducting another test.				
Business System Processing Controls:				
Determine that appropriate processing controls are used to ensure accuracy, completeness, and timeliness of data processed. Evaluate the effectiveness of various processing controls in fulfilling their objectives.				
Some of the commonly used audit techniques include:				
• Use simulated transactions to test processing logic, computations, and control programs in the application. If test transactions are prepared in accordance with user procedures, test data analysis can help the auditor to evaluate these procedures. It can also be used to evaluate individual programs or an entire system. It can direct the auditor to areas where erroneous processing has occurred especially when used in conjunction with data retrieval and program analysis techniques. Test data can be prepared by creating inputs, copying existing master records onto a test master file, or selecting live transactions.				
• Use specialized audit software to analyze the flow of data through the processing logic of the application software and document the logic paths, control conditions, and processing sequences. These techniques analyze the systems command language of job-control statements and the programming languages for the application.				
• Software mapping analysis can be used to review for non-executable codes in software. It documents all the codes in a given application and identifies the use of key data elements.				
• The snapshot audit technique is an automated tool used to trace a specific transaction through software and to document logic paths, control conditions, and processing sequences. This technique can verify program logic flow and help the auditor understand the various processing steps within the application software. Snapshot analysis employs a special code in the transaction record that triggers the printing of the record or data in question to a report format for further analysis. Specific instructions must be written into the application program to generate snapshot reports.				

Questions	Yes	No	N/A	COMMENTS
• The purpose of tracing is to document and analyze the logic paths in complex software. The objective of the tracing audit technique is to verify compliance with specifications, policies, and procedures by documenting how the application software processes transactions. By analyzing the transaction's path through the application, tracing can show instructions that have been executed and the sequence in which they have been executed. Tracing can also be used to verify omissions. Once the auditor understands the instructions that have been executed, analysis can be performed to determine whether the processing steps conform to organizational procedures, policies, and processing rules. Transaction tracing may be used to review transaction types and user identification numbers.				
• An integrated test facility (ITF) permits the internal auditor to examine an application in its normal operating environment. It involves entering and processing selected test transaction input into a live production system simultaneously with live data, tracing the flow of transactions through the various functions in the system, and comparing the actual results of the test transactions with predetermined or pre-calculated results. ITF can be used to test controls and processing of larger automated applications when it is not practical to process test data separately. Test data analysis/ITF may be used for transaction activity simulation, testing edit and validation criteria, testing of database updates and creation of computer-generated transactions, and testing of system output.				
• Embedded audit data collection is similar to continuous control monitoring and uses one or more specially programmed software subroutines embedded in the application software to screen and select input and computer-generated transactions. Distinct from other audit techniques, the method uses in-line code, whereby the application software collects the audit data while it processes data for production purposes. Activity monitoring, sampling, and exception reporting are all controlled by the subroutine parameters. The design and implementation of an embedded audit data-collection application is normally performed as an integral part of the system-development process. As continuous monitoring techniques are refined through use they alert management and auditors to actual or potential problems promptly.				
• Transaction retrieval and analysis are the primary automated tools designed to capture transactions for manual or automated verification analysis. They monitor activity and select transactions using error-based, parameter-based, or sample-based criteria. They are used in compliance testing to monitor transaction processing and to select data for verification.				

Questions	Yes	No	N/A	COMMENTS
• The code-comparison audit technique can be useful in evaluating software maintenance procedures, program library procedures, and program change controls. The auditor compares two versions of application software to identify any changes that have occurred since the earlier version was made and then analyzes the documentation that was prepared to authorize and execute the changes. The technique is used primarily to disclose unauthorized program changes. Either source or object code can be used for comparison. Comparison software can be purchased or developed. The software compares the application code and identifies inconsistencies between the two versions.				

Audit Procedures:

Questions	Yes	No	N/A	COMMENTS
Programmed cut-off controls prevent improper cut-off and reduce the risk of transactions being recorded in the wrong period; for example, an embedded calendar table can be used to compare with transaction dates or provide exception reporting of cut-off discrepancies.				
• Review source codes.				
• Review outputs.				
Cycle processing controls compare pre-established control totals of critical input fields to output totals accumulated by the system.				
• Review source codes.				
• Review outputs.				
Session controls are performed by the application software and designed to emulate a batch procedure. Totals of critical fields by type of transaction are automatically accumulated during a data-entry session and held for subsequent comparison with updated balances.				
• Review source codes.				
• Review outputs.				
File footings are software routines embedded into the application software that verify the dollar values and record counts or any other control fields of an application data file. It provides a primary control against inaccurate/incomplete data and a secondary control over unauthorized modification of application data. File footing is a detective control rather than a preventative control.				
• Develop audit software that performs the same computation.				
Independent confirmation letter is a control to ensure data accuracy.				
• Use software developed and maintained by audit to run confirmation letters and send to independent parties for verification.				
Piece count verification of valuables (i.e., securities) ensures the accuracy of computerized data.				
• Use audit-controlled software to produce count sheets. The assets are verified against the computer records.				

Questions	Yes	No	N/A	COMMENTS
Automated activity log records all activity within an application system.				
• Review application software source code.				
• Review the logs against a list of transactions processed.				
• Use audit software to verify the accuracy and completeness of the automated application log.				
Calculation simulation is a control when performed by a user.				
• Review source codes.				
• Use audit software to re-compute.				
• Manually re-compute.				
On-site and off-site backup of application data and software.				
• Define all the data and software that comprise the application.				
• Verify that copies of this data are created for backup storage for both on-site and off-site storage.				
• Evaluate the ability to meet the processing requirements of the application with the back-up data created.				
• Verify that required copies of back-up data and software are kept at each required location for the proper period of time.				
Restart and recovery procedures are the steps to reinitiate an application after a failure. For most database applications the restart and recovery is controlled by the database software. Most testing of the procedures is done as part of the installation test. The loss of transactions before processing is completed can be especially serious when data are entered in an interactive mode and in systems that use immediate update processing.				
• If the restart and recovery procedures were tested during the installation of the application, review the testing performed.				
• If the application is a database application and the restart and recovery is provided through the database software, they may have been tested as part of the database restart and recovery procedure testing. Review the test results to determine if they satisfy the application test objectives.				
• If there have been recent occasions to use restart/recovery procedures, review the results and determine the adequacy of the procedures employed.				
• Conduct independent tests in the test environment.				
• Determine if shadow file processing is used. This technique involves creating duplicate transaction records that are stored on a different device or, in some cases, at another location for recovery purposes.				
File-level encryption protects data from unauthorized disclosure and modification. It scrambles the data stored on an application file using a pre-determined key.				
• Execute software utility that will dump a few records of the encrypted file and verify that the printed data is encrypted.				

Questions	Yes	No	N/A	COMMENTS
• Review the management of encryption keys and encryption terminal definitions.				
File integrity routines independently verify that only acceptable data is maintained on a computer resident file. Edit criteria can be used as specifications for scanning the file to ensure that program edits have not been circumvented.				
• Use audit software or other programs that have built-in functions that perform frequency distributions on specified fields. Very high or very low occurrence can indicate potential problems and trigger follow-up.				
Having current and complete processing documentation helps ensure that operations are conducted in the correct and authorized manner.				
• Interview employees.				
• Observe compliance with procedures.				
• Review documentation.				
• Review the procedures for updating documentation.				
Transaction sequence verification ensures that all transactions entered have been processed.				
• Review output from the production system.				
• Review source codes.				
• Test transaction sequence verification software.				
Run-to-run reconciliation ensures that the established control is maintained each time the data file is used for processing.				
• Use an independent software test.				
• Review outputs.				
• If the override capability is provided, determine that the use of this capability is properly restricted and recorded.				
Controls over system-generated data are incorporated into systems that automatically generate transactions or perform calculations that are not subjected to human review. These controls validate the integrity and reasonableness of automatically generated transactions and reduce the risk of erroneous transactions (e.g., reports of such transactions or data may be produced for post-processing authorization, review, and reconciliation).				
Additional control over system-generated data occurs when there is a system-to-system interface that includes an automated comparison or reconciliation between the two discrete systems.				
• Review exception report.				
• Review source codes.				
Duplicate transaction testing ensures that the transaction has only been processed once.				
• Review output from the production system.				

Questions	Yes	No	N/A	COMMENTS
• Review source code used for verifying processing sequence.				
• Test transaction-sequence-verification software.				
• Review program source code used to identify and reject suspected duplicate transactions.				
• Conduct an independent test of the application software using copies of the production data and software in a test environment.				
• Review application edit reports that might highlight possible duplicate transactions.				
Programmed balancing controls are incorporated into the application software to ensure the accuracy and completeness of file update and report processing. The opening balance is checked against the closing balance from the previous cycle. The opening balance plus transactions processed equals the current closing balance. This control reduces the risks of processing with the wrong file, with incomplete or missing transactions, and with loss of file integrity.				
• Reconstruct account balances.				
• Review source codes.				
Override of computer edits involves intervention by the application owner by allowing the user the capability to bypass what under normal conditions would be an error that would prevent processing of the transaction to proceed.				
• Review the use of override to determine that it is restricted to an authorized user and that an audit trail of its use is properly recorded. Review the access/resource rules that control who can use the override capability.				
Software-modification controls are normally reviewed as part of a system-development project or as attention to the application-development function. A review of software-modification controls could be performed as part of a business audit if it is directed at reviewing user involvement in the software-modification process. The review could be used to assess user involvement in:				
• Authorization and approval of software modification requests.				
• Acceptance testing of software modifications.				
• Establishment of communications between the user and developers that assures user awareness and involvement in the software-modification process.				
File-label checking verifies that the files being used are correct.				
• Observe procedures.				
• Review source code.				
• Perform independent testing.				
Error reports highlight rejected transactions or errors.				
• Use test deck containing erroneous transactions				
• Review outputs.				

Questions	Yes	No	N/A	COMMENTS
Before/after change imaging.				
When application update programs change databases or application tables, a report of the before and after image of the changed data may be produced. Management can use this report to validate the integrity of the key application tables and databases. • Observe the operation. • Verify changes made to the tables and databases to the report generated by the update program.				
Data-transmission controls cause a proof calculation using a predefined algorithm to be performed on the information included in the transmission. The result of the proof total may be recorded on a header or trailer message segment prior to transmission. The same calculation is then performed when the message is received and the results are compared with information recorded on the header or trailer. If differences are identified, the sender is requested to retransmit the information. • Observe the operation. • Test the application in a test environment.				
Business System Output Controls:				
Determine that appropriate output controls are used to ensure accuracy, completeness, timeliness, and proper distribution of data processed. Evaluate the effectiveness of various processing controls in fulfilling their objectives.				
Review security software access control definitions, logon IDs and associated privileges, authentication methods, access and resource rules, source and shift group definitions, and logical transactional groups for appropriateness.				
Observe the operation and interview staff to determine that terminals are restricted to authorized personnel by these means: • Terminals are located in supervised and secured areas. • Physical identifiers such as cards or keys are required for terminal operation. Cards and keys are given to authorized personnel only. • Terminals are restricted for authorized functions.				
Online acknowledgment for automated output received. • Review source code for the specific application programs used to provide online acknowledgment. • Observe the operation to verify that online acknowledgment is being used and is working as it was intended. • Test the application in a test environment.				
Edit to ensure all hard-copy output is produced. • Review hard-copy output from production process.				
Questions	Yes	No	N/A	COMMENTS
• Observe distribution of output.				

	Yes	No	N/A	COMMENTS

Controlled distribution of hard-copy output.

• Observe manual distribution process.

• Review application job control language (JCL) to identify destinations for all outputs that are distributed automatically.

Input to output reconciliation controls.

• Obtain prior day's ending balance and add and subtract the current day's activity to arrive at ending balance. Reconcile ending balance to output.

• Perform input/output analysis by tracing transactions from initiation to the output phase. The approach relies heavily on the analysis of data and information rather than controls.

Sensitive computer forms are controlled while in storage and in use. Forms are pre-numbered and usage is accounted for in numerical sequence.

• Verify that the current cycle's beginning number is one higher than the last cycle's ending number.

• Re-compute the number of forms on hand.

• Piece count the number of forms on hand.

• Observe the operation.

The output should contain descriptive headings for dates, numbered pages, and data classifications.

• Review output.

If an application maintains sensitive data, screen-masking controls should be employed.

• Review output.

• Observe operation.

User review of computer outputs.

• Observe the reconciliation procedures performed by the users.

• Use audit software to re-create the computer-generated transactions that would serve as a basis for verification during the audit.

Sensitive data destruction procedures provide for secure disposal of all sensitive outputs.

• Walk through the department.

• Observe the destruction process.

Questions	Yes	No	N/A	COMMENTS

Application Access Controls:

Information integrity may be impaired through the transaction processing functions of the application or through direct access to the application's data files or database. Control over the accurate updating of master file or database records is important. Anyone with direct access to master file modification functions (e.g., database utilities) may be able to circumvent established procedures for the initiation, approval, and recording of transactions or access to data and may possibly gain indirect access to assets.			
Information integrity is dependent on the overall data-access-control environment, controls internal to the application system, and access to the data. Access security over applications systems can be incorporated into the application or provided by access-control software; a database-management system or other software may provide some security functions. In addition to application software, there are three common types of systems software used to control access: teleprocessing monitors, access control software, and database management systems (DBMS) software. *Evaluate the effectiveness of access control to the application and its data.*			
Audit Procedures:			
Effective control over access to computer functions and related data is dependent on the use of the application's security features and/or access-control software. A database management system or other software also may provide some security functions. Access controls are designed to enforce the segregation of duties. *Review security packages access-control definitions, logon IDs and associated privileges, authentication methods, access and resource rules, source and shift group definitions, and logical transactional groups for appropriateness.*			
Observe the operation and interview staff to determine that terminals are restricted to authorized personnel by these means: • Terminals are located in supervised and secured areas. • Physical identifiers such as cards or keys are required for terminal operation. Cards and keys are controlled by authorized personnel only. • Terminals are restricted to authorized functions.			
Review approval forms to determine that access to data, terminals, and applications have been approved by data/application owners. • *Review violation reports to determine that exceptions have been resolved promptly.*			

Logical Access-Control Audit Program

Questions	Yes	No	N/A	COMMENTS
The widespread use of communications networks has shown that physical controls provide limited value in protecting the data stored on and processed by the computer. Logical controls restrict access to specific systems to authorized individuals and to the functions each individual can perform on the system. Logical security controls enable the organization to: • Identify individual users of IT data and resources. • Restrict access to specific data or resources. • Produce audit trails of system and user activity.				
Audit Procedures:				
Each type of software has an access path. Access paths are those areas or points where access may be gained to the system. When accessing the computer system, a user may pass through one of multiple software levels before obtaining access to the data resources (e.g., data, program libraries, etc.). a) Review all possible access paths to the data resources to determine that the security features in each piece of software are utilized to minimize the vulnerabilities. Pay specific attention to "backdoor" methods of accessing data by operators and programmers. b) Interview management and review documentation to determine if integrated access-control software is used to streamline security administration and improve security effectiveness.				

Questions	Yes	No	N/A	COMMENTS
c) Control points are those areas on the software's access path that may be used to control and protect data resources. An access-path schematic identifies the users of the system, the type of device from which they access the system, the software used to access the system, the resources they may access, the system on which these resources reside, and the modes of operation and telecommunications paths. The goal of the access path schematic is to assist in the identification of all the control points that could be used to protect the data stored on the system. Review control points for the application to assess their propriety.				
d) Identification is the process of distinguishing one user from all others. Authentication is the process of determining whether individuals are who they say they are.				
Passwords are used to control access to the computer environment. While passwords are widely used for authentication, they are not conclusive identifiers of specific individuals because they may be guessed, copied, overheard, recorded, and played back. If authentication is achieved by use of passwords, review the procedures, observe the operations, and interview user staff to ensure that:				
• Passwords are controlled by the owner.				
• Passwords are changed periodically; the more sensitive the data or the function, the more frequent the changes.				
• Passwords are not displayed when they are entered.				
• Minimum character length is set for the passwords.				
• Use of names, words, or old passwords are prohibited.				
• Users of data and resources are uniquely identified. It is not advisable to use group IDs or passwords.				
• If authentication is achieved by possession of identification devices such as ID cards, access cards, keys, and so on, review the devices and observe the operations to evaluate the effectiveness of this method.				
• Authentication of individuals by physical or behavioral characteristics is also known as a biometric technology. This is an automated method of verifying or recognizing the identity of a person based on physiological or behavioral characteristics. Biometric devices include fingerprints, retina patterns, hand geometry, speech patterns, and keystroke dynamics. If this authentication method is used, review the devices and observe the operations to evaluate the effectiveness of this means.				

Questions	Yes	No	N/A	COMMENTS
• Access-control software allows the identification and authentication of users, the control of access to information resources, and the recording of security-related events and data. Access-control software is important in enforcing the change control process through the segregation of development, testing, and production environments. Many types of software contain features that are designed or may be used to provide security. It is preferable to use access-control software to secure the total environment or to complement the features provided by specific software. Access-control software provides comprehensive and coordinated security.				
a) When security software is initially installed, the protected resources, authorized-user identifiers, and passwords must be identified or defined to that software. Security profiles may include user or resource passwords used to control access to specific program functions of data files. Review the security tables to determine that they are encrypted.				
b) Each user can be assigned a scope of access, and each resource a degree of protection. Resources that should be protected from unauthorized access include: • Application systems program libraries. • System software program libraries. • Data files and databases. • Job-execution-language statement libraries. • Selected processing functions (modules) of applications programs. • Sensitive utilities that can bypass normal security controls • Data dictionary files and programs. • Review the access rules for all the resources that should be protected to evaluate their propriety.				
c) Review responses to security violations for propriety. Responses could include termination of processing, forced shutdown of terminals, issuance of warning or error messages, and writing of audit trail records. • The desired audit trail for security violation is selected during implementation. Evaluate the effectiveness of audit trails; such data may include user ID, resource accessed, date, time, terminal location, and specific data modified during the access.				
Review access-control software to determine that the following controls are in place:				
1. Access to the system is restricted to authorized individuals.				

Questions	Yes	No	N/A	COMMENTS
2. Access to the processing functions of application software is controlled in a manner that permits authorized users to gain access only for purposes of performing their assigned duties and precludes unauthorized persons from gaining access.				
3. Access rules or profiles are established in a way that restricts departmental employees from performing incompatible functions or functions beyond their responsibility, and also enforces proper separation of duties.				
4. Procedures are enforced so that application programmers are prohibited from making unauthorized program changes.				
5. User/application programmers are limited to the specific types of data access (e.g., read, update) required to perform their functional responsibilities.				
6. Security profiles or tables are protected from unauthorized access and modification. Access to these profiles or tables is restricted to certain access paths.				
7. Security tables or profiles are encrypted to restrict unauthorized use.				
8. Security profile-override capabilities are restricted.				
9. Security data and resource access audit trails, including audit trails of the use of the access-control software, are protected from unauthorized modification.				
10. Modifications or changes to the access-control software itself are restricted to the appropriate personnel, and those changes are made according to authorized procedures.				
Certain types of communications software can restrict access to the telecommunication network and to specific applications located on the network.				
• Controls limiting access to a network and to sensitive resources are specified in the communications software through an authorized exit routine or table. Access to this exit or table is restricted to the appropriate individuals.				
• Access to sensitive data and resources in the network is controlled by:				
• Verifying terminal identifications.				
• Verifying logons to applications.				
• Controlling connections between telecommunications systems and terminals.				
• Restricting an application's use of network facilities.				
• Protecting sensitive data during transmission.				

Questions	Yes	No	N/A	COMMENTS
• Automatically disconnecting at the end of a session.				
• Devices and applications sharing similar security requirements are placed in an isolated network with restricted operational and user access.				
• Network software is configured, through the use of optional journals, to provide extensive network activity logs.				
• Tables used to define network options, resources, and operator profiles are protected from unauthorized access and modification.				
• Operator commands that can shut down network components can be executed only by authorized users.				
• Dial-in access to the system is closely monitored and protected.				
• In-house access to communications software is protected, and control over changes to the software is in place.				
• Precautions are taken to ensure that data are not accessed or modified by an unauthorized user during transmission or while in temporary storage.				
• Access to telecommunications hardware or facilities that can monitor transmissions is restricted.				
• Precautions are taken to ensure that data are not accessed or modified by an unauthorized user during transmission or while in temporary storage.				
Application systems consist of data and programs specifically written to perform a business function. Library-management software can be used to store, maintain, and protect source program libraries, job execution language libraries, and in some instances data files and object program libraries. Library management software packages differ in the type of program libraries they can protect, the levels of security they can provide, and the audit trails they can produce. The libraries must be supported by adequate change control and documentation procedures in order to provide a well-controlled change environment.				
• The software system may not be effective unless supported by detailed procedures, including formal authorization to transfer programs; verification by user or Information Systems (IS) management that all changes are authorized and applied correctly; restricting performance of the change-control procedures to a specific change-control function; source programs copied to production libraries and re-compiled; control over emergency changes; emergency access granted for the purpose of resolving the problems should be immediately revoked after the problem is fixed; and all actions taken during the emergency should be automatically logged.				

Questions	Yes	No	N/A	COMMENTS
• Library-management system maintains an audit trail of all activity against the libraries. One important control function performed by the library-management software is the maintenance of a program-change log. Information provided includes the program name, version number, specific changes made, maintenance data, and programmer ID.				
• The library-management software has a facility that compares two source-code program versions and reports any differences.				
• Access to programs or other items stored by the library-management software is limited to certain access paths.				
• Access to passwords or authorization codes is restricted to authorized individuals and passwords are changed on a routine basis.				
• Access to library-management software is protected, and controls over changes to the software are in place.				
• Precautions are taken to ensure that the library-access definition tables are not modified by an unauthorized user.				
• Additional procedures are in place to ensure that the correct versions of production programs reside in object program libraries when these libraries are not protected by the library-management software.				
Database management system software (DBMS) is used to control, organize, and manipulate data; provide multiple ways to access data in a database; and manage integrated data that cross operational, functional, and organizational boundaries within an organization. Data dictionary (DD) software provides a method for documenting elements of a database and may also provide a method of securing data in a database management system. DD software interfaces closely with the DBMS. The ability to add or update the DD should be controlled to ensure the integrity of the documentation. All updates to the DD should produce an audit trail so that an automated record of all changes and a means of recovery from disruptions can be maintained.				
Determine that:				
• Access to data files is restricted at the logical data view, field, or field-value level. Field-level security pertains to the sensitive nature of the fields (salary). Field-value-level security pertains to the contents of a field.				
• Access to the DD is controlled by using security profiles and passwords within the DD software. The DD may use the DBMS to store the information in a database format. Therefore, the database must be secured using the various access-control facilities built into the DBMS software.				
• Because the storage medium for the DD contents is a database, the same audit-trail features that are in place for application databases should also exist for the DD.				

Questions	Yes	No	N/A	COMMENTS
• Inquiry and update capabilities from application program functions, interfacing DBMS or DD facilities, and DBMS utilities are limited to appropriate personnel. Security functions implemented in the DBMS and DD may only be effective when access to the database is made through the DBMS or DD.				
• Access to DBMS software is protected and controls over changes to the software are in place.				
• Procedures for maintaining security profiles in the DD and security tables in the DBMS are adequate to prevent unauthorized access to sensitive information.				
There are two main types of utility software. The first type is used in the system-development process to improve productivity, such as program development aids and on-line editors. The second type is used to assist in the management of the operation of the computer system, such as performance monitors, job schedulers, and disk-management systems. Utility software may have privileged access capabilities at all times, some of the time, or never. Privileged access allows programs or users to perform functions that may bypass normal security.				
Determine that:				
• Access to specific utility files or functions is restricted. Different utilities provide various types of protection. Some utilities establish authorization levels for each protected file or function and check each user's authorization level before allowing access. Other utilities use passwords to prevent unauthorized access.				
• Utility software generates an audit trail of use and activity. Some utilities provide detailed audit trails of activity against protected datasets, libraries, and other resources. These audit trails provide information such as user ID, date and time of access, resource accessed, and the type of access. These audit trails also serve as a record of events, including security violations and unauthorized accesses.				
• Precautions are taken to ensure that library manipulation utilities, such as delete and copy, are protected from unauthorized use.				
• Precautions are taken to ensure that only authorized personnel have access to applications running under the control of the utility.				
• Precautions are taken to ensure that only authorized users have access to utilities that can update production libraries and library members. Certain utilities should not be maintained in the production environment.				
• Audit trails produced by utilities are carefully reviewed to identify possible security violations.				

Operating systems are a series of programs that manage computer resources and serve as an interface between application software and system hardware. These programs manage and control the execution of application programs and provide the services these programs require. Such services may include job scheduling, disk and tape management, job accounting, program compiling, testing, and debugging.				
Determine that:				
• The use of exits is controlled. Operating-system software may be customized by the use of exits to alter its processing. Exits allow insertion of programs of code to perform additional functions.				
• System programmers' activities are closely monitored.				
• System programmers select, install, and maintain systems software. They are highly skilled and have extraordinary access to the most sensitive elements of the computer system.				
• Operating systems use passwords and user IDs to prevent unauthorized users from gaining access to operating-system functions and utilities. Many times these passwords and IDs are defined in a system table or dataset that is activated when the system is generated.				
• Passwords and user IDs are kept confidential. Unauthorized users who can gain access to the system can make unauthorized modifications to systems resources.				
• Access to operating-system software is restricted and controls over changes to the software are in place.				
• Systems and data-security administrators are carefully selected and monitored. They have the authority to modify system functions, including systems-generation procedures and user profiles.				
• Access to operating-system utilities is restricted. Operating systems provide many utilities that can be used to make unauthorized modifications to systems services and resources.				
• Systems generations and re-initializations are monitored because unauthorized generation can result in invalid systems processing.				
• The use of all optional systems-software products, such as on-line editors and TP monitors, is restricted to appropriate authorized individuals.				
• Audit trails are reviewed on a regular basis to determine if any unauthorized access attempts or modifications were made.				

Audit Program for Auditing UNIX/Linux Environments

Questions	Yes	No	N/A	COMMENTS
Preliminary Steps:				
Obtain a description/overview of the UNIX system configuration.				
Obtain a listing of the various systems supported by the UNIX environment.				
Obtain a map of the physical network to include: file servers, bridges, routers, gateways, concentrators/ hubs, and modems.				
Obtain design specifications for the system(s) security.				
Obtain an overview of password management logic.				
Obtain a job description of the system administrator.				
Policies and Procedures:				
• Obtain and review all relevant policies and standards affecting the UNIX environment.				
• Determine if the policies, procedures, guidelines, and standards documents are up-to-date, accurate, complete, signed off by management, and published.				
• Verify that they include information about owners, revisions, scope, roles and responsibilities, and relevant controls. Review system security specifications.				

Questions	Yes	No	N/A	COMMENTS
• Obtain/discuss relevant regulatory requirements with management and review the process management uses to ensure continuous compliance.				
• Review design specifications for system security.				
• Determine if third-party contracts, particularly cloud contracts, include clauses to ensure that consultants and contractors will comply with the company's security policies as well as keeping the company's data confidential.				
• Determine if access is controlled through UNIX password administration facilities or through application(s) user access tables or a combination of both.				
• Check if documentation procedures exist or are planned for security administration.				
• Review procedures for password administration.				
• Review existing security guidelines				
• Users				
• Groups				
• Functions				
Physical Security:				
• Check the adequacy of physical security for each of the network components, especially file servers.				
• Are unused network connectors disabled or physically secured?				
• Is physical access to network components such as cables, routers, taps, repeaters, and terminators adequately restricted?				
• Are entry controls in place to allow only authorized personnel into various areas within the organization where proprietary information is processed?				
• Are proper procedures in place for the administration of configuration changes to the network's physical structure?				
• Is there any security control for third parties or for personnel working in secure areas and is that information only distributed on a need-to-know basis?				
Systems Administration:				
• Has a system administrator been designated for the UNIX/Linux environment?				

Questions	Yes	No	N/A	COMMENTS
• Is the system administrator supported by a backup person?				
• Does the system administrator have a separate account for normal uses that does not require root access?				
• Are adequate procedures used for administering?				
• Managing user logins				
• Managing menu selections				
• File backup and restoration for systems and individual user's files				
• Monitoring of system activity				
• System shutdown				
• Has appropriate administrative responsibility also been assigned to the following activities?				
• Hardware and software installation and maintenance				
• Administration of the password file				
• Maintenance of user's login scripts				
• Assignment of group, owner, and public rights to directories and files				
• Using the UNIX set command, identify and evaluate system variables for appropriateness.				
• Is access to the root ID and password appropriately restricted?				
Account Security:				
• Are account IDs and permissions properly authorized?				
• Do procedures exist for the assignment and maintenance of account passwords?				
• Are obvious password choices prevented by the system?				
• Determine by examining the system password file:				
• If there are active users without a password.				
• If there are users with no password expiration.				
• If there are users defined as root (UID of zero)?				
• If there are users with the same user ID (UIC)?				
• With the exception of root, are all default system logins disabled?				
• Are those who have the su command properly authorized?				
• Are all failed su attempts logged?				
• var/log/messages				

Questions	Yes	No	N/A	COMMENTS
• var/adm/sulog				
Individual users may be grouped into group IDs, for the purpose of accessing specific files, directories, or devices.				
• Review the /etc/group file for appropriateness.				
• Verify that those with GID=0 are appropriate.				
• Identify if those groups can assume (i.e., SU) the capabilities of the root account, and if so, should they be able to do so.				
• Determine who monitors profiles for currency.				
• Determine if privileged accounts are reviewed more frequently.				
• Examine files that indicate system assigned user controls. Are indicated entries in line with current assignments?				
There is seldom a good reason for logging in as root.				
• Determine if the root ID has been changed to accommodate only an SU command so that the root ID could not login or remote login or teleprocess.				
• Examine the file containing the system-wide profile for all users. Check:				
• Are users whose session is inactive logged off after a reasonable period of time?				
• Are all users listed in the group genuine users and is the group ID unique and correctly formed?				
Note that the individual user's profile overrides these parameters.				
File Level Security:				
• Is access to system files properly restricted?				
• Are sensitive or critical data files correctly identified and protected against unauthorized access?				
• Ensure the root path does not contain the current directory. Under normal circumstances in all users, PATH should not include the current directory. If it is essential, it must be placed last on the path.				
• Individual users' home directories must not be readable by world or group. Check that these are properly restricted.				
• Review critical/sensitive files that have set user ID (SUID) or set group ID (SGID) to ensure the settings are proper.				

Questions	Yes	No	N/A	COMMENTS
Device Security:				
• Evaluate devices to ensure they are not world-writable with the exception of the [/dev/tty*] devices.				
• Review the settings for /dev/mem and /dev/kmem to ensure they are not readable to ordinary users.				
Backup and Recovery:				
• Is there a documented backup and recovery plan?				
• Have systems been classified as to their criticality?				
• Is there appropriate off-site storage of backup and recovery files?				
• Have recovery plans been tested periodically?				
• Do they work?				
UNIX Networks–Terminal Security:				
A root ID can only login to a secure terminal. The console should be the only terminal to which the root ID (if it is used) can login directly.				
• Review the terminal definition table to ensure that only the console is labeled as secure.				
• Review the /etc/inittab file to verify what terminals and modems are attached to the server.				
• Review logoff and timeout procedures for terminals. Are they appropriate?				
UNIX Networks–Trusted Hosts:				
The /etc/hosts.equiv file lists trusted hosts. Remote users who log in with rlogin or issue commands with rsh are granted access with no password requirement if they are coming from a system listed in this file and have an account on the local system with the same login name. Only local hosts should be known to this file.				
• Review the systems file used to identify remote users or systems that are permitted to login (rlogin) or remotely execute [rsh] commands without being prompted for a password.				
User entries in the .rhost file permit remote users of a same name to remotely login without being challenged by the systems' restrictions (on remote logins).				
• Review the user home directories for a [.rhost] file to ensure its use is properly restricted.				

Questions	Yes	No	N/A	COMMENTS
• Ensure the version of SENDMAIL program does not support the wiz, debug, and kill commands; all should return error messages, which should take the form of "500 Command Unrecognized."				
UNIX Networks-UUCP Security:				
• Are UUCP and default passwords changed at installation?				
Passwords associated with the UUCP subsystem must be aged on a manual basis.				
• Are these passwords changed periodically?				
• Review the adequacy of protection given to UUCP communication files and programs for adequacy.				
UNIX Networks–FTP:				
A server that allows anonymous FTP allows anyone to connect to the server using the login ".anonymous," and transfer files from a restricted directory. This login allows users who do not have an account on the machine to have restricted access in order to transfer files from a specific directory. If FTP is being utilized:				
• Is the home directory owned by ftp protected from update by all users?				
The directory ftp/bin should be owned by the super user and write protected from everyone. This directory will contain the ls program.				
The ftp/etc directory should be owned by the super user and write protected from everyone. This directory contains the password and group files.				
The password fields should be changed to asterisks (*). A directory ftp/pub, owned by ftp and world-writable, will be available for users to place files that are to be accessible via anonymous ftp. Note that by making this directory world-writable people who are not known are allowed to place files on the system.				

Audit Program for Auditing Windows VISTA and Windows 7 Environments

Questions	Yes	No	N/A	COMMENTS
Layout and Connectivity of the Network				

In order to form a proper audit opinion on the standard of network management, it is essential to document the types and location of all network components.
 	
• Locate all the PCs, peripherals, and other network components in use by the network, and establish:
 	
  • The completeness and accuracy of the hardware inventory
  • The completeness and accuracy of the software inventory
  • The physical location of each PC, printer, cable box, bridge, or router
  • For each machine in the network, establish and document its purpose in the network, identifying:
    • Servers
    • Primary domain controllers
    • Backup domain controllers
    • Workstations
• Determine which servers and workstations are used for:
 	
  • Development and testing
  • End-user production purposes
  • Both				

Questions	Yes	No	N/A	COMMENTS
Examine the network topology and cabling plan.				
• Is one available?				
• Is it up-to-date?				
• Does it clearly identify: • Cabling routes				
• Types of cable in use (twisted pair, ethernet, token ring, etc.)				
Determine the nature of the network protocols used in the network, for example:				
NetBEUI				
TCP/IP				
IPX				
Other				

• Are cabling runs, terminators, cable-jointing boxes, and other points of access to the network secure against:
  • Interference?
  • Accidental or malicious damage?
  • Are the network components examined regularly to detect signs of gradual deterioration, wear and tear, and so on?				

System Administration:				
Because of the design of the Windows security and management system, a very high degree of responsibility rests with the system administrator, who has total control of the operating system and all its resources.				
• Obtain a detailed job description for the system administrator.				
• Does it clearly describe his or her responsibilities and duties?				
• If the organization has scaled up from (say) a single network to multiple domains, is the job description still appropriate?				
• Has the administrator defined a set of procedures for setting up new users?				
• Is it in accordance with the organization's IT security policy (if one exists)?				
• Have the security principles been communicated to all users before they are set up as users of the system?				
• Has the administrator restricted users to the smallest possible amount of privilege they need to carry out their duties?				
• Have users been organized into sensible and well-structured groups for control and management purposes?				
• Identify the persons who are required to have administration privileges on the network. Are they in control of:				

Questions	Yes	No	N/A	COMMENTS
• A single server • A single domain • Multiple domains				
• For each machine or domain controller, establish the following:				
• That a limited number of users have been designated as having administrator privileges • That the administrator account has been renamed • That the administrators use an alternative account name with lower privileges for day-to-day activities				
• *Ensure that the Guest account is properly controlled, and cannot be used with a blank password.*				
• *On sensitive systems, ensure that there is no access for groups such as Everyone and Guest.*				
• *Determine if, where a Windows workgroup or domain is being used as a gateway to another system (e.g., a Novell Netware network), permission has been obtained for the connection to be set up and maintained.*				
Network Capacity Planning:				
Does the network meet the needs of the users and has it sufficient capacity for expansion in the future?				
• Examine the network capacity plan, if available. Does it cover:				
• Disk storage usage and future requirements? Printing volumes and speeds? • Processor utilization on workstations and servers load balancing between servers • The capacity of the network transmission media				
• Is there evidence of regular management review of the above areas?				
• Is the network management and control mechanism appropriate and adequate for:				
• A network of workstations sharing resources • A domain-based network with a single domain controller • A domain-based network with multiple backup domain controllers • A network of domains, each with its own controller • A network of domains with trust relationships				
• Ensure that the administrator keeps the network capacity under review				
• Seek evidence that the Performance Monitoring tools are being utilized to collect information about loadings on processor, disk, and network.				
• Will the Performance Monitor provide an administrative alert whenever the monitored parameters go outside their predefined acceptable limits?				

Questions	Yes	No	N/A	COMMENTS
• Determine if authenticating servers are adequate to handle the user load and are used exclusively for authentication services.				
• Evaluate trust relationships that support the domain model and the security that the client uses.				
Password and Logon Controls:				
An adequate standard of password and logon controls is the first line of defense against unauthorized use of Windows facilities.				
• Is there a legal notice displayed to users as they log in to the system?				
• Are all users required to log on with their own unique user ID and password?				
• Examine the Account Policy menu system in User Manager to determine if appropriate choices have been made for the configurable password restrictions.				
• Examine the Account Policy as regards user lockout in the event of users failing to provide a valid logon.				
• Does the system allow unlimited attempts (not desirable)?				
• Lock out after a certain number of bad attempts and is the number reasonable?				
• Is the lockout duration set to a time period?				
• Is the lockout permanent unless the account is restored by the system administrator?				
• Has the system been set to ensure that users must log on before being allowed to change their passwords?				
• For users accessing the network via the Remote Access Service (RAS), is the Account Policy set to forcibly disconnect their session in the event of permitted logon hours expiring?				
• Examine the User Rights and for each user, establish who can:				
• Use sensitive system functions				
• Take ownership of other users' resources				
• Use administrative programs and functions				
• Check the contents of the system login script to ensure that its contents are appropriate.				
• Ensure the username of the last user is not displayed upon logon.				
• Ensure the auto admin logon registry entry is not used because this embeds the username and password for the domain in the registry in clear text.				

Questions	Yes	No	N/A	COMMENTS
Group Management:				
• Ensure all groups in the domain are necessary and required.				
• List the built-in groups available on the workstation or server to determine:				
• Which users are assigned to each group?				
• Are the appropriate users assigned to each group, according to their responsibilities and duties?				
• Has the appropriate set of user rights been assigned to group members?				
• Examine any global groups that may have been created. Establish:				
• The names of the users who comprise the groups				
• If the users are from multiple domains, and if so, does the composition of the group reflect the overall range of responsibilities applicable to the people comprising it?				
• Identify users who belong to more than one group.				
• Is the additional privilege granted by membership of other groups consistent with:				
• The user's duties?				
• The organization's security policy?				
• Ensure account policies be established to ensure a secure domain structure including:				
• Minimum password length				
• Maximum password age				
• Minimum password age				
• Forced log off when logon hours expire				
• Counts locked out after three attempts in one hour until administrator unlocks the account				
• Password history maintained to prevent repetitive use				
• Ensure all administrator-level accounts within the domain are required and active.				
• Ensure built-in guest account has been disabled.				
• Ensure administrator user account has been renamed to prevent unauthorized access.				
• In Windows 7, ensure Remote Access Service (RAS) does not compromise the security of the domain.				
• Limit RAS access based upon user job requirements.				
• Where RAS access granted ensure the callback feature is utilized.				
• No administrative level accounts with RAS access				

Questions	Yes	No	N/A	COMMENTS
Maintaining the Security of File Systems:				
The directory structure is the key to effective file-system management.				
• Establish the numbers and types of partition on each machine's hard disk.				
• Establish the type of file system that has been set up on each disk.				
• For each file system found, establish whether it is a FAT file system, an HPFS file system, or an NTFS file system.				
• Ensure that, where possible, all partitions holding significant quantities of application and system data are of the NTFS type.				
• Check the permissions over sensitive applications or system directories containing important configuration and system files.				
• Check which groups have the ability to modify or otherwise manipulate the contents of these directories.				
• Examine the arrangements for sharing of directories among workstations, clusters, or from servers.				
• Are shared directories appropriate to the data-sharing needs?				
• Is there a policy of minimum necessary access applied in directory shares?				
• Are share names properly documented and commented in their dialog boxes?				
• Have access-level passwords been set up for share names?				
Auditing and Event Logging:				
• Look for evidence that auditing for specific sensitive system objects has been set:				
• Detection of unauthorized access to files and directories.				
• Detection of authorized changes to critical system files or directories.				
Examine the arrangements for the audit of use of the Remote Access System (RAS).				
• Check for detection of an appropriate set of the following events:				
• User connection				
• User disconnection				

Questions	Yes	No	N/A	COMMENTS

• Inactivity timeout for user
• User failed to authenticate
• User failed to provide login authentication in time
• Disconnection due to network error during login attempt
• Check the settings of the Event Log Settings for size and recording options:
  • Has the log file size been set to an appropriate capacity to hold a typical period's activity?
  • Can the oldest log entries be overwritten at any time if the log files become full, or is a time period set (e.g., seven days)?
• Check that the administrator conducts a security check efficiently and frequently.
• Ensure the audit log was reviewed in a timely manner depending on the risk level of the IT environment.
• Ensure the Auditee policy captures sufficient detail to facilitate review of Auditee events including
  • Logon and log off
  • File an object access
  • Use of user rights
  • User and group management
  • Security policy changes
  • Restart, system, and shutdown				

Backup and Housekeeping:				

Ensure the use of backup and restore user rights is limited and controlled within separate groups.
• Determine the adequacy of the arrangements for:
  • Taking security copies of main data files
  • Copying and securing the registry files
  • Keeping copies of critical configuration files (including system and personal logon profiles)
  • Ensuring that the configuration details of servers and domain controllers are secured
  • Ensuring that emergency startup diskettes are kept up-to-date for all servers and controllers.				

About the Author

RICHARD E. Cascarino, MBA, CIA, CISM, CFE, is well known in international auditing circles as one of the most knowledgeable practitioners in the field. He is a principal of Richard Cascarino & Associates with more than 27 years experience in audit training and consultancy. He is a regular speaker at national and international conferences and has presented courses throughout Africa, Europe, the Middle East, and the United States. Richard is a Past President of the Institute of Internal Auditors in South Africa, was the founding Regional Director of the Southern African Region of the IIA-Inc, and is a member of ISACA and the Association of Certified Fraud Examiners.

Richard has been involved in the development of courses in both internal auditing and IP Security for the school of accountancy, University of the Witwatersrand, Johannesburg, where he continues to act as an external examiner. He has provided consultancy and professional-development services to clients throughout the United States, Africa, Europe, and the Middle East. These include some of the largest corporations, government departments, auditors general, professional bodies, and financial institutions in their respective countries.

He is also a visiting lecturer at the University of the Witwatersrand, lead author of the book *Internal Auditing: An Integrated Approach* (Juta Publishing) as well as the author of the *Auditor's Guide to IT Auditing* (John Wiley & Sons). These books are extensively used as university textbooks worldwide.

About the Website

A S PART OF YOUR PURCHASE OF THIS BOOK, you have been given an education version of IDEA—Data Analysis Software. This software can improve your audit performance and extend your capabilities with IDEA's powerful functionality. With IDEA, you can lower your cost of analysis, add more quality to your work, and meet the new professional requirements regarding fraud and internal control.

IDEA can read, display, analyze, manipulate, sample, or extract from data files from almost any source—from SAP to QuickBooks—including reports printed to a file. IDEA adds depth and productivity to audits and helps users meet the requirements of SAS 99 and Sarbanes-Oxley 404. Examples of how IDEA can be used to meet audit objectives include: accuracy—checking totals and calculations; analytical review—comparisons, profiling, stratifying; validity—duplicates, exceptions, statistical samples; cut-off-date and number sequence analysis; valuation—accounts receivable and inventory provisions analysis.

Included with this version is a combination of extensive HTML-based Help, Informative User Guide with tutorial, "IDEAssistants"—wizards for key functions, Windows-standard features like right-click and drag and drop, plus a carefully designed user interface that makes learning and using a breeze.

IDEA is a registered trademark of CaseWare International Inc.

The link to this software can be found at: www.wiley.com/go/cascarino.

The password is: audit.

Index

Printed and bound by CPI Group (UK) Ltd, Croydon, CR0 4YY

24/04/2025

14661393-0001